Frederick Gard Fleay

Shakespeare Manual

Frederick Gard Fleay

Shakespeare Manual

ISBN/EAN: 9783337055745

Printed in Europe, USA, Canada, Australia, Japan

Cover: Foto ©Thomas Meinert / pixelio.de

More available books at **www.hansebooks.com**

SHAKESPEARE MANUAL.

BY

F. G. FLEAY, M.A.,

13th *Wrangler;* 19th *Classic;* 2nd *Moral Scientist;*
4th *Natural Scientist,* 1852-3.

HEAD MASTER OF SKIPTON GRAMMAR SCHOOL,
FORMERLY SCHOLAR OF TRINITY COLLEGE, CAMBRIDGE.

London:
MACMILLAN AND CO.
1876.

[The Right of Translation and Reproduction is Reserved.]

LONDON:
R. CLAY, SONS, AND TAYLOR, PRINTERS,
BREAD STREET HILL.

TO

ALFRED TENNYSON,

WHO, HAD HE NOT ELECTED TO BE THE GREATEST POET

OF HIS TIME,

MIGHT EASILY HAVE BECOME ITS GREATEST CRITIC,

This Book,

IN CONFIDENCE OF HIS SYMPATHY

WITH ITS INTENTION,

HOWEVER HE MAY DIFFER FROM SOME OF ITS OPINIONS,

Is Dedicated,

(WITH PERMISSION,)

BY FREDERICK GARD FLEAY.

CONTENTS.

PART I.

MANUAL OF REFERENCE.

CHAPTER I.

	PAGE
Shakespeare's Life	1

CHAPTER II.

Contemporary Allusions to Shakespeare	12

CHAPTER III.

On the Plays of Shakespeare	22
Chronological Table	22
Love's Labour's Lost	24
Comedy of Errors	24
Midsummer Night's Dream	25
Richard II.	26
Edward III.	27
Two Gentlemen of Verona	28
Richard III.	30
1 Henry VI.	31

CONTENTS.

	PAGE
John	31
Romeo and Juliet	32
Merchant of Venice	34
1 Henry IV.	35
2 Henry IV.	35
Merry Wives of Windsor	36
Henry V.	37
Much Ado about Nothing	37
Julius Cæsar	38
As You Like It	39
Twelfth Night	40
Hamlet	41
Taming of the Shrew	41
2 and 3 Henry VI.	42
Titus Andronicus	44
Sejanus	45
Measure for Measure	45
All's Well that Ends Well	46
Othello	47
Lear	47
Macbeth	48
Timon of Athens	49
Troylus and Cressida	49
Pericles	51
Anthony and Cleopatra	51
Coriolanus	52
Two Noble Kinsmen	52
Cymbeline	52
Tempest	54
Winter's Tale	54
Henry VIII.	55
Spurious Plays	56

CHAPTER IV.

	PAGE
On various Questions connected with Shakespeare's Plays	56
What **Plays are** Genuine?	58
What Plays **were not** Entirely Written **at one Date?**	60
Early Editions	61
Relative Values of Quartos and Folios	61
Entries **at** Stationers' Hall	**64**

CHAPTER V.

Pronunciation and Metre	65
Pronunciation	66
Metre	69
Distinguishing Metrical Tests	**71**

CHAPTER VI.

How Plays were Presented	73

CHAPTER VII.

On the Early Theatrical Companies	76
Chronological Table	81

CHAPTER VIII.

On the **Theatres, 1576—1642**	82
Chronological **Table**	85

CHAPTER IX.

	PAGE
On Contemporary Dramatic Authors	86
Chronological Table	87
Lilly	88
Peele	88
Greene	88
Marlowe	88
Chapman	89
Jonson	89
Dekker	90
Heywood	90
Middleton	91
Marston	92
Webster	92
Beaumont and Fletcher	93
Rowley	94
Massinger	95
Ford	95
Shirley	96
Randolph	97
Brome	97
Glapthorne	97
Dodsley's Plays, &c.	98
Daniel	109
Alexander	109
Cartwright	109
Suckling	109
Davenant	109

CHAPTER X.

Miscellaneous Chronological Table 101

CHAPTER XI.

	PAGE
List of Desirable Books	104

CHAPTER XII.

Tests of Chronology and Authorship 106

CHAPTER XIII.

On Emendation 110
Canons 110
Causes of **Error** 111

CHAPTER XIV.

On the Actors 113
Table of King's Company 114
    „ **Prince's** 116
    „ Queen's 117
    „ Revel's 117
Other Companies 118

PART II.

ORIGINAL INVESTIGATIONS.

CHAPTER I.

	PAGE
Metrical Tests applied :—i. Shakespeare	121
Table of Dates, as assigned by Drake, Chalmers, **Malone**, Delius, and Fleay	130
Metrical **Tables**	135

CHAPTER II.

On **the** Quarto Editions	139
Tabular View of Quartos	142

CHAPTER III.

Metrical Tests applied :—ii. Beaumont and Fletcher, Massinger	151
On "Henry VIII."	171
On "Two Noble Kinsmen"	172

CHAPTER IV.

On "**The** Taming of **the** Shrew"	175

CHAPTER V.

On "Timon of Athens"—i. (1874)	187
" " ii. (1869)	197

CONTENTS.

CHAPTER VI.

On "Pericles" 209

CHAPTER VII.

On "**All's Well that** Ends **Well**" 224

CHAPTER VIII.

On "Twelfth **Night**" 227

CHAPTER IX.

On "Troylus and Cressida" 232
Canons on Metrical Tests 239

CHAPTER X.

On "Macbeth" 245
Table of **Length of** Shakespeare's Plays 259
Table of **Rhyme Tags** 260

CHAPTER XI.

On "Julius **Cæsar**" 262
Note on "Two Gentlemen of Verona" 270

CHAPTER XII.

Personal Satire **Common** on the Old English Stage ("**Wily** Beguiled.") 272

CHAPTER XIII.

	PAGE
Annals of the Stage, 1584-95	280
"Fair Emm"	281
"London Prodigal"	283
Greene's "Mottoes"	285
Dates of Greene's Plays	286
Dates of Marlowe's Plays	295
Story of the Stage	297

CHAPTER XIV

On "Edward III."	303

CHAPTER XV.

Extracts reprinted from the *Athenæum*—

Is Action Shakespeare?	307
Shakespeare's Arms	311
List of Managers of Companies and Masters of Schools, in the time of Elizabeth	312

INTRODUCTION.

THE object of this little Treatise is to place within the reach of the student of Shakespeare such information as is essential for him to possess, but is at present unattainable unless he purchases many costly books. Hence arises its peculiar construction. The contents of Part I. are strictly limited to such matters as I have found necessary in my own experience for a critical investigation of difficult or disputed questions as to the chronological succession of Shakespeare's plays in order of composition, their relation to the contemporary drama, his manner and method of work, and the subsequent higher problems which bear reference to the development of his artistic faculty. This is as much, I think, as ought to be attempted in so small a compass, as will be more clearly seen on perusing the following summary of Contents:—

In Chapter I. I give a condensed, but I hope not incomplete life of Shakespeare, incorporating Mr. Halliwell's late discoveries, correcting the time-honoured errors as to the shares in Blackfriars Theatre, the date of Shakespeare's first appearance, and the like, but not entering into any discussion as to uncertain or conjectural matters. The sources of information for this Chapter are exhausted in Mr. Halliwell's *Life of Shakespeare*, and his later *Illustrations*. Mr. S. Neil's biography is also a most useful compendium.

In Chapter II., I give collected the principal references to our author made in contemporary writings, and along with them a few allusions to his work from contemporary plays not hitherto pointed out, which serve to limit some disputed dates as to the production of Shakespeare's own dramas. I need hardly say that Dr. Ingleby's *Century of Praise* is the storehouse for contemporary references.

In Chapter III. is contained a summary of the principal grounds on which the authenticity, origin, date, &c. of each play are to be decided. I have, while incorporating the results of my own investigations into this summary, taken care to state other views however opposed to those I think the true ones. In this part of the book there is much that is new: and, even if the new matter be not approved of, it will be of some advantage to have a condensed summary ready to hand, and arranged in approximate chronological order. The usual arrangement of printing such matter as prefatory to each separate play, with the plays themselves in the order of the First Folio, causes great difficulty of reference and prevents any general survey of the evidence as a whole. Hence, we find in some well-known chronological arrangements Shakespeare described as writing four plays in some years, and none in others—even for years together. The works I have found most useful for this Chapter are the *Variorum* Shakspeare of 1821; the writings of G. Chalmers and N. Drake; the modern editions of Dyce and Staunton; and separate works too numerous to mention.

In Chapter IV., I have given a summary of my own views on the genuineness of the plays that pass under Shakespeare's name, the relative value of the early Folios and Quartos, some tables (useful I hope) of the plays divided into Acts and Scenes, and extracts from the books at Stationers' Hall giving the dates of entry of Shakespeare's works. My chief object in this chapter has been condensation and ease of reference; the matter is of course to be found in many places; for the opinions expressed, however, I am solely responsible.

Chapter V. gives summaries of results of late investigation as to pronunciation, metre, and metrical tests. Mr. Ellis's *Early English Pronunciation*, Mr. Sweet's *History of English Sounds*, Dr. Abbott's *Shakespearian Grammar*, S. Walker's *Criticisms*, are laid under contribution for the two former of these three topics; but only for the sake of pointing out how far my own investigations agree or disagree with these high authorities. It does not enter into my plan to discuss these matters in this book.

Chapter VI. embodies in a plain, though inartistic narrative, details of the manner in which plays were presented: had I known before this was in print that Philarète Chasles had written a similar chapter, I would have cancelled my own in favour of a translation of his more elaborate relation.

Chapter VII. is one of the most important chapters

in the book. It gives for the first time an attempt to import order and consistency into the fragmentary notices of theatrical history from 1575 to 1642. In it several important errors are corrected for the first time, and by its aid the dates of many plays of Shakespeare's contemporaries can be for the first time fixed.

Chapter VIII. is a continuation of the same subject; but with the matter arranged under the head of theatrical buildings instead of companies of actors. The two chronological tables accompanying these chapters have cost me more labour than all the rest of the work; and I find them of the greatest usefulness when making chronological investigations. For Chapters VII., VIII., IX., Collier's *Annals of the Stage*, and Malone's *Variorum Shakspeare*, are the great authorities; but I have got at many results from a tabulation of the companies, theatres, printers, publishers (with their addresses), mentioned on the title-pages of published plays. Collation of these frequently leads to unexpected discoveries as to dates of production.

In Chapter IX., I have given lists of nearly all the plays likely to be met with by the student of the Elizabethan drama, with tabulations of companies, theatres, and dates of publication; adding in another column dates of production, as nearly as they can be ascertained. Of course, this last column must be to some extent conjectural, but whenever I have not placed a (?) it must be understood that I give the date on *external* evidence, although I am not able to adduce such evidence for so many plays in a handbook of this kind. As in many of my results I differ much from previous investigators—even from the most care-ful of all of them, **Dyce, I mention this lest it should be** supposed that **these dates were** assigned on internal evi-dence. There must, of course, be some errors in so exten-sive a **list—not,** I trust, many. **The** principal authority for this list is Halliwell's *Dictionary of Old Plays*, it was, how-ever collated with the title-pages of the plays themselves before going to press.

Chapter X. gives a chronological list of miscellaneous matters not incorporable elsewhere, derived from Collier's *Annals of the Stage.*

Chapter XI. gives a **list of** books which form a nucleus of a Shakespearian library.

Chapter XII. enumerates the tests which serve to deter-mine chronological order of writing.

Chapter XIII. lays down some canons **as** to emending corruptions of the text: for these three chapters I am solely responsible.

Chapter **XIV.** which concludes **Part I.** supplies to some extent a desideratum pointed out by Mr. R. Simpson by giving lists of actors taken from various sources for different companies at sundry **dates.** The value of these for inves-tigation may be judged from the fact that they have enabled me to discover errors in Dyce and other accurate critics. The whole of this Part will, I trust, serve as a useful com-panion and supplement to Professor Ward's admirable *History of Dramatic Literature*, as well as a text-book for younger students, and a hand-book of reference for older ones. My **aim has** been to produce a useful, not a showy book. I can say it is the outcome of years of study, and has involved more labour than I should easily get credit for.

I have one omission to explain. I have been urged on very high authority to give an æsthetic estimate (either of my own, or compiled from Schlegel, Hazlitt, and the host of other great critics who have treated the Elizabethan dramas generally) of the relative merits of the minor authors. I avoid, however, all æsthetic criticism in such a work for the same reason as Mr. Wright in the best edited play I know (*King Lear*, Clarendon Press edition) avoids æsthetic notes. "Æsthetic notes," he says, "have been deliberately omitted because one main object of these editions is to induce those for whose use they are expressly designed to read and study Shakespeare himself, and not to become familiar with opinions about him. Perhaps, too, it is because I cannot help experiencing a certain feeling of resentment when I read such notes, that I am unwilling to intrude upon others what I should myself regard as impertinent. They are in reality too personal and subjective, and turn the commentator into a show-man. With such sign-post criticisms I have no sympathy."

With regard to Part II. of this book, I have only to say that much of it was added at the suggestion of Mr. J. R. Green, who pointed out that references abounded in Part I. to papers inaccessible to any but the members of the New Shakspere Society. These papers have, however, been condensed, corrected, freed from some mistakes of my own, and some of the printer's, cleared of interpolations and alterations, and generally reduced to the condition in which they would have been issued **at first**, had I **not had** to write them under great pressure from **other** work (no **paper having** had more than two evenings occupied in writing it), or had I had the opportunity of correcting them before proofs of them **had** been circulated without being submitted to me at all. **All** additions of any importance are inclosed in [brackets]. **In** addition to these reprinted papers I have **given three** chapters, which I **could not insert in Part I.** without introducing **into it an** element which I desired it to be free from as far as possible,—the subjective element. Yet the interpretation **of plays** which contain historical facts disguised under satirical **allegories** is **too** important **to be omitted even in** a **small manual.** That many more such plays exist than have ever been suspected is the chief point I wish to show in these chapters; hence my choice of plays **which are** not generally known as my **typical** examples, in preference **to those** in which Jonson, Dekker, Marston, &c. displayed **their** mutual animosity. **This** latter series, however, has never **yet been** rightly interpreted.

I have said nothing **on the** *poems* of Shakespeare; what I believe to be the true interpretation of the *Sonnets* I have given elsewhere (*Macmillan's Magazine*, March 1875), and **this** article as well as others written by me in the same periodical, **are too** easy of access to justify my reprinting **them, even in** a condensed form, in this Treatise.

I have to express my great regret that Professor Ward's admirable **History of Dramatic** *Literature* did not appear in time for me to avail myself of its guidance in Part I. Chapter III. It would have saved me much trouble. I have also to express my grateful thanks to friends who have assisted me by help or encouragement, in many ways; especially to Mr. S. Neil, Mr. Halliwell, Dr. Abbott, The Poet Laureate, and Professors Delius, Dowden, Ingram, and Ward. To Mr. P. A. Daniel I am yet more indebted for his ready and kindly aid in referring for me to books to which, in this small town, I have no means of access. By his assistance many details have been given which must otherwise have been omitted. Of course, I am also a considerable debtor to the published writings of the abovementioned gentlemen. I shall feel very thankful for any corrections or suggestions, public or private; for errors must exist in so complicated a subject, however carefully treated. All assistance of any kind shall be acknowledged in due course. I ought, however, to anticipate some corrections that will no doubt be offered as to my dates, by stating that, whenever possible, I have adopted the modern epoch for the commencement of the year, 1 January; thus, a date which in Henslow's diary appears as February, 1591, I have written February, 1592. It would have perhaps been better to have written 1591-2, but I have used this notation for cases where it is doubtful in which year an event took place. I should also state that in many instances I may seem to assert too positively: the fact is that there are so many points on which nothing more than strong probability is attainable, that the constant iteration of possibly, probably, it seems to me, I venture to think, and the like, becomes so tiresome, both to writer and reader, that I have preferred **to risk** the accusation of over-confidence in my **own** reasoning, **to** that **of producing lassitude** by perpetual repetitions **of my inability to give** positive statements where it is palpable that nothing **more than great** likelihood can be attained.

F. G. FLEAY.

SKIPTON,
January, 1876.

SHAKESPEARE MANUAL.

PART I.

CHAPTER I.

'SHAKESPEARE'S LIFE.

JOHN SHAKESPEARE of Stratford was a **resident in** Henley Street in that town **as** early as 1552. In 1556 **we** find him buying copyholds of **two houses** and gardens (one **in** Greenhill Street); suing **and being** sued; dealing **in** gloves and barley. **In** 1557 he **was a burgess,** a member **of the** four-year-old corporation of Stratford, chosen by the court-leet **as** borough ale-taster; and married, or **close** on being so, to Mary, youngest **daughter** of Robert Arden of Willmecote, in the parish of Aston Cauntlow, where she inherited "land in Willmecote called Asbies." John Shakespeare had also property in **Snitterfield from** his father. Their first **daughter, Joan, was** baptized **15 September, 1558,** in which year John **was one of the four** constables at Stratford; in 1559 he became an **assessor or** fixer of **fines** under the borough bye-laws. He was in 1561 a municipal chamberlain, and in **1564** a member of the common-hall. At this time he had **lost not only his daughter Joan,** but a second, Margaret. Next to them **succeeded on 23** (?) April, **1564,** William, son of John Shakespeare, so baptized at Stratford on Ar... 6.

Having escaped the danger of the plague which was then ravaging Stratford, the then prosperous family in Henley Street was probably looking forward to a tranquil future. The head of it was of consequence in the borough; he could even afford to allow the chamber to be pretty largely in his debt, and to pay considerable rates for the relief of the poor. He was in this same year appointed to make up the chamberlain's accounts; and in the next, 1565, was elected one of the fourteen aldermen. In 1566 his second son, Gilbert, was born; in 1568 he was made high bailiff; and in 1571 chief alderman, which entitled him to be henceforth called "Magister," or Mr.; in 1575 he bought two freehold houses in Henley Street. Up to this date then, to the year in which Queen Elizabeth visited Kenilworth Castle, which is but thirteen miles from Stratford, John Shakespeare is a prosperous gentleman. William may have been during this time a happy schoolboy at Stratford Grammar School, under Curate Hunt or Thomas Jenkins, enjoying his holidays and witnessing the performances of the various companies of "travelling" players who visited Stratford, and even perhaps the festivities provided by Leicester for the reception of Majesty itself.

But now things begin to change. In 1577 Mr. John Shakespeare becomes irregular in his attendance at corporation meetings; and half his borough taxes are remitted him; in 1578 the land called Asbies is mortgaged to Edmund Lambert for 40*l*., on condition of reversion if repaid before Michaelmas, 1580. John Shakespeare is also excused from a tax of 4*d*. a week for the relief of the poor. Snitterfield may have been sold; certainly Edmund Lambert was security for a debt of 5*l*. due from Mr. John Shakespeare to Mr. Roger Sadler; and in 1579 we find a levy on him for "pikemen, billmen, and archers" unpaid and unaccounted for, reversing the state of accounts we have seen in 1564. But much remains unexplained at this period, from the fact that the registry of the Court of Record at Stratford is wanting from 1569 to 1585. We may, however, fairly take it for granted that William Shakespeare left school about 1578, and then entered on some occupation, what, it is difficult to say. Probably that of a lawyer's clerk is on the whole most likely, in spite of the entire absence of his signature as witness to any known deeds, &c., of that date.

SHAKESPEARE AT STRATFORD.

It may be well to give here a list of the family of John Shakespeare:—

Joan	born 1558 died		in infancy (?).
Margaret	,, 1562 ,,		1563.
WILLIAM	,, 1564 ,,		1616, married 1582.
Gilbert	,, 1566 ,,	before	1612.
Joan	,, 1569 ,,	after	1600.
Anne	,, 1571 ,,		1579.
Richard	,, 1573 ,,		1612.
Edmund	,, 1580 ,,		1607.
Anne Hathaway . .	,, 1556 ,,		1623 William's wife.

Family of William Shakespeare :—

Susanna	born 1583 died	1649, married 1607.
Hamnet	,, 1585 ,,	1596.
Judith	,, 1585 ,,	1662, married 1615.

Family of Richard Shakespeare :—

John	born (?) 1530 died	1601, married 1557.
Henry	,, ,,	1596.
Mary Arden . . .	,, ,,	1608 (John's wife).

For further information see *Variorum Shakespeare*, edition 1821, vol. ii. p. 610, &c.

Premising that I omit the mythical story of Shakespeare's deer-stealing, we now come to one of the most important events of his life—his marriage with Anne Hathaway. The marriage bond in the Worcester registry is of date 28 Nov. 1582; in it Fulk Sandells and John Richardson, farmers, of Stratford, become bound in 40*l*. that "William Shagspere, one thone partie, and Anne Hathwey, of Stratford, in the dioces of Worcester, maiden, may lawfully solemnize marriage together, with once asking of the bannes." On May 26, 1583 (six months after), Susanna, their daughter, was baptized. As to the interpretation to be given to these dates, critics differ. It was certainly frequent at that time to regard betrothal as morally the same thing as marriage, and to act accordingly; yet on the whole I incline to De Quincey's view, that Anne (over twenty-five years old) had entrapped Shakespeare, so much her junior (seven years), into a closer connexion with her than he at first intended, and then obtained from his honour rather than his love an expiatory marriage to atone for the consequences of the connexion. On 2 Feb. 1585 Hamnet and Judith were baptized, his twin children and his last, which is noticeable in regard of the romantic theories that have been put out as to this period of his life.

At this time, 1586, distraint is levied on John Shakespeare; no effects. A writ is then issued against his person three times; he is deprived of his alderman's gown for not "coming to the halls of long time;" and in 1587 he produced a writ of *habeas corpus*, so that he considered himself illegally imprisoned. The imprisonment may have been for debt to Nicholas Lane, to whom he had been surety for his brother Henry. In all probability his fortunes were falling rapidly.

In this same year come to Stratford Burbage's company of players, called the Queen's Company, and receive higher pay than any of the many companies who preceded them. Then or earlier began Shakespeare's London life as a player and dramatist; then certainly ceases his private isolation; it is no longer the life of a citizen of Stratford that we have to consider, but that of the poet, the cosmopolitan, everybody's Shakespeare.

SHAKESPEARE IN LONDON.

AT the time of Shakespeare's early dramatic career, the principal companies of players with whom we are concerned were Lord Strange's, the Earl of Sussex's, the Earl of Pembroke's, the Admiral's (Lord Nottingham's), the Lord Chamberlain's, the Children of the Chapel, and the Children of Paul's. The dramatic writers were Greene, Peele, Marlowe, Lilly, Nash, Lodge, Chettle, Munday, and others. Some of the works of Greene, Peele, Lodge, and Marlowe, were in 1592 produced at the Rose Theatre, where Lord Strange's company were then playing. If, as I believe, Shakespeare was at this time associated with this company, he would, if not before, then become acquainted with the greatest of his forerunners. The allusion made to him in Greene's *Groatsworth of Wit* has been conclusively shown by Mr. Simpson to refer to him as an actor only; and as it is palpable, that, if Greene had known him as an author, he would have referred to him also in that capacity, we may fairly assign as the date of his beginning to write alone 1591; it cannot have well been later, and if earlier Greene would have known it in 1592. John Shakespeare we find in 1591 still in possession of a house in Henley Street, Stratford; in 1591 and in the next year as one of four "credible men" making inventory of goods of one Ralph Shaw, wooldriver, and Henry Field, tanner. At this time Shakespeare was writing his early plays of the rhyming period.

In 1593 the theatres were closed on account of the plague, and Shakespeare found leisure to publish the first piece of his invention, the *Venus and Adonis*, which he dedicated to his patron Lord Southampton. This was followed by a new poem, also dedicated to him, the *Rape of Lucrece*, in 1594. Meanwhile, death had been busy with the band of dramatists; not only had "Learning deceast in beggary" been exemplified in the end of the repentant Greene, who was at enmity with Shakespeare, but his friends Marlowe and Peele had by 1596 also died, the one in a drunken quarrel, the other of a shameful disease. No wonder that he felt disgusted with the theâtre. In that year he probably wrote his great poem to Lord Southampton (*Sonnets* 1—126), in which he expresses himself bitterly as to the position occupied by an actor, especially a travelling or strolling actor. During this time he had also been occupied in retouching, adding to, re-writing plays by other men. *Edward III.* and 1 *Henry VI.;* and I have no doubt *Richard III.* and *Romeo and Juliet*, are rifaccimenti made by him between 1593 and 1596. These plays in their original form were written by Marlowe and Peele, separately or conjointly, except 1 *Henry VI.*, which seems to show Lodge's work in part of it. With them there is no trace of any quarrel on Shakespeare's part. His enemies were Greene and Nash and Lilly. The last of these belonged to rival theatres, which embittered the quarrel. Lilly wrote only for the youths who went under the names of Children of the Chapel and Children of St. Paul's. These "children," as we may see in *Hamlet*, were Shakespeare's particular detestation; with Nash also, the bitter pamphleteer, he had no sympathy; but Marlowe he refers to kindly in *As You Like*

It, iii. 5, "Dead shepherd! Now I find thy saw of might," and Peele seems to have followed him to the Lord Chamberlain's Company. For in that company (whether he joined it along with Lord Strange's company in 1594 or belonged to it earlier) we find Shakespeare fixed in our earliest theatrical notice of him as acting before Queen Elizabeth at Greenwich in December of that year. In 1595 appeared the strange book *Locrine*, a lamentable tragedy "newly set forth, overseen and corrected by W. S." This clever play, which is a new edition of an old work by Charles Tilney and George Peele (1586), contains many lines taken from Greene, and alludes in many places to those plays of his which he produced in 1585-6 in rivalry with Marlowe. It was probably edited by Shakespeare on or just before Peele's death, and one year before the production of *Romeo and Juliet*.

In 1596 his only son Hamnet died. Shakespeare's feelings as a father can be seen in *King John*, iii. 4, which was probably written during his son's illness or very shortly after his decease. In this year also *Romeo and Juliet* was produced at the Curtain Theatre in Shoreditch; a grant of arms to John Shakespeare was applied for at the Heralds' College; his uncle Henry died (to be followed in a few weeks by Margaret his wife); all events which must have in some instances greatly affected the mind of Shakespeare, in others prepared him for a more settled life with more definite aims; in all made him ready for the great change in style and purpose which is shown in the historic and comic plays of his Second Period.

Immediately after the commencement of this, in 1597, begins the publishing of Shakespeare's plays, without his name on the title page; it was, however, inserted in 1598, and in no case (except the noticeable one of *Romeo and Juliet*) was it omitted thereafter. The application for arms is also granted in this year, and William Shakespeare, *gentleman*, has 60*l*. to purchase of William Underhill one messuage, two barns, two gardens, two orchards with appurtenances, in Stratford-on-Avon. This is the celebrated New Place formerly called the Great House, built by Sir Hugh Clopton, in Henry VIII.'s time. John Shakespeare and wife also have money (? from son William) to file a bill in Chancery in the old Asbies matter, to recover that estate from John Lambert, son of Edmund Lambert, the mortgagee of nineteen years back. They had tendered, they allege, the money in release duty; yet the estate is withheld.

The year 1598 is for the critic memorable. In that year Francis Meres published his *Palladis Tamia*, or *Wits Treasury*. In it Meres mentions by name twelve plays, the *Venus and Adonis*, *Lucrece*, and *Sonnets*, and so gives us a most valuable landmark for our chronology. He also shows the estimation in which Shakespeare was held as a dramatist before his name had been affixed to any published play. Nine times is he noticed in this work, oftener than any other; he is praised for Lyricks, Elegies, Comedies, Tragedies, and Knowledge of the English Tongue; and in influence in other matters he was advancing as rapidly as in favour with the critics. Early in this same year Abraham Sturley wrote from Stratford to Richard Quiney (father of Thomas Quiney, the future husband of Susanna Shakespeare) respecting a solicitation to Burleigh, the Lord Treasurer, on behalf of Stratford for exemption from subsidies and taxes, and a grant of money out of 30,000$l.$ set aside by Parliament for relieving decayed towns, in consideration of great fires in Stratford in 1594 and 1595. The passage is worth quoting: "It seemeth that our countryman, Mr. Shakespeare, is willing to disburse some money upon some odd yard land or other at Shottery, or near about us. He thinketh it a very fit pattern to move him to deal in the matter of our tithes. By the instructions you can give him thereof and by the friends he can make therefore, we think it a fair mark for him to shoot at, and not impossible to hit. It obtained would advance him indeed, and would do us much good." Other matters indicate an advance in wealth. He is the third largest holder of corn and malt in his ward, having ten quarters; he is lending Richard Quiney, or at any rate deemed capable of lending, 30$l.$; he is selling stone to the corporation; he is making friends too; he is playing in Jonson's *Every Man in His Humour*. Jonson has joined the Chamberlain's company, and altered into pure English the semi-Italian plot of this play as written at first. Possibly Shakespeare suggested this. At the end of this year the Theatre was pulled down, and in 1599 the building of the Globe Theatre was commenced with the old materials. At this new house in Bankside the rest of Shakespeare's plays were produced; that is in all probability all his dramas that are not included in Meres' list. The theatre at Blackfriars, erected not more than three years earlier, was let out to the Children of the Chapel, and remained in their occupation till 1601, and in that of other children's companies till 1612, to Shakespeare's great annoyance.

In the year 1600 the Fortune Theatre was built by Alleyn for the Admiral's company. In this year ninety extracts from Shakespeare appear in *England's Parnassus;* quotations from him also occur in *England's Helicon* and in *Bel-vedere, or the Garden of the Muses.* Piratical publishers also begin to prefix his name to plays not his. All this shows his rapidly increasing fame.

In 1601 his name is attached to a poem in *Love's Martyr or Rosalin's Complaint,* by Robert Chester: and, which is much more important, his father dies: he was buried on the 8th September. Again we find a division in his works, as shown in style, metre, and dramatic power, coincident with the death of those related to him. He ceases now to write Histories, and almost abandons Comedy. Tragedy of the deepest kind is the subject of his culminating art.

In his Third Period, Shakespeare advances in worldly prosperity as well as in art and reputation. In May 1602 he purchases, for 320*l.*, 107 acres of arable land in Old Stratford parish from William Combe of Warwick, and John Combe of Old Stratford: the indenture, in his brother's absence, is sealed and delivered to Gilbert Shakespeare; in the same year in September, Walter Getley, by his attorney Thomas Tibbottes, at a Court Baron of the Manor of Rowington, surrenders to him and his heirs a house in Walker's Street or Dead Lane near New Place, possession being reserved to the Lady of the Manor, till suit and service had been done by him for the same. At Michaelmas in the same year he bought from Hercules Underhill for 60*l.* one messuage, two orchards, two gardens, two barns, &c. The document of this purchase is in the Chapter House, Westminster. He evidently is looking forward to settling at Stratford, and perhaps to founding a family there.

In 1603, the year of the Queen's death, Sir John Davies compliments him in his *Microcosmos.* We find him also acting in Ben Jonson's *Sejanus,* of which he probably shared the authorship (in its first form). The play, however, was condemned. It is not likely that any play jointly composed by men of such entirely different manners could amalgamate sufficiently to succeed. It did succeed afterwards when Jonson recast the whole. At the end of the same year (December) James I. was entertained at the seat of William Earl of Pembroke, a patron of Shakespeare's, at Walton near Salisbury, by the company to which Shakespeare belonged. It is supposed that Massinger, whose father was a retainer of Pembroke's, on that occasion chose the dramatic career as his business for life.

In 1604 Shakespeare brought an action against Philip Rogers in the Court at Stratford for 1*l*. 15*s*. 6*d*. for malt. A sharp man of business this poet of ours, and looks after details himself; he is by no means the ideal artist of the vulgar. In 1605 he bought of Ralph Hubande a thirty-one years' remainder of a ninety-two years' lease of the tithes of Stratford, Old Stratford, Bishopton, and Welcombe for 440*l*. Prosperity thickens; and the gentle poet is loved as well as prosperous. Augustine Phillips, his co-partner in the profits of the house and fellow-actor, leaves him a 30*s*. gold piece as token of esteem; nay, there is a credible tradition that James I. wrote him an autograph letter at this time.

In 1606 we find he is still in possession of the house in Walker Street, but as he did not fill up the form for the Survey of Rowington Manor (1 Aug.), he was probably absent from Stratford.

In 1607 John Davies of Hereford compliments him in the *Scourge of Folly;* and his daughter Susanna marries Dr. John Hall, a Stratford leech (June 5); but his good fortune is once more interrupted by that which cannot be evaded, Death. On 31 December, 1607, his youngest brother, Edmund, a player, is buried at St. Saviour's, Southwark, aged twenty-seven; on 9 September, 1608, his mother, Mary, is buried at Stratford. Again bereavement, but if we can judge from his works, a softening one; from this time he writes no more cynical tragedies; he takes a healthier if not so grand a view of human life; he returns to history and comedy; but it is Roman and not Chronicle history; and the comedy turns entirely on the rejoining of parents and children after long separation. His last period shows the most human feeling, if not the most perfect art.

In the beginning of his Fourth Period, on October 16, 1608, Shakespeare was sponsor for William Walker, to whom in his will he leaves 20*s*. In 1609 we find him again looking after his business carefully. On 15 March he instituted a process for 6*l*. debt and

24*s.* costs against John Addenbrooke, and as he **could** not be found he pursued his surety, Thomas Horneby, on 7 June. In **1611** his name appears as a donor towards costs of a bill in Parliament for better repair of highways and amending defects in the former statutes; in the same year a fine was **levied on the** property he purchased in May 1602 and **on twenty** acres additional; in 1612, February **4,** Richard Shakespeare, his only surviving brother, was buried; **and now,** having no surviving male relative, all hope of continuing the name and family is gone, **and he** finally **quits** his work after twenty years' hard exertion, having produced an average of two plays each year: about ten in each of his four periods, which curiously enough are each of about five years' duration.

In March 1613 he bought a house near Blackfriars Theatre, abutting on a street leading to Puddle Wharf against the King's Majesty's Wardrobe, for 120*l.*, paying 80*l.* and mortgaging the house for the balance. This house he let to John Robinson for ten years. In the same year the draft of a **bill** in Chancery, **endorsed Lane,** Greene, and Shakespeare complainants, intended **to be** presented to Lord Chancellor Ellesmere, shows that on the moiety of tithes purchased by Shakespeare in 1605 too large a proportion of the reserved rent fell on the share of the complainants. His annual income from these tithes was 120*l.*

In 1613 the Globe Theatre, and probably many **of** his MSS., was burnt down. This theatre **was** rebuilt the same **year.** In **1614** fifty-four houses were burnt in Stratford, and the town was agitated respecting the inclosure of certain common lands, which was opposed by the corporation. On 5 September his name occurs as one of the ancient freeholders **to** be compensated. On 8 October he and Thomas Greene, gent., enter into covenant regarding compensation for inclosure intended by William Replingham. Thomas Greene was clerk to the corporation, and being sent to London **on** this business, **says,** on 17 November:—"My cousin Shakespeare coming yesterday to town I went to see him, and **he** and Mr. Hall say they think there will be nothing done at all." **On 23 December a hall** of the corporation was held, and letters with nearly all **the corporation's** signatures were written to Mr. Manyring and **Mr.** Shakespeare, and Greene **subjoins** that he also writ to his cousin Shakespeare copies of all **the** acts **and a note** of the inconveniences that would happen.

He holds the confidence of the public and of his relatives to the last.

In 1614 his name is on the jury list in a copy of the customs of the manor of Rowington; he had property in fee from that manor. In the same year John Combe leaves him 5*l.* in his will. There is also a notice in the Stratford Chamberlain's accounts of a quart of sack and a quart of claret given to a preacher at New Place, cost 20*d*.

In 1616 Judith, his daughter, was married to Thomas Quiney, vintner, Stratford (February 10); on 25 March he made his will; on his fifty-third birthday he died, and was buried two days after in Trinity Church, Stratford, where the bust, made from a cast taken after death still exists, though, through Malone's want of taste, the hazel eyes, the auburn hair and beard, the scarlet doublet, black tabard, green and crimson cushion, and gilt tassels were all whitewashed.[1] His wife survived him seven years.

Five years' poverty, twenty years' hard work, three years' rest in bereavement, then the final rest in the grave. Such was Shakespeare's life after leaving his home in 1585–6; such is the life of most true men. *La vie c'est le travail*, said Poisson. Without the work he may have been happier; but who would not accept his lot with all its troubles? Loved by his fellows, his relatives, and friends, respected by his citizens, favoured by two sovereigns, he sank into an honoured grave to become the favourite of his countrymen, and the idol of all that care for literature or art. A myriad-minded man, as all great men are, more or less: but more than this, a true-hearted, loving, catholic soul, one to whom nothing in God's universe is strange, nothing despicable; the nearest approach to perfect of all the mighty geniuses our little island has produced.

I append in illustration of the preceding statements extracts from contemporaries alluding to Shakespeare personally, or to passages in his plays chronologically important. These will form the subject of the next chapter.

[1] The whitewash is now removed and the colours restored.

CHAPTER II.

PASSAGES SUPPOSED TO ALLUDE TO SHAKESPEARE, EXTRACTED FROM CONTEMPORARY WRITINGS.

"It is a common practice nowadays among a sort of shifting companions that run through every art and thrive by none, to leave the trade of *noverint* whereto they were born, and busy themselves with the endeavours of art, that could scarce Latinise their neck-verse if they should have need."—NASH, *Preface to Greene's Menaphon*, 1589.

"New found songs and sonnets which every red-nose fiddler hath at his finger's end; .... make poetry an occupation, lying is their living, and fables are their movables .... think knowledge a burden, tapping it before they have half tunned it, venting it before they have filled it, in whom the saying of the orator is verified: *Ante ad dicendum quam ad cognoscendum veniunt.* They come to speak before they come to know. They contemn arts as unprofitable, contenting themselves with a little country-grammar knowledge."—NASH, *Anatomy of Absurdity*, 1590.

"With the first and second leaf he plays very prettily, and in ordinary terms of extenuating verdits Piers Penniless for a grammar-school wit; says his margin is as deeply learned as *Fauste precor gelida.*"—NASH, *Piers Penniless*, 1592.

"Alas, poor Latinless authors. .... For my part I do challenge no praise of learning to myself, yet have I worn a gown in the University, and so hath *caret tempus non habet moribus;* but this I dare presume, that if any Mecenas bind me to him by his bounty, or extend some sound liberality to me worth the speaking of, I will do him as much honor as any poet of my beardless years shall in England."—NASH, *Piers Penniless*, 1592.

"Our pleasant Willy ah is dead of late," &c.
SPENSER, *Tears of the Muses*, 1590, refers probably to Lilly, who "wrote no play after 1589," says Malone.

"An upstart crow beautified in our feathers that, with his

'Tiger's heart wrapt in a player's hide,'

supposes he is as well able to bombast out a blank verse as the best of you, and being an absolute *Johannes Factotum*, is in his own conceit the only Shake-scene in a country."—GREENE, *Groatsworth of Wit*, 1592.

"About three months since died Mr. Robert Greene, leaving many papers in sundry booksellers' hands, among others his *Groatsworth of Wit*, in which a letter written to divers playwriters is offensively by one or two of them taken; and because on the dead they cannot be avenged, they wilfully forge in their conceits a living author; and after tossing it to and fro, no remedy but it must needs light on me.... With neither of them that take offence was I acquainted, and with one of them (Marlowe?) I care not if I never be. The other (Shakespeare?) whom at that time I did not so much spare as since I wish I had.... that I did not I am as sorry as if the original fault had been my fault; because myself have seen his demeanor no less civil than excellent in the quality he professes. Besides, divers of worship have reported his uprightness of dealing, which argues his honesty; and his facetious grace in writing, that approves his wit.... I protest it was all Greene's, and not mine nor Master Nash's, as some have unjustly affirmed."—CHETTLE, *Kind Hart's Dream*, 1592.

"Shakespeare paints poor Lucreece' rape."
Willobie, his Avisa, 1594.

"And there though last not least is Aetion,
  A gentler shepherd may no where he found
 Whose muse full of high thought's invention,
  Doth like himself heroically sound."
SPENSER, *Colin Clout's come Home again*, 1595.

But this more likely means Drayton (Rowland), author **of** *Heroical Epistles* and *Idea* (ἰδέα = αἴτιον).—See extracts from *Athenæum* in Part ii.

Kempe.—" Why here's our fellow Shakespeare puts them all down, ay, and Ben Jonson too. O that Ben Jonson is a pestilent fellow; he brought up Horace giving the poets a pill ; but our fellow Shakespeare hath given him a purge that made him bewray his credit.
Burbage.— "He is a shrewd fellow, indeed."

Return from Parnassus, 1602 (?).

"The sweet witty soul of Ovid lives in mellifluous and honey-tongued Shakespeare. Witness his *Venus and Adonis*, his *Lucreece*, his sugared *Sonnets* among his private friends. **Shakespeare among** the English is the most excellent in both kinds for the **stage. For** Comedy, **witness** his *Gentlemen of Verona*, **his** *Errors*, his *Love's Labour's Lost*, his *Love's Labour's Won*, his *Midsummer's Night's Dream*, and his *Merchant of Venice*; for Tragedy, his *Richard the* 2, *Richard the* 3, *Henry the* 4, *King John*, *Titus Andronicus*, and his *Romeo and Juliet*.

"The Muses would speak with Shakespeare's fine-filed phrase if they would speak English," &c., &c.—MERES, *Palladis Tamia*, 1598.

" And Shakespeare, thou whose honey-flowing **vein**
  Pleasing the world thy praises doth obtain,
  Whose *Venus* and whose *Lucreece*, sweet and chaste,
  Thy **name in** Fame's immortal book hath placed," &c.
    R. BARNEFIELD, *Poems and Divers Persons*, 1598.

"*Ad Gulielmum Shakespeare.*

" Honey-tongued Shakespeare, when I saw thine issue
  I swore Apollo got them and none other :
  Their rosy-tainted features **clothed in tissue**
  Some heaven-born goddess **said to be their** mother **:**
Rose cheekt *Adonis*, with **his amber tresses,**
  Fair firehot *Venus*, charming **him to love her,**
Chaste *Lucretia*, virgin-like her **dresses,**
  Proud, lust-stung *Tarquin* seeking still to prove her ;

Romeo, Richard, more whose names I know **not,**
  Their sugar'd tongues and power-attractive **beauty,**
Say they are saints, although that saints they show **not,**
  For thousands vows to them subjective duty;
They burn in love thy children, Shakespeare, het them,
Go woo thy Muse! More nymphish brood beget them!"
                           WEEVER, *Epigrams,* 1596.

" Players, I love ye and your quality,
    As ye are men that pastime **not abused,**
  And some I love for painting poesy, (W. S. R. B.)
  And say fell Fortune cannot **be excused**
  That hath for better uses you refused.
Wit, courage, good shape, good parts, and all good
  As long as all these goods are no worse used,
And though the stage doth stain pure gentle blood,
    Yet generous ye are in mind and mood."
              SIR JOHN DAVIES, *Microcosmos,* 1603.

" Nor doth the silver-tongued *Melicert*
    Drop from his honey'd Muse **one sable tear**
To mourn her death that gracèd **his desert**
    And to his lines open'd her royal **ear.**
Shepherd, remember our *Elizabeth,*
And sing her rape done by that *Tarquin,* Death!"
              HENRY CHETTLE, *England's Mourning*
                     Garment, 1603.

" There shalt thou learn **to be** frugal (for players were never so thrifty as they are now about London); and to feed upon all men, **to let** none feed upon thee, to make thy hand a stranger to thy pocket, thy heart slow to perform thy tongue's promise; and when thou feelest thy purse well lined, buy thee some place of lordship in the country, that, growing weary of playing, thy money may then bring thee to dignity and reputation; then thou needest care for no man; no, **not** for them that before made thee proud with speaking **their words on the stage.** Sir, I thank you (quoth the player) for **this** good counsel. I promise you I will make use of it, for I have heard, indeed, of some that have **gone to** London very meanly, and have come in time to be exceeding wealthy."—*Ratsei's Ghost*, 1605-6.

> " You poets all, brave Shakespeare,
> Jonson, Greene,
> Bestow your time to write
> For England's **Queen.**"
> *A Mournful Ditty*, &c., 1603.

" To our English Terence, Mr. Will Shakespeare.

> "Some say, good Will, **which I** in sport **do sing,**
> Hadst thou not play'd some kingly **parts in sport**
> Thou hadst been **a companion for a king,**
> And been a king among **the meaner sort.**
> Some others rail; but rail as they think **fit,**
> Thou hast no railing **but a** reigning **wit;**
> And honesty thou sowst which they **do reap,**
> So to increase their **stock which they do** keep."
> JOHN DAVIES, *Scourge of Folly*, 1607.

"That full and heightened style of **Master** Chapman, the laboured **and** understanding works **of** Master Jonson, the no less worthy composures of the both worthily **excellent** Master Beaumont and Master Fletcher; and lastly (without wrong last to be named), the right happy and copious industry of Master Shakespeare, Master Dekker, and Master Heywood."—JOHN WEBSTER, *Dedication to the White Devil*, **1612.**

*" To Master **Wm.** Shakespeare.*

> "Shakespeare, that nimble Mercury, **thy brain,**
> Lulls many hundred Argus' eyes asleep:
> So fit for all thou fashionest thy vein,
> At th' horse-foot fountain thou hast drunk full deep.
> Virtue's or vice's theme to thee all **one is:**
> Who loves chaste life, **there's** *Lucreece* for a teacher;
> Who lists read lust, there's *Venus and Adonis,*
> True model of a most lascivious lecher;
> Besides, in plays thy wit winds like Meander,
> Whence needy new composers borrow more

Than Terence doth from Plautus or Menander,
  But to praise thee aright I want thy store.
Then let thine own work thine own worth upraise,
And help t' adorn thee with deservèd days."
THOMAS FREEMAN, *Rub and a Great Cast*, 1614.

"To him that impt my fame with Clio's quill,
  Whose magic rais'd me from Oblivion's den,
That writ my story on the Muses' hill,
  And with my actions dignified his pen;
He that from Helicon sends many a rill,
  Whose nectar'd veins are drunk by thirsty men,
Crown'd be his style with fame, his head with bays,
And none detract but gratulate his praise.

Yet if his scenes have not engrost all grace,
  The much famed actor could extend on stage,
If Time or Memory have left a place
  For me to fill t' enform this ignorant age;
In that intent I show my horrid face,
  Imprest with fear and characters of rage,
Nor acts nor chronicles could e'er contain
The hell-deep reaches of my soundless brain."
C. B., *The Ghost of Richard III.*, 1614.

"A hall, a hall!
Room for the spheres, the orbs celestiall
Will dance Kempe's jig. They'll revel with neat jumps;
A worthy poet hath put on their pumps.
O wit's quick travers, but *sance ceo's* slow,
Good faith, 'tis hard for nimble Curio.
Ye gracious orbs, keep the old measuring,
All's spoild if once ye fall to capering.
  Luscus, what's playd to-day? Faith, now I know;
I set thy lips abroach, from whence doth flow
Nought but pure *Juliet and Romeo*.
Say who acts best, Drusus or Roscio?

"Now **I have him that ne'er of** aught did speak
But when of plays or players he did treat.
H'ath made a commonplace-book out of plays,
And speaks in print, at least whate'er he says
Is warranted by Curtain *plaudities*.
If ere you heard him courting Lesbia's eyes,
Say, Courteous Sir, speaks **he not** movingly
From **out** some new pathetic tragedy?
He writes, he rails, he jests, he courts, what not,
And all from out his huge long-scrapèd **stock**
Of well-penn'd plays."
     . MARSTON, *Scourge of Villany*,
      Satire x., 1598.

"A man, **a** man, a kingdom for **a man**."
     From the same, Satire vii.

Compare with the foregoing *Romeo and Juliet* :—

"Earth-treading stars that make dark **heaven light**."
     i. 2, 25.

"A hall, a hall, give room and foot it, girls."
     i. 5, 24 (not in first quarto).

"You have dancing shoes with nimble soles . . . .
 Mer. Soar with them above a common bound."
     i. 4, 12.

"Two of the fairest stars in all the heavens,
Having **some** business, do entreat her eyes
To twinkle in their spheres till they return."
     ii. 2, 14.

and ii. 4, 60,' &c., **for** "wit's quick traverse."

The following parallels are from contemporary plays :—

"Now to the next tap-house, there drink down this, and by the operation of the third pot, quarrel again."—*Ram Alley*, ii. 2.

"He enters the confines of a tavern . . . . **and by** the operation of the second cup draws him on the drawer."—*Romeo and Juliet* iii. **1,** 6.

"Dash, we must bear some brain."
Ram Alley, ii. 4.

"Well I do bear a brain."
Romeo and Juliet, i. 3.

"Is there no trust, no honesty in men?"
Ram Alley, ii. 4.

"There's no trust, no faith, no honesty in men."
Romeo and Juliet, iii. 2, 88.

"He stirreth not, he moveth not, he waggeth not."
Ram Alley, iv. 2.

"He heareth not, he stirreth not, he moveth not."
Romeo and Juliet, ii. 2, 16.

"But why speak I of shame to thee, whose face
Is steel'd with custom'd sin, whose thoughts want grace.
The custom of thy sin so lulls thy sense,
Women ne'er blush though ne'er so foul th' offence,
To break thy vow to me, and straight to wed
A doating stinkard."
Ram Alley, v. 3.

Imitated from *Hamlet*, iii. 4, 161 ; i. 4, 48 :—

"That monster custom, who all sense doth eat
Of habit's devil," &c. (not in Folio.)

"What a falling off was there!
From me, whose love was of that dignity
That it went hand in hand even with the vow
I made to her in marriage, and to decline
Upon a wretch."

This shows that at the date of the acting of *Ram Alley* (published 1611) the quarto form (Q 2) of *Hamlet* was acted : the alterations in the folio must be of subsequent date ; the play is one continuous parody of Shakespeare; contains allusions to *Othello* ("Villain, slave, thou hast wrong'd my wife !"), to *Much Ado About Nothing*, *Measure* for *Measure*, *All's Well that Ends Well*, and other **plays**. It was **acted** by the Revells Children **between 1607 and 1611**, probably not so near **the** later date, when it was published, **as the** former.

The *Dumb Knight*, by Lewis Machin **and Gervase** Markham, acted by the Revells Children, and published **1608, in** addition to indirect allusions to and parodies on *Lear, Merry Wives of Windsor, Othello, Macbeth*, as well as **earlier plays, contains this** passage :—

"**A book** that never an **orator's clerk** in this kingdom but is beholden unto; it is called *Maids' Philosophy*, or *Venus and Adonis*."

If the character of Alphonso is **imitated from Iachimo**, *Cymbeline* cannot **be later than** 1608; **but I** think **this** not likely.

Another play filled with allusions to Shakespeare **is the** *Puritan*, by W. S., 1607, acted by the Paul's Children; **for instance :—**

"Instead **of a** jester **we'll have the** ghost in a white sheet set at the upper **end of** the table."

Macbeth was the first **of** Shakespeare's plays that had **no jester** in it.

Act iv. Sc. 3 is distinctly imitated from *Pericles*, iii. 2, which fixes the date of that play as not later than 1607. Compare also *Richard III.*, i. 2, 33.

"*Pyeboard.* Let me entreat the corpse to **be set down**.

Sheriff. Bearers, set down the coffin. This were wonderful and worthy Stowe's Chronicle.

Pye. I pray bestow the freedom of the air upon our wholesome art. Mass! **His** cheeks begin to receive natural warmth. . . . O, he stirs, he stirs **again**; look, gentlemen! he recovers, he starts, he **rises.**

Sher. O, O defend us! out, alas!

Pye. Nay; pray be still; **you'll make him** more giddy else. He knows nobody yet.

Oath. Zounds, where am **I?** **Covered** with snow! I marvel.

Pye. **Nay;** I knew he would swear **the** first thing, &c. &c."

In comparing *Pericles*, note that Thaisa says, "O, dear Diana! Where am I?" on awaking.

Locrine, 1595, edited by W. S., is **a** remarkable play; it contains allusions to, **parodies on** lines in, or the lines themselves borrowed from, the plays of Peele, Greene, and Marlowe; the so-called plays of Shakespeare, *Titus Andronicus*, *Henry VI.*, and *Richard III.*; Kyd's *Jeronimo* and other old dramas. But in no instance can I trace any allusion to any undoubted play of Shakespeare. The wooing of Eshild, Act iv. Sc. 1, seems to be imitated from *Richard III.*, i. 2. and

"Methinks I see both armies in the field,"
echoes .
"I think there be six Richmonds in the field."

If this be so, *Richard III.* cannot have been written later than 1595, which agrees with the date I give to it.

Here we must leave this subject, not from deficiency of material, but because a fuller exposition of the question would require a volume, and is unfit for an elementary treatise. We next proceed to consider Shakespeare's plays individually as regards—1, their authenticity; 2, the origin of their plots; 3, the date of their production; 4, miscellaneous observations which do not fall under the above headings. Throughout the next chapter the numbers 1, 2, 3, 4, refer to the headings now enumerated.

I take the plays in their chronological order as nearly as it can be ascertained; this being the natural order for study or investigation of any writer whose development we care to become acquainted with; and therefore I prefix a table of the time-succession of Shakespeare's works. The reasons for the order will be found under the heads of each play.

CHAPTER III.

ON THE PLAYS OF SHAKESPEARE.

Approximate Chronological **Table of** *the production of Shakespeare's*
Works.

	1588—Venus and Adonis.
	1589—Taming of a Shrew (part).
	Corambis Hamlet (part)
i.	1591—Love's Labour's **Lost (revised 1597).**
	Love's Labour's **Won.**
ii.	1592—Comedy of Errors.
iii.	Midsummer Night's Dream (revised 1599).
	1593—**Lucrece.**
iv.	**Richard II. (revised** 1597).
v.	1594—Edward III. (part).
	Troilus and Cressida and Twelfth Night (begun).
vi.	**1595**—Two Gentlemen **of Verona (completed).**
vii.	Richard III. (quarto).
viii.	? Scene in 1 Henry VI.
ix.	John.
x.	1596—Romeo and Juliet (first **revision).**
xi.	Merchant of Venice.
	Sonnets.
	1597—Romeo and Juliet (finished).
	Love's Labour's Lost (revised).

xii.		1 Henry IV.
xiii.	1598—	2 Henry IV.
xiv.		Merry Wives of Windsor (first draught).
xv.	1599—	Henry V.
xvi.		Much Ado About **Nothing**.
xvii.	1600—	Julius Cæsar.
xviii.		As You Like **It**.
xix.	1601—	Twelfth Night.
xx.		Hamlet (first draught).
xxi.	1602—	Taming of the Shrew (part).
xxii.		? Sejanus (part).
		Richard III. (folio).
xxiii.	1603—	**Measure for Measure.**
		Hamlet (complete)
xxiv.	1604—	All's Well that Ends **Well** (re-written).
xxv.		Othello.
xxvi.	1605—	Lear.
		Merry Wives of Windsor **(complete).**
xxvii.	1606—	Macbeth.
xxviii.		Timon (part).
xxix.	1607—	Troilus and Cressida (finished).
xxx.		Pericles (part).
xxxi.	1608—	Antony and Cleopatra.
		Cymbeline (begun).
xxxii.	1609—	Coriolanus.
xxxiii.		Two Noble Kinsmen (part).
xxxiv.	1610—	Cymbeline (finished).
xxxv.		Tempest.
xxxvi.	1611—	Winter's Tale.
xxxvii.		Henry VIII. (part).

I.—LOVE'S LABOUR'S LOST.

1. Certainly Shakespeare's.

2. Origin unknown.

3. **Dated by** Drake and Delius (rightly) 1591; Chalmers, 1592; Malone, 1594. It was printed in 1598, as "presented before her highness [Queen Elizabeth] last Christmas (1597), and **newly corrected and augmented.**" **Among** the added parts are probably, i. **2, 171—192**; iii. **1**, 166—207; iv. **3**, 1—25; v. **2**, 575—590; 726—833; 847—879; and the corrected parts, i. **1**, 1—48; ii. **1, 1—177**; iv. **1, 1—12**; iv. **3**, 290—380; v. **2**, 1—40. The conceit of A-jax and **ajakes** being perhaps **taken** from Harrington's *Metamorphosis of Ajax*, 1596 (cf. v. **2**, **579**), and "the first **and second cause,** passado, **duello,**" &c., alluding to Saviolo's *Treatise* **of** *Honour and Honourable* **Quarrels, 1595** (cf. i. **2**, 184).

4. Berowne and Rosaline in **this** play are first sketches of Benedick and Bettris in *Much Ado About* **Nothing**. There was **a** companion play called *Love's Labour's* **Won,** **mentioned** by Meres, but not extant. This is generally, and no doubt rightly, considered to have been the nucleus of *All's Well that Ends Well.* Mr. Brae inclines to *Much Ado About Nothing:* I think as good a case as his could be made out for *Twelfth Night* **or for** several other plays of Shakespeare's. The title is alluded to in *Two Gentlemen of Verona*, Act. i. Sc. **1, 6.**

II.—COMEDY OF ERRORS.

1. Undoubtedly Shakespeare's (though all the doggrel lines are suspected by Ritson).

2. Taken from the *Menæchmi* of Plautus; in great part of the **plot.** There is a translation of this comedy by W[illiam] W[arner], **1595.** From the last line of the prologue to this, "Much pleasant *error* ere they meet together," Shakespeare may have taken his title;

but the foundation of the play was probably not this translation, but
"The *Historie of Error* shewn at Hampton Court on New Yere's
daie at night (1576-7), enacted by the Children of Pawles." Yet
Warner's play was entered at Stationers' Hall 10 June, 1594, and
the printer's advertisement states it had been circulated for some time
in MS.

3. Assigned by Drake, Chalmers, and Delius to 1591, by Malone
to 1592. I agree with Malone. The only note of time is

"*Ant. S.* In what part of her body stands *France?*

"*Drom. S.* In her forehead, arm'd and reverted, making war
against her *hair.*"

The *heir* of France was Henri IV.; the war about his succession
began August 1589. Henri became a Roman Catholic 25 July,
1593, and was crowned February 1594. This limits the date.

4. In this play, as in the preceding, the unity of time is observed;
and the action is confined to one town. The plot is so improbable
as to distinctly mark the play as one of the first group, of plays of
fancy. It is seldom acted, the extreme difficulty of obtaining two pairs
of actors sufficiently like to realize the "errors" enough for modern
taste being insurmountable. Nor is it in any sense one of Shakespeare's best plays. It is more like *Midsummer Night's Dream*
than any other in the fantastic tangle of events on which the plot is
founded. The opening scenes also are very similar in their motives.
For the likeness of the twins compare Viola and Sebastian in *Twelfth
Night.* It is noticeable that in this the first play in which Shakespeare
treats of jealousy it is the woman who is jealous.

III.—MIDSUMMER NIGHT'S DREAM.

1. Undoubted.

2. Hints for the framework of Theseus and Hippolyta were
probably received from Chaucer's *Knight's Tale;* for the interlude
of Thisbe from Chaucer's *Thisbe of Babylon;* for the fairies from
popular tales of *Robin Goodfellow;* but Oberon from Greene's
James IV.

3. Dated by Drake, 1593; Chalmers, 1598; Malone, 1594; Delius later than 1594; I should place it in 1592.

Oberon and Titania were introduced in a dramatic entertainment before Queen Elizabeth in 1591. Act v. 1, 52, "The thrice three muses' mourning for the death of learning, *late* deceased in beggary," alludes to the *Tears of the Muses* by Spenser, published in 1591, or possibly to the death of Greene in 1592, or to both.

4. This play is full of young poetry, fanciful and lively; the story is very poor, and there is little development of character in any of the personages except Bottom and his company. The unity of time is not so strictly kept as in the *Comedy of Errors*; the time occupied is two days and a half. It is very like the *Errors* in its embroilments and its framework. For the name compare *Winter's Tale*, if it be taken in the sense of a "summer's story" (*Sonnet* 98); but the allusions to the name in the play itself (iv. 1, end; Epilogue, &c.) do not confirm this interpretation. Similar allusions are found in *Comedy of Errors*, v. 1, 388; *Measure for Measure*, v. 1, 416; *All's Well that Ends Well*, iv. 4, 35; v. 1, 24.

IV.—RICHARD II.

1. Certainly Shakespeare's.

2. Founded on Holinshed's *Chronicle*.

3. Dated 1596 by Drake, Chalmers, and Delius; 1593 by Malone (rightly).

4. There was an earlier play (called *Henry IV.*) in which Richard was deposed and killed on the stage. It was performed at a public theatre, at the request of Sir Gilly Merick and other followers of Lord Essex, the afternoon before his insurrection. Merick gave forty shillings extra to Phillips to play it, as the play was old and would not draw. In Shakespeare's play the deposition scene was not printed till 1608. It was probably not acted, and suppressed in the edition of 1597 because the Pope had published a bull against Elizabeth in 1596 exhorting rebellion. In 1599 Hayward was

censured in the Star Chamber, and imprisoned for publishing his *History of the First Year of Henry IV.*, which is simply the deposition of Richard II.

The time comprised in the play is two years, 1398-1400. It was Shakespeare's earliest historical play, and rightly called a tragedy in the title of the old quarto. So was *Richard III.;* but not *Henry IV., Henry V.,* or *John.*

It is less suited to the stage than the other histories.

V.—EDWARD III.

1. Supposed by Collier, Ulrici, and others, to be entirely Shakespeare's. In my opinion only the love story, Act i. Sc. 2, Act. ii., is his. Mr. Tennyson tells me, however, that he can trace the master's hand throughout the play at intervals. See my paper from the *Academy*, 25 April, 1874, in Part II.

2. Founded on Holinshed, and the Shakespeare-part on the *Palace of Pleasure.*

3. Published in 1596 as having been "played sundry times about the city of London." Written probably a year or two before this.

4. Unlike Shakespeare's undoubted historical plays in containing a love story and involving the principal personage in unhistorical adventures. In these and other respects it is like Peele's *Edward I.;* but the flow of metre is not like Peele. Did Shakespeare finish and correct this play as he did *Richard III.?* The metre is like that of this play as corrected. Or is it by Lodge?

VI.—TWO GENTLEMEN OF VERONA.

1. Mr. Upton and Sir Thomas Hanmer have supposed this play to be spurious. Mr. Halliwell (Phillipps) and I at one time suspected a second author to have written part of it; we have both withdrawn this opinion, which was founded on the ground of numerous expressions not found elsewhere in Shakespeare. They are, however, Shakespearian in manner.

2. The greater part of this play is taken from the *Story of the Shepherdess Filismena* in the *Diana* of Montemayor. Bartholomew Young published a translation of the *Diana;* his dedication is dated November 1598. It had **been previously** translated by Thomas Wilson **in** 1595-6; and parts by **Edward Paston and Sir Philip** Sidney. Young's was the only one published, **and** was probably **completed as** early as 1582-3. The ending of the play is, however, taken **from** *Apollonius* **and** *Sylla,* a **novel by** Bandello, extant (untranslated) **in** 1554. **The** original **of** the *Diana* dates **1560.** There is an English translation of *Apollonius and Sylla* in Riche, *his farewell to militaire profession* 1606. This and *Felix and Felismena* are reprinted in Collier's *Shakespeare's Library*. The encomium **on** solitude (v. 4) and Valentine's consenting to head the robbers, are taken from P. Sidney's *Arcadia*, **B. i.** Chap. 6, where Pyrocles acts in a similar way (published 1590).

3. This play is assigned by Malone to 1591, **by** Delius to **an** earlier date still; by Chalmers and Drake to **1595.** I assign the two first acts to the beginning **of** 1593, the three last to 1595. The external evidence is very **slight.**

> "Some to the wars **to try their** fortunes there;
> Some, to discover **islands far** away," (Act i. Sc. 3,)

may refer to the following circumstances:—

In 1595 Sir W. Raleigh undertook a voyage to Trinidado, whence he made an expedition up the Oronoque to discover Guiana. Sir Humphrey Gilbert had made a similar voyage in 1594. A second invasion by the Spaniards was expected in 1595. Soldiers were levied, fleets were equipped, troops were sent **to aid** Henri IV. of France in consequence.

Speed says,

> "Like one that had the pestilence," (Act ii. Sc. 1.)

There was a great plague in London in 1593, and 11,000 died there. But this kind of evidence has little value; Essex had been joined by many volunteers when he went to France in 1591. There was a plague in 1583.

Marlowe's *Hero and Leander* was entered at Stationers' Hall 18 September, 1593. Marlowe was buried on 1 June, the same year.

There is an allusion to that story in Act i. Sc. 1, probably from Marlowe's poem, which *may* have circulated in MS. some time before. This is, however, not likely. Shakespeare alludes to the same story in other plays, of which the earliest is *Romeo and Juliet* (probably 1596), Act iii. Sc. 1. The allusion to "Merops' son" is likely to be taken from the old play of *King John* (1591),

" As sometimes Phaeton
Mistrusting silly Merops for his sire."

This play Shakespeare certainly read before 1596, as his own *King John*, founded on it cannot be placed later than that year. Mr. Boaden (who has been followed by many later critics) observed that the germs of other plays are contained in this comedy.

4. This play, whether from being an early work, as some think, or from being an attempt at an entirely new kind of comedy, that of social life as distinguished from that of mere fancy, as illustrated in the three preceding plays; or from having been produced at a period of depression (compare *Sonnet* 29, &c.), as I think, is certainly one of the weakest and least satisfactory of all Shakespeare's plays. It is less poetic than any other, though some lines are eminently beautiful and quotable. It is more careless, not only in sending Valentine to Milan by sea, but also in twice having Verona in the text where Milan is required. There is also a strange confusion between duke and emperor, similar to confusions which I notice elsewhere. It is unnatural in some of its incidents; in Silvia's giving Proteus her picture, though she rejects his suit; in Valentine's surrendering Silvia to the perjured Proteus; in Proteus's threat to employ force to Silvia. It has many weak versions of incidents and situations that are much better rendered in other plays. For instance, compare the character of Valentine with that of Mercutio in *Romeo and Juliet;* of Launce with Lancelot Gobbo, and of Lucetta with Nerissa in the *Merchant of Venice;* the incidents of the rope ladder and the banishment of the principal character with those in *Romeo and Juliet.*

This inferiority must not, however, be taken as absolute evidence as to relative date, since it often happens in plays known to be later than those in which the better version occurs. Compare, for example, the Constable in *Measure for Measure* with Dogberry in *Much Ado About Nothing.*

It is to be noted that this is the earliest comedy and, except *Richard II.*, the earliest play in which the unity of time is altogether neglected in defiance of Sir Philip Sidney. That of place had also been given up in *Richard II.*

The plots of many of these early plays are built up of the same or very similar materials. The following table may be useful as showing the characters to be compared in some of them, and in the tales from which this play is taken :—

Romeo and Juliet.	*All's Well.*	*Two Gentlemen.*	*Felix and Fel.*	*Apol. and Sylla.*	*Twelfth Night.*
—	—	Sebastian.	Valerio.	Silvio.	Cesario.
Rosaline.	Helena.	Julia.	Felismena.	Sylla.	Viola.
Juliet.	Diana.	Silvia.	Celia.	Juliana.	Olivia.
Romeo.	Bertram.	Proteus.	Don Felix.	Apollonius.	Count.
Mercutio.	—	Valentine.	—	Silvio.	Sebastian.

Some of the weaknesses of the play arise from an exaggerated carrying out of the main idea, which is certainly that of friendship; first broken then restored; the corresponding play is the *Merchant of Venice.* Antonio is the contrast to Proteus; Launce and Lucetta are clearly germs of Launcelot and Nerissa.

VII.—RICHARD III.

1. Halliwell thinks that the turbulent character of this play as we now have it is due to an older one. I have no doubt that it was originally written by G. Peele, left unfinished by him, completed and partly corrected by Shakespeare as we have it in the Quartos, and that Shakespeare afterwards altered it into the shape in which it was printed in the Folio. No other hypothesis can, I think, account for its similarity to much of *Henry VI.* which is not Shakespearian, and also for the unparalleled differences between the Folio and Quarto. (See my essay in *Macmillan's Magazine* for November, 1875, on *Henry VI.*)

2. Founded on Holinshed's *Chronicle* and a preceding play on the same subject produced by the Queen's Company in 1594.

3. Date of first production probably 1595.

4. **Period** involved, eight years : 1477–85. This, like the *Taming of the Shrew*, has always been a favourite acting piece.

VIII.—1 Henry VI.

1. Condemned by nearly all critics; and assigned in various divisions to Marlowe, Greene, &c. I have little doubt that Marlowe wrote i. 1, i. 3, iii. 1, iv. 1, v. 1 ; Lodge wrote i. 2—6, ii. 1—3, iii. 2, 3, [? iv. 2—7, v. 2] ; Shakespeare wrote ii. 4, and perhaps ii. 5 ; and possibly he in his very early time, but more likely Lodge, wrote iv. 2—7 and v. 2. Some fourth and unknown hand certainly wrote iv. 4, v. 1, v. 5, which are quite different from the rest of the play.

2. Founded on Holinshed ; but not following him so closely as the histories by Shakespeare do.

3. Certainly before 1592, when it was acted by L. Strange's men at the Rose. The Chamberlain's Company had it before 1599. See Epilogue to *Henry V.*

4. This play is independent of 2 *Henry VI.* and 3 *Henry VI.* It was tacked to them by the writer of the last scene after 1600. It probably passed to the Chamberlain's Company when L. Strange's men joined them in 1594.

IX.—John.

1. Certainly Shakespeare's.

2. Founded on *The Troublesome Raigne of John, King of England, with the Discoverie of King Richard Cordelion's base Son, vulgarly named the Bastard Fawconbridge ; also the Death of King John at Swinstead Abbey.* 1591. Falsely attributed to Shakespeare in title-page of 1622 and to W. Sh. in that of 1611.

3. Hamnet, Shakespeare's only son, died in August 1596. Constance's lament for Arthur's loss (Act iii. Sc. 4) would appear to be written soon before this event.

> "A braver choice of dauntless spirits
> **Than now the** English bottoms have waft o'er,
> **Did** never float upon the swelling tide
> **To do** offense and scathe **to Christendom**," (Act ii. Sc. 1,)

was probably suggested by the great fleet then preparing to be **sent** against Spain in 1596. **It sailed** on 3 June, the great armada **was** destroyed, Cadiz sacked, and **the** fleet returned by 8 August, four days before Hamnet died.

The *Spanish Tragedy, Solyman and Perseda*, and *Captain Thomas Stukely* are **quoted or** alluded to ; but they do not help to fix **the** date, which Drake and Chalmers place **in 1598.** Malone **and** Delius in **1596.** I prefer 1595.

4. The action extends through the whole **of John's** reign from 1199 **to** 1216. It is the first historical **play, properly so** called, among Shakespeare's works.

X.—ROMEO AND JULIET.

1. Boswell has conjectured that in the first Quarto (1597) there are embodied remains of an older play on which Shakespeare founded his. I believe that G. Peele wrote the early play about 1593; that Shakespeare in 1596 corrected this up to the point where there is a change of type **in** Q 1 (to end of Act ii. Sc. 3), and in 1597 completed his corrections as in Q 2.

2. Luigi da Porto's novel, *Hystoria di dui nobili Amanti* (Venice, 1535), followed by Bandello's novel (Lucca, 1554), was the origin of Boisteau's. From Boisteau, Painter **took** his *Rhomeo and Julietta* (*Palace of Pleasure*, 1567), and Arthur Brooke his poem of *The Tragical History of Romeus and Juliet, containing a Rare Example of True Constancie*, &c. (1562, 2nd Edition, 1587). Shakespeare copied the poem, using the novel occasionally, as is clear from the following table :—

ON THE PLAYS OF SHAKESPEARE. 33

	Novel.	*Play.*	*Poem.*
Name of prince.	Signor Escala.	Eskales.	Escalus.
Romeo's family.	Montesches.	Mountagues.	Montagues.
Friar's messenger.	Anselmo.	John.	**John.**
Act i. Sc. 2, l. 68-75.	Omitted.	Given.	Given.
Capulet's residence.	Villa Franca.	Freetown.	Freetowm.
Romeo's name.	Rhomeo.	**Romeo.**	Romeus; Romeo(once).
Juliet's sleep.	40 hours.	**42 hours.**	omitted.

3. Dated by Chalmers, 1592; Drake, 1593 (rightly for George Peele's share); Delius, 1591; Malone, 1596 (rightly for Shakespeare's corrected edition). Malone's argument is this:—Shakespeare, Burbage, and others, "the Lord Chamberlain's men," on the death of Henry Lord Hunsdon the Lord Chamberlain (22 July, 1596), were protected and sanctioned by George Lord Hunsdon. In August 1596 William Brooke, Lord **Cobham**, was appointed Chamberlain, who died 5 March, 1596-7; on 17 April George Lord Hunsdon succeeded him. The company could therefore only be called Lord Hunsdon's men (as they are in title-page of Quarto, 1597,) between July 1596 and April 1597. [But this only **shows** that **the** piece **was produced in that** interval, not that the original play was then written.]

In Act iii. Sc. 1, Q 1, the "first and second **causes**" are mentioned: that **passage (not** the whole play) was **therefore** written after Saviolo's *Book* **on** *Honour* and *Honourable Quarrels* had been published (1594); see *Love's Labour's Lost*, Act i. Sc. 2. This fixes the earliest date for the play, say some critics; but Peele may have known this book in the original language.

There are passages in Act v. very like some in Daniel's *Complaint of Rosamond* (entered February 1591-2).

The comedy of *Doctor Doddipoll*, which appeared, Malone says, before 1596, imitates (?) this play; compare Act iii. Sc. 2, line 22, &c., Q 2, with

> "**The glorious** parts of fair Lucilia,
> Take them and join them in the heavenly spheres,
> And fix them there as an eternal light
> For lovers to adore and wonder at."

In v. 2, 9, Q 1, the practice of sealing up the **doors** of plague-infected houses is alluded to. This may refer to the plague of **1593**.

In Act i. Sc. 3, line 23, **Q 1, the nurse's** speech probably alludes to **the** earthquake in **1580 as Juliet's weaning day**; and as Juliet is nearly fourteen **years old, this** brings us to **1593.** The nurse's miscalculation, that fourteen less one makes eleven, **adds to the** humour of the passage.

Weever's *Epigrams* (published before **1595) allude to this** play. See page 15.

4. This is certainly Shakespeare's earliest tragedy. **It was probably** meant as a companion to *Troylus and Cressida,* **the** love-story in which **is,** I think, of the **date** 1594. Faithful Juliet **is the contrast** to faithless Cressid. The only other instances of **similar** titles of paired names are *Benedick* **and** *Betteris* (*Much Ado About Nothing*) and *Antony and Cleopatra.* **The play was** acted at **the** Curtain Theatre; it is rather to be classed **with the** other early ones **as a love play** than with the great tragedies, **which** form a group by themselves. Mercutio is like Valentine (*Two Gentlemen of Verona*) before he meets **with** Silvia. Romeo **in his** inconstancy is like Proteus; also like the **Count in** *Twelfth Night.* The time occupied in the play is five days.

XI.—MERCHANT OF VENICE.

1. Undoubted.

2. The main plot **is** from the *Pecorone* of San Giovanni Fiorentino; **Fourth** day, first novel, *Gianetta* (1378). The casket story from an old translation **of** the *Gesta Romanorum* (1577). Both stories are condensed in the **Variorum** *Shakspeare* (1821). Gosson (1579) mentions *The Jew* shown at the Bull, representing the greediness of worldly choosers (casket-scene) "and the bloody minds of usurers" (Shylock).

3. Malone identifies **this play** with *The Venesyan Comedy*, acted at the Rose, 1594. But Shakespeare's plays were not at **any** date acted there. Drake and Chalmers date it, nearly rightly, **1597.** I prefer 1596.

XII.—1 Henry IV.

1. Undoubtedly Shakespeare's.

2. Founded on **Holinshed's** *Chronicle*, and *The Famous Victories of King Henry the Fifth*, *containing the honourable Battle of Agincourt*, **1594**.

3. **Entered** 25 February, 1597-8. Written in **1596** (Drake), or more probably **1597** (the general opinion).

4. The period comprised in this play is about **ten** months, from 14 September, **1402** (Holyrood **Day**), to **21** July, 1403 (Eve of St. Mary Magdalen). In this **and the** succeeding plays Shakespeare reaches his highest **point in** comedy in the character of Falstaff. Prose appears here **for** the first time as an essential part of the drama in his historical **plays**.

XIII.—2 Henry IV.

1. Certainly Shakespeare's.

2. Same as preceding.

3. Dated by Drake, 1596; Chalmers, **1597**; Malone, 1598, I think rightly.

In Act iv. 4, **118**, Clarence says :—

> "The incessant care and labour **of** his mind
> Hath wrought **the mure**, that should confine it in,
> So thin, that life **looks** through and will break out."

In Daniel's *Civil Warres*, l. iii. st. **116** (entered October 1594, published **1595**,) we find :—

> "Wearing the wall so thin that **now the mind**
> Might well look thorough and **his frailty find**."

In Act v. :—

> "**Not Amurath an Amurath** succeeds,"

alludes to **Mahomet's** strangling his brothers on his succeeding to his father, **Amurath III.**, in February **1596**.

Pistol's distich, "**Si** fortuna **me tormenta**," &c., appeared in *Wits, Fits, and Fancies*, entered **at Stationers'** Hall in 1595. Justice Shallow is alluded to by name in *Every Man in His Humour*, acted 1598, hence the date is fixed to **1596**, 1597, or 1598.

4. The period comprised **is nine years, 1403—1412**.

XIV.—MERRY WIVES OF WINDSOR.

1. Certainly Shakespeare's.

2. Founded on *The Lovers of Pisa*, **a tale** in Tarleton's *News out of Purgatorie* (1589); printed in the *Variorum Shakspeare* (1821).

3. Said to have been written **at** the desire of Queen Elizabeth, to show Falstaff in love. Certainly written after *Henry IV.;* possibly after *Henry V.* This play does not form one **of the** *Henry IV. and V.* series, and consistency with them is **not to be** looked for in it. Malone and Drake date it **1601**. I prefer **1598 for** the first sketch, as in Q 1. The revised **form** of it, Q 2, **is said to have been** written about 1605, because "king" is substituted for "council" in **Act i. 1, 113**. "These knights will hack," iii. 1, 79, is supposed **to allude to the** 237 knights made by James I. before May 1603. So "**When** the court lay at Windsor," Act ii. Sc. 2, l. 63, means probably July 1603: it was held usually at Greenwich in the summer. "Coach after coach," Act ii. **Sc.** 2, l. 66, could not be much before 1605, when coaches came into general use (Howe's *Continuation of Stowe's Chronicle*). "Outrun on Cotsale," **Act i.** Sc. 1, l. 92, alludes to the Cotswold games instituted by Robert Dover about 1603.

4. The surreptitious copy of the **first** form of this play was the **only** one published before the First Folio, the MS. of the improved form being in the hands of the proprietors of the Globe Theatre.

The title Sir, given to priests, is a translation of Dominus; it was restrained to Sir Knight, Sir Priest, Sir Graduate, and Sir Esquire. **See** *A Decacordon of Ten Quodlibeticall Questions*, &c., 1602.

XV.—HENRY V.

1. Undoubted.

2. Same as *Henry IV*.

3. Written while the Earl of Essex was in Ireland (see Act. v., Chorus,) between April and September 1599, as promised in Epilogue of 2 *Henry IV*.

The allusion in the prologue to *Every Man in His Humour* is of no use to fix the date, not being written till 1601.

4. The early Quartos of this play are not first sketches, but surreptitious copies grossly mutilated. The period comprised is from the first to the eighth year of Henry V. The allusions to Oldcastle (1 *Henry IV*., i. 2, 48, 2 *Henry IV*., Epilogue,) refer not to the play of *Sir John Oldcastle*, wrongly attributed to Shakespeare, but to the character who takes Falstaff's place in the worthless old play of *The Famous Victories*. The French scene, Act iii. Sc. 4, is quite exceptional. I hope it is not Shakespeare's, and believe it to be Lodge's.

XVI.—MUCH ADO ABOUT NOTHING.

1. Certainly Shakespeare's.

2. Taken indirectly from a novel of Belleforest's after Bandello. There is a similar story in Ariosto, *Orlando Furioso*, Book v., and in the *Geneura* of Turbervil.

3. Written in 1599 or 1600.

4. The characters of Benedick and Betteris are founded on those of Berowne and Rosaline in *Love's Labour's Lost*. The old tale, "It is Not So," is given in the *Variorum Shakspeare*, 1821.

XVII.—JULIUS CÆSAR.

1. Hitherto undoubted. I have, however, given reasons for supposing that Jonson either revised the play or superintended its revision. Antony is throughout it spelled without an *h*, as Jonson spells it. Shakespeare elsewhere always uses the *h*. There are phrases, such as "bear me hard," "I will come home to you (to your house)," "quality and kind," &c., which are used by Jonson, not elsewhere by Shakespeare. The play is singularly free from the words of Shakespeare's coinage that abound in his other plays; it is shorter than the average of plays of similar character by 1,000 lines; the metre shows clear traces of having been abridged like the surreptitious copies of *Romeo and Juliet* and *Hamlet*. The passage quoted by Jonson as ridiculous, "Cæsar did never wrong but with just cause," does not occur in it, but has been altered into "Know Cæsar doth not wrong, nor without cause will he be satisfied" (see Jonson's *Discoveries*). Compare the *Induction* to the *Staple of News*, "Cry you mercy! You never did wrong but with just cause."

2. Founded on North's translation of *Plutarch's Lives* of Julius Cæsar, Marcus Brutus, and Marcus Antonius.

3. Assigned by Drake, Chalmers, and Malone to 1607; by Halliwell to 1600-1; by Delius to a time before 1604. I think it was produced in 1600, again in 1607, and in the abridged form we now have it after 1613.

Malone argues for 1607 being the date of original production on the ground that Lord Sterling's play was written then or not long before; and he "would not have been daring enough to enter the lists with Shakespeare." The inference is stretched too far; it is only fair to conclude from the printing of Sterling's *Julius Cæsar*, and also of the second edition of the *Tragedy of Cæsar and Pompey*, or *Cæsar's Revenge*, in 1607, that a production or revival of Shakespeare's piece took place that year. A much stronger argument would have been the probability that all the Roman plays were produced in successive years, like the groups of the great tragedies, or the historical plays. The internal evidence for an early date is, however, overwhelming (especially in metre), and Mr. Halliwell has found an allusion to this play of the date of 1601.

4. Shakespeare makes Cæsar be killed in the Capitol, though Plutarch expressly says in Pompey's portico ; he was probably continuing the tradition of the earlier poems and plays. Compare *Hamlet*, iii. 2, 108, &c. (also in Q 1), and Chaucer. The quarrelling scene in *The Maid's Tragedy* (? 1609) is imitated from that between Brutus and Cassius. This confirms the guess that the play was represented in 1607. It was called also *Cæsar's Tragedy* (1613), probably in its altered form. Gosson mentions a *History of Cæsar and Pompey* in 1579. The time included in the play is nearly three years. The real hero of the tragedy is Marcus Brutus. The treatment is more like that in *Henry IV.* and *V.* than that of the other Roman plays, and forms a connecting link between the histories and tragedies. See Part II. on this play.

XVIII.—AS YOU LIKE IT.

1. Undoubted.

2. Founded on Lodge's novel of *Rosalynd, or Euphues' Golden Legacy* (1590). The characters of Jaques, Touchstone, and Audrey are entirely Shakespeare's. For Lodge's novel, see Collier's *Shakespeare's Library*.

3. "Staied," in the Stationers' books, 4 August (year not given, but either 1600, 1601, or 1602, and almost certainly 1600), along with *Henry V.*, which was entered again 14 August and published in the same year; *Much Ado About Nothing*, which was entered 23 August and published the same year ; and *Every Man in His Humour*, published 1601.

Rosalind says :—

"I will weep like Diana in the fountain."—iv. 1, 145.

Stowe mentions this image of Diana as set up in 1598 and decayed in 1603. The date of the play is fixed then between 1598 and 1600. Malone says 1599.

A line of Marlowe's *Hero and Leander* is quoted (iii. 5, 83); this poem was published 1598.

4. Shakespeare played Adam in this play; he continued to act till 1603, when he played in *Sejanus;* he also acted the Ghost in *Hamlet,* &c.

XIX.—TWELFTH NIGHT.

1. Undoubted.

2. See under the *Two Gentlemen of Verona* for the story of Viola; that of Malvolio is Shakespeare's own.

3. Used to be dated as one of the last of Shakespeare's plays on the ground of allusions to "undertakers," Dekker's *Westward Ho!* Sir Robert Shirley coming as ambassador from the Sophy; and the internal evidence of perfection of style, &c. It is now certain that it was produced before February 1602; and there are clear indications in the metre that some parts of the Viola story were written much earlier—about 1594. I date the completion 1601. The early parts are, I think, traceable all through the verse scenes, specially in Act iii. Sc. 1, and Act v. Sc. 1.

4. The Count in this play is called Duke in Act i. Sc. 2 and Sc. 4, just as the Emperor is called Duke in *Two Gentlemen of Verona* and the King is called Duke in *Love's Labour's Lost*. The second name of the play, *What You Will*, is a strange one; it is very like that of *As You Like It*. Mr. Staunton's conjecture that Shakespeare not having named these plays answered hurriedly to the inquiring manager, "Call it what you will; name it as you like it," is the most plausible explanation of their origin. Marston took the name *What You Will* for a play of his own in 1607. The name *Twelfth Night* was probably that of the date of the first production of the play.

XX.—HAMLET.

1. Undoubted.

2. Founded on an older play now lost; and on the *Hystorie of Hamblett* (black letter; date of earliest edition unknown), which was translated from one of Belleforest's novels. He took it from "Saxo Grammaticus."

3. Dated by Malone, 1600; Chalmers, 1598; Drake, 1597 (revised 1600); Delius (more rightly), 1602. Steevens mentions a reference to *Hamlet* in Gabriel Harvey's handwriting as made in 1598, which may have been written any time before 1620; and the reference to the inhibition of the players (Act ii. Sc. 2, l. 346) is not necessarily to be applied to the first order of the Privy Council for the restraint of the immoderate use of playhouses (made 22 June, 1600), for this order proved ineffectual; but rather to their second order, made 31 December, 1601. The Fortune and the Globe were allowed to remain open; the others were closed owing to the personal allusions indulged in by some of the companies. The play was probably revised in 1603.

4. The allusion in Nash's epistle to "whole Hamlets or handfuls of tragical speeches" must allude to the old play now lost; and so must Lodge's allusion to the Ghost that cried, "Hamlet, revenge! so miserably." Shakespeare's play was entered 26 July, 1602. I should place the first draft in 1601, the complete play in 1603. I have little doubt that the early *Hamlet* of 1589 was written by Shakespeare and Marlowe in conjunction; and that portions of it can be traced in the First Quarto as "Corambis" *Hamlet*.

XXI.—TAMING OF THE SHREW.

1. Declared spurious by Dr. Warburton. Dr. Farmer assigned only the Induction and the character of Petruchio to Shake-

speare, with occasional touches elsewhere. Mr. Collier advocated the same opinion. I assign to the second writer the following parts:—i. 1, i. 2; ii. 1, except l. 168—326; iii. 1, iii. 2, 129—150; iv. 2, iv. 4; v. 1, and perhaps, v. 2, 176—189. This second hand was probably T. Lodge. It is observable that in all these parts there is scarcely a trace of the old play *The Taminge of a Shrewe*; while in the other parts, plot and even language is freely borrowed; exactly in the way in which Shakespeare revised his first drafts of *The Merry Wives of Windsor* and *Hamlet*. See Part II.

2. Founded on the play mentioned above and on the *Supposes* of Gascoigne "englished" from Ariosto, 1566.

3. Dated by Drake and Delius, 1594; Chalmers, 1599; Malone, 1596; Collier, I think rightly, 1601-2.

The play is not mentioned in Meres' list (1598). The line,

"This is the way to kill a wife with kindness,"

seems to allude to Heywood's play, *A Woman Killed with Kindness*, the date of which is 1602. The play of *Patient Grissel* by Dekker, Chettle, and Haughton, was brought out in 1599; this play of Shakespeare's is clearly a rival piece, in opposition to which again came out Dekker's *Medicine for a Curst Wife* (July 1602).

4. The old play, *The Taming of a Shrew*, was probably written by Marlowe and Shakespeare in conjunction in 1589. Shakespeare certainly wrote much, if not all the prose in it. This early drama, along with the old *Hamlet*, 2 and 3 *Henry VI.*, and *Titus Andronicus*, almost certainly came into the possession of the Chamberlain's company in 1600. They previously belonged to the Earl of Pembroke's.

2 AND 3 HENRY VI.

1. The Quarto editions have always been regarded as earlier works than the Folio. They are quoted under the names of: *The Contention* and *The True Tragedy*. The full titles are *The first part of the Contention betwixt the two famous Houses of York and Lancaster* and *The True Tragedy of Richard Duke of York*. The theories that have been held as to the authorship are—1, Malone's,

that Marlowe, Greene, &c., wrote *The Whole Contention* (that is, both Quartos), and that Shakespeare enlarged and completed them into 2 and 3 *Henry VI.;* 2, Knight's, that Shakespeare was author of both Quartos and Folio; 3, Grant White's, that Shakespeare, Marlowe, and Greene, wrote the Quartos from which Shakespeare transferred his own work to the Folio, the additions also being his; Hudson, Steevens, Johnson, Hazlitt, Ulrici, and the Germans generally, hold the Shakespearian authorship of the Quartos in more or less entirety. Other critics (except myself) hold the additions to be his. I believe the whole of 2 and 3 *Henry VI.* to be by Peele and Marlowe: the latter writing Act iii. Sc. 3 and Act iv. Sc. 1 of 2 *Henry VI.* and Acts ii. v. of 3 *Henry VI.* and Peele, the rest.

N.B.—3 *Henry VI.* iv. 8 should form part of Act v.—The grounds of my view, æsthetic, artistic, and metrical, are given in a paper by me in *Macmillan's Magazine* (Nov. 1875). Of course Shakespeare revised (though he did not write) these plays about 1601.

2. Founded on Hall's *Chronicle;* not Holinshed's; but follows him loosely. See the blunders as to the side espoused by Lady Grey's husband; the marriage of the Prince of Wales to Warwick's eldest daughter, &c., &c.

3. Written not later than 1592. See the quotation of "A tiger's heart wrapt in a player's hide," in Greene's *Groatsworth of Wit.*

4. The Quarto editions are merely piratical versions taken down in shorthand (in my opinion) at a theatrical representation. There is scarcely anything in the Quartos not in the Folio; and what little there is seems to be introduced for the groundlings. Malone's numbers are altogether deceptive, from the manner in which they are evolved. The plays were written for Pembroke's company, and the earliest notice of them in connexion with the King's is on the title-page of *The Whole Contention* in 1619, three years after Shakespeare's death. There are in the Quartos, and in the parts peculiar to the Folio, many classical allusions, similes, and expressions in the styles of Marlowe and Peele. Malone's dissertation is the store from which most of the modern arguments concerning authorship have been taken.

TITUS ANDRONICUS.

1. In 1687 there was a tradition reported by Ravenscroft that this play was only touched by Shakespeare. **Theobald,** Johnson, Farmer, Stevens, Drake, Singer, Dyce, Hallam, **H.** Coleridge, **W. S. Walker,** reject it entirely. **Malone, Ingleby, Staunton,** think it **was touched** up by him. Capel, **Collier, Knight,** Gervinus, **Ulrici, and many** Germans, **think it to be** Shakespeare's; **R. G. White, that it** is a joint work **of Greene, Marlowe, and Shakespeare! The fact that it** was acted **by the companies of Sussex, Pembroke, and Derby, and** printed as so acted **before it came into the possession of the** Chamberlain's company, is far **more important than the mention of it** in Meres, or the reception **of it in the Folio. It was** not published with Shakespeare's name **as author in his** lifetime. Halliwell **thinks Shakespeare's** play (? *Titus and Vespasian*) is lost, and was **the one entered by J.** Danter **in 1594. I hold** this play to **be Marlowe's.** See my paper in *Macmillan's Magazine* (Nov. 1875).

2. May have been founded **on a** ballad. **The story** was known to Painter, who alludes to it **in his** *Palace of Pleasure.*

3. Probably 1590. See **Jonson's** allusion to it in *Bartholomew Fair* (1614) as some 25 or 30 years old. He couples it with Kyd's *Jeronimo.* Certainly written before 1592, when it was acted at the **Rose.**

4. A stilted, disagreeable play with a few fair touches. It has many classical allusions in it; many coincidences in the use of words and phrases with Marlowe's work, and with *Henry VI.*; in style and metre **it is** exactly what a play of Marlowe's would be if, corrected by Shakespeare as he corrected *Richard III.* of Peele's.

A play called *Titus and Vespasian* was also acted at the Rose, which appears from a German translation to have treated of the same story as *Titus Andronicus* (see Cohn, *Shakespeare in Germany*). In this form of the play Vespasian is a friend of Titus. It is very likely a remnant of the form into which Shakespeare cast his play, with or without the aid of Marlowe. Our present play is not Shakespeare's; it is built on the Marlowe blank-verse system, which Shakespeare **in** his early work opposed: and did not belong to Shakespeare's company till 1600.

XXII.—SEJANUS. (?)

1. Jonson tells us that in the first form of this play as acted on the public stage "a second pen had good share; in place of which I have rather chosen to put weaker and no doubt less pleasing of mine own than to defraud so happy a genius of his right by my loathed usurpation." This second pen was usually, until lately, supposed with good reason to be Shakespeare's. Most critics now reject this hypothesis: but no other likely name has been advanced in his place,[1] unless we admit Dr. Nicholson's view that Sheppard was the "second pen." I cannot think so.

2. Founded on *Tacitus, Suetonius, Seneca,* &c.

3. Produced in 1603.

4. As the early form of the play is lost, the question of authorship is of little importance.

XXIII.—MEASURE FOR MEASURE.

1. Undoubted.

2. Founded on Whetstone's *Promos and Cassandra,* 1578, printed in *Six Old Plays on which Shakespeare founded, &c.* Nichols, 1779.

3. Generally and rightly dated 1603. It apologises for King James' ungracious entry into England.

> "I'll privily away. I love the people,
> But do not like to stage me to their eyes.
> Though it do well, I do not relish well
> Their loud applause and aves vehement."
> Act i. Sc. 1.

> "The general subject to a well-wisht king,
> Quit their own part, and in obsequious fondness
> Crowd to his presence, where their untaught love
> Must needs appear offense."
> Act ii. Sc. 4.

---

[1] Beaumont did not begin to write till 1606, nor Fletcher till 1607, as far as we know. Chapman and Marston wrote commendatory verses on the play. Surely none of these can have been the second hand.

James had issued a proclamation forbidding the people to resort to him.

"What with the war, what with the sweat . . . . Heaven grant us peace!"—Act i. Sc. 2.

The war with Spain still existed in 1603: but James had shown he meant to end it, as he did on 19 August 1604. In 1603 there was a plague, which carried off more than 30,000 in London.

The list of prisoners, Act iv. Sc. 3, contains four stabbers; the roaring boys, bravados, roysters, &c., were so outrageous in 1603 that the statute of Stabbing was passed in the first half of 1604.

4. This play is the central one for the metre of the third period; it has more lines with extra syllables before a pause in the middle of a line than any other. It is freer in rhythm than any play in the first and second periods.

XXIV.—ALL'S WELL THAT ENDS WELL.

1. Undoubted.

2. **The main** plot is founded on Painter's *Giletta of Narbonne*, in the *Palace of Pleasure* Vol. **1**. The comic part with Parolles, &c., is Shakespeare's.

3. Dated by Malone and Chalmers, 1606; by Drake and Delius, 1598; I assign **it to** 1604, as near to *Measure for Measure* as possible. It contains some parts of very early work (1591-2), perhaps remains of *Love's Labour's Won*, namely, the rhymed parts of—i. 1, 230—244, i. 3, 133—142; **ii.** 1, **130—214, ii.** 3, 80—210, ii. 3, 130—150; iii. **4;** sonnet, and **end of scene.**

4. The scene Act iii. **Sc.** 5, **should be** compared with *Two Gentlemen of Verona* (Act iv. Sc. 2); the device by which Bertram is deceived into meeting Helen, his wife, with that in *Measure for Measure*.

ON THE PLAYS OF SHAKESPEARE. 47

XXV.—OTHELLO.

1. Undoubted.

2. Founded on a novel by Giraldi Cinthio (Decade iii. Novel 3).

3. Date earlier than November 1604. This used to be looked on as one of the latest of Shakespeare's plays.

4. The names Othello and Iago occur in Reynolds' *God's Revenge against Adultery*. The date of the action is 1570. Mustapha, the general of Solymus II. attacked Cyprus in May in that year. The Turkish fleet first sailed towards Cyprus, then went to Rhodes, met another squadron, and resumed its course for Cyprus; which was taken in 1571. The accounts of the cannibals and "men whose heads do grow beneath their shoulders" are taken from Sir Walter Raleigh's narrative of the *Discovery of Guiana* (1600); he says, "I am resolved they are true." For the passion of jealousy compare Othello with Troylus, Leontes, Ford, and Posthumus.

XXVI.—LEAR.

1. Undoubted.

2. Founded on Holinshed's *Chronicle* and *The True Chronicle History of King Leir and his three Daughters, Gonorill, Ragan, and Cordella* (entered 1594, printed 1605). This is contained in Steevens' reprint of the Quarto editions of Shakespeare; also in *Six Old Plays, &c.* The episode of Gloster and his sons is taken from the story of the blind king of Paphlagonia in Sidney's *Arcadia*, reprinted in the *Variorum Shakspeare*, 1821. It also often alludes to Harsnet's *Declaration of Egregious Popish Impostures*, 1603.

3. The date must lie between 1603 and 1606. The play was entered November 1607 as having been played in December 1606. It was probably produced early in 1605, as the old play was then reprinted and entered 8th May, "as lately acted," in order to deceive the public.

"I smell the blood of a *British* man " (Act iii. Sc. 6 end), stands

"I smell the blood of an *English* man,"

in Nash's pamphlets, 1596. England and Scotland were united in name and James proclaimed king of Great Britain, **24** October, 1604.

4 Compare Hamlet and Ophelia with Lear, for the phenomena of madness.

XXVII.—MACBETH.

1. Messrs. Clark and Wright reject as Middleton's—i. **1**, i. 2, i. 3, 1-37; ii. 3 (Porter's speech); iii. **5; iv.** 3, 140—159; **v. 2, v.** 8 last forty lines, besides many rhyming tags: I reject also (but not, in all, forty lines) various other rhyming tags: but **retain i.** 2; ii. 3; v. **2.** I must refer to my essay on the subject in Part II., the reasons cannot be condensed here.

2. Founded on Holinshed's *Chronicle*, and Reginald Scot's *Discovery of Witchcraft*.

3. **Dated** almost without **exception 1606** (Middleton's revision being much later). In Act ii. **Sc. 3.** "The expectation of plenty." Wheat was lower in Windsor **market** in 1606 than for thirteen years afterwards, also **lower** than **the** year before. So were barley and malt. The "equivocators" in **the** same year must mean the Jesuits, specially Garnet their superior, who was tried for gunpowder treason on 28 March, **1606** (see Malone). Again the "stealing out of a French hose" implies **that they were at** that time **short** and **strait.** Now in 1606, in Anthony **Nixon's** *Black Year* we find that tailors took more **than** enough **for the new fashion's** sake. **In 1605** King James at Oxford was addressed **by** three students **of St. John's** College in Latin verses founded on the weird-sisters' **predictions** to Macbeth. It is not likely they would choose this subject **after** Shakespeare had treated it. Middleton's *Witch* was certainly **produced** after 1613. There are two passages from Plutarch's **life of** *Antony* alluded **to in** this play. **"The** insane root that takes **the reason**

prisoner," Act i. Sc. 3, l. 84, and "My genius is rebuked as it is said Mark Anthony's was by Cæsar," Act iii. Sc. 1, l. 57. Shakespeare was then probably reading for *Anthony and Cleopatra*, which was produced before May 1608.

4. For treatment of Ghost compare *Hamlet*; for Witches in Act iv. Sc. 2, compare Middleton's *Witch*, the *Witch of Edmonton* by Ford, Dekker, and Rowley (Witch-part by Ford), and Jonson's Masque of *Queens* and *The Sad Shepherd*.

XXVIII.—TIMON OF ATHENS.

1. By two authors. Shakespeare undoubtedly wrote i. 1 (verse part); ii. 1, ii. 2 (verse part); iii. 6 (verse part); iv. 1, iv. 3 ; v. 1, v. 2, v. 4. Cyril Tourneur I think (Delius says Wilkins) wrote the rest. Shakespeare's part was certainly written first, though C. Knight denies this.

2. Founded on a passage in Plutarch's *Life of Antonius*, and the 28th novel in voL 1 of Painter's *Palace of Pleasure*; also on Lucian's *Dialogues*.

3. Evidently to be dated between the great tragedies (which it closely resembles in tone), and *Anthony and Cleopatra*, in reading for which Shakespeare met with the story. I assign it therefore to 1606, a year before the other plays left unfinished by Shakespeare, *Pericles* and *Troylus and Cressida*. Delius says 1608, others 1610. The date of the completion of the play is doubtful ; it may have been 1608, or 1623, when the Folio was printed.

XXIX.—TROYLUS AND CRESSIDA.

1. Nearly the whole of the fifth Act has been suspected as spurious, so has the Prologue.

2. Founded on Chaucer's *Troilus and Creseide* for the love story ; Caxton's *Troy Book* for the story of Hector and Ajax ; Thersites, Patroclus, &c., are taken from Chapman's *Homer*.

3. I have tried to show **that these three** portions were written at different dates **about** 1594, 1595, and 1607. **The whole** play was printed in 1608 as never having been acted. **Thersites** is referred to in *Cymbeline*—

> "Thersites' body is as good as Ajax
> When neither **are alive**."—Act iv. Sc. **2, l. 252.**

This scene in *Cymbeline* I assign to 1607-8, which agrees with my date for *Troylus;* which Malone places in 1602, on account of an **entry in the** Stationers' **books, referring, not to** the play of 1599 by Dekker and Chettle, **but to one** acted by the Chamberlain's **men**; and there is a reference to the story of Troylus and Cressida in the comedy of *Histriomastix*, which seems to imply that Shakespeare had written some play on **this** subject before Elizabeth's death : she is spoken of as alive **in** the last **Act.**

> " *Troy.* Come Cressida, my cresset light,
> Thy face doth shine both **day** and night.
> Behold, **behold** *thy garter blue*
> *Thy knight his valiant elbow wears,*
> That when he SHAKES his furious SPEARE,
> The foe, **in shivering fearful sort**
> May lay **him down in death** to snort.
> *Cress.* O Knight, **with valour** in thy face
> Here take **my** skreene, wear it for grace ;
> Within thy **helmet** put the same,
> Therewith to **make** thy enemies lame."

This **surely refers to the** changing of sleeve and glove in the play in direct connexion with Shakespeare's name. Was the play by him, not containing the Thersites and **Achilles** part, exhibited soon after 1595? Troylus is referred to **in** *Much Ado about Nothing* (1599) as the first employer **of** Pandars. **I cannot** hesitate on this matter. Shakespeare's **play** in its first form was exhibited before 1599, probably in 1597.

4. The love part **of** this play is **a** pendant to *Romeo and Juliet;* Pandarus should be compared with the Nurse.

XXX.—PERICLES.

1. First two Acts and Gower throughout unquestionably by Wilkins, who founded a novel on this play afterwards. The brothel scenes in Act iv. Sc. 5 and 6 by Rowley, I think; S. Walker says by Dekker, who did not write for the King's Company. Acts iii., iv., v., with these omissions, by Shakespeare. The play put together by Wilkins.

2. Founded on a novel by T. Twine; *The Patterne of Painful Adventures, &c., that befell unto Prince Appolonius, the Lady Lucina his wife, and Tharsia his daughter, &c.*, re-published in 1607, entered in 1576. Gower tells the story in *Confessio Amantis* 1554. The play follows this version sometimes. The *Gesta Romanorum* story (nearly the same) does not seem to have been used.

3. Certainly before 2 May, 1608, when it was entered; probably before the re-publishing of Twine's novel in 1607. I should date 1607. Delius tells me that he prefers 1608.

4. The Shakespeare part should be carefully compared with the corresponding stories in *Cymbeline* and *Winter's Tale*, especially the latter, in which the same extraordinary lapse of time is permitted between the Acts. This play and Rowley's *New Wonder*, and Marston's *Insatiate Countess*, are probably the three most incorrectly printed plays in the language. The beginning of the Shakespeare part, Act iii. Sc. 1, should be compared with the opening of *The Tempest*. Restorations to life after apparent death occur in *Romeo and Juliet*, *Much Ado about Nothing*, *Cymbeline*, and *Winter's Tale*.

XXXI.—ANTHONY AND CLEOPATRA.

1. Undoubted.

2. Founded on Plutarch's *Life of Marcus Antonius*.

3. Dated unanimously early in 1608.

XXXII.—CORIOLANUS.

1. Undoubted.

2. Founded on Plutarch's *Life of Coriolanus*.

3. Usually dated 1609-10; I prefer 1609. Menenius' fable (Act i. Sc. 1) is taken from Camden's *Remaines* (1605), and not from North's *Plutarch*. The play must have been written before 1612 for this reason; Mr. Halliwell has found that in every edition of North's *Plutarch* up to 1603 "unfortunately" is printed for "unfortunate" in the passage corresponding to Act v. Sc. 1, L 98. This is an evident misprint, as it spoils the meaning. Shakespeare corrected it, and wrote "unfortunate," which was adopted in the 1612 edition of North's *Plutarch*. As to Shakespeare's own copy being the one in the Greenock library dated 1612, if it was so he must have used another. He did not write *Julius Cæsar* after that date.

XXXIII.—THE TWO NOBLE KINSMEN.

1. Written by Shakespeare and Fletcher as stated in the Quarto of 1634. Shakespeare's part consists of Act i.; Act iii. Sc. 1, 2; Act v. Sc. 1, 3, 4.

2. Founded on the *Knight's Tale* of Chaucer.

3. The date of Shakespeare's share I fix from internal evidence as 1609; that of Fletcher's completion of the play is probably the same as that of his finishing *Henry VIII.* 1613.

XXXIV.—CYMBELINE.

1. The wretched vision in Act vi. Sc. 4 cannot be Shakespeare's; the rest of the scene is also doubtful.

2. Dated by Drake, 1605; Chalmers, 1606; Malone, 1609; Delius, 1610. Some scenes are probably earlier, about 1607-8; for

the rest, Delius is probably right, or nearly so. The name Leonatus is from Sidney's *Arcadia*, which Shakespeare used for his *Lear*. The story of *Cymbeline* in Holinshed is near that of *Lear* and that of *Macbeth*; and the story of Hay and his sons staying his countrymen in a lane in a battle against the Danes is near that of *Macbeth* in Holinshed's *Chronicle of Scotland*. Shakespeare, therefore, probably wrote *Lear*, *Macbeth*, and *Cymbeline* nearly at the same time. There is also an allusion to Cleopatra's sailing on the Cydnus to meet Anthony; he had therefore been reading for the play of *Anthony and Cleopatra*. The character of Imogen is distinctly imitated in the Euphrasia of Beaumont's *Philaster* (dated by Dyce 1608, possibly 1610-11). Compare also:

"I hear the tread of people; I am hurt :
The gods take part against me, could this boor
Have hurt me thus else?"
Philaster iv. 1.

with

"I have bely'd a lady,
The princess of this country; and the air of 't
Revengingly enfeebles me; or could this carle,
A very drudge of Nature's, have subdued me
In my profession?"
Cymbeline iv. 2.

I date the play as completed 1609-10, after *Coriolanus*, *Lear*, *Macbeth*, and *Anthony and Cleopatra*.

3. Founded on Holinshed's *Chronicles* and a novel of Boccaccio (Day 11, Novel 9). The story is also found in *Westward for Smelts* (1603). The scenes containing the story of Bellario and Imogen's flight I assign to an earlier date than the rest of the play; the whole of the scenes with Iachimo are certainly of the later date (1609-10 ?).

4. The date of the commencement of the play is A.D. 16, Cymbeline's 24th year of reigning, Augustus' 42nd.

XXXV.—THE TEMPEST.

1. The masque in Act iv. Sc. 1 has been considered by the Cambridge editors an insertion, like the vision in *Cymbeline*.

2, 3. The pamphlet describing the tempest of July 1609, which dispersed the fleet of Sir George Somers and Sir Thomas Gates, in which the Admiral-ship was wrecked on the island of Bermuda, was published in December 1609, or January 1609-10. The narrative of Jourdan, in which "the Bermudas" is called the Isle of Devils, is dated 13 October, 1610. *The True Declaration of the Councill of Virginia* was also published in 1610. Shakespeare's play was produced either late in 1610 or early in 1611. There can be no doubt of the play having been founded on these narratives. (See Malone's essay in *Variorum Shakspeare*, 1621.)

4. This is one of the plays that observes the unity of time. Mr. Staunton conjectured that one of the characters at least (the Duke of Milan's son, Act i. Sc. 2, l. 438) is lost. He thought that each player had a property in his own part, and that sometimes all the parts could not be bought up by the publishers. The play is certainly very short, only 2,068 lines, the average being 3,000; and it is strange that this character of the Duke's son is not brought on the stage. Perhaps Francisco is what is left of him. The pronunciation of Stephăno (pronounced Stephāno in the *Merchant of Venice* 1596) was probably learned from Ben Jonson's *Every Man in His Humour* (1598), in which Shakespeare acted. Compare with this in *Cymbeline*, Act iv. Sc. 2, the proparoxyton pronunciation of Posthumus.

XXXVI.—WINTER'S TALE.

1. Undoubted.

2. Founded on Greene's *Dorastus and Fawnia* (1588).

3. Dated 1610-11. Mentioned in Sir Henry Herbert's *Office Book* as an olde playe called *Winter's Tale*, formerly allowed of by

Sir George Bucke, who took possession of the office of Master of the Revels in August 1610.

4. To be compared with *Pericles* and *Cymbeline* for the stories of Perdita and Marina and Imogen; with *Henry VIII.* for the queen's trial. Said to be sneered at by Jonson in the *Induction* to his *Bartholomew Fair*, 1614, along with *The Tempest*.

"If there be never a *servant-monster* (Caliban) in the *Fair* who can help it, nor a *nest of anticks?* (The twelve Satyrs: *Winter's Tale*, iv. 4. 352.) He is loth to make Nature afraid in his plays, like those that beget *Tales, Tempests*, and such like drolleries." In his *conversations* with Drummond of Hawthornden (1619), he said that Shakespeare wanted art and sometimes sense; for in one of his plays he brought in a number of men saying they had suffered shipwreck in Bohemia, where is no sea near by 100 miles.

XXXVII.—HENRY VIII.

1. This play was written by Shakespeare and Fletcher jointly; Shakespeare's part is Act i. Sc. 1, 2; Act ii. Sc. 3, 4; Act iii. Sc. 2; Act v. Sc. 1. (See Mr. Spedding's essay, *Gentleman's Magazine*, Aug. 1850.)

2. Founded on Holinshed's *Chronicle*, Cavendish's *Life of Wolsey*, and Fox.

3. Date 1613. In Act v. Sc. 5, l. 51, we read:

"Wherever the bright sun of heaven shall shine,
His honour and the greatness of his name
Shall be, and make new nations.

A State lottery was set up expressly for the establishment of English Colonies in Virginia in 1612. Rowley's *Henry VIII.* and the drama of *Lord Cromwell* were reprinted in 1613 with the usual fraudulent intentions. Sir Henry Wotton says in his letters, that the Globe was burnt down on 30 June O. S., St. Peter's day 1613, while a *new* piece named *All is True* was performing; this piece from his minute description was certainly *Henry VIII.* Yet Shakespeare's part may have been written earlier than Fletcher's, say in 1611.

4. In 1613 the titles of many of Shakespeare's plays were changed. I *Henry IV.* was called *Hotspur;* and *Henry IV.* (or *Merry Wives of Windsor* ?), *Sir John Falstaff; Much Ado About Nothing, Benedick and Beatrix; Julius Cæsar, Cæsar's Tragedy.* In both plays completed by Fletcher, Shakespeare introduces and completely sketches all the principal characters. For the vision in Act iv. Sc. 2, compare *Pericles,* Act v. Sc. 2; and *Cymbeline,* Act v. Sc. 4. None of these are Shakespeare's work. The time involved in the play is twelve years, 1521-33. Historically Katherine survived the birth of Elizabeth three years.

Spurious Plays.

Other plays have been assigned to Shakespeare without reasonable ground ; for instance :—

1. The *London Prodigal,* printed in 1605 by T. Creede for N. Butter ; acted at the Globe.

2. The *Yorkshire Tragedy,* printed in 1608 by T. Pavier ; acted at the Globe.

3. *Sir John Oldcastle,* printed in 1600, entered on the Stationers' books by T. Pavier, acted by the Admiral's Company.

All these three had Shakespeare's name in full on the title-page ; all were printed for piratical booksellers. N. Butter was the publisher of the shamefully garbled Quarto of *King Lear.* *Sir John Oldcastle* was written in 1599 by Munday, Drayton, Wilson, and Hathway.

4. *Lord Cromwell,* printed in 1602, entered on the Stationers' books by W. Cotton, acted by the Queen's Company.

5. *The Puritan,* published by G. Eld in 1607, acted by the Children of Paul's.

6. *Locrine,* "newly set forth, overseen, and corrected by W. S.," printed by T. Creede, 1595.

These latter three have W. S. on the title-page. The relation of *Locrine* to Shakespeare has never been fully worked out. It is

ON THE PLAYS OF SHAKESPEARE.

worth investigation. The whole six were printed along with *Pericles* in the Third Folio as additions to the collection in the First Folio.

7. *The Birth of Merlin* was printed by T. Johnson in 1662 for Francis Kirkham and Henry Marsh, as by Shakespeare and Rowley; "several times acted."

8. *The Troublesome Reign of King John* was published by S. Clarke in 1591, and again by J. Holme (printed by V. S[immes]) in 1611. It was acted by the Queen's Company. "By W. Sh." was inserted on the title-page in 1611.

9. *The Merry Devil of Edmonton* was published by J. Hirst and T. Archer in 1608. Acted at the Globe. The author, T.B., was probably Tony Brewer.

10. *Fair Em.* was published in 1631. Acted by Lord Strange's Company before 1591, in which year it was criticised by Greene.

11. *Mucedorus* was published in 1598; acted at the Globe; probably written by Lodge.

12. *Arden of Feversham* was printed in 1592.

None of these plays can be Shakespeare's. In addition to the decisive internal evidence, note, with regard to Nos. 3, 4, 5, 8, that no company except the Chamberlain's (afterwards the King's) and possibly Lord Strange's ever acted any play of Shakespeare's. Yet many German critics and one or two English believe in the authenticity of many of these dramas. Mr. Simpson has in the press a volume of various other plays in which he thinks Shakespeare may have been concerned.

[Note on *Richard II.*—Since p. 26 was in type Mr. Hales has shown reason for identifying the play of *Henry IV.* performed for Sir Gilly Merrick with Shakespeare's *Richard II.* I find this confirmed by Camden's account of the trial. Another play called *Richard II.*, mentioned by Forman in his *Diary*, I identify with *The Life and Death of Jack Straw*, mentioned in a subsequent chapter.]

CHAPTER IV.

ON VARIOUS QUESTIONS CONNECTED WITH SHAKESPEARE'S PLAYS.

(A.)—What plays published in Shakespeare's name are genuine?

1. There are some plays included in all editions of his works which he probably never wrote a line of, namely :—

   1. *Titus Andronicus.*
   2. *2 Henry VI.*
   3. *3 Henry VI.*

The first of these is by Marlowe, the other two by Peele and Marlowe jointly. The division of their work is given under the heading of each play.

The original editing of 1 *Henry VI.* was probably Marlowe's. Shakespeare having added ii. 4 and (?) 5 about 1596 without retouching the rest.

Many persons, however, still believe that Shakespeare wrote large portions of these plays; they have never succeeded in separating his work.

2. There are plays finished by Shakespeare and rewritten by him, viz. :—

   1. *Romeo and Juliet.*
   2. *Richard III.*
   3. *Taming of the Shrew.*

WHAT PLAYS ARE GENUINE?

The two first of these in the Quarto editions show us Peele's work after Shakespeare's first corrections, the Folios after his rewriting; he probably corrected them after Peele's death. In the *Taming of the Shrew* his share is confined to the Petruchio story; the rest of the play is most likely by T. Lodge.

3. There are plays left unfinished by Shakespeare and completed by others, viz. :—
   1. *Timon.*
   2. *Pericles.*
   3. *Troylus and Cressida.*

His share of *Timon* was confined to the story of Timon himself; Cyril Tourneur probably writing the rest. Of *Pericles* he wrote the story of Marina; Rowley (?) wrote the brothel scenes, and Wilkins the rest; Wilkins being also the plotter and editor. Of *Troylus and Cressida* the part not Shakespeare's is confined to the last Act. This is probably taken from the old play by Dekker and Chettle; acted in 1599.

4. There are plays which are joint productions of Shakespeare and Fletcher, namely :—
   1. *Two Noble Kinsmen.*
   2. *Henry VIII.*

He also possibly helped Ben Jonson in his first draft of *Sejanus*.

5. There are plays to which Shakespeare contributed isolated scenes :—
   1. *1 Henry VI.* (as noticed above).
   2. *Edward III.* (Act i. 2; ii. all).

6. Some of Shakespeare's plays have been greatly abridged for theatrical purposes, namely :—
   1. *Tempest.*
   2. *Julius Cæsar.*

7. One has not only been abridged, but interpolated :—
   1. *Macbeth.*

8. Similar interpolations may be found in *Cymbeline*, and possibly in *The Tempest*, *Henry V*. (French scene), and *Merry Wives*, Q 1 (Fairies).

Of these results those concerning the *Two Noble Kinsmen* (Hickson and Spalding, after Weber), *Henry VIII.* (Spedding), *Troylus and Cressida* (Dyce and Fleay), *Timon of Athens* (Fleay), *Pericles* (Fleay), *Taming of the Shrew* (Fleay), are granted by all the best critics; those concerning *Macbeth* (Clark, Wright, and Fleay), *Tempest* (Staunton), *Romeo and Juliet* (Fleay), *Richard III.* (Fleay), *Henry VI.* (Fleay), *Edward III.* (Fleay), *Julius Cæsar* (Fleay), are yet disputed.

N.B. The names in parentheses in the above indicate not the first proposers of the theory of combined authorship in each case, but the first critics who brought the several theories to distinct tests by separating the Shakespearian portions from the second writers. The theory of double authorship in *Timon* has been previously advanced by Knight and Delius; in the *Taming of the Shrew* by Collier; in *Pericles* by Delius and Tennyson (forty years since he tells me); not to mention earlier statements for the most part very indefinite. For details, see the notices under the heading of each play.

Besides this question of authenticity it may be well here to notice a question which involves similar critical investigation. There are certain plays that were not entirely written at one date.

1. *All's Well that Ends Well* was probably a recast of *Love's Labour's Won*. Traces of the early work may be found in it. (See p. 46.)

2. *Troylus and Cressida* was certainly written at three dates :—

    1. The Troylus love story.
    2. The Hector story.
    3. The Achilles story.

The last of these dates about 1608. The two earlier of these written about 1593-6, probably constituted the play entered in 1602 on the Stationers' books by J. Roberts, as acted by the Chamberlain's men.

3. The verse part of *Twelfth Night* (in my opinion) was first written about 1594 and recast 1601, when the rest of the play was added.

4. We know that the *Merry Wives of Windsor* and *Hamlet* were thus written, since we have the first drafts (imperfectly) in the first quartos.

5. *Love's Labour's Lost* certainly, and *Midsummer Night's Dream* and *Richard II.* probably, were recast previously to publication.

(*B.*)—*The* **Early** *Editions of Shakespeare's works* :—

Besides the Folio of 1623, the first collected edition of the plays, there were a number of separate plays published in quarto before that date. In the table in Part II. will be found the printers' and publishers' names of every one of these editions anterior to 1623. The later copies are of no critical value. The symbols, Q 1, Q 2, &c., are those used in Clark and Wright's excellent "Cambridge Shakespeare;" a * indicates all the editions published without Shakespeare's name on the title-page; a † that the printers of the Folio used that edition to print from.

The Folio editions were published in 1623 (F 1), 1632 (F 2), 1664 (F 3), 1685 (F 4).

(*C.*)—*On the Relative Value of the Quarto* **and Folio** *Texts of Shakespeare* :—

The following results are derived from a careful examination of the Quarto and Folio editions, aided by but not dependent on the collations in the "Cambridge Shakespeare" :—

1. The Cambridge editors are quite right in stating that the following plays in the Folio are printed from the Quarto texts, and therefore the earliest complete Quarto must be looked to in each case as being the highest authority :—

   1. *Richard II.*
   2. 1 *Henry IV.*
   3. *Love's Labour's Lost.*
   4. *Much Ado about Nothing.*
   5. *Romeo and Juliet.*
   6. *Titus Andronicus.*

2. I also agree with them that the Fisher Quarto of *Midsummer Night's Dream* gives better readings than the Roberts, which was used by the Folio editors. But for the *Merchant of Venice* the Heyes Quarto used for the Folio seems to me better than the Roberts Quarto.

3. In no other case did the Folio editors use the Quarto texts, which were undoubtedly, as they state in their preface, all surreptitious.

4. All omissions of passages in the Folio texts may be reduced to two classes: one of accidental omissions of words or lines in printing, the other of intentional cancelling of long passages for purposes of stage representation. The passages found in the Folio but not in the Quarto, on the other hand, are generally such as would not be so omitted.

5. The Quarto *Lear* abounds with errors of ear, and was clearly surreptitiously taken down by notes at the theatre. *Henry V.*, the *Contention*, and the *True Tragedy* were similarly though still more clumsily stolen.

6. *Romeo and Juliet*, Q 1, the *Merry Wives of Windsor*, Q 1, and *Hamlet*, Q 1, though surreptitious and abridged, still represent the earliest forms of these plays; they were all rewritten afterwards, but they are very valuable to the Shakespeare student, as showing his manner of work, as well as sometimes preserving lines or expressions which we would not willingly lose. *Richard III.* in some respects belongs to this class. One other Quarto, which might be thought to be analogous (*Henry V.*), is merely an imperfect piratical issue, and utterly worthless. The *Contention* and the *True Tragedy*, on which *Henry VI.* has been supposed to be founded, are in like manner merely piratical issues grossly imperfect, by the same publisher, T. Pavier, possibly touched up by his partner, H. Chettle.

7. *Hamlet*, Q 2, and *Othello*, Q 2, were not derived from sources independent of their first quartos, but were formed by corrections being made in copies of Q 1 at subsequent representations. The same thing is true for the *Whole Contention* of 1619, which does not give an intermediate stage of composition between the Quartos and

Folios as has been supposed. This conclusion, which is quite certain, is most important. So *Hamlet* and *Othello*, Q 2, are founded on Q 1, with corrections from the Folio.

8. The *Troylus and Cressida* Quarto has been printed from a written transcript of a copy belonging to the theatre, hastily and not quite accurately made.

9. The *Richard III.* Quarto represents Shakespeare's first correction of an earlier play; so does the First Quarto of *Romeo and Juliet*.

10. The Quartos of 2 *Henry IV.* and *Othello* are useful for correction of many readings: they are transcripts of the stage copies as first used, obtained in somewhat the same way as the *Troylus and Cressida*.

From all this it results that in every instance except the first two groups, eight plays in all, our text must be founded on the Folio of 1623. But for these eight the Quarto readings are generally better. As, however, even in these, the Folio spelling and punctuation agrees more nearly with the rest of the plays in the Folio, it is preferable to correct the Folio text from the Quarto for a revised edition than conversely. For a scholar's text the Folio with the Quarto variations noted (and introduced where desirable), is the one thing needful. Booth's wonderfully accurate reprint of this edition, or Chatto and Windus's photographic reproduction, if interleaved, will enable any student to make such an edition for himself without great labour. In any case he had better use the Folio as the foundation of all his work. No published edition except Knight's has done this, and he has gone too far by rejecting the Quarto readings even in the eight plays mentioned.

(D.)—*On the division into Acts and Scenes of Shakespeare's Plays*:—

There is no authority for this division for any play (except *Othello*, Q 1, 1622) anterior to the Folio edition of 1623. And in that edition not all are divided. The exceptions are :—

1. Plays printed from Quarto editions :—

   Love's **Labour's** *Lost.*
   Midsummer Night's Dream.
   Merchant of Venice.   } Divided into Acts only.
   Much Ado about Nothing.
   Titus **Andronicus.**

   Romeo and Juliet.   Not divided at all.

2. Plays probably produced between 1606 and 1609 :—

   Timon.
   Troylus and Cressida. } Not divided at all.
   Anthony and Cleopatra.

   Coriolanus.
   Julius Cæsar.   } Divided into Acts only.
   Pericles.

3. Plays produced before **1604.**

   Comedy of Errors.
   All's Well that Ends Well.
   Taming of the Shrew.   } Divided into Acts only.
   Henry V.

   2 *Henry VI.*
   3 *Henry VI.*   } Not divided at all.

The other eighteen plays in the Folio (just half) are divided into **Acts and Scenes.**

Lists **of** the *Dramatis Personæ* (Actors' Names) are **given only in** seven plays :—

   Two Gentlemen of Verona.
   Measure for Measure.
   Timon.
   Pericles.
   Henry V.
   Tempest.
   Winter's Tale.

(*E.*)—*Dates of Entries at Stationers'* **Hall** :—

   Venus and Adonis.   1593 April 18.
   Titus Andronicus.   1594 February 6.

EARLY EDITIONS. 65

First Contention.	1594	March 12.
Taming of a Shrew.	,,	May 2.
Lucreece.	,,	May 9.
Locrine.	,,	July 20.
Edward III.	1595	December 1.
Romeo and Juliet (ballad ?)	1596	August 6.
Richard II.	1597	August 29.
Richard III.	,,	October 20.
1 Henry IV.	1598	February 25.
Merchant of Venice.	,,	July 22.
As You Like it.		August 4. [("To be
Henry V.	1600	stayed") Note at be
Much Ado about Nothing.		ginning of Register.]
Henry V.	,,	August 14.
Much Ado about Nothing.		
2 Henry IV.	,,	August 23.
Midsummer Night's Dream.	,,	October 8.
Merchant of Venice.	,,	October 28.
Merry Wives of Windsor.	1602	January 18.
Henry VI. First and Second Parts; (2 and 3 Henry VI.)	,,	April 19.
Titus Andronicus.		
Hamlet.	,,	July 26.
Troylus and Cressida.	1603	February 7.
Romeo and Juliet		
Love's Labour's Lost.	1607	January 22.
Taming of a Shrew.		
Hamlet.		
Taming of a Shrew.	,,	November 19.
Romeo and Juliet.		
Love's Labour's Lost.		
Lear.	,,	November 26.
Pericles.	1608	May 20.
Anthony and Cleopatra.		
Troylus and Cressida.	1609	January 28.
Sonnets.	,,	May 20.
Othello.	1621	October 21.
First Folio.	1623	November 8.

CHAPTER V.

PRONUNCIATION AND METRE.

TABLE of Vowel Pronunciation, extracted from **Mr. A. J. Ellis's** large work on the subject:—

Spelling.	Pronunciation.
a long	as *a* in father.
e ,,	{ as *a* in mare. { rarely as *e* in eve.
i ,,	as *i* in time (Scotch).
o ,,	{ as *o* in uomo (Italian). { rarely as *oo* in pool.
u ,,	as *u* in flûte (French).
a short	as *a* in chatte (French).
e ,,	as *e* in met.
i ,,	as *i* in river.
o ,,	{ as *o* in homme (French). { rarely as *ou* in po**u**le (French). { or *u* in p**u**ll.
u ,,	{ as *ou* in po**u**le (French). { or *u* in p**u**ll.
ai	{ as *ay!* { rarely as *a* in mare.
ei	{ as *ey* in they. { or *a* in mare. { rarely as *ay!*

Spelling.	Pronunciation.
ee	as *e* in *e*ve.
ie medial	
ie final	as *i* in t*i*me (Scotch).
y ,,	or as *i* in r*i*ver.
eo ,,	as *e* in *e*ve.
	or *a* in m*a*re.
oi ,,	as *eu* in n*eu* (N. German).
au ,,	as *aw* in *aw*n.
eu ,,	as *Eu* in *Eu*ropa (Italian).
oo ,,	as *oo* in p*oo*l.
ou ,,	as *ow* in kn*ow* (occasional English).
	or as Dutch *ou*.
ea ,,	as *a* in m*a*re.
	rarely as *e* in *e*ve.
	very rarely as *a* in ch*a*tte (French).
	occasionally as *e* in m*e*t.

These conclusions are no doubt nearly accurate as to the normal pronunciation of Shakespeare's time. I have found, however, by an independent investigation, that great **laxity prevailed from 1580 to 1630, and** that scarcely any vowel **sound was** determinate in popular use. The statements given below embrace the varieties of sound allowed by the poets and dramatists of that period. I have not attempted to give them accurately; indeed, the nature of the case would not permit it; but I have given the nearest sounds now in use to those which formed the limiting pronunciations in each case. Mr. Ellis's table will supply some corrections necessary to those who desire more exact information.

1. I believe the short vowels were sounded nearly as in *bill, dell, ran, doll, pull*, at the present time; $\breve{o}$ occasionally taking the sound of $\breve{u}$; $\breve{a}$ that of $\breve{o}$; $\breve{e}$ that of $\breve{a}$; and $\breve{i}$ that of $\breve{e}$.

2. The long vowels were sounded nearly as in *time, mare, father, Rome, pool*.

$\bar{i}$ sometimes	taking the sound	of *ee* in f*ee*l.
$\bar{e}$,,	,, ,, ,,	*e* in *e*ve.
$\bar{a}$,,	,, ,, ,,	*au* in d*au*nt.
$\bar{o}$,,	,, ,, ,,	*oo* in p*oo*l.

So far I differ little from Mr. Ellis; but in the diphthongal spellings I venture to assert that in many of them the pronunciation was not fixed, but varied from that of one of the component signs to that of the other. Thus:—

ai varied between *a* in m*a*re, and *i* in *i*sland.
ei ,, ,, *ei* in d*ei*gn, and *i* in *i*sland.
oi ,, ,, *oy* in j*oy*, and *i* in *i*sland.
ui ,, ,, *u* in r*u*le, and *i* in *i*sland.
ou ,, ,, *o* in n*o*, and *u* in r*u*le.
eo ,, ,, *e* in *e*ve, and *o* in n*o*.
ea ,, ,, { *e* in *e*ve, and *a* in m*a*re; *ea* was sometimes also shortened.

As to the sounds of *au, eu, oo, ie* medial, *ie* and *y* final, they were, I think, respectively those of *aw* in *aw*n, *eu* in *Eu*rope, *oo* in p*oo*l, *e* in *e*ve, *i* in t*i*me (or *y* in easil*y*), which are nearly the same as those given by Mr. Ellis. The reasons for these statements are too lengthy to be here given, even in a condensed form. I may say, however, that they depend partly on the nature of the rhymes (supposed generally to be imperfect) that were admitted by the Elizabethan writers, and partly on variations in the spelling of words that were of common recurrence.

There are some other laws of pronunciation which have been not at all or imperfectly recognised. At the risk of infringing on the office of the grammarian it may be well to give them here :—

1. *Laws of Contraction.*—S. Walker has noticed that where two syllables end in *s* with a short vowel between them, the latter syllable may be omitted; thus *horses* is often contracted into *horse'*; *this is* into *this'*. But he has not noticed that the law extends to all dentals thus: *let it* may be contracted into *let'*; *committed* into *commit'*; *proceeded* into *proceed'*, &c. &c.

2. It has often been observed that *heaven, even,* and the like, are frequently one syllable; and that in some cases, as *sennight* for *seven-night*, the *v* is not pronounced; but it has not been noticed that *any* word containing *v* between two vowels may omit the *v* in pronunciation, so that *driven* becomes *dri'en*; *love, lo'e*; *corsive, corsie,* &c. The same omission takes place sometimes for other letters, as *ta'en* for *taken*.

3. *Laws of Resolution.*—The separation of final *-tion*, *-sion*, &c., into two syllables, *ti-on*, *si-on*, is well known: not so the following.

4. Any two consecutive consonants, whether initial or medial, may be separated by a slight sound corresponding to the Hebrew *Shwa*, and so give rise to an extra syllable. Thus we have *G'ratiano*, *kin'sman*, *lor'd*, pronounced nearly as *Geratiano*, *kinisman*, *lorud*, &c.

5. Any syllable involving a *w* or *y* sound in it may be resolved into two; no matter whether the sound be diphthongal or the *w* or *y* be consonantal. Thus *twelve* becomes *too-elve*; *ay* becomes *ah-ee*; *sweet* becomes *soo-eet*; *boy* becomes *baw-ee*; &c. &c.

6. The pronunciation of vocal *r*, in *fi-er* (fire), *su-er-ly* (surely), is well known.

For other questions of contraction, accent, resolution, &c., see Abbott's *Shakespearian Grammar*.

METRE.

The following canons as to Shakespeare's metre are derived either from Sidney Walker's excellent criticisms or from my own personal observation:—

1. Shakespeare admits, in addition to the regular 5-foot blank verse line, the Alexandrine, short lines of 1, 2, or 3 feet, and rhyming lines of 4 or 5 feet.

2. He does not admit blank lines of 4 feet (Walker).

3. Nor does he admit lines in blank verse deficient by an initial syllable (Walker).

4. Wherever there is an appearance of a 4-foot line, it is either made up of two shorter lines (3 + 1, 2 + 2), or it is corrupt. Thus:—

{ " What I shall think is good.
{ The princess."

{ " Stands for my bounty.
{ But who comes here?"

are according to Shakespeare's usual manner.

"To let these hands obey my blood,"

is corrupt either by omission or misarrangement. (Fleay.)

5. Shakespeare admits an extra syllable before a pause either in the middle or at the end of a line. In fact, he treats any line containing a full stop or even a colon as if it were two lines (Walker). Thus :—

{ " Have sure more lack of rea*son*.
{ What would you say?"

{ " Forerunning more requi*tal*.
{ You make my bonds still grea*ter*."

The end of a line always counts as a pause whether stopt or not.

6. Shakespeare's metre varies at different periods of his life to an extent unknown to any other writer; for instance :—

a. Doggrel lines abound in his earliest comedies. *Love's Labour's Lost* has 194; the *Comedy of Errors*, 109; *Two Gentlemen of Verona*, 18; *Merchant of Venice*, 4. They never occur after this.

b. Alternately rhyming lines abound in his early plays, but gradually decrease, and at the end of his second period are for ever thrown aside.

c. The use of rhyme couplets diminishes gradually from a proportion of two rhyme lines to one of blank verse, down to an absolute absence of rhyme.

d. Alexandrines, which are absent in his earliest plays, increase gradually, though irregularly, until his latest.

e. Alexandrines not only increase in frequency, but assume a freer form, having pauses in the later plays after the 2nd, 7th, 8th, or 10th syllable, like Spenser's, instead of being confined to the French form with pause in the middle, as in his first and second periods.

f. Lines with an extra syllable before a pause are most frequent in his third period.

g. On adopting the use of lines with weak or unemphatic endings (*with, of, you, and*, &c., for final words), he gave up in some measure the lines mentioned in *f*.

h. Lines with extra end-syllable, or female lines, as they are often called, increase in frequency from none to 726.

i. Lines of less than 5 measures are more abundant in the later plays; but how far this is due to omissions and alterations for stage purposes we cannot tell.

j. The use of weak-ending lines increases regularly throughout the fourth period of these plays.

k. On the combined use of these facts as foundations, it is possible to construct a scheme of chronology for the plays which shall not contradict any external evidence, and shall be in accordance with critical dicta derived from higher considerations. Such a scheme is given in Part II. with the numerical data on which it is founded.

As these peculiarities of metre have been applied not only to the determining the chronological succession of our author's works, but also to the distinguishing his work from that of others, it may be well here to note the characteristics of a few authors sufficiently to ensure the recognition of their work.

Fletcher can be at once distinguished by the number of female lines, in which he exceeds every other English author. His lines are usually "stopt," and often end in an extra *emphatic* syllable. Thus:—

"And stand upon as strong and honest guards *too*."

Massinger is known instantly by his numerous weak endings, in which he indulges beyond any other writer; his lines are usually not stopt; he avoids lines of less than 5 feet.

Neither of these writers admits prose.

Jonson is known by jolting rough tri-syllabic feet where there is no pause.

"Best put yourself in yŏŭr case again and keep."

He avoids lines of less than 5 feet, and is singularly regular in his metre.

Ford has many female lines, but avoids short lines, which distinguishes him from Fletcher. The chronological order of his plays exactly agrees with the proportions of rhymes and female lines in them.

Chapman can be known by his use of such rhymes as *gárland, hand; pálace, face;* by his frequent elision of *v* between two vowels, as in *clo'en, gi'en,* &c., and his regular verse not admitting lines of less than 5 feet, except in a very few instances.

Peele uses rhymes (like Chapman) such as *gárland, hand,* &c., and indulges in tri-syllabic feet like Jonson, but to a much greater extent.

Beaumont is distinguished from *Fletcher* by admitting prose, not using the extra emphatic syllable, allowing rhymes in the middle of his blank verse, and frequent unstopped lines.

Marlowe is distinguished from *Peele* by his not using the Chapman rhymes nor the tri-syllabic feet of Jonson; from *Greene* by his frequent omissions of the initial syllable in his blank verse. It is very doubtful if any prose in his plays, as published, is of his writing.

Greene is distinguished by his regular see-saw unmelodious rhythm and his abundance of stopped lines. He never acquired any proficiency in his handling of blank verse.

Lodge is remarkable for the similarity of his metrical style to that of the earliest plays of Shakespeare. He belongs to the rhyming school as opposed to the blank verse school of which Marlowe was the founder.

Tourneur uses lines of irregular length to an extent unknown in other authors.

Similar marks or tests can be given for every author who is not a mere imitator; but my object here is to illustrate not exhaust this subject, merely with regard to the authors who have been supposed to have written portions of plays commonly attributed to Shakespeare.

CHAPTER VI.

ON THE MANNER IN WHICH PLAYS WERE PRESENTED.

WE shall be able to conceive the nature of our early theatrical performances most readily if we give details for the earliest house known, and then mention such alterations as were introduced in later theatres in due course. Let us imagine, then, what would be our mode of proceeding if we were visiting the Curtain in 1596 to see the performance of *Romeo and Juliet*. Having ascertained from the displaying of the flag on the pole on the theatre roof that exhibitions were going on, we should, if we had come from any distance, first look out for some one to care for our horses while we were in the theatre; for the Curtain stood well out of the town in Shoreditch Fields. If one of the traditional Shakespeare boys could be procured, we should of course give him the preference. The next point to determine would be which part of the house we should go to. The Pit, or "ground," was the cheapest place (1*d.*); but standing in the Pit is not comfortable, especially as the whole central part of the theatre is open to the sky; neither are the "groundlings" the best society for appreciating such a play as this. The twopenny Galleries, on the other hand, are not well placed for seeing the actors. Shall we then try the "Rooms" or Boxes?—the cost will be 3*d.* at least if we do. We should prefer if we could to go on the stage itself and take a "stool" as they do in the new private house, along with the "gallants," even at a cost of another 6*d.* or 1*s.*, according to the convenience of the place we can obtain. Having taken our place, let us look round before the curtains are drawn aside; the "musics" are collecting themselves in their usual station over the "room" nearest the stage; the critics and wits are "drinking tobacco," or discussing the author, or getting their "tables" ready to make notes; an emissary of Pavier or some other pirate of the time is arranging his paper to take down as much of the play in shorthand as he can, with a view to surreptitious publication; the rushes are strewn upon the stage; the inner curtain which covers the balcony where Juliet is to speak "aloft," and where the "scroyles of Angiers" flouted King John last year, is carefully drawn; the "flourishes" are sounded by the trumpets; the front curtains separate, and the play commences. As the stage is hung with black we know that a tragedy is to be performed, and that man in a long black cloak is of course the Prologue. The board on which the name of the scene is written tells us that the plot is laid in Verona; and the erection over the trap, which we can see from our place in the rooms, hints that a "tomb" will be required in the fifth Act. It is hard to follow the changes of scene; we cannot help wishing that some of those mechanical devices so lavishly expended on Court pageants could be introduced here. Why should not the stage be more real? Would it lower the character of the plays by appealing too much to the groundlings behind the pales there? We have plenty of time to think on such matters while the trumpets, cornets, organs, viols, hautboys, or recorders are playing between the Acts. Another thought that will haunt us is how much will the poet get for this play? Will the profits of his "second day" be large? Twenty nobles (6*l.* 13*s.* 4*d.*) seems a small sum for such a noble piece of work. But perhaps he will publish it himself and get something out of the sale of copies. I am ready for one with my sixpence, for I like the play. He gets something, however, as an actor, probably more than as a poet. He has shares, too, I am told, in the theatre; and when they perform at Court the Queen gives 18*l.* or 20*l.* for each performance. Perhaps he'll be rich yet if he's prudent. But the curtain is drawn; the play is over, shall I stay for the jig? I think I will. I don't care much for the clown's dancing and singing, but Kempe's a clever fellow; I'll see him for once, and "throw up a theme or two for him to extemporize on." But it's past three already; the play must have lasted more than two hours; a long performance to-day. I shall have to switch and spur to get home as I appointed.

MANNER OF PRESENTING PLAYS.

Such would be as near as I can judge a description of our earliest theatre. I add further details for the others. The Bull, **Curtain**, and Globe were public theatres. The **Cockpit**, Whitefriars, and Blackfriars were "private houses." The Globe was round; the Curtain was square.[1] At the Bull, Fortune, and Theater, the lowest price for the "ground" was 2d.; at the Globe, Blackfriars, Phœnix, and Hope, it was 6d., the "rooms" being 1s., and places on the stage an additional 6d. or 1s. The time of commencing performances grew gradually later; in 1609 it was 2 P.M.; in 1632, 3 P.M. Two or three new plays were produced each year at a house, consequently Shakespeare must have nearly sufficed for the requirements of the Globe. The lists I have given of the plays of other authors will enable the student in great measure to reconstruct the history of other houses. The poet was allowed the profit of either the second or third night; poets were often admitted gratis. An office fee for licensing new plays of 6s. 8d. had to be paid to the Master of the Revels. At the private houses the performance was usually by candlelight. The common statement that the Globe was a summer theatre only, does not apply to Shakespeare's theatre, but to the re-erection after the fire of 1613.

[1] The Fortune as built in 1599 was square; as rebuilt after the fire of 1621 it was round. The confusion of one of these erections with the other has been a prolific source of **error**.

CHAPTER VII.

ON THE EARLIEST ENGLISH THEATRICAL COMPANIES.

(From the Athenæum, July, 1875.)

OUR stage historians have repeatedly asserted that as many as fifteen distinct companies of actors existed in the time of Elizabeth, independently of the companies of "children." I have found that a closer investigation shows that more than six companies of men and four of children never existed in London at one time; and that these can all be traced down to three companies of men and two of children. The obscurity of the history of these times does not arise from the paucity of our material, as our great critic, Mr. Halliwell, has recently complained, but from want of sufficiently minute investigation on the one hand, and the existence of different companies, in successive times, under the same name, on the other. I have been much gratified by finding that Mr. Halliwell's investigations, unrivalled for comprehensive research, have confirmed the only point in what I shall have to say that needed confirmation.

The companies enumerated by Chalmers, in his "Farther Account of the English Stage," are: of adults,—Lord R. Dudley's, Sir R. Lane's, Lord Clinton's, the Earl of Warwick's, the Lord Chamberlain's, the Earl of Sussex's, Lord Howard's, the Earl of Essex's, Lord Strange's, the Earl of Darby's, the Queen's, the Lord Admiral's, the Earl of Hertford's, the Earl of Pembroke's, and the Earl of Worcester's: and of boys—the Children of Paul's, of the Chapel, of Westminster, and of Windsor. He is also careful to tell us that Shakespeare was admitted into the Chamberlain's company, started in 1575; that whether W. Elderton and R. Mountcaster were then the leaders of it is uncertain; that Lord Strange's company of tumblers began to play at the Rose in 1592; and other matters which I have found to be unfounded. I will treat of these companies in groups.

Group I.—Lord Darby's company of 1580-2 were in all probability the same company as his son Lord Strange's of 1592-3. These must be carefully distinguished from Lord Strange's group of tumblers of 1580-2, who were not the players at the Rose; and from the later company, also called Lord Darby's, formed under Brown in 1600.

Lord Hunsdon's company of 1582 took the name of Lord Chamberlain's on his accession to that office in 1585, and retained it till his death in 1596. In the few months of Lord Brooke's chamberlainship (during which, as Malone proved, *Romeo and Juliet* was produced at the Curtain Theatre) they passed to his son, just as Lord Darby's did to his son Lord Strange, and were then called Lord Hunsdon's. On this second Lord Hunsdon being made Chamberlain, in 1597, they again took the title of the Chamberlain's servants, and retained it till King James's accession in 1603, when they became the King's company.

Into this company, Lord Strange's (which, and not the Lord Chamberlain's, was very probably the company in which Shakespeare made his first appearance) was absorbed in 1594. Mr. Halliwell has given evidence of this union in his latest work.

The houses generally used by this group were the Theatre, the Curtain, and the Cross Keys (in winter only), until they removed to the new Globe in 1599.

We must now recur to an earlier time. From 1574 to 1582 a company played under the names indifferently of the Earl of Sussex's or the Lord Chamberlain's servants. These have been confused by all the writers I have seen with the later Lord Chamberlain's men, yet nothing is more certain than that my statement is right; the evidence is positive. After the appointment of Lord Hunsdon as Chamberlain, they were called only by the name of the Earl of Sussex till 1594.

From 1594 to 1597 the Earl of Pembroke **too,** had a body of players, perhaps the same as Lord Seymour's (the Earl of Hertford's) of 1592.

These were almost certainly united **with the Sussex company to** form the second Earl of Darby's company (under **Brown),** about 1599.

The **Earl** of Pembroke's **company** was incorporated into **the Lord** Chamberlain's in 1600; but probably not directly, but passing through **an** intermediate stage as the company **of the** Earl of **Darby.**

Group **2.—Lord** Philip **Howard, Earl of Arundel, had** a company from **1574 to 1580, which afterwards** passed **to Lord** Charles Howard, **and was called indifferently the Lord Admiral's or the** Earl of Nottingham's **servants.**

In 1603 they became the Prince's servants.

This company played first at the Theatre and Curtain; then (with Henslow) at the Rose**; finally at the Fortune (built in 1600), where they remained** permanently **till 1622.**

Group 3.—In 1562 **Lord R.** Dudley had a company of players, **called** afterwards the **Earl of** Leicester's (1565–1582), on his accession to that title.

In 1564, J. Dudley, Earl **of Warwick,** had a company, which was **afterwards united** with **Sir R. Lane's** (1571–3) about 1574. It retained **the title** of the Earl **of** Warwick's till 1582.

In 1582, **out of** the Earl of Warwick's and the Earl **of Leicester's the** Queen's **company** was formed, which continued till 1594.

This company **may** have been absorbed into the Earl of Worcester's, **which became the** Queen's (Queen Anne's) in 1603, after a **year or two, during** which they kept the designation of the Earl of **Worcester's men.** They played chiefly **at** the Red **Bull** and the Curtain. If the above be true—and there are not more than a very few conjectural points in it, and those of the slightest possible importance; all the rest is proven by **statements** in our records hitherto overlooked—then the history of all the adult companies is traced down to the three that we know existed at the accession of James the First.

Now let us look to the children.

Group 1.—Consists of only the **Children of** Paul's, established 1563, who played at their own house till 1591, and also from 1601 to 1605.

Group 2.—The Chapel Children, **established** 1565, gradually absorbed the Children of **Westminster (1567–1575)** and the Children of Windsor (1571–1577). **They acted at Blackfriars from** 1596 to 1601, and about 1605 they took the name of **Children** of the Revels. In 1612 they **removed to Whitefriars, and were ultimately** formed by Beeston into the *Company* **of the Revels.**

One chief point **to note here is the singular blunder that** has confused Elderton and **Mountcaster with managers of the Chamberlain's** company, besides confusing **that** company (Sussex's) with Lord Hunsdon's. Elderton and Mountcaster were masters of "boys." Elderton is expressly stated to **be master of the** Westminster boys, and **Mountcaster** of Merchant **Taylors'.** The erection of these into separate **companies is purely imaginary.** The Earl of Oxford's company were **also boys.** I have, of course, **not given here the mass of material** from which these results have **been obtained. Slender as** they may seem when thus abstracted from their foundations, **they are** the outcome of many hours' labour, it having been **necessary in** order to obtain **them to** tabulate every entry of whatever **kind for** every play mentioned **in our** dramatic literature up **to 1603 in** three separate forms.

At the accession of James I. (1603) there were then four companies. **The King's (formerly the** Chamberlain's), the Queen's (formerly the **Earl of Worcester's), the** Prince's (formerly the **Admiral's), and the Children of Paul's.** This last was succeeded by **the Revels** Children **in 1605, who in turn were** incorporated with Queen Anne's about 1613, **to form** the company **of the Revels.** Lady Elizabeth had also **a company of** actors from about **1612** onwards, or even earlier.

In 1622, great changes took place **in all** these companies, and a **new one (the** Palsgrave's) was formed. **It** lasted, however, only to 1624. **After 1625, the** companies **in existence** were the Queen's (Henrietta's), **the** Bull, the Fortune, **and the** King's, which outlasted all changes till **1642. In** 1629 a new Company of Revels is started, which becomes the Prince's on the birth of Charles II.

This company must not be confused with the former Princes' (Henry's and Charles I.) any more than the two Chamberlain's companies above noticed, or Queen Henrietta's with Queen Anne's or Queen Elizabeth's. The new Prince's company had not one actor in common with the old one. In 1637 another company (Beeston's boys) was established, and in 1640, under the same manager, the "King's-and-Queen's" was incorporated. This concludes our enumeration of changes till 1642, when the theatres were closed.

It will be found easy to follow these complicated alterations, if constant reference be made to the chronological tables of theatres and companies at the end of this chapter. They have been carefully compiled, and although they are contradictory to many received notions, may be depended on as accurately giving all information at present attainable.

In the annexed Table the top line gives dates at intervals of two years; a line, thus ——, indicates the period during which the company whose name is over it is known to have existed; changes of name are indicated by printing the names in succession over a line broken at the date of change, thus Chamb. King's; union of two companies to form a third, by a brace, thus —L. Strange / L. Hunsden — Lord Chamberlain; absorption of a company into another by an arrow, thus— Chamberlain / Pembroke↑.

If from the small scale of the Table any date appear doubtful refer to pp. 76-80.

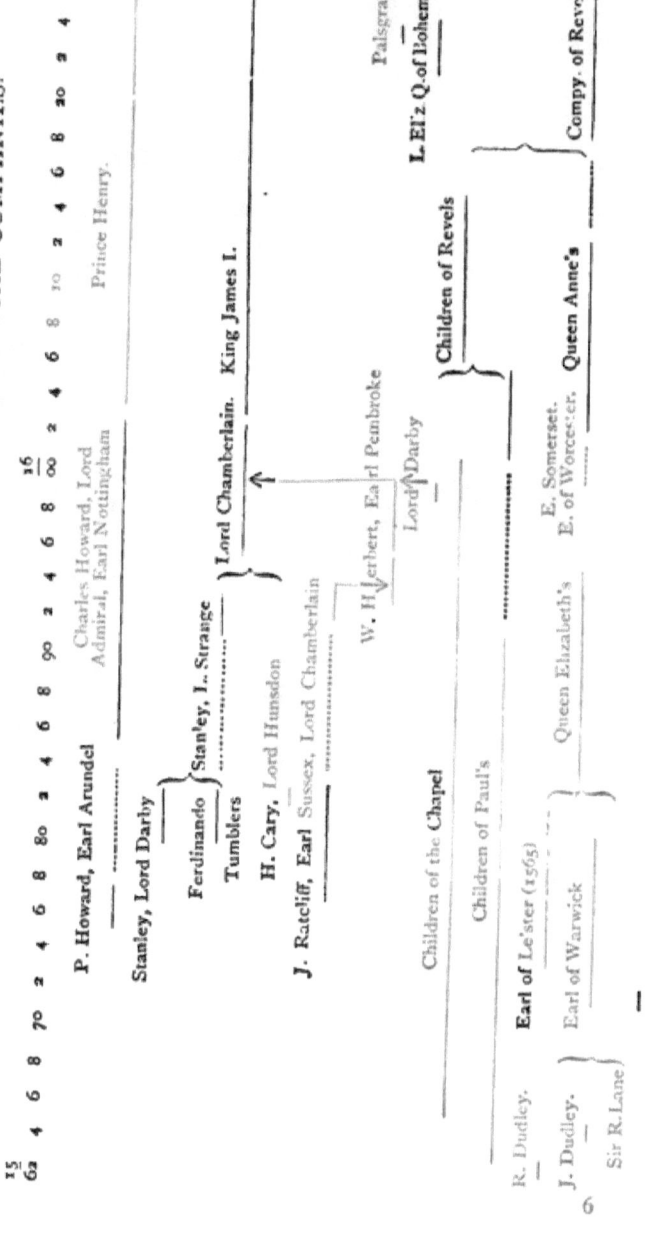

CHAPTER VIII.

ACCOUNT OF THE THEATRES FROM 1576 TO 1642.

THE earliest theatres of which we have record were—the Curtain (1576), the Theater (1576), and the private room belonging to the Children of Paul's (1574). The two former theatres were both public, and occupied by various companies, the Queen's, the Admiral's, Lord Strange's, the Earl of Sussex's, the Earl of Pembroke's, &c., of whose occupancy we have no precise records. The Queen's Company (under Tarleton) also acted at the Red Bull. Henslow opened the Rose theatre in 1592, where the following companies played successively :—

>Lord Strange's, beginning 19 February, 1592.
>Earl Sussex's, **27 December,** 1593.
>**Sussex's and the** Queen's, 2 April, 1594.
>**Admiral's, 14 May,** 1594.
>**Admiral's** and Chamberlain's, **3 June, 1594.**
>**Admiral's,** 27 October, **1596.**

In 1596 Blackfriars **was** adapted **for theatrical** purposes by J. Burbage, and let **out to the** Children of **the Chapel, who** occupied it till 1601. They were then possibly **succeeded by the** Children of Paul's, who had been suspended **in 1591, and who,** in 1605, gave place in like manner to the **Children of the Revels.**

Meanwhile, **in 1599,** J. Burbage pulled down the Theater, where the Chamberlain's company had settled about 1595-6, and built the Globe. To this new building that company moved in 1599-1600, and occupied **it till 1642, except during** the **short** time of its rebuilding after the fire of **1613**. They took possession of the Blackfriars theatre in 1613, and used it as well as the Globe till 1642.

In 1600, Alleyn built **the Fortune theatre, to** which the Admiral's **company** moved from the **Rose and** continued **there** until 1621, **when** the **Fortune was burnt down. In that year** the same company (then called **the Prince's) left the Fortune for** the Curtain, where they remained two or **three years, the new** company (the Palsgrave's) taking their place at the Fortune in 1622, on its rebuilding. This company died **out in 1624; and** the Company **occupying this house** was called the **Fortune** company simply: **it remained there till 1640,** when it exchanged **with the** Prince's **(Charles II.) and went to the Bull.**

When the Children of **the** Revels were turned out of Blackfriars in 1612 they went to **Whitefriars, and** remained there till 1613. In that year they ceased **to exist as a** children's company, and the company of the Revels was formed out of them and the Queen's company (formerly **the** Earl of Worcester's), who had **occupied** the **Red Bull and** the Curtain since 1599. The Revels company occupied the **same** two houses from 1613 to 1622, when the Prince's came there. As the Prince became King in 1625, this company **ceased** to exist, and the **Curtain** was abandoned. The Bull was **still** kept in action, (the company playing there being simply called **the** Bull Company) till **1637, when the Salisbury** Court company (Prince's or Revels) **came to the Bull and** played there as the Prince's company till 1640, when they **exchanged with the Fortune.**

The Curtain theatre **followed the** Red Bull in all its changes.

In **1619,** the Cockpit (Phœnix), **which had** been destroyed, was **rebuilt and occupied** by the **company of the** Lady Elizabeth (afterwards **Queen of** Bohemia) **which had previously performed some** time at **the Swan:** this company **lasted till 1624. In 1625, the** Queen's (Henrietta's) **actors set up at this house. In 1637, William** Beeston's boys succeeded **the Queen's, who went to Salisbury Court,** where the Prince's **(Charles II.) or Revels company had acted previously. They** had at first been called the Revels Company, but on the birth of Charles (1630) took the name of the Prince's. Salisbury **Court was built in Whitefriars in 1629. In** 1640, Beeston's **boys were formed, with new recruits,** into the King-and-Queen's company.

We have now gone through the history of the principal theatres in detail: omitting nothing but a few occasional changes of a very temporary kind (probably only for a night or two). The facts here stated differ in many details from those in any previously published account of our theatres; but for every statement made I have positive evidence which I hope some day to give in full. It would be out of place in so small a work to enter into minute particulars.

In the annexed Table the names of the principal theatres are given in the left-hand column: dates (at intervals of two years) are printed along the top line: the line ——— under these dates opposite the name of a theatre shows the years during which performances were exhibited in it: wherever dates can be ascertained the companies who occupied the theatre are printed over the line. Thus, the Red Bull was successively occupied by the Queen's company (Elizabeth's); the Earl of Worcester's (afterwards Queen Anne's); then by the Revels company: then by the Prince's, &c.; this is plain at a glance. In like manner we can see that the Revels Children on leaving Blackfriars went to Whitefriars, and were afterwards incorporated with the Queen's into the Revels company, &c., &c. If from the small scale of the table any doubt as to a date arises, reference should be made to pp. 82–84.

CHRONOLOGICAL TABLE OF THE PRINCIPAL THEATRES.

	15/76	8	80	2	4	6	8	90	2	4	6	8	16/00	2	4	6	8	10	2	4	6	8	20	2	4	6	8	30	2	4	6	8	40	2
Theater............	Chamberlain's																																	
Globe													Chamblin's=King's															King's						
Paul's	Paul's Children												? Paul's																					
Blackfriars													Chapel. ? Paul's. Revels Prince's. Children. L. Eliz.															King's						
Cockpit (Phœnix) (Drury Lane)																						Lady Eliz.		Queen's			Beeston's.	King & Queen's						
Salisbury Court..																											Revels (Prince's) Queen's							
Whitefriars........															Revels Children																			
Red Bull...........												Queen's					Worcester's=Queen's					Revels Cy. Prince's.	Bull Company.	Prince's.	Fortune Cy.									
Curtain																	Worcester's=Queen's					Revels Cy. Prince's												
Rose.................																																		
Fortune																	Admiral's=Prince's									Palsgrave's. Fortune Company			Prince's					

CHAPTER IX.

ON THE DRAMATIC AUTHORS CONTEMPORARY WITH SHAKESPEARE.

It does not come within the scope of this book to treat of any author except Shakespeare critically. It is however indispensable for the accurate determination of the chronological arrangement of his plays, and for the understanding of his relations to his contemporaries, that Tables of their plays arranged in order of time should be accessible. Such Tables have never hitherto been formed. I annex therefore lists of the plays of all the dramatists whose works have been republished in a collected form, and a list of plays of other authors contained in Dodsley (Hazlitt's edition) &c., with dates of publication (and production, where possible), and notices of the theatre and company to which each play belonged. The dates of production will be found to differ largely from those hitherto assigned in many instances, but never without reasons grounded on external evidence and confirmed by internal. This evidence I hope to give in a future work. For information concerning plays now lost or not republished in modern times, Halliwell's *Dictionary of Old Plays* will supply all necessary information. With a few exceptions (for which special reasons exist) only published plays are noticed here.

In the annexed Table a dotted line .... indicates the period of the author's life; a line not broken ———— that of his working career.

CHRONOLOGICAL TABLE OF THE PRINCIPAL DRAMATISTS.

	BORN	Companies / Theatres	DIED
i. Lilly	1553	Chapel and Paul's	1601
ii. Peele	1552	Chap. Adml's. Queen's	1596–7
iii. Greene	1561	Queen's	1592
iv. Marlowe	1564	Adm. Pem.	1593
v. Shakespeare	1564	Strange. Chamb. King's	1616
vi. Chapman	1557	Adm. Paul's. Revels	1634
vii. Jonson	1574	Chm.Chp.Chm. King's — Phœ.	1637
viii. Dekker	1575	Adm.Paul's Prince's and Queen's	1641
ix. Heywood	1582	Darby Queen's — King's	1640
x. Middleton	1574	Adm. Paul's Prince's & Rev. King's	1624
xi. Marston	1575	Ad.Pls. Revels	1624
xii. Webster	?1582	Paul's Queen's and King's	1652
xiii. Fletcher	1576	King's, 5 Revels	1625
xiv. Beaumont	1586	King's, 1 Paul's, 3 Revels	1616
xv. Tourneur	1583	King's	1627
xvi. Rowley	?1591	1 Prince's, 1 Curtain, Rev. King's	1629
xvii. Massinger	1584	King's and Queen's	1640
xviii. Ford	1586	King's and Queen's	1639
xix. Shirley	1595	Phœ.,Sal.Ct.&Blkfrs.	1666
xx. Randolph	1605		1639

I.—LILLY (JOHN), born 1553, began work 1578, died 1601 :—

Name of Play.	Company.	Published.
1. Woman in the Moon	—	1597
2. Love's Metamorphosis	Chapel, Paul's	1601
3. Campaspe	Chapel, Paul's	1584
4. Sappho and Phao	Chapel, Paul's	1584
5. Galathea	Paul's	1592
6. Endymion	Paul's	1591
7. Midas	Paul's	1592
8. Mother Bombie	Paul's	1594
9. ? Maid's Metamorphosis	Paul's	1600

These (except 9) were all produced before 1589 (Malone).

II.—PEELE (GEORGE), born 1552, **began work 1584**, died 1596-7 :—

Name of Play (and Author)	Company.	Pub.	Written.
1. Arraignment of Paris	Chapel	1584	1584
2. David and Bethsabe		1599	1585
3. Locrine (Tilney)	L. Strange's	1595	1586
4. Battle of Alcazar	—	1594	1587
5. Edward I.	—	1593	1588
6. Old Wives' Tale	Queen's	1595	1589
7. ? King John (Troublesome Reign)	Queen's	1591	1590
8. ? 2 & 3 Henry VI. (Marlowe)	Pembroke's	1594	1591-2
9. ? Edward III. (Shakespeare)	? L. Strange's	1596	1594
10. ? Richard III. (Shakespeare)	Chamberlain's	1597	1595
11. ? Romeo and Juliet (Shakespeare)	Hunsdon's	1597	1596

III.—GREENE (ROBERT), born 1561, began **work** 1585, died 1592 :—

Name of Play.	Company.	Pub.	Written.
1. Alphonsus	—	1599	1585
2. Orlando Furioso	Queen's	1594	1586
3. Friar Bacon	Queen's	1598	1588
4. James IV.	Queen's	1598	1589
5. Looking-glass for London (with Lodge)	Queen's	1594	? 1589

IV.—MARLOWE (CHRISTOPHER), born 1564, began work 1585, died 1593 :—

Name of Play.	Company.	Pub.	Written.
1. Tamburlaine I.	Admiral's	1590	1585
2. Tamburlaine II.	Admiral's	1590	1586
3. Faust	Admiral's	1609	1587
4. Jew of Malta	(Cockpit 1633)	1633	1588
5. Massacre of Paris	Admiral's	n. d.	1589
6. ? Taming of a Shrew (Shakespeare)	Pembroke's	1594	1589

Name of Play.	Company.	Pub.	Written.
7. ? Titus Andronicus	{Sussex, Pembroke, Darby ... ...}	1600	1590
8. ? 2 & 3 Henry VI. (Peele) ...	Pembroke's	1594	1591
9. Edward II.	Pembroke's	1598	1592
10. Dido (Nash)	Chapel	1594	1593

V.—SHAKESPEARE (WILLIAM). See Chapter iii.

VI.—CHAPMAN (GEORGE), born 1557, began work 1597, died 1634:—

Name of Play (2nd Author).	Company.	Theatre.	Pub.	Writ.
1. Blind Beggar of Alexandria ...	Admiral's ...	Rose	1598	1598
2. Humorous Day's Mirth	Admiral's ...	Rose	1599	1599
3. Bussy d'Ambois	Paul's	—	1607	1602-4
4. Eastward Ho (Jonson, Marston).	{Her Maj. Revels ...}	Blackfriars ..	1605	1605
5. All Fools	[Revels] ...	Blackfriars ..	1605	1605
6. Gentleman Usher	—	—	1606	—
7. Monsieur d'Olive	{Her Maj. Children}	Blackfriars ..	1606	1606
8. Cæsar and Pompey	—	—	1607	—
9. 10. Byron's Conspiracy and Tragedy.		Blackfriars ..	1608	1608
11. Mayday	[Revels]	Blackfriars ..	1611	1611
12. Widows' Tears		Blkfrs, Whtfrs.	1612	1612
13. Revenge of Bussy d'Ambois ...		Whitefriars ..	1613	1613
14. Ball 15. Chabot } (finished by Shirley) ...	[Queen's]	{Drury Lane. Drury Lane.}	1639 1639	*1632 *1635
? Alphonsus of Germany†	King's ...	Blackfriars ...	1654	—

For the *Second Maiden's Tragedy* and *Revenge for Honour* usually attributed to Chapman, see page 99.

VII.—JONSON (BENJAMIN), born 1574, began work 1596, died 1637:—

Name of Play (2nd Author).	Company.	Theatre.	Pub.	Writ.
1. Every Man in his Humour ...	Chambln's	Globe ...	1601, 1616	1598
2. Every Man out of his Humour	{Chapel Children}	Blackfriars ...	1600	1599
3. Case is Altered	Children ...	Blackfriars ...	1609	1599
4. Tale of a Tub	{Cockpit list 1639} ...	—{(licensed 1633) 1640}	1603- 4‡
5. Cynthia's Revels	Chapel ...	Blackfriars ...	1600	1600
6. Poetaster	Chapel ...	Blackfriars ...	1602	1601
7. Sejanus (? Shakespeare)	Chambln's ...	Globe	1605	1603
8. Eastward Ho (Chapman, Marston)	Revels ...	Blackfriars ...	1605	1605

---

* These dates are those of Shirley's completion of the plays. There is no clear evidence of Chapman's writing for the stage after 1613. *Alphonsus* is not Chapman's; nor did he write for the King's Company.
† Probably acted by the King's Company at Blackfriars, May 5. 1636.
‡ The parts concerning Inigo Jones (Act v. Sc. 2), and the masque at the end, were added in 1633.

90   SHAKESPEARE MANUAL.

Name of Play (2nd Author.)	Company.	Theatre.	Pub.	Writ.
9. Volpone	King's	Globe	1605	1605
10. Epicœne	King's	Globe	1609	1609
11. Catiline	[King's	Globe]	1611	1611
12. Alchemist	King's	Globe	1612	1612
13. Bartholomew Fair	L. Eliz.	Hope	1614	1614
14. Devil is an Ass	—	—	1641	1616
15. Staple of News (entered 1626)..	—	—	1631	1625
16. New Inn	King's	[Blkfrs.]	1631	1629
17. Magnetic Lady	—	—	1640	1632
18. Sad Shepherd } unfinished {	—	—	1640	1637
19. Mortimer's Fall	—	—	1640	1637

VIII.—DEKKER (THOMAS), born 1575, began work 1598, died 1641 :—

Name of Play (2nd Author).	Company.	Theatre.	Pub.	Writ.
1. Old Fortunatus	Admiral's	Rose	1600	1596
2. Patient Grissell (Haughton, Chettle)	Admiral's	Rose 28 Mar.	1600	1597
3. Satiromastix	{Chamber- lain's, Paul's}	[Globe]	1602	1602
4. Westward Ho (Webster)	Paul's	—	1607	1602-4
5. Northward Ho (Webster)	Paul's	—	1607	1602-4
6. Sir Thomas Wyatt (Webster)	Queen's	[Bull]	1607	1603-4
7. Honest Whore I. (Middleton)	Prince's	Fortune	1604	1604
8. Roaring Girl (Middleton)	Prince's	Fortune	1611	?1606
9. Whore of Babylon	Prince's	Fortune	1607	1607
10. Honest Whore II.	[Prince's	Fortune]	1630	1608
11. If it be not good, &c.	Queen's	Bull	1612	1612
12. Match me in London	[Queen's]	Bull	—	—
	[Queen's]	Phœnix	1631	—
13. Guy of Warwick (Day)	—	—	1619	—
14. Virgin Martyr (Massinger)	Revels	Bull	—	?1614
15. Witch of Edmonton (Ford)	Prince's	Cockpit	1658	1623-4
16. Sun's Darling (Ford)	Their Maj.	Cockpit	1657	1624
17. Wonder of a Kingdom	—	—	1636	—
18. Shoemaker's Holiday (Wilson)	Admiral's	Rose	1600	—

IX.—HEYWOOD (THOMAS), born 1582, began work 1599, died 1640 :—

Name of Play (2nd Author).	Company.	Theatre.	Pub.	Writ.
1, 2. Edward IV.	Darby's	—	1600	—
3. Woman Killed with Kindness	(Queen's, 1607)	{see Henslow's Diary}	1607	1602
4. Four Prentices of London	[Queen's]	Bull	1615	?1604
5. Fair Maid of Exchange	—	—	1607	—
6, 7. If you Know not Me, &c.	—	Cockpit 1632.	1606	—

Name of Play (2nd Author).	Company.	Theatre.	Pub.	Writ.
8. Rape of Lucreece	Queen's	... Bull 1638 ...	1608	—
9. Golden Age	Queen's	... Bull	1611	—
10. Silver Age	—	—	1613	—
11. Brazen Age	—	—	1613	—
12, 13. Iron Age	—	—	1632	—
14. Royal King and Loyal Subject.	Queen's	... —	1637	—
15, 16. Fair Maid of West	Queen's	... —	1631	—
17. Life of Duchess of Suffolk ...	—	—	1631	—
18. English Traveller	—	Cockpit ...	1633	—
19. Maidenhead well Lost	—	Cockpit ...	1634	—
20. Love's Mistress	Queen's	... Cockpit ...	1636	—
21. Amphrisa	—	—	1637	—
22. Love's Masterpiece	—	—	1640	—
23. Wise Woman of Hogsdon ...	—	—	1638	—
24. Fortune by Land & Sea (Rowley)	Queen's	... —	1655	—
25. Late Lancashire Witches (Broome)	[King's]	... Globe	1634	—
26. Challenge for Beauty	[King's]	... Globe & Blkfs.	1636	—

X.—MIDDLETON (THOMAS), born 1574, began work **1599**, died 1624 :—

Name of Play (2nd Author).	Company.	Theatre.	Pub.	Writ.
? Mayor of Quinborough (Hengist)	Admiral's	... Rose	1661	1597
1. Old Law (part)	—	—	1656	1599
2. Blurt Master Constable	Paul's	—	1602	1601-4
3. Phœnix	Paul's	—	1607	
4. Michaelmas **Term**	Paul's	—	1607	
5. Mad World, my **Masters**	Paul's	{(Queen's, Salsb Court 1640)}	1608	
6. **Trick** to Catch the **Old One** ...	Paul's	Blackfriars ...	1608	
7. Honest Whore (Dekker)	**Prince's**	... Fortune ...	1604	**1604**
8. **Your** Five Gallants	[Revels]	... Blackfriars entd.	1608	
9. Mayor of Quinborough	—	? Blackfriars..	1661	1605-8
10. **Family** of Love	Revels	... [Blackfriars]..	1608	
11. **Chaste** Maid in Cheapside ...	Lady Eliz.	... Swan	1630	—
12. **Roaring** Girl (Dekker)	**Prince's**	... Fortune ...	1611	? 1606
13. **Fair Quarrel** (Rowley)	Prince's	... [Fortune] ...	1617	1611-15
14. **World Tost at** Tennis (Rowley)	Prince's	... — ... entd.	1620	
15. **Changeling** (Rowley)	[Prince's]	...{Drury Lane (1623) Salsb. Ct.(1631-3)}	1653	1611-15
16. **Spanish Gipsy** (Rowley)	[Prince's]	...		
17. **Widow** (Jonson, Fletcher) ...	King's	... Blackfriars ...	—	1615-16
18. **More** Dissemblers besides Women	King's	... Blackfriars ...	1657	{old in 1623}

Name of Play (2nd Author).	Company.	Theatre.	Pub.	Writ.
19. Anything for Quiet Life ...	King's	Blackfriars	1662	
20. No Wit : no Help, &c. ...	—	—	1657	1617-23
21. Women beware Women ...	—	—	1657	
22. Witch ...	King's	Blackfriars	MS.	
23. Game at Chess ...	[King's]	Globe ...	[1625]	1624

XI.—MARSTON (JOHN), born 1575, began work 1602, died 1624 :—

Name of Play (2nd Author).	Company.	Theatre.	Pub.	Writ.
1. 2. Antonio and Mellida ...	Paul's ...	—	1602	—
3. Malcontent (cf. Webster) ...	Admiral's	Rose ...	1604	—
4. Eastward Ho (Jonson, Chapman)	{ Her Maj. Revels ... }	Blackfriars ...	1605	—
5. Dutch Courtisan ...	{ Her Maj. Revels ... }	[Blackfriars].	1605	—
6. Fawn ...	{ Her Maj. Revels ... }	[Blackfriars]..	1606*	—
7. Sophonisba ...	[Revels]	Blackfriars	1606	—
8. What you Will ...	Revels	[Blackfriars]..	1607	—
9. Insatiate Countess (Barksted)...	[Revels]	Whitefriars ...	1613	—

XII.—WEBSTER (JOHN), born ?1582, began work 1602, died 1652 :—

Name of Play (2nd Author).	Company.	Theatre.	Pub.	Writ.
1. Malcontent (additions to) ...	King's	Globe ...	1604	1604
2. Northward Ho (Dekker)...	Paul's ...	—	1607	1602-4
3. Westward Ho (Dekker) ...	Paul's...	—	1607	1602-4
4. Sir T. Wyatt (Dekker) ...	Queen's	[Bull] ...	1607	1603-4
5. White Devil ...	Queen's	{ [Bull] ... Phœnix }	1612 1631	1611 —
6. Duchess of Malfi ...	King's	Globe & Blkfs.	1623	1616
7. Devil's Law Case ...	Queen's	—	1623	1622†
8. Appius and Virginia ...	(Cockpit 1639)'	—	1654	—
9. Cure for Cuckold (Rowley)	[probably only begun by Webster]		1651	—
10. Thracian Wonder (Rowley)			1651	—

---

* *Fawn* was acted also at Paul's before 1606.
† This is Dyce's date; I date the play between 1608-15; rather earlier than later.

XIII.—FLETCHER, born 1576
XIV.—BEAUMONT, born 1586 } began work 1607, died { 1625.
1616.

Title.	Author.	Date.
1. Woman Hater	Beaumont (B.)	1607
2. Faithful Shepherdess	Fletcher (F.)	before 1610
3. Four Plays in One	B. and F.	
4. Wit at Several Weapons	do.	
5. Thierry and Theodoret	do.	
6. Maid's Tragedy	do.	before 1611
7. Philaster	do.	,, 1611
8. King and No King	do.	1611
9. Knight of Burning Pestle	do.	1611
10. Cupid's Revenge	do.	1612
11. Scornful Lady	do.	1609-12
12. Coxcomb	F.	1612
13. Captain	do.	1613
14. Henry VIII.	F. and Shakespeare	1613
15. Two Noble Kinsmen	do.	?1613
16. Honest Man's Fortune	B. and F.	1613
17. Masque	B.	1613
18. Wit without Money	F.	before 1619
19. Bonduca	do.	,, 1619
20. Valentinian	do.	,, 1619
21. Knight of Malta	F. and Middleton (Md.)	,, 1619
22. Queen of Corinth	do.	1616-19
23. Mad Lover	F.	before 1619
24. Loyal Subject	do.	1618
25. Humorous Lieutenant	do.	before 1620
26. Woman's Prize	do.	after 1619
27. Chances	do.	,, 1619
28. M. Thomas	do.	,, 1619
29. Double Marriage	do.	,, 1619
30. Women Pleased	do.	,, 1619
31. Island Princess	do.	at Court 1621
32. Pilgrim	do.	,, 1621
33. Wild Goose Chase	do.	,, 1621
34. Custom of the Country	do.	1621
35. False One	F. and Massinger (M.)	after 1618
36. Little French Lawyer	do.	,, 1619
37. Very Woman (Woman's Plot)	do.	1621
altered by Massinger probably	—	1634
38. Laws of Candy	do.	after 1619
39. Beggar's Bush	do.	at Court 1622
40. Prophetess	do.	licensed 14 May, 1622
41. Sea Voyage	do.	,, 22 June, 1622
42. Spanish Curate	do.	,, 24 Oct. 1622
43. Lover's Progress	do.	before 1623
44. Love's Cure	F., M., Rowley (R.)	after 1622

Title.	Author.	Date.
45. Maid in the Mill	F. and Rowley (R.)	licensed 29 Oct. 1623
46. Wife for a Month	F.	,, 27 May, 1624
47. Rule a Wife, &c.	do.	,, 19 Oct. 1624
48. Bloody Brother	F. and ?...	after 1623
49. Elder Brother...	F. and M.	,, 1625
50. Fair Maid of the Inn	F. M. R.	licensed 22 June, 1626
51. Noble Gentleman	F. and ?...	,, 3 Feb. 1626
52. Nice Valor	F. and ?...	after 1624
53. Night Walker	F. and Shirley ...	,, 1625
54. Love's Pilgrimage	do. ...	,, 1625

Whether Fletcher wrote any part of *The Widow* (by Middleton and Jonson, about 1615) is very doubtful. He certainly had **no** share in the *Faithful Friends*, which I assign to Beaumont alone, date 1606. **All these** plays were produced **by the** King's company except No. **1, by** Paul's **Children; 9, 10, 11, by** Revels **Children; 53** by the Cockpit company.

XV.—TOURNEUR (CYRIL). See page 99.

XVI.—ROWLEY (WILLIAM), born **1591** (?), began work 1607, died **1627** :—

Name of Play (2nd Author).	Company.	Theatre.	Pub.	Written.
1. Travels of Three Brothers (Day, Wilkins) ... ...}	—	Curtain ...	lost	1607
2. Match at Midnight ...	Revels ...	[Bull] ...	1633 ...	before 1622
3. Fair Quarrel (Middleton)	Prince's ...	—	1617 ...	,, 1623
4. World Lost at Tennis (Middleton) ... ...}	Prince's ...	—	entd. 1620	,, 1623
5. Old Law (Middleton) ...	—	{ Salisbury Ct. 1631-3 }	1656 ...	,, 1623
6. SpanishGipsy(Middleton)	—	{ Drury Lane, 1623 }	1653 ...	,, 1623
7. Changeling (Middleton)	—	{ Salisbury Ct. 1631-3 }	1653 ...	,, 1623
8. Witch of Edmonton (Ford and Dekker) ... ...}	Prince's ...	Cockpit ...	1658 ...	1623-4
9. All's Lost by Lust	{ L. Eliz.} Queen's.}	Phœnix ...	1633 ...	1623
10. Maid in the Mill(Fletcher)	King's ...	Blackfriars.	—	1623
11. New Wonder	[King's] ...	Blackfriars]	1632 ...	1624-6
12. Cure for Cuckold (Webster) ... ...}	[King's] ...	—	1651 ...	1624-6
13 ThracianWonder(Webster)	[King's] ...	—	1651 ...	1624-6
14. Birth of Merlin (? Shakespeare) ... ...}	[King's] ...	—	1662 ...	1624-6

XVII.—MASSINGER (PHILIP), born 1584, began work 1613, died 1640 :—

Name of Play (2nd Author).	Company.	Theatre.	Pub.	Written.
1. Virgin Martyr (Dekker)	Revels ...	Bull	1622	... ? 1613
2. Fatal Dowry (Field) ...	King's ...	Blackfriars	1632 ...	? 1614
3-13. Eleven Plays with Fletcher (see under Fletcher).				
14. Unnatural Combat ...	King's ...	Globe ...	1639	... before 1622
15. Duke of Milan	King's ...	Blackfriars	1623	... ,, 1622
16. New Way to pay Old Debts	—	Phœnix ...	1633	... ,, 1622
17. Maid of Honour	{Queen's} {[1632]}	Phœnix ...	1632	... ,, 1622
18. Bondman	—	Cockpit ...	1624 licensed Dec. 1623	
19. Renegado'	{Queen's} {[1630]}	Drury Lane 6Mar.1630	17 Apl. 1624	
20. Parliament of Love ...	—	Cockpit ...	29June,1660	3 June, 1624
21. Roman Actor	King's ...	Blackfriars	1629	... 11 Oct. 1626
22. Great Duke of Florence	Queen's...	Phœnix ...	1636	... 5 July, 1627
23. Picture	King's ...	{Globe and} {Blackfriars} 1630		... 8 June, 1629
24. Believe as you list	—	sent back	11 Jan. 1631	
25. City Madam	King's ...	{(Globe or} {Blackfriars)}1658		... 25May,1632
26. Guardian	King's ...	Blackfriars	1655	... 31 Oct. 1633
27. Bashful Lover	King's ...	Blackfriars	1655	... 9 May, 1636
28. Old Law (revised from Rowley and Middleton)	—	{Salisbury} {House}	1656	... {after 1629} {? 1637}

XVIII.—FORD (JOHN), born 1586, began work 1621, died 1639 :—

Name of Play (2nd Author).	Company.	Theatre.	Pub.	Written.
1. 'Tis Pity she's a Whore ...	Queen's [1633]	Phœnix ...	1633	? 1621
2. Love's Sacrifice	Queen's [1633]	Phœnix ...	1633	? 1622
3. Witch of Edmonton (Dekker, Rowley)	Prince's	Cockpit ...	1658	1623-4
4. Sun's Darling (Dekker) ...	(TheirMaj.1657)	Cockpit ...	1657	1624
5. Lover's Melancholy	King's	{Globe and} {Blackfriars}	1629	1628
6. Broken Heart	King's ... —	Blackfriars	1633	1633
7. Perkin Warbeck	Queen's	Phœnix ...	1634	1634
8. Fancies Chaste and Noble ...	Queen's	Phœnix ...	1638	1637
9. Ladies' Trial	TheirMajesties	Drury Lane	1639	1638

XIX.—SHIRLEY (JAMES), **born 1595, began** work 1625, died 1666 :—

Name of Play (2nd Author).	Company.	Theatre.	Pub.	Written.
1. Constant Maid	—	Nursery	1640	? 1624
2. (Love Will Find Out the Way; ? T. B.)	—	Hatton Garden	1661	—
3. Humorous Courtiers	—	Drury Lane	1640	? 1624
4. Arcadia	—	Phœnix	1640	? 1624
5. Bird in Cage	—	Phœnix	1633	? 1624
6. Wedding	—	Phœnix	1629	before 1625
7. School of Compliments (Love Tricks)	—	Drury Lane	1631	{ licensed 10 Feb. 1625
8. Maid's Revenge	—	Drury Lane	1639	9 Feb. 1626
9. Brothers	—	Blackfriars	1652	4 Nov. 1626
10. Witty Fair One	—	Drury Lane	1633	3 Oct. 1628
11. Faithful (Grateful) Servant	—	—	lost	3 Nov. 1629
12. Traitor (Rivers)	—	—	1635	4 May, 1631
13. Duke	—	—	lost	7 May, 1631
14. Love's Cruelty	—	Drury Lane	1640	Nov. 1631
15. Changes	Revels	Salisbury Court	1632	10 Jan. 1632
16. Hyde Park	—	Drury Lane	1637	20 Apr. 1632
17. Ball (Chapman)	—	Drury Lane	1639	16 Nov. 1632
18. Beauties	—	—	lost	21 Jan. 1633
19. Young Admiral	—	Drury Lane	1637	3 July, 1633
20. Gamester	—	Drury Lane	1637	11 Nov. 1633
21. Example	—	Drury Lane	1637	24 June, 1634
22. Opportunity	—	Drury Lane	1640	29 Nov. 1634
23. Coronation	Her Maj.	Drury Lane	1640	6 Feb. 1635
24. Chabot (Chapman)	—	Drury Lane	1639	29 Apr. 1635
25. Lady of Pleasure	—	Drury Lane	1637	15 Oct. 1635
26. Duke's Mistress	—	Drury Lane	1638	18 Jan. 1636
27. Royal Master	—	Dublin	1638	23 Apr. 1638
28. St. Patrick for Ireland	—	—	1640	? 1624
29. Gentleman of Venice	—	Salisbury Court	1655	30 Oct. 1639
30. Look to the Lady	—	—	lost	10 Mar. 1639
31. St. Albans (entered 14 Feb. 1639)	—	—	lost	—
32. Rosania (Doubtful Heir)	—	—	1652	1 June, 1640
33. Politic Father (Politician)	—	Salisbury Court	1655	26 May, 1641
34. Cardinal	—	Blackfriars	1652	25 Nov. 1641
35. Sisters	—	Blackfriars	1652	26 Apr. 1642
36. Court Secret	—	Blackfriars	1653	—
37. Imposture	—	Blackfriars	1652	—
38. Honoria and Mammon (from Masque of Honor and Riches, 1633) (see also under Fletcher)	—	—	1659	—

XX.—RANDOLPH (THOMAS), born 1605, died 1639 :—

Name of Play.	Written.
1. Conceited Pedlar	before 1630
2. Aristippus	,, 1630
3. Jealous Lovers	,, 1632
4. Amyntas	,, 1638
5. Muses Looking Glass	,, 1638
6. Hey for Honesty	—

XXI.—BROME (RICHARD) :—

Name of Play (2nd Author).	Company.	Theatre.	Pub.	Written.
1. Fault in Friendship (Jonson, jun.)	—	Curtain	—	entered 2 Oct. 1623
2. Late Lancashire Witches (Heywood)	—	Globe	1634	—
3. Northern Lass	—	Globe and Blackfriars	1632	—
4. Sparagus Garden	Revels	SalisburyCourt	1640	before 1635
5. Antipodes (for Cockpit)	Queen's	SalisburyCourt	1640	,, 1638
6. Novella	—	Blackfriars	1653	1632
7. City Wit	—	—	1653	—
8. Damoiselle	—	—	1653	—
9. Court Beggars	King's	Cockpit	1653	1632
10. Mad Couple Well Matched	—	Cockpit (1639)	1653	—
11. Queen's Exchange	—	—	1657	—
12. Weeding of Covent Garden	—	—	1658	—
13. New Academy	—	—	1658	—
14. Lovesick Court	—	—	1658	—
15. English Moor	Queen's	—	1659	—
16. Queen and Concubine	—	—	1659	—
17. Jovial Crew (Merry Beggars)	—	Cockpit	1652	1641

XXII.—GLAPTHORNE (HENRY) :—

Name of Play.	Company.	Theatre.	Published.
1. Hollander (written 1635)	—	Cockpit	1640
2. Argalus and Parthenia	—	Drury Lane	1639
3. Ladies' Privilege	—	Drury Lane	1640
4. Wit in a Constable	—	Cockpit	1639
5. Alb. Wallenstein	King's	Globe	1639
? Parricide (Revenge for Honor) probably altered from Chapman.	Prince's	[Bull]	entered 27 May, 1624

The dates of writing given in the last column of these tables are only approximations in many instances: but where a month and day are given a definite entry is referred to and an inferior limit of time is thus fixed.

XXIII.—List of **Plays** which are not included in the foregoing, but which **have been republished (most of them** in the new edition of Dodsley) :—

Name of Play.	Author.	Company.	Theatre.	Pub.	Writ.
1. Royster Doyster	Nicholas Udall	—	—	1566	1550
2. Ferrex and Porrex	Norton, Sackville	—	—	1565	1562
3. Appius and Virginia	R. B.	—	—	1575	1563
4. Damon and Pythias	Rich. Edwards	—	—	1571	1565
5. Gammer Gurton's Needle	S[till]	—	—	1575	1566
6. Cambyses	Th. Preston	—	—	1570	1569
7. Promos and Cassandra	G. Whetstone	—	—	1578	—
8. Sir Clyomon	—	Queen's	—	1599	? 1582
9. Three Ladies of London	R. Wilson	[Queen's]	—	1584	1584
10. Locrine	Tylney and Peele (edited by W. S.)	L. Strange's	—	1595	1586
11. Marius and Sylla	T. Lodge	Admiral's	—	1594	1586-8
12. Three Lords and Ladies of London	R. Wilson	[Queen's]	—	1590	1588
13. Jeronimo	T. Kyd	—	—	1605	before 1589
14. Spanish Tragedy	T. Kyd	—	—	[1594]	before 1589
15. Soliman and Perseda	?T. Kyd	—	—	[1599]	1589
16. Taming of a Shrew	—	Pembroke's	—	1594	1589
17. Sir T. More	—	—	—	—	1590
18. Troublesome Reign of King John	[G. Peele]	Queen's	—	1591	1590
19. Fair Emm	—	L. Strange's	—	1631	1590
20. London Prodigal	—	L. Strange's	(King's, 1605)	1605	1591
21. King Leir	—	Queen's	—	1605	1592
22. Two Angry Women	H. Porter	Admiral's	—	1599	? 1592
23. Summer's Last Will	T. Nash	Chapel	—	1600	1592
24. Arden of Feversham	—	L. Strange's	—	1592	1592
25. Grim the Collier	J. T.	—	—	[1662]	after 1590
26. Look about You	[A. Munday]	Admiral's	—	1600	? 1592
27. Downfall of Robin Hood	A. Munday	Admiral's	—	1601	? 1593
28. Death of Robin Hood	A. Munday, H. Chettle	Admiral's	—	1601	? 1593
29. Richard III.	—	Queen's	—	1594	1593
30. Knack to Know a Knave	[? T. Lodge]	Alleyn's	[Lord Strange's]	1594	1593

CONTEMPORARY AUTHORS.

Name of Play.	Author.	Company.	Theatre.	Pub.	Writ.
31. Mucedorus	[T. Lodge]	—	—	1598	1594
	—	King's	Globe	1613	1610
32. George a Green	—	Sussex's	—	1599	1594
33. How a Man may, &c.	J. Cooke	Worcester's	—	1602	? 1597
34. Englishmen for My Money	W. Haughton	Admiral's	—	1616	1598
35. Sir John Oldcastle	Munday, Drayton, Wilson, Hathaway. [ascribed to Shakespeare]	Admiral's	—	1600	1599
36. Timon	—	—	University	—	? 1600
37. Return from Parnassus	—	—	S. John's Camb.	1606	1602
38. Hoffmann	H. Chettle	Admiral's	Phœnix, 1631	1631	1602
39. Cromwell	—	Chamberlain	—	1602	—
40. Lingua	—	—	—	1607	1602
41. Wily Beguiled	—	—	—	1606	1603
42. Yorkshire Tragedy	—	—	—	1605	—
43. Puritan	—	Paul's	—	1607	—
44. Dumb Knight	G. Markham L. Machin	King's Revels	Blackfriars	1608	1607
45. Miseries of enforced Marriage	G. Wilkins	King's	Globe	1607	1607
46. Merry Devil of Edmonton	T. B.	King's	Globe	1608	1607
47. Revenger's Tragedy	C. Tourneur	King's	Globe	1607	1607
48. Atheist's Tragedy	C. Tourneur	King's	Globe	1611	? 1609
49. Ram Alley	L. Barry	King's Revels	Blackfriars	1611	1611
50. Second Maiden's Tragedy	—	—	—	31 Oct. 1611	
51. Woman's a Weathercock	N. Field	Queen's Revels	Whitefriars	1617	1612
52. Amends for Ladies	N. Field	Prince's, L. Eliz.	Blackfriars	1618	1613
53. Albumazar	J. Tomkis	—	Trinity Camb.	1614	1613
54. Hog hath Lost his Pearl	R. Tailor	Apprentices	Whitefriars	1614	1613
55. Heir	T. May	Revels	—	1633	1630
56. Old Couple	T. May	—	—	1658	—
57. Revenge for Honour	? Glapthorne	Prince's	—	1654	1624
58. City Nightcap	R. Davenport	Queen's	Phœnix	1661	1624
59. Microcosmus	T. Nabbes	—	Salisbury Court.	1637	—
60. Ordinary	W. Cartwright	—	—	1651	—

7—2

Name of Play.	Author.	Company.	Theatre.	Pub.	Writ.
61. London Chanticleers	—	—	—	1659	1636
62. Shepherd's Holiday	Rutter	Queen's	—	1635	—
63. Fuimus Troes	J. Fisher	—	{Magdalen Oxon.}	1633	1633
64. Lost Lady	W. Barclay	—	—	1639	—
65. City Match	J. M[ayne]	King's	Blackfriars	1639	1639
66. Queen of Arragou	W. Habington	—	—	1640	—
67. Antiquary	S. Marmion	Queen's	Cockpit	1641	—
68. Rebellion	T. Rawlins	Revels	—	1640	—
69. Andromana	J. G.	—	—	1660	—
70. Parson's Wedding	T. Killigrew	—	—	1664	—
71. Five Wise Men and all the rest Fools	—	—	—	—	—
72. Sophy	Sir J. Denham	King's	Blackfriars	1641	—

The following are of inferior importance, and a simple enumeration of them will suffice for our purpose :—

DANIEL (SAMUEL), born 1562, died 1619; wrote *Philotas* (printed 1605), *Cleopatra* (printed 1594), *Queen's Arcadia* (presented 1605), *Hymen's Triumph* (acted 1614), *Vision of Twelve Goddesses* (1604), and *Tethys' Festival* (1611).

ALEXANDER (WILLIAM, Earl of Stirling), born 1580, died 1640); wrote four "Monarchicke" tragedies; *Darius* (printed 1603), *Crœsus* (1604), *Julius Cæsar* (1604), and *The Alexandræan Tragedy* (1605).

CARTWRIGHT (WILLIAM), born 1611-15, died 1643; wrote *The Royal Slave* (acted 1636), *The Lady Errant* (printed 1651), *The Siege* (printed 1651), besides *The Ordinary* already mentioned.

SUCKLING (SIR JOHN), born 1608, died 1641-2; wrote *The Goblins, Aglaura, Brennoralt* (all printed 1646), and *The Sad One* (1658).

DAVENANT (SIR WILLIAM), born 1606, died 1669; wrote before 1642; *Albovine* (printed 1629), *Cruel Brother* (1630), *Just Italian* (1630), *Platonic Lovers* (1636), *Wits* (1636), *Love and Honor* (licensed 1634, printed 1649), *News from Plymouth* (licensed 1635), *Unfortunate Lovers* (licensed 1638, printed 1643), *Fair Favorite* (licensed 1638), and *Distresses,* or *Spanish Lovers* (licensed 1639). He also wrote other plays after 1656.

CHAPTER X.

A CHRONOLOGICAL TABLE OF MISCELLANEOUS MATTERS PERTAINING TO THE THEATRE,

FROM 1558 TO 1642.

1558. Queen Elizabeth's accession.
1561. T. Beyer made Master of the Revels.
1566. Still's Gammer Gurton's Needle produced.
1574. The Earl of Leicester's players licensed. Burbage, Perkin, Langham, Johnson, R. Wilson, &c.
   Plays performed on Sundays out of prayer time.
1576. The Theater and the Curtain built in Shoreditch.
1578. The Privy Council limited plays in the City to the companies of the Chapel Children, Paul's Children, Earl of Warwick, Earl of Leicester, and Earl of Essex.
1579. 24th July, E. Tilney made Master of the Revels.
1580. Plays on Sundays abolished. Newington Butts built.
1581. Whitefriars built. Pulled down soon after by the Queen's order, as well as the Cross Keys, Bull, Bell and Savage, and Paul's.
1583. The Queen's company selected.
1585. The Rose and the Hope opened.
1588. Paris Garden opened.
1589. A Commission of Censure appointed.
1591. No plays allowed on Thursdays because of bear-baiting being interfered with by them. Interdict on Paul's Children imposed after 1591.
1592. Dr. Rainolds and Dr. Gager hold forth at Oxford on the unlawfulness of stage plays.

1593. The Queen's company dispersed.
1594. Lord Strange's company absorbed into the Chamberlain's.
1595. Swan opened.
1596. Blackfriars building adapted for a theatre. Chapel Children put in by Burbage.
1599. The Fortune built by Alleyn for the **Admiral's** company.
1600. **The** Globe built by Burbage.
1601. **The** interdict on Paul's Children removed before 1601.
    All theatres ordered to be shut except the Fortune and the Globe.
1603. King James I. succeeds to the throne. He licenses Shakespeare, Burbage, Philipps, Hemings, Condell, &c., who **usually** play at the Globe.
    No plays allowed, except at **Court and in** private, on Sundays.
    The **King takes the** Chamberlain's **company for** his own; the **Queen the Earl** of Worcester's; **the** Prince the Admiral's.
1604. **Prince's** company at the Fortune (not the **Curtain**).
    Blackfriars bought by the Globe company.
1605. Children of the Revels at Blackfriars (formerly **the Chapel Children**).
    First moveable scenes at Christ Church.
1607. T. Coryat at Venice.
    Plays in Lent forbidden early in this reign.
1610. November 7. Sir G. Buck Master of the Revels.
1612. **Lady** Elizabeth's company join the Revels, separating **next** year (Collier).
    Revels Children at Whitefriars.
1613. J. **Taylor head of** Queen Elizabeth's company at the Hope.
    Globe burnt.
    Swan and Rose shut up before 1613.
    Lady Elizabeth becomes Queen of Bohemia.
1614. Globe rebuilt. Hope burnt down.
1616. Dispensation granted for playing in Lent, except Wednesdays and **Fridays**. The Red Bull and Fortune have tumblers at this season.
1617. The Cockpit (*nuper erectum*) pulled **down.**

1619. Queen Anne's death.
Cockpit rebuilt.
The Queen's Revels company become the King's.
The united Four Companies formed.
1621. December 15. The Fortune burnt.
Sir J. Astley Master of the Revels
1622. The Revels company at the Red Bull formed from Queen Anne's, which was licensed to bring up children for the Revels.
Sir Henry Herbert Master of the Revels.
The Red Bull not one of the Four Companies.
1625. King Charles married, and succeeds to the throne.
Prince's servants at the Curtain for last time.
1627. Red Bull company forbidden to play Shakespeare.
1629. Women on stage at Blackfriars.
Whitefriars rebuilt as Salisbury Court.
A French company performs at Blackfriars, the Bull, and the Fortune.
1630. Playhouses shut from April to November on account of the plague.
1633. Histriomastix published.
Prynne's ears cut off.
1634. Henrietta Maria at Blackfriars.
1635. French players at the Cockpit.
1636. First scenery used in a *private* performance of *Love's Mistress*, at Denmark House.
Theatres shut on account of the plague.
William Beeston ordered to make a boys' company at the Cockpit (King and Queen's).
1639. Poets receive second day's money taken at door.
1640. The Prince's company go to the Fortune; the Fortune company to the Bull.
Beeston dies; Davenant succeeds him.
1642. Theatres shut. War breaks out.

NOTE.—Stage plays were suppressed definitely in 1647, and the first scenery *on the stage* was introduced in 1662.

CHAPTER XI.

A LIST OF BOOKS MOST DESIRABLE FOR A STUDENT OF SHAKESPEARE TO POSSESS.

1. The reprint of the Folio edition of 1623, now sold by Glaisher, Holborn; or the reproduction by photolithography published by Chatto and Windus.
2. The Globe edition (Macmillan), for reference, the lines being numbered.
3. The *Variorum* edition of 1821. 20 vols. This is the storehouse of all important facts concerning Shakespeare from which the main part of modern editions is derived.
4. Mrs. Cowden Clarke's Concordance to the plays.
5. Mrs. Furness's Concordance to the Poems.
6. Schmidt's Shakespeare Lexicon, 2 vols. (Williams and Norgate.)
7. Clark and Wright's Cambridge edition, for the Collations. 9 vols. (out of print). (Macmillan.)
8. Dr. Abbott's Shakespearian Grammar. (Macmillan.)
9. S. Walker's Criticisms, 4 vols. (A. R. Smith.)
10. S. Neil's Shakespeare: a Biography. (Houlston and Wright.)

The large modern editions by Knight, Staunton, Dyce, and Halliwell are all useful for reference; but for anyone with limited means, after getting Nos. 1, 2, 4, 6, 8, 10, which are almost indispensable, a better investment is to procure copies of the old dramatists, viz.:—

(*a*) Beaumont and Fletcher, by Dyce, 2 vols. (Phillips and Sampson, Boston, 1854), if possible: if not, then that by Darley, 2 vols. (Routledge and Co.).

(*b*) Massinger, by Cunningham. (Chatto and Windus.)

(c) Ben Jonson, by Cunningham, 3 vols. (Chatto and Windus.)
(d) Webster, by Dyce. (Routledge.)
(e) Marlowe   ditto   (ditto).
(f) Greene and Peele   (ditto).
(g) Chapman's works, 3 vols. (Chatto and Windus.)
(h) Marston (A. R. Smith), 3 vols.
(i) Lilly   (ditto)   2 vols.
(j) Randolph (Kerslake).
(k) Brome, 3 vols.; Dekker, 4 vols.; Heywood, 6 vols.; Glapthorne, 2 vols.; Chapman, 3 vols.; are published in Pearson's reprints. Middleton and Shirley, by Dyce, are out of print. A more useful expenditure than these *éditions de luxe* would be:—
(l) Dodsley's Old Plays, by W. C. Hazlitt, 14 vols.
(m) The best selection for those who do not care to have the minor dramatists complete, is the *Ancient British Drama* by Sir W. Scott, 3 vols.

Other important works are:—

11. Halliwell's Dictionary of Old Plays.
12. Halliwell's Dictionary of Archaic words, 2 vols. (very useful).
13. W. C. Hazlitt's Handbook to Early English Literature.
14. W. C. Hazlitt's edition of Collier's Shakespeare Library, 6 vols.
15. Arber's reprints of Old English Literature are very useful and cheap.
16. Professor Ward's History of Dramatic Literature, 2 vols. (Macmillan), is very valuable.

Books *about* Shakespeare, called æsthetic, are best eschewed entirely until a distinct opinion has been formed from independent study. Among the best of these are Gervinus; Ulrici; Dowden; Hazlitt. Schlegel is useful, but not trustworthy. The publications of the (older) Shakspeare Society are valuable. So will be the Quarto reprints of the New Shakspere Society, a cheap edition of which is promised for non-subscribers in the prospectus. It is impossible to give anything like full information on this subject in this Manual. Hence I omit from the list given above such books as Cotgrave, Florio, Minsheu, and many other old dictionaries, with other books equally desirable but not necessary.

CHAPTER XII.

ON THE TESTS BY WHICH CHRONOLOGY AND AUTHORSHIP CAN BE DETERMINED.

THESE tests are made up of two distinct classes, *External* and *Internal*. The *External* tests divide into :—

1. *Direct.*—These consist of definite and positive statements made by authorities whose veracity and ability can be depended on.

2. *Indirect.*—These consist of deductions made from direct statements : for instance, from the facts that certain actors were engaged in representing a play, one or more of whom joined or left the company for which it was written at a given date ; or, that the play was produced at a theatre of known name at which the company to whom the play belonged only acted at a certain time ; and the like.

The former of these is the only kind of direct evidence that has hitherto been successfully used. The latter is that which has been of the greatest service to me in correcting erroneous statements hitherto admitted as accurate, and in determining the dates of plays not previously chronologically placed.

Of *Internal* evidences there are several kinds, namely :—

3. *Allusive.*—It is not uncommon for a play to contain allusions to other plays, or to political, theatrical, or other public matters whose dates are known from other sources. This evidence is usually more valuable by way of confirmation than of positive determination. It must be carefully watched and not strained too far, not only because such allusions are often imagined to exist without

sufficient grounds, but also because the custom of altering and rewriting plays was extremely prevalent in the Elizabethan era.

4. *Æsthetic.*—Under this head I include all evidences (usually separated into several branches) that depend on the taste or capacity of the critic who uses them, such as the estimate he forms of the power of the writer in forming a plot or in distinguishing his characters, or the knowledge he displays of human nature, or the general poetic merit of the work examined. Of course the verdict of a great critic based on the result of an attentive reading is of value, even when no grounds are alleged; but the lamentable mistakes that all critics of this kind have fallen into should make us very careful in doing anything more than making their decisions the ground for further investigation. No evidence based on impressions should be allowed to overweigh one definite fact, any more than evidence to character is allowed to overweigh positive evidence of events or actions in a court of law.

5. *Language.*—So far as mere "style" is concerned, this in some measure falls under the last head, and is liable to the same objections as are there adduced. The practice of the old dramatists of writing plays in which one man furnished the plot and another wrote the dialogue, has led to great error in determinations based on this ground. But so far as the use of peculiar phrases, unusual words, and above all of *idiotisms* or specially individual grammatical forms, is concerned, the test is of high value, and has not been at all sufficiently attended to. Among such forms, not only the use of particular affixes, prepositions, inflexions, &c. must be included, but also inversions and other peculiarities in the formation and arrangement of sentences.

6. *Metre.*—This is the most valuable of all internal tests, because in it, and in it only, can quantitative results be obtained. This has been completely overlooked by some, who seem to think that results may be grounded on the number of times that an author uses a certain form of expression, such as "for to go," for instance. This would be absurd. It is impossible to determine the number of times that such an expression *might have been* introduced in a play of (say) 3,000 lines, and therefore it is impossible

to say how often he has preferred this mode of expression to any other. But in a play of 3,000 lines of verse every line must have a masculine or feminine termination; hence, the number of feminine terminations gives us a quantitative test. In like manner every line must rhyme or not rhyme with the line next to it; every line must have a definite number of beats or measures; rhyming passages must be heroic, or alternate, or follow some other definite system: in all these cases we can get quantitative positive results. And it is certain that these results do, when properly used, give true and important consequences. On the other hand, such tests as the so-called weak-ending test, the pause test, &c., which partly depend on the æsthetic sense of the critic and are consequently indefinite as to quantity, can only be depended on as affording a basis for subsequent investigation. The great need for any critic who attempts to use these tests is to have had a thorough training in the Natural Sciences, especially in Mineralogy, classificatory Botany, and above all, in Chemical Analysis. The methods of all these sciences are applicable to this kind of criticism, which, indeed, can scarcely be understood without them.

As to their history, it will suffice here to say that Malone used them as *qualitative* tests only; that Mr. Spedding applied the female ending test to the play of *Henry VIII.* quantitatively; that Professor Hertzberg counted the female endings in some of the plays of Shakespeare but failed in obtaining any satisfactory results from them; that I reduced the theory of such tests to a system, established the canons for their use, assigned special distinctive tests to each of the Elizabethan dramatists and worked out the results for the whole of their plays. I have also applied the same kind of tests to some of the Greek dramatists and obtained satisfactory results for Æschylus and Sophocles; while in the case of Homer, I find that *language* tests are conclusive as to the existence of an *Achilleis* completed afterwards by the author of the *Odyssey* into the present form of the *Iliad*. My results (independently worked out) on this author agree in most points with those of Professor Geddes; but Books XIII.—XV., XVII. do not form part of my *Achilleis*.

I have been thus explicit on this kind of test, because it is not as yet at all generally understood, and because I attach to it the highest importance. As in the Second Part of this book several instances of its application occur, I need give no further detail here; but I must specially notice the extremely careful manner in which the weak-ending test has been applied to Shakespeare by Professor Ingram. Although I do not agree with him as to its value in chronologising the plays of the Fourth Period (for the reasons given above), yet to him is due the pointing out its perfection as a discriminating test between the plays of the Third Period and the Fourth when used as a class test; and his steady, careful work, and entirely courteous treatment of those who differ from him, make his Essay a model to be imitated by critics on this subject.

CHAPTER XIII.

ON EMENDATION OF THE TEXT.

THE text of Shakespeare has been made to so great an extent the pretext for ingenious persons to display their cleverness by rewriting, altering, inserting, omitting, and otherwise tampering with the old editions, and on the other hand the old copies are in many places so undoubtedly incorrect, that it seems desirable to attempt to lay down here a few general principles as to the limits within which it is permissible to propose any alteration of the text as originally published; at present the general system of editors seems to be to alter not only everything they do not understand, but also everything that they think could be written better. The following canons would exclude two-thirds of the emendations that have been proposed.

1. That no emendation however plausible can be admitted, unless either the passage as it stands is inexplicably absurd, or in direct violation of the author's metrical system. Thus the well-known passage, "his nose was as sharp as a pen and a table of green fields," was absolute nonsense and required emendation; and the lines

"They say she hath abjured the sight
And company of men. O that I served that lady!"

are so palpably unmetrical that they could not have been so written by Shakespeare. Hence the readings "a' babbled" "company and sight" were rightly proposed by Theobald and Steevens, and adopted by all the best editors. On the other hand, there are hundreds of instances in which Pope and Steevens endeavoured to reduce Shakespeare's free metre to regular Iambic five-foot lines; and numerous alterations by such critics as Warburton, who evidently thought he could improve his author, are absolutely unjustifiable.

2. No emendation can be admitted unless the mode in which the reading of the old editions originated from it can be clearly explained. This point seems almost entirely disregarded by editors.

3. The character of the copy under consideration, as shown by the known or admitted errors in other parts of it, must be taken into account. Thus an emendation which would be easily admissible in the Quarto Edition of *Lear*, could not be allowed in a play of Ben Jonson's, if it depended for its justification on similarity of sound with the printed edition. The former being a surreptitious copy carelessly printed, the latter seen through the press by the author himself.

4. The most usual errors arise from these causes:—

a. Errors in Writing:—Every one who writes much and thinks rapidly knows how often he omits or repeats words in his writing; these errors are usually corrected in modern times in subsequent revision by the author, or by the reader for the press. In older times dramatic authors were often careless in this matter, and readers for the press did not exist.

b. Errors in Reading:—These arise from the setter-up of the type not being clever in deciphering MSS., or from want of clearness in the author's handwriting; both fruitful causes of error. In the case of Shakespeare, every instance of certain emendation ought to be tabulated and the cause of the corruption assigned.

c. Errors of Hearing:—These occur when "copy" has been taken down from dictation: sometimes an author dictates his work originally,—but more frequent cases arise from the production of surreptitious editions derived from notes taken in shorthand at the theatre or from recitations of actors in private.

d. Errors of Printing:—These arise from the type being sorted into wrong compartments of the compositor's case, or from the compositor dipping his hand into the wrong compartment to take out a type, or from his eye being caught by a wrong word (especially where the same word occurs twice or oftener near together); these causes give rise to such misprints as *b* for *c* (compartments for these letters being in close proximity); to such errors as *r, c, t; a, e; C, G;* &c., being substituted for each other (similarity of type leading to wrong sorting); to omissions and repetitions from the eye catching the first of two like words, or conversely, and so on.

e. Errors of Correction:—These are caused either by the author's not clearly pointing out to the printer alterations in "copy," whether made on MS. or on a previous edition, or by the printer not understanding the directions given to him. This kind of error has scarcely been noticed heretofore.

f. Errors of partial Alteration:—These arise from an author's writing a second part of a sentence on a plan different from that on which he originally began it, and forgetting to alter the first part to correspond. These occur most often through the exigences of rhyme. They were pointed out by me in the *Provincial Magazine*, article "Shelley," 1857.

g. The players often inserted oaths, obscene jests, &c., at their will: sometimes these got into the text, especially in surreptitious copies.

h. Errors of Accident:—These cannot be classified. Under this head I should place accidental destruction of part of MSS. from any cause; obliteration of words or lines; falling out of a type; and all the numerous conceivable occasions of error which, occurring only rarely, are not deserving of special notice.

5. The errors resulting from these causes are—

A. Errors of omission.
B. ,, ,, insertion.
C. ,, ,, transposition.
D. ,, ,, substitution.
E. ,, ,, corruption.
F. ,, ,, repetition.

It would be inconsistent with our plan to go into this question in greater detail: but any error not falling under one of the heads in (5), not traceable to one of the causes in (4), not corrigible in accordance with (1) (2) (3), ought not to be assumed to exist. The curse of modern editing is unnecessary emendation.

CHAPTER XIV.

ON THE ACTORS OF THE ELIZABETHAN PLAYS.

IT is not part of our scheme to give details of the lives of these men. The *Variorum Shakspeare* and **Collier's** *History of Dramatic Literature* are the great storehouses of facts on that subject, and they are easily accessible; but as hitherto tabulated lists of the several companies arranged in chronological order have never been published, such lists are here appended. They are of the highest value for determining dates in many instances, and have been far too much neglected for that purpose. The tables here given are derived —the first nine from the old editions of such plays as have lists of actors prefixed, and from the *Variorum Shakspeare*, vol. ii.; the last four from the (old) Shakspearian Society papers vols. i. and iv. The arrangement of the tables is self-explanatory.

    i. Chamberlain's (King's) Company 1594—1619
    ii. King's   ,,   1619—1642
    iii. Prince's   ,,   1598—1615
    iv. Queen's (Revels)   ,,   1622—1639
    v. Revels Children   ,,   1609—1613.

The rest are single lists, requiring no parallel columns. Of course the sign — opposite an actor's name and under the title of a play, &c., indicates his forming one of the company of that date. The Roman numerals in the last column indicate that the actor's name to which they are opposite will be found also in the table indicated by the numeral. All the actors given in the Folio Shakespeare list are indicated by their having the date of their death or a (?) in a special column in Table I.

I.—KING'S (Chamberlain's.)	1594 Lord Strange's Men.	Seven Deadly Sins.	1 Henry VI.	1598 Every Man in Hum.	1599 Every Man out of H.	Malcontent.	1603 List.	1603 Sejanus.	1605 Fox.	1610 Alchemist.	1611 Catiline.	1613 Captain.	Valentinian.	Bonduca.	1616 Duchess of Malfy.	Loyal Subject.	Queen of Corinth.	Knight of Malta.	Mad Lover.	Humorous Lieutenant.	Died.	See also Table
Belt, T.	—																					
Goodall, T.	—	—																				
Allen, Edw.	—	?																				xi.
Duke, Jno.	—																					
Beeston, Chr.	—																					vi., x.
Sinkler	—	—																				
Bryan, Geo	—	—																				
Pope, Thos.	—		—																		1598	
Phillips, Aug.	—	—																			1603	
Kempe, Wil.	—	?	—																		1605	
Armin, Rob.																					1608	
Sly, Wil.	—																				1611	
Cook, Alex.		?																			1612	
Shakespeare, W.			—		—																1614	v.
Cowley, Ric.	—	—			—																1616	
Burbage, Ric.	—	—			—																1619	
Hemings, Jno	—	—			—																1619	
Condell, Hen.		?			—																1630	
Gough, Rob.																					1629	
Ostler, Wil.												—			—						?	
Tooley, Nic.		?											—								?	viii.
Pallant, Ric.																					1623	
Lowin, Jno.														—	—	—	—	—	—			x.
Underwood, Jno															—	—	—	—	—	—	1658	
Eccleston, Wil.														—	—	—	—	—		—	1624	viii.
Rice, Jno.															—						1629	v.
Robinson, Ric.															—	—					1629	
Pollard, Tho.																				—	? 1650	
Sharp, Ric.																						
Thomson, Jno.																				—		
Field, Nat.																						
Holcome, Tho.																—	—				1641	v., viii.
Benfield, Rob.																	—	—			? 1650	v.
Taylor, Jos.																					1653	v., vi., xii.
Gilburn, Sam.																					1597	
Cross, Sam																					? 1600	
Shank, Jno																					1650	iii.

ACTORS OF THE ELIZABETHAN PLAYS. 115

II.—KING'S.	1621 Custom of Country,&c.	1621 Pilgrim.	1621 Island Princess.	1621 Lover's Progress.	Double Marriage.	False One.	1622 Prophetess.	1622 Spanish Curate.	1622 Sea Voyage.	Laws of Candy.	1623 Maid in Mill.	1623 Wife for a Month.	Wildgoose Chase.	1623 Duchess of Malfy.	1624 List.	1626 Roman Actor	1629 Picture.	1629 List.	1629 Deserving Favourite.	1631 Believe as you list.	1636 List.	1649 List.	See also Table
Tooley, Ric.	—																						i.
Lowin, Jno	—																						i.
Eccleston, Wil.			—	—																			i.
Underwood, Jno	—																						i.
Rice, Jno																							i.
Pollard, Tho	—																					—	i.
Sharp, Ric.																							i.
Thomson, Jno	—																						i.
Robinson, Ric.																						—	i.
Holcome, Tho				—																			i.
Benfield, Rob	—																						i.
Taylor, Jos	—	—		—																			i.
Shank, Jno																		—	—				i.
Birch, Geo	—																						
Horne, Jas.	—																						
Rowley, Wil.												—											iii., xii.
Penn, Wil.																	—	—					v.
Swanston.Eliard													—							—			vi.
Hamerton, Step													—					—					
Trigg, Wil.													—										
Gough, Alex													—							—			
Honeyman, Jno																							
Pallant, Ric																							
Patrick, Wil.																	—					—	
Greville, Curtis																							vii.
Smith, Ant																							
Vernon, Geo																—							
Hobbes, Tho																		—	—				
Baxter, Ric																				—			?viii.
Horton, Edw																							
Clerk, Hugh																						—	iv.
Bird, Theo. (= T. Bourne																						—	iv.
Allen, Wil.																						—	

III.—Prince's (Admiral's.)	1598 (Diary)	Tamar Cham.	Fred. and Bas.	Shoemaker's Holiday, 1600.	1603? List.	1607 List.	1615.	See also Table
Heywood, Tho.	—							
Hearne, Tho.	—							
Munday, Ant.	—							
Spencer, Gab.	—							
Jones, Jnb.		—						
Gregory, Jno		—						
Deryghten (boy)		—						
Gideon		—						
Gibbs		—						
Will. (boy)		—						
Rowley, Tho		—						
Kester		—						
Brown, [? Rob.]		—						xi.
Brown, Edw.		—						xi.
Gill's boy		—						
Red-faced fellow		—						
Barne, Will. (boy)		—						
George		—						
Parson, Tho		—						
Marbeck, Tho.		—						
Denyghten								
Pigge			—					
Ledbeater			—					
Dutton, Edw.			—					
Martin			—					? viii.
Hunt, Tho.			—					
Griffin								
Dunstan, Jas.	—	?						
Juby, Ric.								
Day								
Flower			—					
Wilson			—					
Jones, Ric.	—		?					
Shaw, Rob.			—					
Dutton. Edw. (boy)								
Price, Ric.			?					vii.
Singer, John	—	—	—					
Allen, Ric.	—							v.
Shank, Jno					—			i.
Grace, Fra					—			vii.
Stratford, Wil.					—			
Pryone, Ric. (? = R. Pryce)					—			
Colbrand, Edw.					—			
Parr, Wil.		—						
Cartwright, Wil.		—			—			
Towne, Tho.					—			
Rowley, Sam.	—	?			—	—		
Massey, Cha	—	—				—		vii.
Jeffes, Hum.		—				—		
Jeffes, Ant.		—				—		
Barne, Wil. (Bird)	—					—		
Dow(n)ton, Tho.	—				—	—		
Juby, Edw.					—	—		
Daniel, Jno.							—	
Rowley, Wil.								ii, xii.

ACTORS OF THE ELIZABETHAN PLAYS. 117

IV.—QUEEN'S, &c.	Revels, Bull, 1612.	Revels, Cockpit, 1624.	Wedding, Queen's, 1609.	Fair Maid of W., Queen's 1631.	Han. and Scip., Queen's, 1633.	John and Nat., Queen's, 1639.	See also Table	V.—REVELS (Children.)	Epicene, 1609.	Coxcomb, 1612.	Honest Man's Fortune, 1613.	See also Table
Worth, Ellis.	—						ix.	Cook, Alex........	—			i.
Basse, Tho.........	—						v.	Cary, Gilb.	—	—		
Cumber, Jno.....	—							Atawell, Hugh.	—			
Blaney, Jno.....	—						v.	Smith John,.....	—			
Robins[on], Wil	—	—						Barksted. Wil...	—	—		
Perkins, Ric.....	—							Penn, Wi..........				ii.
Sumner, Jno. ...	—	—						Allen, Rich.				iii.
Bowyer, Mich..	—	—						Blaney, Jno......	—			iv.
Reynolds, Wil..	—	—						Field, Nat.		—		i.
Allen, Wil.	—	—		—				Benfield, Rob...	—	—	—	i.
Shakerly, Edw.	—	—						Taylor, Jos.......	—	—		i.
Rogers, Edw....	—	—						Read, Emm.	—	—		
Bourne, Theo...	—	—		—				Basse, Tho.......		—		iv.
Sherlock, Wil...	—	—	—	—		—	vi.	Eccleston, Wil..		—		ii.
Turner, Ant.....	—	—		—	—	—	vi.					
Wilbraham, Wil.		—		—								
Young, Jno......		—		—								
Dobson, Jno.....		—										
Clerk, Hugh....		—										
Pass, Jno.		—										
Read, Tim.......			—									
Axel, Rob........			—									
Goat			—									
Hatfield, Geo...			—									
Fenn, Ezek......			—									
Jackson			—									

VI.—PHŒNIX COMPANY, 1622.

Lady Elizabeth's.

Beeston, Christopher (Queen's 1624; see i., x.)
More, Joseph
Swanston, Hilliard (see ii.)
Cane, Andrew (see **vii.,** ix.)
Greville, Curtis **(see vii.)**
Sherlock, William (see **iv.)**
Turner, Anthony (see iv.)

Taylor, Joseph (see ii.)
Blagrave (King's, 1629).

The two last names are not in the list of 1622; I take them from Malone.

VII.—FORTUNE COMPANY, 1622.

Palsgrave's.

Grace, Francis (see iii.)
Massey, Charles (see iii.)
Price, Richard **(see** iii.)
Fowler, Richard (see ix.)
Cane, Andrew (see vi., ix.)
Greville, Curtis (see ii., vi.)

VIII.—CYNTHIA'S REVELS, 1600; AND POETASTER, 1601.

Chapel Children.

Field, Nathaniel (see i.)
Pavy, Salathiel (died young)
Day, Thomas
Underwood, John (see **ii.)**
Baxter, Robert **(1600 only; see ii.)**
Frost, John (1600 only)
Ostler, William (see i.)
Martin, John (? see iii.)

ACTORS OF THE ELIZABETHAN PLAYS. 119

IX.—HOLLAND'S LEAGUER, 1633.

Prince Charles' (II.) **Company.**

Brown, William
Worth, Ellis **(see iv.)**
Keyne, Andrew (see vi., **vii.)**
Smith, Matthew
Sneller, James
Gradwell, **Henry**
Bond, Thomas
Fowler, Richard (see vii.)
May, Edward
Huyt, Robert
Stafford, Robert
Godwin, Richard
Wright, **John**
Fouch, Richard
Saville, Arthur
Mannery, Samuel

X.—QUEEN'S COMPANY, 609.

Greene, Thomas
Beeston, Christopher (see **i.**, **vi.**)
Heywood, Thomas
Pallant, **Richard** (see i.)
Swinnerton, **Thomas**
Duke, John
Hault, James
Beeston, Robert

XI.—WORCESTER'S COMPANY, 1586.

Browne, Robert (see iii.)
Tunstall, James
Allen, Edward **(see i.)**

Harrison William
Cooke, Thomas
Johns, Richard
Browne, Edward (see iii.)
Andrews, Richard.

XII.—SERVANTS OF THE DUKE OF YORK AND ROTHSAY.

(Afterwards Charles I.) 1610.

Garland, John
Rowley, William (see ii., iii.)
Hobbes, Thomas
Dawes, Robert
Taylor, Joseph (see i., vi.)
Newton, John
Reason, Gilbert.

XIII.—CURTAIN COMPANY, 1582.

Wilkinson, Thomas
Wilkins, Thomas
Medley, Robert
Hicks, Richard
Lanman, Henry
Manne, Robert

Dowle, Isaac, 1580
Stoddard, Thomas, 1582
Ainsworth, John (died) 1582
Bent, Richard, 1583
Tarleton, Richard (died) 1588
[   ] Humphrey (died) 1592
Burbage, Cuthbert, 1597
Cowley, Richard, 1597
Burbage, Richard (died) 1619
Wilkins, George, (died) 1613.

PART II.

CHAPTER I.

ON METRICAL TESTS AS APPLIED TO DRAMATIC POETRY.

PART I.—SHAKESPEARE.

(Read before the New Shakspere Society, March 13, 1874.)

THIS subject has scarcely at all, and never sytematically, been hitherto worked out. The portion of the dramatic literature of England to which I have directed my attention in this respect has been that which is usually called the Elizabethan period, and **comprises** the **following authors** : Greene, Peele, Marlowe, Ben Jonson, Beaumont **and Fletcher, Webster,** Chapman, Massinger, Ford, Marston, and **Shakespeare, in their** entire works ; and portions of Dekker, Middleton, Rowley, Heywood, and others. My first two papers are **designed to** gather together **the** results I have arrived at with regard to some of the greatest of these, viz. Massinger, Beaumont, Fletcher, and especially Shakespeare. But before entering into details it may be advisable, as the subject **is new to so** many, to endeavour to clearly point out the nature **of** these tests and their object. First, then, as to their nature. Malone and others had long ago been **struck** by the difference of style **in** Shakespeare's plays produced at different periods, and had in a vague sort of way used one of **these** tests at any rate as an indication of chronological arrangement. I allude to **the frequency of rhyming lines.** Bathurst has since also indicated a metrical test for the same purpose, viz. the unstopped line. But the vague manner in which the rhyme test has been used may be shown by one example: Hallam in his *Literature of Europe* says, "Were I to judge by internal evidence, I should be inclined to place this play" (i.e., *Romeo and Juliet*) "before the *Midsummer Night's Dream:*" and then alleges, among other reasons as a justification of this inference, "the great frequency of rhymes" in *Romeo and Juliet*. Now, in fact, there are, as will be seen on reference to the table, p. 16, nearly twice as many rhymes in *Midsummer Night's Dream:* so that the argument actually tells the other way. I cannot speak definitely as to the stopped-line test, not having worked it out; but Bathurst's arrangement is evidently based only on the general impression derived from reading the plays,—which in the case of plays that were not written all at one time, or in one style, is sure to be deceptive,—and to be founded chiefly on the last acts. Beyond this I know of nothing that has been done of a similar kind, except that in his examination of *Henry VIII.* Mr. Spedding tabulated the number of double endings in that play.[1] This, however, is the great step we have to take; our analysis, which has hitherto been qualitative, must become quantitative; we must cease to be empirical, and become scientific: in criticism as in other matters, the test that decides between science and empiricism is this: "Can you say, not only of what kind, but how much? If you cannot weigh, measure, number your results, however you may be convinced yourself, you must not hope to convince others, or claim the position of an investigator; you are merely a guesser, a propounder of hypotheses."

But is not metre too delicate a thing to be put in the balance or crucible in this way? Is it possible so to examine the outer form in which genius has clothed itself, as to obtain any definite results? Do not the great men of any particular time resemble each other? Do not the lesser men imitate them? Can we always distinguish a poet from his imitators? and is not any trick of melody easily acquired and reproduced? There is something in these objections, but not much. We can always distinguish the

---

[1] Professor Ingram has since done an admirable paper on Shakespeare's weak endings (September 1875).

great men from each other by sufficient care ; and imitators, who have no style of their own, seldom survive their own time to trouble us. If they do, their intrinsic worthlessness shows up in some way or other, as we shall see in the course of these inquiries.

In order to show, however, the kind of work before us more distinctly, I have taken a piece of Dryden's "*All for Love,*" (10 lines), and rewritten it, as far as metre (and metre only) is concerned, in the styles of Fletcher, Beaumont, Massinger, Greene, and Rowley. The original runs thus :—

" I know thy meaning.
But I have lost my reason, have disgraced
The name of soldier with inglorious ease :
In the full vintage of my flowing honors
Sat still and saw it prest by other hands :
Fortune came smiling to my youth and wooed it,
And purple greatness met my ripen'd years.
When first I came to empire, I was borne
On tides of people crowding to my triumphs ;
The wish of nations and the willing world
Received me as its pledge of future peace."

Fletcher's Metre.

"I know thy meaning :
But I have lost my reason, and have disgraced me :
Inglorious ease has shamed my name of soldier.
In the full vintage of my flowing honors
I saw it prest by others hands and sát still :
Fortune came smiling to my youth and wooed it,
My ripend years were clothed in purple greatness :
When I first came to empire I was bórne forth
On tides of people crowding to my triumphs,
The wish of nations and the willing world
As a dear pledge of its future peace received me." [1]

---

[1] " What should I do there then? You are brave captains,
Most valiant men: go up yourselves: use virtue:
See what will come on't: pray the gentleman
To come down and be taken? Ye all know him :
I think ye've felt him too : there ye shall find him,

Beaumont's.

"I understand; but now my reason 's lost:
My soldier's name by ease of little boast
I have disgraced; yea, while my honor flowed
In vintage of the fullest, sat and saw
It prest by other hands: then to my youth
Came Fortune, wooing smilingly, and with
Th' imperial purple **met** my ripened years:
When first I came to empire, on **full** tide
Of populous crowds to triumph I did ride,
The wish of nations: all men willingly
Received me as a pledge **of peace to be.**"[1]

But Beaumont's **style is** often more like Massinger's.

Massinger's.

"**I** know thy meaning, but have lost **my sense,**
And have disgraced the name of soldier with
Inglorious ease; in the full vintage of
My flowing honors I sat still, and saw
It prest by other hands: and smiling Fortune
Came to my youth and wooed it. Purple greatness
Met my ripe years. When first I came to empire,
On tides of crowding people I was borne
To triumph. Yet the wish of nations and

> His sword by his side: plumes of a pound weight by him,
> Will make your chops ake: you'll find it a more labour
> To win him living than climbing of a crów's nest."
> FLETCHER, *Bonduca,* v. 2.

[1] "Insatiate Julius, when his victories
Had run o'er half the world, had he met her,
There he had stopt the legend of his deeds,
Laid by his arms, been overcome himself,
And let her vanquish th' other half: and fame
Made beauteous Dorigen the greater name.
Shall I thus fall? I will not: no, my tears
Cast in my heart shall quench these lawless fires;
He conquers best, conquers his lewd desires."
BEAUMONT, *Triumph of Honor,* Sc. 2.

The willing world received me as its pledge
Of future peace." [1]

Greene's.

" I know thy sense : but with inglorious ease
I've shamed my soldier's name ; **my** reason's **fled.**
Erewhile my honor flow'd in vintage full :
I sat and saw it prest by other hands :
Then Fortune came, and smiling woo*d my youth :
And purple greatness met my ripen'd years.
And **I was borne,** when first I came to reign,
Triumphant on the tides of peopled crowds ;
The wish of many **a race ;** and the glad world
Received me as its pledge of future peace." [2]

Rowley's (at his worst, doing job-work).

"I know thy meaning, but have lost reason :
I have disgraced the name of soldier
With inglorious ease : in the full vintage
Of flowing honors, I sat still and saw
It prest by other hands. Smiling Fortune

---

[1] " To all posterity may that act be crowned
With a deserved applause, or branded with
The mark of infamy! stay yet—ere I take
This seat of justice or engage myself
To fight for you abroad or to reform
Your state at home, swear all upon my sword,
And call the gods of Sicily to witness
The oath you take, that whatsoe'er I shall
Propound for safety of your commonwealth,
Not circumscribed or bound in, shall by you
Be willingl, obeyed."
      MASSINGER, *Bondman*, i. 3.

[2] " Fair queen of love, thou mistress of delight,
Thou gladsome lamp, that wait'st on Phœbe's train,
Spreading thy kindness through the jarring orbs,
That in their union praise thy lasting powers :
Thou that hast stayed the fiery Phlegon's course,
And made the coachman of the glorious wain
To droop in view of Daphne's excellence,
Fair pride of morn, sweet beauty of the even,
Witness Orlando's faith unto his love !"
      GREENE, *Orlando*.

Came to my youth and wooed it, and purple
Greatness met my ripen'd years. When at first
I came to empire, I was borne on tides
Of people crowding unto my triumphs;
The wish of nations and the willing world
Received me as its pledge of future peace."[1]

This hardly seems metre at all : but it has its own law; and passages like the above have passed with some editors as Fletcher's.

These examples are sufficient to show what variety of styles may exist in blank verse, and what I shall prove do exist in the authors named. Moreover, these differences can be tabulated ; the number of lines with double endings ; the number of rhyming lines ; the number of lines with more or less than five measures can be stated. But to what purpose? If we learn nothing further from these tables, they are useless. There are two ends to be served by such lists. If an author has distinctly progressed in the manipulation of his art, if he has different manners of work in different periods of his life, such tables are very valuable for determining the chronological order of his productions. This is the main use which the Director of our New Shakspere Society anticipated from the application of metrical tests, and the table I have formed for Shakespeare's plays will, I have no doubt, be useful for this purpose. But the far more important end from my point of view will be the determination of the genuineness of the works traditionally assigned to a writer. These metrical tests made me suspect the genuineness of the *Taming of the Shrew*, parts of *Timon*, *Pericles*, and *Henry VIII.*, when I was not aware that they had ever been suspected ; I hope the evidence I have gathered on these, and on *Henry VI.*, will be some furtherance to the objects of our Society. These, however, must be treated in separate papers ;—this one will, I fear, be too long as it is ;—and so must the examination of Fletcher and

[1] "*Ant.* But is it possible that two faces
    Should be so twinn'd in form, complexion,
    Figure, aspect, that neither wen nor mole,
    The table of the brow, the eyes lustre,
    The lips cherry, neither the blush nor smile
    Should give the one distinction from the other?
    Does Nature work in moulds?
Mart. Altogether!
                                 ROWLEY, *Maid o' Mill*, ii. 2.

Massinger, which I regard as far the most valuable result of my work. I will only say here that I have discoverd distinctive tests of their manners; that some of the plays have been quite wrongly assigned by every editor ; that Massinger's hand is distinct in about nine of Fletcher's plays ; and that if the results of the examination of Shakespeare's text be unsatisfatory to any one (as I doubt not they will be to some, the problem is so very complicated), at any rate let them suspend their judgment as to the value of metrical tests generally, till they see how simply that easier problem of Fletcher's authorship is disposed of by them. I was of opinion myself that this question should have been discussed first ; but our Director overruled me, partly, no doubt, to get the Shakespeare table in print as a guide for future workers in the same track.

I must now ask you to refer to the table constantly, so as to verify the following conclusions. I suppose that no one will doubt on other than metrical grounds, that *Love's Labour's Lost* is one of the earliest, and *Winter's Tale* one of the latest, of Shakespeare's comedies. Let us, then, for simplicity begin by comparing these two. In *Love's Labour's Lost* we find more than 1,000 rhyming lines in the dialogue ; in *Winter's Tale* none. In *Love's Labour's Lost* only seven lines with double endings ; in *Winter's Tale* 639. In *Love's Labour's Lost* few incomplete lines ; in *Winter's Tale* many. In *Love's Labour's Lost* one Alexandrine ; in *Winter's Tale* 16. In general terms, then, we may expect to find, that in Shakespeare's development he gradually dropped the rhymed dialogue, adopted double endings, Alexandrines, and broken lines ; and this is undoubtedly true. On reference to the table, however, you will see that a chronology founded on any of the last three tests would lead to the strangest results, *e.g.* the double endings would place *Richard III.* very late indeed, and *John* very early ; the two parts of *Henry IV.* would be widely separated. The Alexandrine test would make *Measure for Measure* the latest of the comedies ; the test by broken lines would make *Lear* far the latest of all the plays ; the rhyme test—and the rhyme test only of all that I have as yet applied —is of use *per se* for determining the chronological arrangement of Shakespeare's works. It is, however, worth while to print the table *in extenso*, as it will be valuable for reference for many other purposes, as we shall see in the questions of the genuineness of disputed plays. In using it, however, we have another important consideration to allow for. We know from the title-pages to the Quartos that Shakespeare was in the **habit** of making additions to his works, and we have strong reason to believe that in some instances, viz. in the *Merry Wives of Windsor*, *Romeo and Juliet*, and *Hamlet*, we are in possession of early sketches of these plays, or at any rate of the *acting versions* of these early sketches. We also find that in *Lear*, *Hamlet*, and *Richard III.*, we have **two versions, one** of which differs much from the other in quantity; and in these as well as in *Othello*, 2 *Henry IV.*, and *Troylus and Cressida*, there are many various readings that affect such a table. Now my table is made **from** the Globe edition, as being the most convenient portable one with **numbered lines**; but any conclusions drawn from it will be subject to some discount on account of these variations. **The chronological scheme, then, that I shall propose, is only provisional, and to serve as a basis for more accurate investigation of each play, based on all its editions.** Such an investigation I **am** making as to *Romeo and Juliet*, and the results will, I hope, be given in the edition **to** be edited for our Society by Mr. P. **A. Daniel.** We must also **consider,** when we have Quartos, the relative accuracy of the printers, **and** I may refer you to my table of these editions as useful on this **point.** The following, then, are the results, **as** I interpret **them, to** be drawn from my metrical table as to the succession of Shakespeare's plays :—

1. *Henry VI.* and *Titus Andronicus* are not Shakespeare's **in the** main bulk; they are productions of what I may call the Lodge, **Peele,** and Marlowe School. **I shall** not go into the evidence here, **as I** shall give **it in** full in separate papers.

2. *Henry* **VIII.** and **The** *Two* **Noble** *Kinsmen* **are** partly Fletcher's, **as has** been shown by others.

3. The *Taming of the Shrew*, *Pericles*, and *Timon of Athens* are **also** only partly Shakespeare's : **these plays I shall** also discuss separately.[1] The plays fall distinctly **into four periods** :—

---

[1] Since writing this I have investigated *Romeo and Juliet*, **and** *Richard III.*, **and** found reason to believe that they are founded on earlier plays by George **Peele.**

METRICAL TESTS.

I. The Rhyming period, including *Love's Labour's Lost, Midsummer Night's Dream, Comedy of Errors, Romeo and Juliet,* and *Richard II.*

II. The History period, including *Two Gentlemen of Verona, Merchant of Venice, Twelfth Night, As You like It, Taming of the Shrew, Merry Wives of Windsor, Much Ado about Nothing, Richard III, John, Henry IV., Henry V.,* and *Julius Cæsar.*

III. The Tragedy period, including *Macbeth, Hamlet, Othello, Lear, Timon, Troylus and Cressida* (which was partly written much earlier), *Measure for Measure,* and probably *All's Well that Ends Well,* which is certainly a revision of an earlier play, probably *Love's Labour's Won.*

IV. The Final period, including *Pericles, Cymbeline, Coriolanus, Anthony and Cleopatra, Henry VIII., Two Noble Kinsmen, The Tempest,* and *Winter's Tale.*

FLEAY.	DATE	DRAKE.	CHALMERS.	MALONE.	DULIUS.	DATE
Ven. and Ad.	1588					
Taming a Shrew (part)	1589				Tit. And. 1589, Two \} before	1591
					Gen. of Verona	
L. L. Lost, L. L. Won.	1591	Love's L. L., Com. of E.	Comedy of Errors.	Two G. of V., H. VI	Rom. and Jul., C. of \} about	1591
Errors, Mid. N. D.	1592	Henry VI.			E., L. L. L.	
Lucrece, Rich. II.	1593	Mid. N. D., Rom. & J.	Love's L. L., R. and J.	Comedy of Errors.	1 H. VI., Trui T., C. before	1592
Edw. III (part), 2 Gent.	1594	Taming of the Shrew.		Rich. II., Rich. III.		
				L. L. L., M. N. D.,	Rich. III., T. of S. about	1594
Rich. III., John.	1595	Two Gen. of Verona,	Hen. VI., Two Gen. of	M. of V.		
		Rich. II.	Verona,		M. of V., M. N. D. "	1595
Rom. and Jul., M. of \}	1596	\{ Hen. IV., 2 Hen. IV.,	Rich. II., Rich. III.,	Rom. and J., John, \}	John, Richard II. "	1596
V., Sonnets.		Rich. II	M. W. of W.	Tam. of S.		
R. & J.(Q²), L. L. L. \}			M. of V., 1 Hen. IV., \}		\{ 1 Hen. IV., 2 Hen. IV	
(revised) 1 Hen. V. \}			2 Hen. IV., H. V. \}	1 Hen. IV.	after Rich. II.	
2 Hen. IV., M. W. W.	1598	John, All's Well.	Mid. N. C., John, Ham		All's Well, Merry Wives,	—
					after Hen. IV.	
Hen. V., M. A. N.	1599	Much Ado, Henry V.	Taming of the Shrew,	\{ 2 Hen. IV., Hen. V. \}	Henry V., Much Ado,	1599
Cæsar, A. Y. L.	1600	Hamlet (revised).	Much Ado.	As you like it.	As You Like It, about	1600
				Much Ado, Hamlet		
12th N., Ham. (Q1)	1601	\{ As Y. L., M. W. of W. \}	Winter' Tale.	Merry W. of W.	12th Night, before Feb.	1602
T. of S., Ric. III. (F).	1602	T. and C.	As You Like It.	Troilus & Cressida.	Hamlet,	1602
M. f. M., Ham. (Q2)	1603	Henry VIII., Timon.	Henry VIII.	M. for M., Hen. VIII.	\{ M. for M., Jul. \} before Dec.	1604
		Measure for Measure.			Cæsar,	
Othello, A. W. W.	1604	Lear.	Measure for Measure.	Othello.	Othello, before Nov.	1604
Lear, M. W. W. (F).	1605	Cymbeline.	Lear.	Lear.	Macbeth, after 1603, before	1610
Macbeth, Timon.	1606	Troylus and Cres., Mac.	All's Well, Mac., Cym.	All's Well, Macbeth	1604 or	1605
T. and C., Pericles.	1607	Julius Cæsar.	Julius Cæsar.	Jul. Cæsar, 12th N.	A. & C., Cori., before May	1608
Cym. (begun), A. & C.	1608	Anthony and Cleopatra	Anthony and Cleopatra.	Anthony and Cleo.	\{ Troy. & Cres., Tim., \} about	1608
Cor., 2 N. K.	1609	Coriolanus.	Corio'anus.	Cymbeline.	Per.,	
Cym. (finished), Tem.	1610	Winter's Tale.	\{ Troylus and Cressida, \}	Timon, Coriolanus.	Tempest, before Nov.	1611
			Timon.		Cymb., Winter's Tale, 1610-1611	
W. T., Hen. VIII.	1611	Tempest.	Winter's Tale, Tempest.	Winter's Tale, Tem.		
	1612	Othello.				
	1613	12th Night.	Othello, 12th N., Tem.		Henry VIII.	1613

I give above, in parallel columns, the scheme proposed, and those of Delius, Malone, Drake, and Chalmers. I quote these three latter from Allibone. Before remarking on the scheme, I desire to add that it is by no means final : I have myself several other tests in course of application, and I have no doubt other workers in the same field will find additional ones, now that the subject is ventilated. As a provisional scheme, however, I place some confidence in it, for this reason : that, although it is based solely on the metrical table, it *in no instance* contradicts any external evidence. It also distributes the work much more equally than the other schemes ; never requiring more than two plays to be written in one year.

Remarks on the Position of certain Plays in this List :—

First Period.—These five plays are distinctly marked off as a separate class by the vast preponderance of rhyming lines. *Love's Labour's Lost* has more than 1000, *Midsummer Night's Dream* 850, *Romeo and Juliet* 650, *Richard II.* 530, and *Comedy of Errors* (though a very short play) 380, which is equivalent to 600 in a play of ordinary length. Now, no other of Shakespeare's plays reaches to the number of 200 rhyming lines ; and as the battle between rhymed and unrhymed compositions was fierce at this time, I feel that there is no doubt that Shakespeare joined the advocates of rhyme at first, and gradually learned to feel the superiority of blank verse ; at any rate, the difference between these Five Plays of the first period, as to amount of rhyme, is too great, in my opinion, to admit any other play, however inferior, to be ranked with them. I know how strongly some think that the *Two Gentlemen of Verona* must have preceded *Midsummer Night's Dream*, because this latter is so beautiful a "work." I do not say a "play ;" for I agree with N. Drake and others in the view that the *Two Gentlemen* is superior as an acting piece, however inferior as a poem. I must, for want of space, refer to Drake's Treatise for a full statement of his arguments. For myself, I find it impossible to believe that the *Two Gentlemen* was not written some two years before as the *Merchant of Venice*, which is so like it in metrical handling ; and equally impossible to regard the *Midsummer Night's Dream* as a production of any but the earliest period, when fancy was strong, and the sense of the prose realities of life comparatively weak. Note also that the three comedies in this first period all **observe** the unity **of** time, no action extending to the second day, and that they are **all** similar in their **nature**, turning on the solution, as it were, of an embroilment produced under circumstances **barely or** only hypothetically possible. The almost total absence of Alexandrines in *Romeo* **and** *Juliet*, and **their absolute** absence in **the** three comedies (**the one** instance in *Love's Labour's Lost* I think **is corrupt**), is **another very** striking difference from all the other **plays**. In *Richard II.*, however, **these Alexandrines are** admitted, **and this is** therefore the play in which **this, the first** sign of the Second Period, begins to show itself. In other respects this play is, to my thinking, far removed from *John* or *Henry IV*. It bears something of the same relation to Marlowe's *Edward II.* that the *Two Gentlemen of Verona* does to the *Taming of a Shrew*, or *Richard III.* to *Henry VI*. Shakespeare in it seems not to move with the same freedom that he does in his later plays, and the whole work has an artificial air. Another point that distinctly separates the earlier from the later historic plays is, the absence of prose: *Richard II.* and *John* have none, *Richard III.* only one bit, but that reads like, **and I believe is, a** portion of Peele's work; and of these **earlier plays** *Richard III.* is the only one that is absolutely **devoid of Comedy. This also** marks its position.

Second Period.—The positions I have given to the plays in this period so nearly coincide with those generally assigned (except as to the *Two Gentlemen of Verona*, which has already been noticed) that no special remarks seem needed. One general characteristic of the period is the diminution of the number of rhyming lines, which number about 100 to 200 in this period for a full play. *Much Ado* and *Merry Wives* have a smaller number, but are almost entirely in prose, being quite exceptional in this respect. Also the number of short lines is considerably increased, though not nearly so much as in the next period. Alexandrines **are admitted from 5 to** 20 in a play (but in *Richard II.* there **are** 33?); the number of feminine endings increases, but not in any regular progression, and doggerel lines, stanzas, sonnets, and alternate rhymes (which abound in the earliest plays) gradually die out: there are not many in any plays of this period.

Third Period.—In this a few words may be needed on the position I have assigned to *Macbeth*. I agree with Clark and Wright that this play has been much altered since its first composition, and has now many interpolations in it; in Act iv. Scene 3—the passage on the touching for the evil—the marks of interpolation are palpable; l. 159 follows metrically on l. 139,

"'Tis hard to reconcile—See who comes here"

making a perfect line: the Doctor (unknown elsewhere in the play) is dragged in for the express purpose of introducing the subject; and "Comes the king forth, I pray you," l. 140, is inconsistent with "Come, go we to the king," l. 236.

In this Third Period the metre is much freer; prose and verse are intermingled in the same scene; tri-syllabic feet abound; short lines are very abundant; double endings very greatly multiplied; Alexandrines *not* composed of two lines of six syllables are introduced; the Alexandrines with regular cæsura increase greatly; the number of rhyming lines gradually falls off. The plays are difficult to test, as to metre, in this period; partly from the similarity of style in the great plays, partly from the great variations in the Quarto and Folio texts. I am, however, applying further tests, which I hope will be decisive.

Fourth Period.—In this the rhymes fall off rapidly, and in the Comedies actually disappear; the metre becomes more regular and less impassioned,[1] and the general impression left by these later works is, that they were produced at greater leisure, and more carefully polished. The dates given by metrical considerations agree too nearly with those assigned on external evidence to need comment.

And here I think I may fairly point out how singular the coincidence of the order here given is with that assigned by the best English critics on external evidence. This order was first made out from the rhyme-test only; and, except in the instances of plays which are not undoubtedly authentic or written at two different periods, I have not changed the relative position of one since I first

---

[1] Professor Ingram has since shown that "weak endings" are the characteristic test of the Fourth Period.

sent this list to Messrs. Clark and Wright in 1870. At that time I had not read any treatise on the external evidences, and was not even aware that any attempt had been made to classify the plays into periods. I own this with some shame; but claim, at the same time, some additional confidence in the results of the rhythmical tests. It may seem to some ludicrous to speak even of the application of mathematics to such a subject; but it will be seen from the table that the plays assigned to the period ending in 1598 by the rhyme test, exactly agree with those in Meres's list (setting aside questions of genuineness). Now, the doctrine of chances gives us as the odds against these 10 plays being selected out of the 30 which are undoubtedly more or less Shakespeare's, more than 20 millions to one: in exact numbers, one chance only out of 20,030,010 would hit on this exact selection of plays. To a mind accustomed to the exact sciences, this fact alone is conclusive as to the immense value of the rhyme test.

I might go into detail concerning the reasons for the position of each particular play; but I think it better to consider all special matter separately. The table itself is subjoined. It is only necessary here to add a caution as to the amount of subjectivity to be expected in such a table as this; there must be some until the laws of metre are more definitely laid down than they are at present. (I.) As to the rhymes, it is sometimes doubtful if a rhyme is intentional or accidental. In such cases the rhyme is counted in this table. (II.) It is sometimes doubtful if one line of six feet, or two lines, one of five feet, and one of one, be intended. In the following table the line is, if possible, reckoned as divided. (III.) In some instances, lines of four feet in the Globe Edition can be avoided by re-arranging the lines without altering the reading; this has been sparingly done in *Pericles*, and in cases where the arrangement of the lines is made by modern editors without authority in the original texts. (IV.) All Alexandrines proper with cæsura at the end of the third foot are counted in the six-measure lines, and not as two lines of three measures, except where, as in *The Two Gentlemen of Verona* and *Richard III.*, lines of six syllables are repeated many times together. In the larger tables from which this one is abridged, all peculiarities are noted for each scene; perhaps when our text is settled, it may be worth while to print such

METRICAL TESTS.

tables in full for each play. The four last lines in the table are from the imperfect editons in the first Quartos.

With regard to the position of the *Taming of the Shrew* as assigned by me, as also indeed for *Timon*, *Pericles*, and *Henry VI.*, I must ask for absolute forbearance, until my special papers on these plays are read. I hope the first-mentioned of these plays especially will not appear so misplaced as it must do now after the paper devoted to it has been studied.

N.B. The columns headed *Alternates*, *Sonnets*, and *Doggerel* are included in the totals summed in the column headed *Rhymes*, 5 *measures*, which gives the number of *all* rhyming-lines not shorter than the ordinary blank-verse line.

METRICAL TABLE OF SHAKESPEARE'S PLAYS.

Play.	Total of Lines.	Prose.	Blank.	Rhymes, 5 Measures.	Rhymes, Short Lines.	Songs.	Double Endings.	Alternates.	Sonnets.	Doggerel.	1 Measure.	2 Measures.	3 Measures.	4 Measures.	6 Measures.
I.—PLAYS OF FIRST (RHYMING) PERIOD.															
Love's L. Lost...	2789	1086	579	1028	54	32	9	236	71	194	4	12	13	—	1
Midsum. N. D...	2251	441	878	731	138	63	29	158	—	—	—	5	3	—	—
Com. of Errors...	1770	240	1150	380	—	—	137	64	—	109	3	8	9	—	—
Rom. and Juliet..	3002	405	2111	486	—	—	118	62	28	—	10	20	16	?4	6
Richard II......	2644	—	2107	537	—	—	148	12	—	—	11	17	26	22	?33
II.—HISTORIES OF SECOND PERIOD.															
Richard III......	3599	?55	3374	170	—	—	570	—	—	—	20	39	13	23	16
King John.......	2553	—	2403	150	—	—	54	12	—	—	1	9	4	4	2
1 Henry IV......	3170	1464	1622	84	—	—	60	4	—	—	16	17	16	16	13
2 Henry IV......	3437	1860	1417	74	7	15	203	[Pistol 64 l.]	—	—	3	13	7	—	6
Henry V.........	3320	1531	1678	101	2	8	291	[Pist. 157 l.] 14	—	—	2	13	10	4	23
Julius Cæsar.....	2440	165	2241	34	—	—	369	—	—	—	14	31	55	6	16
III.—COMEDIES OF SECOND PERIOD.															
Two Gent. of V..	2060	409	1510	116	—	15	203	16	—	18	8	15	32	8	5
Merchant of Ven.	2705	673	1896	93	34	9	297	4	—	4	8	16	22	2	14
Twelfth Night...	2684	1741	763	120	—	60	152	—	—	—	8	21	23	5	10
As you Like it...	2904	1681	925	71	130	97	211	10	—	2	3	10	33	1	5
Merry Wives.....	3018	2703	227	69	—	19	32	[Pistol 39 l.]	—	—	3	3	—	3
Much Ado, &c...	2823	2106	643	40	18	16	129	22	—	—	2	7	15	4	4

Play.	Total of Lines.	Prose.	Blank.	Rhymes, 5 Measures.	Rhymes, Short Lines.	Songs.	Double Endings.	Alternates.	Sonnets.	Doggerel.	1 Measure.	2 Measures.	3 Measures.	4 Measures.	6 Measures.
IV.—COMEDIES OF THIRD PERIOD.															
All's Well.........	2981	1453	1234	280	2	12	223	8	14	—	7	31	31	5	14
Measure for M...	2609	1134	1574	73	22	6	338	—	—	—	10	29	66	5	47
V.—TRAGEDIES OF THIRD PERIOD.															
Troylus & Cres...	3423	1186	2025	196	—	16	441	—	—	—	10	46	62	13	43
Macbeth............	1993	158	1588	118	129	—	399	—	—	—	8	28	43	8	18
Hamlet	3924	1208	2490	81	—	60	508	[86 l. in play]			20	53	55	11	47
Othello.............	3324	541	2672	86	—	25	646	—	—	—	19	66	71	13	78
King Lear.........	3298	903	2238	74	—	83	567	—	—	—	18	34	116	22	50
VI.—PLAYS OF FOURTH PERIOD.															
Cymbeline........	1448	638	2585	107	—	32	726	[84 l. in vision]			8	15	31	18	42
Coriolanus........	1392	829	2521	42	—	—	708	—	—	—	3	33	76	19	42
Anthony and C..	3964	255	2761	42	—	6	613	—	—	—	14	38	84	31	16
Tempest............	2068	458	1458	2	—	96	476	[54 l. masq.]			2	16	47	5	11
Winter's Tale.....	2750	844	1825	—	—	57	639	[32 l. chor.]			8	14	19	13	16
VII.—PLAYS IN WHICH SHAKESPEARE WAS NOT SOLE AUTHOR.															
Taming of Shrew	2671	516	1971	169	15	—	260	—	—	49	4	18	22	23	5
Henry VIII.......	2754	?67	2613	16	—	12	1195	[46 l. in Prol.]			2	15	18	3	32
Two Noble Kins.	2734	179	2468	54	—	33	1079	& Epilogue]			9	15	46	17	5
Pericles.............	2356	418	1436	225	89	—	120	[292 l. Gower]			17	4	59	26	18
Timon of A.......	2358	596	1560	184	18	—	257	—	—	—	15	28	54	30	37
VIII.—FIRST SKETCHES IN EARLY QUARTOS.															
Rom. and Juliet.	2066	261	1451	354	—	—	92	28	—	—	7	26	30	21	92
Hamlet	2068	509	1462	54	43	—	209	[36 l. in play]			13	45	76	37	30
Merry Wives.....	1395	1207	148	40	38	[fairies]19	—	—	—	-	—	1	—	5	4
Henry V.	1672	898	774	30	—	—	104	—	—	—	1	25	35	31	15
IX.—DOUBTFUL PLAYS.															
Titus Andron. ..	2525	43	2338	144	—	—	154	—	—	—	4	8	9	9	12
1 Henry VI.......	2693	—	2379	314	—	—	140	—	—	—	5	5	4	7	12
2 Henry VI.......	3032	448	2562	122	—	—	255	—	—	—	8	25	15	21	12
3 Henry VI.	2904	---	2749	155	—	—	346	—	—	—	13	11	14	11	7
Contention.......	1952	381	1571	44	—	—	54	—	—	—	—	14	16	32	44
True Tragedy ...	2101	—	2035	66	—	—	148	—	—	—	14	21	29	38	34

POSTSCRIPT TO PAPER I.

Table of Ratios of rhyme-lines in rhyme-scenes to blank-verse lines in each play :—(First approximation.)

COMEDIES.   HISTORIES AND TRAGEDIES.

First Period.

Love's Labour 's Lost	·6		
Mid. Night's Dream	1	Richard II.	4
Comedy of Errors	3	Romeo and Juliet	4·3

Second Period.

{ 1st Plot of 12th Night	7·5	1st Plot of Troyl. & Cres.	8·4
{ 2 Gent. of Ver.	11	2nd do. do.	13·6
		Richard III.	*
Merchant of Venice	16	John	16
{ Much Ado, &c.	21	{ 1 Henry IV.	19
{ Merry Wives (Quarto)		{ 2 Henry IV.	19
{ As You Like It	19	{ Henry V.	19
		Julius Cæsar	*
} Compln. of 12th Night. Prose.			
{ Com. of Tam. of the Shrew	20		

Third Period.

{ Measure for Measure	22	{ Hamlet	about 30
{ All's Well, &c. (rewrit.)	22	{ Othello	,, 30
Merry Wives (Folio)	22	{ Lear	,, 30
		Macbeth?	,, *
		Part of Timon	33
		Compln. of Troyl. & Cres.	54·5

Fourth Period.

Cymbeline	about 30	{ Coriolanus	60
Part of Pericles	32	{ Anthony and Cleopatra	66

COMEDIES.		HISTORIES AND TRAGEDIES.

Fifth **Period.**

| { Tempest | 729 | { Part of Two N. Kinsmen 281 |
| { Winter's Tale | infinity | { Part of Henry VIII. infinity. |

The above table is corrected up to the date of my present investigations (Sept. 1875) from one published in *The Academy* by me (March 28, 1874).

My reasons for all alterations will be given in my special paper on each play. They are based chiefly on a more scientific application of the *rhyme-test*, aided by the *weak-ending test*, the *middle syllable test*, and above all by the *cæsura test*, which is next in importance to the *rhyme-test*; and has helped me much in making a different division of the plays in some instances. *Cymbeline*, however, was misplaced through another cause, a numerical blunder; which I have now corrected. As these investigations extend, this table will require further correction.

CHAPTER II.

ON THE QUARTO EDITIONS OF SHAKESPEARE'S WORKS.

A LIST of these has long been wanted, drawn up in such a way as to afford ready reference to students in search of such information as can be obtained from the title-pages of the various volumes. These have often been reprinted; but such a table as is annexed will give readier access to the inquirer, and also, from the manner of its arrangement, supply information that would otherwise require many separate documents.

Explanation of the Table.—In the extreme left-hand and right-hand columns are placed the dates of publication, and in the horizontal lines between these the names of the works published in those years, as well as the names of the printers and publishers; and the symbols (Q 1, Q 2, &c.) by which the Cambridge editors refer to each edition. The works are divided into four groups, partly with a view to avoid the straggling arrangement which would be necessary were no such division adopted; partly with regard to certain peculiarities in each group, which will presently be pointed out in the Notes. The first of these groups contains poems only, viz. *Venus and Adonis*, *Lucreece*, and the *Passionate Pilgrim*. The second group contains the *Sonnets*, *Richard II.*, *Richard III.*, 1st and 2nd *Henry IV.*, and *Much Ado about Nothing*. The third group contains three plays originally published in imperfect editions, *Romeo and Juliet*, *Hamlet*, and *The Merry Wives of Windsor*; three plays that differ much from the Folios, viz. *Troylus and Cressida*, *Lear*, and *Othello*; two plays, of which two editions each were published originally in the same year, viz. *Midsummer Night's* **Dream** and the *Merchant of Venice;* and Shakespeare's probably **earliest play**, *Love's Labour's Lost*. In the fourth group are placed plays more **or** less spurious, viz., the Quarto *Romeo and Juliet*, *The Contention* **of** *the Houses* **of** *York and Lancaster*, *The* **True Tragedy** *of* **Richard** *Duke of York*, *Henry V.* (as first issued), *Pericles*, and *Titus Andronicus.* The abbreviations used **for the titles of these plays, &c., are** given on p. **144, and it is** hoped will **require no further explanation.** One or two other signs may however require it, *e.g.* "Q 4 f. Q 3," in the second column for each group, **means** "**the fourth** edition published **in quarto**, which edition is considered **by the** Cambridge editors to have been printed from the third ;[1]" *Q, means "an edition without Shakespeare's name on the** title page;" †Q, means "the edition from which, **in** the opinion **of the** Cambridge editors, the Folio **was** printed ;" **J.** R[oberts] means that J. R. is printed on the title-page, and that J. **R.** is ascertained from the **entries in** the Stationers' books or other reliable **evidence to mean J.** Roberts. There is nothing else in the table that requires explanation. Nor is it necessary to point out in detail its use for showing at a glance **the** successive editions of each work, **the dates** at which the copyright of each **changed hands, the** number **of** works published in each year, the **date of** the maximum number of publications (1598—1600), the sudden appearance of Shakespeare's name on all his authentic works **in 1598** (except **the** edition of *Romeo and Juliet* in 1609), &c. But **in the Notes will** be found **some** additional particulars which are **of interest.**

[1] **The** Ven. & Ad *Q 4 is the Isham copy found at Lamport by Mr. Charles Edmonds, and edited by him. It was not discovered till after the Cambridge Shakespeare was published, and consequently all our notation will have to be altered in a future edition. The 1630 Ven. and Ad. (now in the Bodleian) with title-page, was formerly in the Ashmole Museum, but I have not seen it. According to Edmonds it was "printed by J. H., and are to be sold by Francis Coules." He adds that it is different from our Q 10, which is in the Bodleian, without title, but catalogued with date 1630.—W. ALDIS WRIGHT.

Mr. Wright has consequently altered the notation in the table to that to be adopted in the next edition of the Cambridge Shakespeare.—F. G. F.

TABULAR VIEW OF THE QUARTO EDITIONS OF SHAKESPEARE'S WORKS,

FROM 1593 TO 1630 A.D.

Supplementary List of Quartos from 1630 to 1652, which could not conveniently be put in the Table, pp. 142-3.

GROUP.		NAME OF PLAY.	EDITION.	PRINTER.	PUBLISHER.
III.	1631	Love's Labour's Lost	Q2 from F1	W. S.	J. Smethwicke
	?	Hamlet	Q5 from Q4	do.	do.
	1631	Taming of Shrew	Q1 from F1	do.	do.
II.	1632	1 Henry IV.	Q7 from Q6	J. Norton	W. Sheares
	1634	Richard II.	Q5 from F2	do.	
	,,	Richard III.	Q8 from Q7	do.	
IV.	1635	Pericles	†Q6	T. Cotes	
I.	1636	Venus and Adonis	*Q13	J. H.	F. Coules.
III.	1637	Hamlet	Q6 from Q5	R. Young	J. Smethwicke
	,,	Romeo and Juliet	Q5 from Q4	do.	do.
	,,	Merchant of Venice	Q3 from Q2	M. P.	L. Heyes
II.	1639	1 Henry IV.	Q8 from Q7	J. Norton	H. Perry
III.	1652	Merchant of Venice	Q4 from Q3		W. Leake

GROUP I.—POEMS. GROUP II.

Date of Publication	Name of Work	EDITION	PRINTER	PUBLISHER	Name of Play	EDITION	PRINTER	PUBLISHER
1593	V. A.	*Qto. 1	R. Field	see Note				
1594	do	*Q2 f. Q1	do.	do.				
,,	Luc.	*Q1	do.	J. Harrison				
1595								
1596	V. A.	*Q3 f. Q2	do.	do.				
1597					R. II.	*Qto. 1	V. Simmes	A. Wise
					R. III.	*Q1	do.	do.
1598	Luc.	*Q2 f. Q1	P. S[hort]	do.	1 H. IV	*Q1	P. S[hort]	do.
,,					R. II.	Q2 f. Q1	V. Simmes	do.
					R. III.	Q2 f. Q1	T. Creede	do.
1599	P. P.	Q1	for W. Jaggard	W. Leake	1 H. IV	Q2 f. Q1	S. S[tafford]	do.
,,	V. A.	*Q4 f. Q3		do.				
1600	V. A.	*Q5 f. Q4	J. H[arrison]	J. Harrison	2 H. IV	Q1	V. Simmes	A. Wise and W. Aspley
,,	Luc.	*Q3 f. Q2	do.	do.				
,,					M. A.	†Q1	do,	do.
,,								
1602	V. A.	*Q6 f. Q5 *Q7		W. Leake	R. III.	Q3 f. Q2	T. Creede	A. Wise
1603								
1604					1 H. IV	Q3 f. Q2	V. Simmes	M. Law
1605					R. III.	Q4 f. Q3	T. Creede	do.
1607	Luc.	*Q4 f. Q3	N. O[kes]	J. Harrison				
1608					1 H. IV	Q4 f. Q3		do.
,,					R. II.	Q3 f. Q2	W. W[aterson]	do.
1609					Son.		G. Eld.	J. Wright and W. Aspley
,,								
1611								
,,								
1612	P. P.	Q2		W. Jaggard	R. III.	Q5 f. Q4	T. Creede	M. Law
1613					1 H. IV	†Q5 f. Q4	W. W[aterson]	do.
1615					R. II.	†Q4 f. Q3		do.
1616	Luc.	Q5	T. S.	R. Jackson				
1617	V. A.	*Q8		W. B[arret]				
1619								
1620	do	*Q9		J. P[arker]				
1622					R. III.	Q6 f. Q5	T. Purfoot	do.
					1 H. IV	Q6 f. Q5	do.	do.
1624	Luc.	Q6 f. Q5	J. B[enson]	R. Jackson				
1627	V. A.	*Q10	J. Wreittoun					
1629					R. III.	Q7 f. Q6	J Norton	do.
1630	do.	*Q11?	do.					
,,	do.	*Q12	J. H.	F. Coules.				

QUARTO EDITIONS OF SHAKESPEARE. 143

GROUP III.

Name of Play.	EDITION	PRINTER.	PUBLISHER.
L.L.	†Q to 1	W. W[aterson]	C. Burbie
R. J.	*Q 2	T. Creede	do-
M.D.	†Q 2		J. Roberts
do.	Q 1		T. Fisher
M. V.	†Q 2	J. Roberts	L. Heyes
do.	Q 1	do.	
M. W.	Q1. imp.	T. C[reede]	A. Johnson N. L[ing] and J. Trundell
Ham.	Q 1		
do	Q 2	J. R[oberts]	N. L[ing]
do.	Q3 f. Q2	do.	do.
Lr.	Q1 Q2		N. Butter
R. J.	†*Q3 f. Q2		J. Smethwicke
T. C. (bis)	Q1	G. Eld.	R. Bonian and H. Whalley.
Ham.	Q4 f. Q3		J. Smethwick
? R. J.	Q4 f. Q3		do.
M.W.	Q2 f. Q1		A. Johnson
Oth.	Q 1	N. O[kes]	T. Walkley
do.	Q 2	A. M.	R. Hawkins
M. W.	Q3 f. F1	T. H.	R. Meighen

GROUP IV.

Name of Play.	EDITION	PRINTER.	PUBLISHER.	Date of Publication
? T. A.	n. e.	J. Danter		1593
Con.	*Qto. 1	T. Creede	T. Millington	1594
T. T.	*Q 1	P. S[hort]	do.	1595
R. J.	*Q1 imp.	J. Danter.	entered for E. White	1596
				1597
				1598
				1599
Con.	*Q2 f Q1	V. Simmes	do.	1600
T. T.	*Q2 f. Q2	W. W[aterson]	do.	,,
H. V.	*Q1 imp.	T. Creede	T. Millington and T. Busbie	,,
T. A.	*Q 1	J. R[oberts]	E. White	,,
H. V.	*Q2 f. Q1	T. Creede	T. Pavier	1602
				1603
				1604
				1605
				1607
H. V.	*Q3 f. Q2	T. P[avier]		1608
				,,
Per.	Q1 Q2		H. Gosson	1609
				,,
do.	Q3 f. Q2 †*Q2 f. Q1	S. S[tafford]	E. White	1611
T. A.				
				1612
				1613
				1615
				1616
				1617
M. C.	Q3 f. Q2		T. P[avier]	1619
Per.	Q4 f. Q3			
				1620
				1622
				,,
				1624
				1627
				1629
Per.	Q5 (inc.)	J. N[orton]	R. B[irde]	1630
				,,

ABBREVIATIONS USED FOR NAMES OF PLAYS, &c.,
in pp. 142-3.

V. A.	Venus and Adonis.	⎫
Luc.	Lucreece.	⎬ Group I.
P. P.	Passionate Pilgrim.	⎭
R. II.	Richard II.	⎫
R. III.	Richard III.	
1 H. IV.	First Part of Henry IV.	
2 H. IV.	Second do. do.	⎬ Group II.
M. A.	Much Ado about Nothing.	
Son.	Sonnets.	⎭
R. J.	Romeo and Juliet.	⎫
L. L.	Love's Labour's Lost.	
M. D.	Midsummer Night's Dream.	
M. V.	Merchant of Venice.	
M. W.	Merry Wives of Windsor.	⎬ Group III.
Ham.	Hamlet.	
Oth.	Othello.	
Lr.	Lear.	
T. C.	Troylus and Cressida.	⎭
Con.	Contention of York and Lancaster.	⎫
T. T.	True Tragedy of Duke of York.	
H. V.	Henry V.	
Per.	Pericles.	⎬ Group IV.
T. A.	Titus Andronicus.	
W. C.	Whole Contention of York and Lancaster including Con. and T. T.	⎭
imp.	imperfect.	
inc.	incorrect.	
n. e.	not extant.	

Notes on the Table.

Group I.—The edition of **Venus and Adonis**, **1593**, was to be sold at the White Greyhound, St. Paul's Churchyard, where we find, from the title-page of *Lucrece*, Q 1, that in 1594 J. Harrison was carrying on his business; in 1599, however, W. Leake is in possession of the Greyhound, and from this date J. Harrison's books have no address. In 1602 (cf. *Venus and Adonis*, Q 5), W. Leake had given up the Greyhound, and had taken a new shop with the sign of the Holy Ghost (or did he change his sign only?).

W. Jaggard, the printer of the *Passionate Pilgrim*, was one of the proprietors of the 1st Folio.

The entries in the Stationers' books give some further information. On 18 April, 1593, the *Venus and Adonis* was entered by R. Field, and was not assigned to J. Harrison till 25 June, **1594**, which assignment is also entered: the dates of the other **entries are by W. Leake, 25 June,** 1596; W. Barret, 16 February, **1616;** and J. Parker, **8 March,** 1619.

Group II.—M. Law evidently became possessor of A. Wise's copyright about **1594.**

W. Aspley, at one time in connection with A. Wise, was one of the proprietors of the 1st Folio.

Group III.—Arthur Johnson's *Merry Wives of Windsor* is the imperfect copy.

Othello and *Lear* differ much from the 1st Folio, and do not come from the same source as it does.

J. Roberts, the printer of *The Merchant of Venice* and **Midsummer Night's** *Dream,* seems to have been given to piracy and invasion of copyright.

J. Smethwicke was one of the proprietors of the 1st Folio.

From the entries in the Stationers' books we can trace some of the copyrights. On 18 January, 1601-2, the *Merry Wives of*

Windsor was transferred from **T.** Busbie to A. Johnson. This **T.** Busbie was partner with T. Millington **in the** spurious copy of *Henry* **V.**, and it is probable that the *Merry Wives*, Q 1, was surreptitious. It had, however, Shakespeare's name on the title-page, and has remains of **an** earlier sketch from his hand; it should perhaps be **placed in the fourth group.** On **7** February, 1602-3, *Troylus and Cressida* **was entered by Mr. Roberts.** On 22 January, **1606-7,** Nich. Ling entered, with consent of Mr. Busbie, *Romeo and Juliet*, *Love's Labour's Lost*, **and** *The Taming of a Shrew* (viz. the old play entered **by P. Short in 1594)**; he did not print the **two former, though** he did the **latter;** and accordingly, on 19 **November, 1607, we find** John Smethwicke enters *Hamlet* (the imperfect **sketch),** *The Taming of a Shrew, Romeo and Juliet*, and *Love's Labour's Lost*, al of which had belonged to Ling. Smethwicke also took Ling's house of business, under (the dial **of)** St. Dunstan's, **Fleet Street.** Smethwicke's son sold *Romeo and Juliet* to Flesher **in 1642.**

The *Lear*, published by N. Butter, was entered on 26 November, 1607, for N. Butter and **T.** Busbie. We have seen that Busbie had **to** do with the spurious *Merry Wives;* and the printing of the *Lear* **is not** like that of a genuine copy, though it has **much** matter not in **the Folios.**

In **1619** Lawrence Heyes entered *The Merchant of Venice*, but **did not print** it till 1637.

Group IV.—On 19th April, 1602, Millington's copyrights were sold to **Pavier,** and among them **a** *Titus Andronicus*, which the Cambridge **editors** think **to** be the one entered by J. Danter in 1593. It cannot be the one published by White, as he issued editions in 1600 and in 1611; *i.e.* both before and after the transaction between Millington and Pavier.

All the publications in this **fourth group** are clearly surreptitious.

From the Stationers' books we learn **that** the same E. White mentioned above entered the spurious *King Leir*, afterwards published by J. Wright in 1605. The date **of** entry is 14th May, 1594. This White also entered the surreptitious 1st Quarto of *Romeo and Juliet*.

QUARTO EDITIONS OF SHAKESPEARE. 147

There is an interesting entry in 1626, when E. Brewster and R. Birde acquired J. Pavier's right in "Shakespeare's plays or any of them." *Sir John Oldcastle*, *Titus and Andronicus*, and *Hamblet*, are mentioned. And on 8th November, 1630, is entered the assignment to Richard Coates, by R. Birde, of *Henry V.*, *Sir John Oldcastle*, *Titus and Andronicus*, **York and** *Lancaster*, *Agincourt*, *Hamblet*, *Pericles*, and *The Yorkshire* **Tragedy**. Evidently Pavier was a wholesale dealer in spurious issues.

I add **the addresses** of some publishers **and** printers mentioned in the above table:—

I.—R. Field,   Anchor, Blackfriars, near Ludgate.
    Francis Coules   In the Old Bailey without Newgate.
    J. Harrison,   White Greyhound, St. Paul's.
    W. Leake,   1. Greyhound, St. Paul's.
         2. Holy Ghost, St. Paul's.
    R. Jackson,   Conduit, Fleet Street.
    J. Benson,   St. Dunstan's.
    L. Heyes,   On Fleet Bridge.

II.—A. Wise.   Angel, St. **Paul's**.
    M. Law,   Fox, St. Paul's, near **St. A**ugustine's gate.
    J. Wright,   Christ Church **gate**.
    R. Bonian and   { Spread Eagle, **St. Paul's,** over against
         H. Whalley,   Great **North door**.
    V. Simmes,   { White Swan, near Barnard Castle,
            Adling Street.
    T. Creede,   { Catharine Wheel, near Old Swan,
            Thames Street.
    Th. Purfoot,   1. Lucretia, St. Paul's.
         2. Within New Rents, Newgate.
         3. Opposite St. Sepulchre's, &c.
    J. Norton.   Queen's Arms.

III.—C. Burbie,   Near the Exchange.
    T. Heyes,   **Green** Dragon, St. Paul's.
    T. Walkley,   Eagle **and** Child, Britain's Burse.
    R. Hawkins,   **Chancery** Lane, near Serjeant's Inn.

T. Fisher,	White Hart, Fleet Street.
N. Ling,	**Under St.** Dunstan's, Fleet Street.
J. Smethwicke,	do. (under the dial).
N. Butter,	{ Pied Bull, St. Paul's, **near** St. Austin's gate.
W. Leake (1652),	{ Crown, Fleet Street, between the **two** Temple gates.
R. Meighen,	{ Middle Temple Gate and St. Dunstan's Churchyard, Fleet **Street.**

IV.—T. Millington,   Under **St.** Peter's Church, **Cornwall.**
 do. with T. Busbie, Carter Lane, next Powle's **Head.**

T. Pavier,	{ **Cat** and **Parrot,** Cornhill, **near** Exchange.
E. White,	{ **Gun,** near **Little** North door, St. Paul's.
A. Johnson,	{ Flower de' **Luce** and **Crown,** St. Paul's.
H. Gosson,	Sun, Paternoster **Row.**
R. Birde,	**Bible,** Cheapside.

In order finally to point out the importance of ready reference **to** such **a** table **as** the above, **I** subjoin a list of the results which **it** manifestly leads to as to the **work** needed at the present time in **the way of** reprinting those old **texts.**

I.—We **want** texts printed in parallel columns of—

Romeo and Juliet	Q 2	
Hamlet	Q 2	
Merry **Wives** of Windsor	F 1	**and** the imperfect sketches
2 Henry **VI.**	F 1	(**with** collations **of** other editions).
3 Henry VI.	F 1	
Henry V.	F **1**	

These are needed to give a basis to determine Shakespeare's manner of work, if the early sketches are from his hand (as I believe the **first** three are), and if not, to disprove the genuineness of the sketch **plays.**

II.—We want texts in parallel columns of—

Richard III.   Q 1 ⎫
2 Henry IV.   Q 1 ⎪
Troylus and Cressida   Q 1 ⎬ and **F** 1 (with collations).
Lear   Q 1 ⎪
Othello   Q 1 and Q 2 ⎪
Hamlet   Q 1 ⎭

to ascertain the relation of the Folio text with that of the previous editions.

III.—We want **texts of the two earliest** Quartos in parallel columns of—

Midsummer Night's Dream,
Merchant of Venice,

to ascertain which edition **should have** the preference for a **revised text.**

IV.—Of—   Much Ado about Nothing,
          Love's Labour's Lost,
          Richard II.
          1 Henry IV.

we **want single-text reprints** of Q 1, as being **preferable to F** 1, which was printed **from the Quartos in** these **plays.** *Pericles*, Q 1, and *Two Noble* **Kinsmen,** Q 1, would also be desirable reprints. It is clearly **useless to reprint the** Folio **for plays** where it is merely copied from **the Quartos.**

It should **be noticed that of the eight** plays **which the proprietors** of the **Folio printed from the Quartos,** three, **viz.** *Love's Labour's Lost,* **Romeo** *and* **Juliet,** and *Much Ado about Nothing,* had become their **property ; so that** (setting *Titus Andronicus* aside as spurious) they had only to get permission **to** print four ; viz. *Richard II.,* 1 *Henry IV., Midsummer Night's* **Dream,** and *Merchant of Venice;* and even of these four we have **no positive evidence** that they did not **buy** up three; as there are **no reprints after** 1623 for the **previous** proprietors of the Quartos (except *Merchant of Venice,* 1637 ?)

As I have spoken above of reprints needed in **parallel columns**, I may here mention as a cognate matter the **need of** reprints of the passages from North's *Plutarch*, **Holinshed's *Chronicle*,** &c., parallel to *revised* texts of the Historical and Roman plays founded on them; and of reprints of plots of the old plays of *The **Taming** of a Shrew, Promos and Cassandra, The troublesome raigne of King John*, &c., parallel with the plots of the plays founded on them.

I am also strongly of opinion that *revised* texts of the early sketches of *Romeo and Juliet, Hamlet, The Merry Wives of Windsor, The Contention*, and the *True Tragedy*, should be printed parallel with revised texts of the plays in their fuller and later forms. Such revised texts of the early sketches have never been printed.

[P.S.—When I wrote this paper I was not aware that *Romeo and Juliet* had been edited, on the plan proposed in page 148, by Mommsen (with a most valuable introduction and collations), and that an edition of *Hamlet* on a somewhat similar plan had been issued in England.—F. G. F. *Jan.* 1876.]

CHAPTER III.

ON METRICAL TESTS AS APPLIED TO DRAMATIC POETRY.

PART II.—FLETCHER, BEAUMONT, MASSINGER.

(*Read March* 27, 1874.)

THE fact that Fletcher was aided in his plays by Massinger has long been known, and in one or two instances conjectures have been made that Massinger helped him in specific plays; but on this point, as well as on the question of what share Beaumont had in the plays produced in the joint names of himself and Fletcher, no definite conclusion has been arrived at. It will be convenient for future reference if, before entering on our present inquiry, I subjoin a Table of the plays passing under the names of Beaumont and Fletcher, with the dates of their production (when known) and the authors to whom I assign them, pointing out the instances in which I differ from Mr. Dyce in this respect.

GROUP I.—PLAYS PRODUCED BEFORE BEAUMONT'S DEATH.

Date.	Name of Play.	Authors (F. G. Fleay).	Authors (Dyce).
1607	*Woman Hater	B	F. only.
Before 1610	Faithful Shepherdess.....	F.	F.
?	Four Plays in one	B. and F..........	B. and F.
?	Wit at several Weapons	B. and F..........	B. and F.
?	Thierry and Theodoret...	B. and F..........	B. and F.
Before 1611	Maid's Tragedy	B. and F..........	B. and F.
Before 1611	Philaster	B. and F..........	B. and F.
1611	King and No King.........	B. and F..........	B. and F.
1611	Knight of B. Pestle	B. and F..........	B. and F.
1611-12	Cupid's Revenge	B. and F..........	B. and F.
?	Scornful Lady................	B. and F..........	B. and F.
1612	Coxcomb	B. and F..........	B. and F.
1613	*Captain	B. and F..........	F, (after Weber).
1612	Masque...........................	B.	B.
1613	*Honest Man's Fortune	F. and Anon. ...	B. and F.
1613	Henry VIII.	F. and Shakes.	
1613	Two Noble Kinsmen......	F. and Shakes..	F. and Shakes.

GROUP II.—PLAYS BY FLETCHER ONLY (FLEAY).

Date.	Name of Play.	Author according to Dyce.
After 1614	Wit Without Money	Probably F. only.
Before 1619	Bonduca	F. (B. and F., Weber)
Before 1619	Valentinian	F. (B. and F., Darley)
Before 1619	Mad Lover	F.
1618	Loyal Subject	F.
?	Humorous Lieutenant	F.
Old in 1633	Woman's Prize	F.
?	Chances	F.
?	Monsieur Thomas	F.
After 1618	Double Marriage	F.
?	Women Pleased	F.
1621	Island Princess	F.
1621	Pilgrim	F.
1621	Wild-Goose Chase	F.
1621	Custom of Country	Probably F. only.
1624	Rule a Wife and Have a Wife	F.
1624	Wife for a Month	F.

GROUP III.—PLAYS BY FLETCHER AND ANOTHER AUTHOR.

Date.	Name of Play	Other Autho. (Fleay).	Other Author (Dyce).
After 1618	False One	Massinger	Massinger (after Weber).
?	*Little French Lawyer	Do.	Beaumont.
1621	Very Woman	Do.	Altered by Massinger.
1622	*Beggar's Bush	Do.	No other.
1622	*Prophetess	Do.	Do.
1622	*Spanish Curate	Do.	Do.
1622	Sea Voyage	? Do.	Altered.
After 1621	*Laws of Candy	? Do.	Beaumont (perh.)
After F.'s death	*Elder Brother	Do.	No other undoubtedly.
After F.'s death	Lover's Progress	Do.	Massinger (after Weber).
Before 1619	*Knight of Malta	Middleton	No other.
	*Queen of Corinth	Do.	Rowley.
1622	*Love's Cure	Mid. and Row.	No other.
1623	Maid of Mill	Rowley	Rowley.
1624?	*Bloody Brother	?	Rowley.
1625-6	*Fair Maid of Inn	?	No other.
?	Nice Valour	?	?
1625-6	*Noble Gentleman	?	Shirley (after Weber).
1633	Night Walker	Shirley	Shirley.
After F.'s death	Love's Pilgrimage	Do.	Do.

In these Tables B. and F. stand for Beaumont and Fletcher respectively. I have formed the plays into three groups: the first of these extends to Beaumont's death; the second includes all the plays in which Fletcher's hand alone is perceptible; the third includes the rest of the plays. It will be seen that I have starred in the table all the plays as to the authorship of which I hold an opinion different from Mr. Dyce. This is the case as to three in the first group; which are important, and as to which I think him decidedly wrong. In seven cases in the third group I find traces of a second author where Dyce does not; and in four cases I differ from him as to who the author is; but in the second group we agree entirely that it is solely Fletcher's work. It will be well, then, to begin with these plays, and examine what are their peculiarities in rhythm. They are distinguished—

(1) By number of double or female endings: these are more numerous in Fletcher than in any other writer in the language, and are sufficient of themselves to distinguish his work.

(2) By frequent pauses at the end of the lines: this union of "the stopped line" with the double ending is peculiar to Fletcher: Massinger has many double endings, but few stopped lines.

(3) By moderate use of rhymes: this distinguishes him from Beaumont, who has more rhymes than Fletcher or Massinger, and who in serious passages has few double endings.

(4) By moderate use of lines of less than five measures: he has more than Massinger, however.

(5) By using no prose whatever. Massinger also admits none: there are two little bits in his work; both, I think, intercalated.

(6) By admitting abundance of tri-syllabic feet, so that his (Fletcher's) lines have to be felt rather than scanned; it is almost impossible to tell when Alexndrines are intended.

I now give a Table of the rhythmical pecularities of this group; and a similar Table of Massinger's plays in which he worked alone; these are rightly given in the editions, with one exception; viz. *A Very Woman*, which is, as Dyce conjectured, an alteration of Fletcher's *A Right Woman*, which was previously supposed to be lost.

Name of Play.	No. of Double Endings.	Rhyming Lines.	Alexandrines.	Lines of less than 5 Measures
Custom of Country	1756	14	5	8
Bonduca	1500	42	50	20
Valentinian	1947	38	10	26
Mad Lover	1507	8	—	26
Loyal Subject	2266	20	21	29
Double Marriage	1762	36	5	27
Humorous Lieutenant	2193	12	5	20
Women Pleased	1823	12	—	7
Woman's Prize	1678	22	5	57
Chances	1236	18	8	29
Island Princess	2059	12	6	29
Pilgrim	1845	18	6	18
Wild-Goose Chase	1949	6	3	24
Monsieur Thomas	1800	2	5	28
Wit Without Money	1543	6	50	21
Rule a Wife, &c.	1595	4	—	42
Wife for a Month	1764	8	—	21
Average	1777	16·3	10·6	25·5

N.B.—The *Chances* is a very short play, about four-fifths of an average one; and the *Laws of Candy* is so corrupt as to be uncountable with accuracy.

TABLE OF MASSINGER'S PLAYS.

Name of Play.	No. of Double Endings.	Rhyming Lines.	Alexandrines.	Lines of less than 5 Measures
Unnatural Combat	934	10	1	2
Duke of Milan	1146	34	2	6
Bondman	1085	32	2	3
Renegado	1121	32	1	3
Parliament of Love	915	14	7	5
Roman Actor	960	32	1	3
Great Duke of Florence	1006	10	1	4
Maid of Honour	1056	22	3	—
Picture	1227	22	2	4
Emperor of East	1058	8	2	—
A New Way, &c.	1228	20	—	2
City Madam	1081	6	6	3
Guardian	1075	8	2	4
Bashful Lover	1070	24	4	3
Believe as You List	925	12	3	—
Average	1059	16·8	2·5	2·3

On comparing these Tables, it is evident that, as to the authorship of a play, it would not be safe to conclude to which of these two authors it belonged, on the evidence of the number of rhymes; but that the double endings would be conclusive. Fletcher's range is from 1500 to 2000, in round numbers, with an average of 1775; while Massinger's ranges from 900 to 1200, with an average of 1000. A play, having between 1200 and 1500 double endings and divisible into parts of distinctly different styles, would probably be a joint production of Massinger's and Fletcher's, especially if the part containing the greater proportion of female endings had also the larger share of short lines and Alexandrines. Now examine the following Table of the plays which I assign to Fletcher and Massinger jointly.

TABLE OF FLETCHER'S AND MASSINGER'S JOINT PLAYS.

Name of Play.	Part assigned to each Author.	No. of Double Endings.	Rhyming Lines.	Alexandrines.	Lines of less than 5 Measures
Little French Lawyer ...	F., Act ii. Sc. 1, 2, 3; iii. 2, 4, 5; iv. 1, 2, 3, 4; 6b, 7; v. 1a, 2, 3a..............................20 pp. M., Act i. Sc. 1, 2, 3; iii. 1, 3; iv. 5, 6a, 7a; v. 1b, 3b..12 pp. F., Act ii. Sc. 1, 2, 3; iii. 1, 2, 3, 4; iv. 1,	937 479	16 14	21 —	23 4
False One	2, 3 ....18 pp. M., Act i. Sc. 1; v. 1, 2, 3, 4..................11 pp.	953 339	4 22	1 —	3 5
Prophetess...............	F., Act i. Sc. 1, 2, 3; iii. 1, 2, 3; v. 2, 3 ...15½ pp. M., Act ii. Sc. 1, 2, 3; iv. Ch. 1, 2, 3, 4, 5; v. Ch. 1 ....11 pp.	1002 383	4 26	10 3	12 —
Spanish Curate...........	F., Act ii Sc. 1, 2, 3, 4, 5; iii. 1, 2, 4; iv. 2, 3, 5, 6, 7; v. 2..................................20 pp. M., Act i. Sc. 1, 2, 3; iii. 3; iv. 1, 4; v. 1, 3 ...13 pp.	1201 374	— 10	2 1	5 1
Beggar's Bush............	F., Acts ii., iii., iv., v. ....26 pp. M., Act i. .... 4 pp.	1075 164	24 6	1 —	26 —
Elder Brother............	F., Acts ii., iii., iv., v. ....21½ pp. M., Act i. .... 5½ pp.	1164 495	— —	— 5	11 —
Lover's Progress.........	F., M. cannot be distinguished by Scenes. Hand of M. apparent in Act iii. Sc. 1; iv. 2; and of F. in i. 2; iii. 2, &c...............	1411	14	5	4
Very Woman	F., Act iii. Sc. 1, 2, 3, 4, 5; iv. 1, 3 ....12 pp. M., Act i. Sc. 1; ii. 1, 2, 3; iv. 2; v. 1, 2, 3, 4, 5, 6 ....21 pp.	631 702	2 20	6 —	16 —
? Sea Voyage	Parts cannot be separated; rewritten for theatrical purposes..	937	22	4	228
? Laws of Candy	I cannot separate the authors of this play; but there are two. Act ii. Sc. 1; iii. 3, differ from the rest. Has it been treated like Sea Voyage, &c.?	762	4	9	82

It is evident at once that all the metrical conditions required are fulfilled by the division here made. In every instance the proportion of double endings is that which would be expected from the tables previously made for Fletcher and Massinger. There is the same irregularity as to the number of rhymes; the same excess of Alexandrines and short lines on the part of Fletcher, to a similarly varying amount. Now let us turn to evidence of a different character. We all know Sir Aston Cockayne's lines addressed to Charles Cotton concerning Beaumont:—

> "His own renown no such addition needs
> To have a fame sprung from another's deeds,
> And my good friend, old Philip Massinger,
> With Fletcher writ in some that we see there."

In another poem he says,

> "For Beaumont, of those many, writ in few,
> And Massinger in other few."

And in a third place, speaking of Fletcher and Massinger, Sir Aston says:—

> "Plays did they write together, were great friends."

If these plays which I have selected, and which do fulfil the necessary metrical requirements, are not the plays in question, are we to look for them among those which do not fulfil the requirements? But again. Although these tests are satisfied by the division, the division was not made by means of these tests: the weak-ending test was the one I selected for this purpose. Massinger often ends his lines with words that cannot be grammatically separated from the next line; articles, prepositions, auxiliaries, &c., am, be, of, in, the, this, &c. Fletcher uses the stopped line, usually. On this ground I made the separation: I then made tables of the Acts and Scenes in which each character appears, to see if the manner of work and the apportionment of it between the authors could be traced; and having found my first judgment invariably confirmed, I then applied the tabular test. As yet I have found all the tests give the same result. It would not be possible to give all the investigations in one paper: but for an example I will take the play of the *Little French Lawyer*, the first on our list. A simple reading of the text shows the existence of two authors, from the frequent changes of style and treatment: a marking of the unstopped lines makes the division exactly as I give it in the table: and an examination of the plot shows that, of the three stories contained in this play, namely, that of La Writ, and that of Annabella, were assigned to Fletcher; the third, that of Lamira, being given to Massinger.

Nor does our evidence end here: on looking into the text we find that in every place where Dinant's name occurs in the scenes assigned to Fletcher, it is pronounced Dínant, paroxyton: but in the Massinger scenes it is oxyton, Dinánt. The fact being settled, then, that there are two authors, and one of these Fletcher, and it being quite evident (as we shall presently see) that Beaumont was not one,—Beaumont introduces prose scenes, eschews double endings, and rhymes abundantly,—our choice probably lies between Massinger, Middleton, and Rowley, as being the only playwrights known to have worked with Fletcher. But the phenomena are exactly the same for eight plays in our list, and nearly so for the two marked with a (?), and the dates of three of these are about 1622; this gives another argument against Beaumont, who died in 1615-16; and conclusively disposes of Rowley, whose style is utterly unlike the writer's we are in search of, and who had not the poetical faculty shown in the Massinger part of these eight (or ten?) plays. And besides this, three of these plays have already been conjecturally assigned to Massinger, as part author, by Dyce (in two instances following Weber), who has also given us his opinion that *A Very Woman* is a rifacimento of *A Right Woman* by Fletcher, which it certainly is. It is strange that, having got so far on the right track, Dyce did not anticipate our restoring all eight (or ten?) of these plays to Fletcher and Massinger; and still more strange, that Seward and Weber should single out the character of La Writ, who never speaks a line that is not pure Fletcher in every way, as being the unassisted work of Beaumont.

There is another point of external evidence yet to notice: five (or seven?) of these plays were produced, three of them certainly in 1622; two of them probably very near that date. The other three were not produced till after Fletcher's death. Now, 1622 and 1623 are just the dates in which no play of Fletcher's (unassisted) is on our list; and after the notice of the *Virgin Martyr*, October 1620, in the book of Sir George Buck, Master of the Revels, there is no entry as to Massinger till December 1623, when the *Bondman* was produced. This may be regarded as finally settling this question.

With regard to the other subdivisions of the third group, as only four of the ten plays contained in them were produced in Fletcher's lifetime, they are far less interesting, and do not give aid in examining the method of the poet's work. I give a Table of their Rhythm, however, for the sake of completing our scheme; and for the same reason add a Table of the plays in which Massinger worked with other authors.

Note.—R. stands for Rowley in this table, aud Md. for Middleton.

[I ought also to state that the lines of demarcation are much more definite in this and the preceding Tables than in that which embraces the works on which Beaumont and Fletcher wrought together; for these two friends and these only, as far as I can discover, habitually aided each other, not only by writing scenes separately in each play, but also by writing portions of scenes, speeches, or even lines, in the same scenes, jointly; for instance, Act ii. Sc. 2, in the *Maid's Tragedy*, tabulated as Fletcher's, unquestionably contains some of Beaumont's writing, though much more of his coadjutor's. Fletcher's hand can also frequently be traced in Beaumont's prose-scenes, though he never *introduces* prose himself.

—F. G. F. *Jan.* 1876.]

TABLE OF JOINT PLAYS BY FLETCHER AND MIDDLETON (?); FLETCHER AND ROWLEY; FLETCHER AND SHIRLEY; MASSINGER AND FIELD; MASSINGER AND DEKKER; MIDDLETON AND ROWLEY

Name of Play.	Part assigned to each Author.		No. of Double Endings.	Rhyming Lines.	Alexandrines.	Lines of less than 5 Measures
Queen of Corinth	F., Act i. Sc. 1, 2, 3, 4; ii. 1, 2, 3, 4; v. 4 (ii. only all Fletcher)	15 pp.	754	8	—	1
	Md.? Act iii. Sc. 1, 2; iv. 1, 2, 3, 4; v. 2, 3.	14 pp.	210	50	4	31
Bloody Brother	F., Act ii. Sc. 1, 2, 3; iii. 1*b*, 2; v. 1*b*, 2	10 pp.	601	4	3	13
	Md.? Act i. Sc. 1; iii. 1*a*, *c*, 2, 3; v. 1*a*, *c*	18 pp.	538	84	—	6
Knight of Malta	Md., Act i. Sc. 1, 2, 3; iii. 1, 2, 3; v. 1, 2	14 pp.	312	44	—	10
	F., Act ii. Sc. 1, 2, 3, 4, 5; iii. 1, 4; iv. 1, 2, 3, 4	19 pp.	1041	2	2	25
Love's Cure			622	66	5	18
Maid of Mill	F., Act i. Sc. 1, 2, 3; iii. 2, 3; v. 2*a*	13 pp.	776	—	4	8
	R., Act ii. Sc. 1, 2; iii. 1; iv. 1, 2, 3; v. 1, 2*b* (much prose; metre too irregular to tabulate)					
Noble Subject	Recast by some one in same way as preceding; little Fletcher left		—	—	—	—
Nice Valour	Act iv. Sc. 1 is tolerably pure Fletcher, the rest has been treated like preceding		605	72	12	119
Fair Maid of Inn	F. and some other author (not Massinger); not separated; partly prose		876	72	8	75
Night Walker	F. to end of Act iii. Sc. 2; after this so altered by Shirley, as to defy separation		953	12	8	22
Love's Pilgrimage	F., Acts i., ii., iii. N.B. Act i. Sc. 1, inserted from Jonson		1254	6	19	155
	Shirley, Acts iv., v. Partly prose	21 pp.	1050	3	14	21
	Massinger, Act i. Sc. 1, 2; iii. 1*a*; iv. 2, 3, 4; v. 1, 2	11 pp.	259	12	2	8
Fatal Dowry	Field, Act ii. Sc. 1, 2; iii. 1*b*; iv. 1	22 pp.	559	22	—	6
Virgin Martyr	Massinger, Act i. Sc. 1, 2; iii. 1, 2; iv. 3; v. 2	12 pp.	133	24	4	12
	Dekker, Act ii. Sc. 1, 2, 3; iii. 3; iv. 1, 2; v. 1	17½ pp.	577	34	1	6
	Middleton, Act i. Sc. 1*b*; ii. 1, 2; iii. 2; iv. 2; v. 1 (partly)	16½ pp.	235	70	2	18
Old Law	(No Massinger.) Rowley, Act i. Sc. 1*a*; iii. 1; iv. 1; v. 1 (partly)	25 pp.	605	45	26	81
		9 pp.	(prose.)	—	—	—

The work in the *Bloody Brother* is curiously arranged. Fletcher wrote all the parts connected with the poisoning attempted by La Torch,—namely, ii. 1, 2; iii. 2; and the parts involving Edith,— namely, iii. 2; v. 2; and the impassioned speeches of Edith in iii. 1; v. 1; the rest is not his. The *Maid in the Mill* is noticeable as being one of the plays containing prose in which Fletcher had a share that were produced after Beaumont's death and during Fletcher's lifetime. Fletcher's part was the story of Ismenia, and Rowley's that of Florimel, at the outset; but they soon changed the parts, and after changing kept them distinct to the end. I cannot agree with Dyce in assigning *Rollo* and *The Queen of Corinth* partly to Rowley; they seem much more like Middleton, and are far removed from Rowley's style.

We have now left for consideration only the group of plays produced before Beaumont's death. The dates of most of these are known; but some we cannot determine from external evidence. I have assigned conjectural dates to them, for reasons which will appear. Before examining these, it is necessary to determine the general characteristics of Beaumont's metre. This has been hitherto regarded as an insoluble problem. The habit, of which we are traditionally and rightly informed, which Beaumont and Fletcher had contracted, namely, that of writing together in the same scene, seems to forbid any analysis being applied which can separate the two authors' work. This separation can, however, be made, to some extent. We know from our second group (of Fletcher's undoubted plays) what his characteristics are—no prose; many double endings; pauses at the end of lines. If we find any work in which these characteristics are entirely absent, that work will probably not be Fletcher's. Now, there is a work called *Four Plays in One*, that is evidently by two authors. The first two of these short plays are in every respect different from the other two. The latter two are in Fletcher's usual style. In 7 pages we find 673 double endings; 5 rhymes; 4 incomplete lines In the former two plays, in 18 pages there are only 172 double endings; 85 rhymes; 13 incomplete lines, and a considerable amount of prose; the lines also are in Shakespeare's later manner, ending on particles, &c., so as to run on continuously with the succeeding line. These must be by Beaumont. We have then, here, the characteristics of his style unmixed with Fletcher's, which gives us the key we require. We can now separate their work.

It may seem strange that, since Weber had rightly apportioned these plays to our authors, characteristics so salient should never have led any critic to assign the other plays rightly. This, I think, may be explained. There is an inveterate habit among editors to read their authors too much in the order in which the old editions were printed. I can, in many recent issues of great value, trace the mischief and inaccuracy that is still produced by this cause, and in none more than in Dyce's "Beaumont and Fletcher."

The *Woman Hater* was first published in Quarto, and was undoubtedly the earliest of these plays that has reached us. Therefore Dyce studies it first ; finds it to be almost or entirely by one author ; finds, moreover, that it was first published in the name of Fletcher only, and concludes that it was mainly by him. Hence he gets a false notion of Fletcher's style that invalidates all his conclusions as far as this first group is concerned. I doubt not that other editors have been similarly influenced ; and for myself, I can say that the acceptance of this conclusion of Dyce's kept me two years from seeing the proper starting-point, namely, the plays written by Fletcher alone after Beaumont's death. As to the title-page of the *Woman Hater*, it does not stand alone. The first play published in the names of Beaumont and Fletcher jointly was *The Scornful Lady*, in 1616; but *Cupid's Revenge* was published in 1615 in Fletcher's name singly. The *Woman Hater* (1607), *Knight of the Burning Pestle* (1613), *Maid's Tragedy* (1619, 1622), and *Thierry and Theodoret* (1621), were published without authors' names. In 1648, *Thierry and Theodoret* and *The Woman Hater* were published in Fletcher's name singly ; in 1649 both of them in the joint names of Beaumont and Fletcher, as *Cupid's Revenge* had already been in 1630. Now, that *Cupid's Revenge* and *Thierry and Theodoret* were joint works, all the editors admit. This one play, *The Woman Hater*, is treated differently by them ; in opposition, I think, to the external evidence, and certainly to the internal. I must, however, before giving my theory on this group, call your attention to the following Table, which is similar to those already under our notice for the other groups.

TABLE OF BEAUMONT AND FLETCHER'S JOINT PLAYS.

Name of Play.	Part assigned to each Author.	No. of Double Endings.	Rhyming Lines.	Alexandrines.	Lines of less than 5 Measures
Woman Hater	B., nearly or quite all (prose in every scene)	213	84	23	70
Wit at several Weapons	B., Act i. Sc. 2; ii. 2, 3, 4; v. 1, 2	156	30	2	37
	B. and F., Act i. Sc. 1; ii. 1; iii. 1; iv. 1, 2, 3.	599	52	9	37
Thierry and Theodoret	F. traceable in Act i. Sc. 1; ii. 2, 3; iv. 1; v. 2.	921	46	15	77
Maid's Tragedy	B., Act i. 1, 2; ii. 1; iii. 1, 2; iv. 2; v. 4 ...25 pp.	200	40	7	103
	F., Act ii. Sc. 2; iv. 1; v. 1, 2, 3 ....7½ pp.	264	4	5	35
Philaster	F., Act v. Sc. 4. B., Act i. Sc. 2; ii. 1, 3; iii. 1; iv. 2, 3, 4; v. 1, 5	427	28	22	178
King and No King	B., Act i. Sc. 1, 2; ii. 1, 2; iii. 1, 2, 3; iv. 4; v. 2, 4	240	24	2	57
	F., Act iv. Sc. 1, 2, 3; v. 1, 2, 3 .....26 pp., 9 pp.	304	—	9	53
Knight of Burning P.	Prose Beaumont's; rest mixed	205	328	1	7
Cupid's Revenge	F. traceable in Act i. Sc. 16; ii. 5; iv. 3	583	34	16	184
Scornful Lady	Text very incorrect; verse printed as prose.	855	14	24	239
Coxcomb	F. traceable in Act i. Sc. 1, 2, 3, 5; ii. 1; iii. 1, 2; iv. 2, 4, 5, 6; v. 1, 3	678	22	10	198
Captain	F. chiefly traceable in Act iv. Sc. 3 (23 pp. out of 33)	1124	20	14	54
Honest Man's Fortune	Act v. Sc. 1, 2, 3 .... 7 pp.	277	10	1	16
	Other author (? Beaumont), Acts i., ii., iii., iv...28 pp.	258	54	13	49

I have still to make a few remarks as to the points where I differ from Dyce. As to the authorship of the *Captain*, the difference is not important, as that play certainly is two-thirds Fletcher. Had Dyce not been misled by the *Woman Hater* in which Fletcher had no share, and had he been aware that **Fletcher** wrote *no prose*, he would not have made any mistake. The play of the *Honest Man's Fortune* is partly by Fletcher; but that the other part is Beaumont's I am not sure: it reads to me differently from his other works. Still I have not entirely examined this play, and prefer to leave the question open: it may be Beaumont's; at any rate, only one act is Fletcher's.

Before concluding this paper I must again repeat that it is only preliminary. The matters I believe to be absolutely fixed in it by the application of metrical tests are, the part authorship of Massinger in the plays given in the table above; the relative amount of Beaumont's work; and the classification of these plays. If on these points I have not produced conviction, the fault lies in the narrow limits which I feel it right to impose on a first work of this kind; or more probably in defective manner of exposition. I am certain that no one can go through the detailed evidence in the way I have done and remain unconvinced. To produce conviction in others who can have set before them only part of the mass of statistics on this subject, is very difficult. In my next paper I hope to produce all the evidence in full as to one or two plays that have passed under Shakespeare's name. To do this for all the plays I have considered would require many volumes; but I hope the sample will be a fair one, and that my work will be judged from it.

TABLE OF QUARTO EDITIONS.

(FOR REFERENCE.)

Woman Hater, 1607 (n.n.); **1648 (F.)**; 1649 (B. and F.).
Faithful Shepherdess, no date (F.); 1629 (F.); 1634 (F.), &c.
Knight of Burning Pestle, 1613 (n.n.); 1635 (B. and F.).
Masque, no date (n.n.); ascribed to B. in Folio.

PASSAGES FOR ILLUSTRATION.

Cupid's Revenge, 1615 (F.) ; 1630 (B. and F.) ; 1635.
Scornful Lady, 1616 (B. and F.) ; 1625 ; 1630; 1635 ; 1639, &c.
Maid's Tragedy, 1619 (n.n.) ; 1622 (n.n.) ; 1630 (B. and F.) ; 1638 ; 1641, &c.
King and No King, 1619 (B. and F.) ; 1625 ; 1631 ; 1639, &c.
Philaster, 1620 (B. and F.) ; 1622 ; 1628 ; 1634 ; 1639, &c.
Thierry and Theodoret, 1621 (n. n.) ; 1648 (F.) ; 1649 (B. & F.).
Wit without Money, 1639 (B. and F.), &c.
Monsieur Thomas, 1639 (F.).
Rule a Wife, &c., 1640 (F.).
Elder Brother, 1637 (F.).
Bloody Brother, 1639 (by B. J. F.) ; 1640 (F.).
Night Walker, 1640 (F.).
Two Noble Kinsmen, 1634 (F. and Shakespeare).

None of these were printed in the first Folio 1647, but all were in the second, 1679.

PASSAGES FOR ILLUSTRATION.

Evadne. "Alas, Amintor, thinkst thou I forbear
To sleep with thee because I have put on
A maiden's strictness? Look upon these cheeks,
And thou shalt find the hot and rising blood
Unapt for such a vow ! No ! in this heart
There dwells as much desire and as much will
To put wish'd act in practice as e'er yet
Was known to woman : and they have been shown
Both. But it was the folly of thy youth
To think this beauty, to what land soe'er
It shall be call'd, shall stoop to any second.
I do enjoy the best, and in that height
Have sworn to stand or die. You guess the man."

Maid's Tragedy, Act ii. Sc. 1. (BEAUMONT.)

Evadne.   " No, **I** do not!
I do appear the same, the same Evadne
Drest in the shames I lived in, the same monster.
But these are names of honour to what **I am**:
I do present myself the foulest creature,
Most poisonous, dangerous, and despised of men,
Lerna e'er bred or Nilus. **I am hell**
Till you, **my dear lord, shoot your light into me,**
The beams of your **forgiveness : I am** soul-sick,
And wither with the fear of one condemn'd,
Till I have got your pardon."
     Maid's Tragedy, Act iv. Sc. 1. (FLETCHER.)

Cler,*mont.* " They are both brave fellows,
Tried and **approved : and** I am proud **to** encounter
With men **from whom no honour can be lost.**
They will play **up to a man and set him off.**
Whene'er I go to **the field,** Heaven **keep me from**
The meeting of an **unflesh'd youth or coward.**
The first to get a name **comes on too hot ;**
The coward is so swift in giving ground,
There is no overtaking **him** without
A hunting nag, well-breath'd too."
    Little French Lawyer, Act i. Sc. 2. (MASSINGER.)

Cleremont. '"**Colour'd** with smooth excuses. **Was't a friend's part,**
A gentleman's, a man's **that wears a sword**
And stands upon the point of reputation,
To hide his head then when his honour call'd **him,**
Call'd him aloud and led him **to** his fortune?
To halt and slip the collar? **By my life**
I would have given my life **I'd never known thee !**
Thou hast eaten canker-like into **my** judgment
With **this** disgrace, thy whole life cannot heal again."
    Little French Lawyer, **Act ii. Sc. 3.** (FLETCHER.)

Antonio.   " Give me that face
And I am satisfied, upon whose shoulders
So e'er it grows. Juno, deliver us
Out of this amazement! beseech you, goddess,
Tell us of our friends! How does Ismeria?
And how does Isabella? Both in good health
I hope as you yourself are."
Maid in the Mill, **Act iv. Sc. 1.** (ROWLEY.)

Antonio.   "**Oh** 'tis a spark of beauty!
And where **they appear so excellent** in little
They will but flame in great. Extension spoils 'em.
Martine, **learn this! the narrower** that our eyes
Keep **way unto our object, still the** sweeter
That **comes unto us; great bodies** are like great countries,
Discovering still, **toil and no pleasure** finds 'em."
Maid in the Mill, **Act i. Sc. 2.** (FLETCHER.)

Sophia.   " Alas, my son, nor Fate nor Heaven itself
Can or would wrest my whole care **of your good**
To any least secureness in your ill!
What I **urge** issues from my curious **fear,**
Lest you should make your means to scope your snare:
Doubt of sincereness is the only mean
Not to incense it, but corrupt it clean."
Rollo, Act iii. Sc. 1. (? MIDDLETON.)

Sophia.   "**Oh my** blest boys, the honour of my years,
Of all my **cares the bounteous** rewarders!
Oh let me thus **embrace you, thus for** ever
Within a **mother's** love lock **up your** friendship!
And my sweet **sons** once more with **mutual twinings**
As one chaste bed begot you, **make one** body!
Blessings from Heaven in thousand showers fall on you!"
Rollo, **Act ii. Sc. 3.** (FLETCHER.)

Philippo.   "Appeal to **Reason**:
She will reprieve you from the power of grief
Which rules but in her absence: **hear** me say
A sovereign message from her, which in duty
And **love** to your own safety you ought hear.
Why do you strive so? Whither would you fly?
You cannot wrest yourself away from care:
You may from counsel: you may shift your **place**
But not your person: and another clime
Makes you no other."
                    Love's Pilgrimage, Act v. Sc. 4.   (SHIRLEY.)

Philippo.   "For my sister
I do believe you: and so near blood has made us,
With **the dear love** I ever bore your virtues,
That I will be a brother to your griefs too.
Be comforted 'tis **no** dishonour, sister,
To love nor to love him you do: **he's a gentleman**
Of as sweet hopes as years: as many promises
As there be growing truths and great **ones**.
  Theodosia.   **Oh, sir!"**
                    Love's Pilgrimage, Act. i. Sc. 2.   (FLETCHER.)

Dorothea.   "**Be** nigh me still, then!
In golden **letters** I'll **set** down that day
That gave thee to me. Little did I hope
To meet **such** worlds of comfort in thyself,
This little pretty body: when I coming
Forth of the temple heard my beggar boy,
My sweet-faced godly beggar-boy, crave an alms,
Which with glad hand I gave, with lucky hand!
And **when** I took thee home, my most chaste bosom
The thought was filled **with** no hot wanton fire,
But with a holy flame mounting still higher
On wings **of** cherubims than it did before."
                        Virgin Martyr, Act ii. Sc. 1.   (DEKKER.)

Dorothea.   "Even thy malice serves
To me but as a ladder to mount up
To such a height of happiness, where I shall
Look down with scorn on thee and on the world:
When circled with true pleasures placed above
The reach of death or time 'twill be my glory
To think at what an easy price I bought it.
There's a perpetual spring, perpetual youth:
No joint-benumbing cold or scorching heat.
Famine nor age have any being there.
Forget for shame your Tempe! Bury in
Oblivion your feign'd Hesperian orchards!"
          Virgin Martyr, Act. iv. Sc. 3.   (MASSINGER.)

Charalois.   "And though this country, like a viperous
       mother
Not only hath eat up ungratefully
All means of thee her son, but last thyself,
Leaving thy heir so poor and indigent
He cannot raise thee a poor monument
Such as a flatterer or a usurer hath:
Thy worth in every honest breast builds one,
Making their friendly hearts thy funeral stone."
          Fatal Dowry, Act ii. Sc. 1.   (FIELD.)

Charalois.   "I but attended
Your lordship's pleasure. For the fact as of
The former, I confess it, but with what
Base wrongs I was unwillingly drawn to it,
To my few words there are some other proofs
To witness this for truth. When I was married,
For then I must begin, the slain Novall
Was to my wife in way of our French courtship
A most devoted servant."
          Fatal Dowry, Act v. Sc. 2.   (MASSINGER.)

Simonides.   " By my troth, Sir,
I partly do believe it : conceive, Sir,
You have indirectly answered my question.
I did not doubt the fundamental ground
Of law in general for the most solid :
But this particular law that me concerns,
Now at the present, if that be firm and strong
And powerful, and forcible, and permanent,
I am a young man that has an old father.

       Old Law, Act i. Sc. 1. (ROWLEY.)

Simonides. " **Know then, Cleanthes**, there is none can be
A good son and bad subject ; for if princes
Be called the people's fathers, then the subjects
Are all his sons, and he that flouts the prince
Doth disobey his father : there you're gone.

. . . . .

I say again, this act of thine expresses
A double disobedience ; **as** our princes
Are fathers, so they **are our** sovereigns too,
And he that doth rebel 'gainst sovereignty
Doth commit treason in the height of degree.
And now thou art quite gone."

       Old Law, **Act** v. **Sc. 1.** (MIDDLETON.)

The above passages **have** been taken at random from the authors quoted under **the** following limitations :—

1. For **every pair of** authors that wrote together in the plays considered **in this paper, two** corresponding quotations are given.

2. These **pairs of** quotations are in each instance taken from the *same* **play** and from speeches **of** the *same* personage : **in** order **to** insure more accurate comparison. They are also as near as may **be** of the *same* length.

POSTSCRIPT I.—ON "HENRY VIII."

In order to determine the question of the date of the Shakespeare part of this play, so as to settle the difference between Mr. Spedding and Professor Elze, I have subjected the Shakespeare and Fletcher portions to metrical tests: with the following results:—

	Shakespeare.	Fletcher.
Total number of lines	1146	1467
Number of rhyme lines	6	10
,, ,, short lines	19	27
,, ,, Alexandrines	23	8
,, ,, double endings	380	863
Proportion of double endings to blank verse	1 : 3	1 : 1·7

It is manifest that Mr. Spedding is right, and Professor Elze wrong. The rhyme-test here, as always, is decisive; in the Shakespeare part there are only six rhyme lines, and these rhymes *all three accidental*. The date of the Shakespeare work is thus determined as the very latest—as late, at least, as the *Tempest* and *Winter's Tale*, as Mr. Spedding says. All the other metrical peculiarities agree with this.

It will also be seen in my paper on Beaumont, Fletcher, and Massinger, that Fletcher did not work in conjunction with other authors than Beaumont till 1613. The only exception apparent is *The Two Noble Kinsmen;* but although the Shakespeare part of this play was earlier than 1613 there is no reason to believe that the Fletcher part is. This gives another instance of the consistency obtained in all our theories by careful application of the rhyme-test.

[Is it not a probable conjecture that Shakespeare originally wrote a complete play; that part of the MS. was burnt in the Globe fire of 1613; that Fletcher was employed to re-write this part; that in doing this he used such material as he recollected from his hearing of Shakespeare's play? This would account for the superiority of his work here over that elsewhere.—F. G. F. *Jan.* 1876.]

POSTSCRIPT II.

ON "THE TWO NOBLE KINSMEN."

This play has been already so conclusively shown to be a joint production of Shakespeare and Fletcher, and the portion written by each author has been so accurately assigned, that I should not have thought it necessary to re-open the question, were it not that every instance in which the results of critical examinations based on different grounds can be obtained, is valuable, not only as to the immediate end in view, but also as a test of the worth and power of the methods employed. So in this instance; if the examination as to authorship based on considerations of an æsthetic nature, coincides with that based on metrical criticism, we shall have not only an enormously strong addition to the evidence of Fletcher's share in this work, but also a remarkable example of the value of metrical tests in determining authorship. It is for the latter reason that I now proceed to give the results of metrical examination of this play of *The Two Noble Kinsmen*. I may add that having had to work in a small country village, with no library within reach, and my whole critical apparatus consisting of the Folio reprint, Mrs. Clarke's "Concordance," Dyce's "Beaumont and Fletcher," and Sidney Walker's Notes, my results were obtained quite independently of previous investigators, whose essays I had never seen.

To come to the point, then: In this play there are two prose scenes, Act ii. Sc. 1*a*; Act iv. Sc. 3. Both these belong to the underplot. In my paper on Fletcher I have shown that Fletcher never wrote *prose* in any of his plays. I should therefore assign these to Shakespeare. Mr. Hickson has given strong reasons for the same course, on other considerations.

Looking next to the number of rhymes, we find no aid as to discriminating these authors. Except in the masque, there are only five in the whole play: two in the parts we assign to Shakespeare; three in the Fletcher parts. Not only does this agree with Fletcher's usual practice, but it enables us to say with confidence that Shakespeare's **part of this play was** written as late as 1610 A.D.: as **only** in *The Tempest* and *Winter's Tale* do we find that he had **given up rhymes to anything like such an extent:** even in the Roman plays we find **twenty rhymes in a play.**

From the number of Alexandrines, we obtain no aid whatever. **There are three in** the Shakespeare **parts, six in the** Fletcher.

From the number of lines of one, **two, or three measures,** we also obtain no aid: **there** are forty-one in **the** Shakespeare parts, twenty-seven in the Fletcher. But the **number of** double endings and of incomplete lines of **four** measures, which **are the most** important metrical means **of** distinguishing between **these writers,** will require tabulation *in extenso.*

TABLE (SHAKESPEARE).

Act.	Scene.	No. of Lines.	Double Endings.	Lines of 4 feet.	Proportion of lines with Double Endings.
I.	1.	209	51	—	1 in 4·1
	2.	116	37	—	1 ,, 3·1
	3.	100	37	—	1 ,, 2·7
	4.	49	12	—	1 ,, 4·1
	5.	6	—	—	
III.	1.	122	36	—	1 ,, 3·4
	2.	38	9	—	1 ,, 4·2
V.	1.	173	50	—	1 ,, 3·5
	3.	46	42	—	1 ,, 3·5
	4.	147	47	1	1 ,, 3·1
Total	—	1124	321	1	1 in 3·5

This Table contains all the scenes **assigned** to Shakespeare, except the two prose scenes which are certainly his. I now give a similar Table for **the other parts.**

SHAKESPEARE MANUAL.

TABLE (FLETCHER).

Act.	Scene.	No. of Lines.	Double Endings.	Lines of 4 feet.	Proportion of lines with Double Endings.
II.	1b.	275	158	1	1 in 1·7
	2.	82	38	3	1 ,, 2·2
	3.	33	18	2	1 ,, 1·8
	4.	64	45	1	1 ,, 1·4
	5.	39	23	—	1 ,, 1·7
III.	3.	53	32	—	1 ,, 1·6
	4.	20	11	—	1 ,, 1·9
	5.	107	51	2	1 ,, 2·1
	6.	308	192	3	1 ,, 1·6
IV.	1.	150	61	4	1 ,, 2·5
	2.	156	78	2	1 ,, 2·0
V.	2.	111	64	1	1 ,, 1·7
Total.	—	1398	771	19	1 in 1·8

It will be seen that the metrical **evidence confirms the results** of the higher criticism in the strongest **manner.** The average number of double endings in the Shakespeare **parts is exactly** that of the latter part of his career (4th period, time **of** *Winter's Tale*); the number in the Fletcher part exactly agrees **with** that deduced in my paper on Fletcher from all his undoubted works. In one scene only (Act iv. Sc. 1) does his average fall **as** low **as 2·5;** and in **this scene** there is, I think, some Shakespeare material **(not much) used by him in** the jailer's speeches. Moreover, the imperfect **four-measure lines occur in the** Fletcher parts in the proportion of **15 to 1 in the** Shakespeare **parts.** There is, therefore, **not only** the strongest confirmation of **the conclusions** of the best critics as to this play, **but** also **the** firmest **ground for confidence in our** metrical arguments. In every case **when** examination **careful** enough for **firm** conclusions has been previously **given, our results** are found in agreement with **them;** while, **at the same** time, **we have** in the examination **of metres an instrument far more** powerful, because more exact and more scientific, than **any other** that has ever been brought to bear on subjects of this nature.

CHAPTER IV.

ON "THE TAMING OF THE SHREW.

(Read April 24, 1874.)

THERE is something in the first aspect of this play so different from the generality of Shakespeare's work as to have long since excited suspicion as to its authorship. Mr. Hallam, for instance, quotes, apparently with approval, Mr. Collier's opinion that Shakespeare had nothing to do with any of the scenes in which Katherine and Petruchio are not introduced. In support of this opinion many general considerations may be urged; *e.g.* :—

1. It does not occur in Meres's list; and, as Meres mentions every undoubted play that is at all likely to have been written by Shakespeare before 1598, and even includes *Titus Andronicus*, which has been given up by many critics whose opinions are of importance on these questions, it is very unlikely that he should have omitted this one, and this only.

2. This is the only instance of a play with an Induction, so as to form a play within a play, in all Shakespeare's work; and this Induction is most clumsily managed : there is no provision for getting Sly off the stage. Shakespeare could never have been guilty of this blunder, especially as the old play, *The Taming of a Shrew*, winds up satisfactorily in this respect.

3. There is no other comedy of Shakespeare's, except the *Merry Wives*, in which there is not a Duke or King; and in which all the

characters are taken from the middle classes. The tone of this work is quite *sui generis* in this respect.

4. As Hazlitt remarks: "This is **almost the only one** of Shakespeare's comedies which has a regular **plot and** downright moral." I would rather omit the "almost," and **add** that no work of Shakespeare's is so narrow **in feeling,** so restricted in purpose, so **unpleasing in** general **tone.**

5. This play **was made** a special **object of** ridicule by Fletcher in his *Woman's Prize, or the Tamer Tamed;* the date of this latter play is uncertain, but **it** lies between 1616 and 1621, probably nearer the former date than **the latter.** Now, would Fletcher have chosen for ridicule a work by **his friend,** whom he admired and respected, **and that, too,** within **three or** four years at most **of** his friend's death, **not long** after **he had been** remodelling *Henry VIII.,* and working **with** him **in** *The Two Noble Kinsmen?* But we have much **stronger arguments than** these general **ones**; to which **we** now pass on.

I.—*Argument from* **Metrical** *peculiarities.*

The irregular lines **in this play fall** into **several** well-defined **classes.**

1. **There are** lines deficient **by a whole measure or foot.**

Examples :—

  i. **1,** **51.** I pray **you,** sir, is it **your will.**
  ii. **1, 259.** Go, fool, and whom thou keeps', command.
  ii. **1, 300.** I'll see **thee** hang'd on Sunday first.
  iii. **2, 185.** Hark, **hark,** I hear the minstrels play.
  iii. **2, 233.** My household stuff, my field, my barn.
  iv. **1, 164.** 'Tis burnt, and so is all the meat.
  iv. **4, 46. The** match **is made,** and all is done.
  v. 2, 66. Let's each **one send** unto his wife.

2. There are lines deficient by **a** syllable in some part of the line marked ▲ in the following examples :—

  i. **1,** 14. Vincentio's son **brought** up in Florence ▲
  2. 190. No; say's' me so ▲ friend? What countryman?

i. 2, 251. Sir, let me be so bold as ask ₄ you.
ii. 1, 73. Beccare! you are marvellous ₄ forward.
iii. 2, 168. What said the wench when ₄ he rose again?
iv. 1, 124. Where be these knaves? What no man at ₄ door.
iv. 3, 30. Why, then, the mustard ₄ without the beef.
iv. 3, 62. Lay forth the gown! What news with you, Sir ₄?
iv. 4, 33. No worse than I ₄ upon some agreement.
iv. 4, 34. Me shall you find ready and willing ₄.
iv. 4, 55. Then at my lodging, an it like you ₄.

3. There **are lines in which one syllable** constitutes the first measure.

Examples:—

i. 1. 48. Gentlemen, importune me no farther.
i. 1, 73. Well said, **master! Mum,** and gaze your fill.
i. 1, 74. Gentlemen, **that I may** soon make good.
i. 1, 90. Gentlemen, **content ye!** I'm resolved.
i. 2, 160. O this learning, what a thing it is!
i. 2, 161. O this woodcock, what an ass it is!
i. 2, 198. Will he woo her? Ay, **or I will** (Ile, F.) hang her.
i, 2, 247. What! this gent'man will **out-talk us all.**
ii. 1, 109. **Sirrah,** lead these gent'men **to my daughters.**

If the Globe arrangement be taken, **the line is still worse,** viz.:—

To my daugh'ters and tell **them both.**

ii. 1, 202. **No such jade as** you, if me you mean.
iii. 2, 89. **Come,** where be these gallants? Who's **at home?**
iii. 2, 92. Were it better **I should rush in thus?**

[Lines **130 and 132** have both been plausibly emended. I therefore do **not quote them.**]

iv. 1, 150. Out, you rogue! **You pluck** my foot awry.
iv. 1, 163. What's this? Mutton? **Ay.** Who brought **it?** I.
iv. 2, 120. Go with me to clothe you **as** becomes **you.**
iv. 4, 2. Ay, what else, and but I be deceived.
iv. 4, 71. Come, Sir, we will better it in Pisa.
v. 2, 38. **How** likes Gremio these quick witted folks?

v. 2, 40. Head and butt : a hasty-witted body.
v. 2, 93. Not quoted ; pronounced " wor'se " (*r* vocal).
Ind. 2, 114. Madam wife, they say that I have dream'd.

4. There are lines of six measures, with the first measure monosyllabic.

Examples :—

iv. 1, 153. Where's my spaniel, Troilus ? Sirrha, get you hence !
iv. 2, 4. Sir, to satisfy you in what I have said.
iv. 2, 11. Quick proceeders, marry ! Now tell me, I pray.
iv. 2, 33. Never to marry with her, though she would entreat.
(1st foot 2 syll. but no cæsura.)
i. 2, 194. O Sir, such a life, with such a wife, were strange.

5. The doggerel lines are chiefly of four measures in each line.

Examples :—

i. 1, 68. Hush, máster, hére's some good pástime tóward !
The wench is stark mád or wónderful fróward.
i. 2, 11. Víllain, I sáy, knock mé at the gáte ;
And ráp me wéll, or I'll knóck your knave's páte.
i. 2, 16. Faith, sírrha, an yóu'll not knóck I'll ríng it,
I'll trý how yóu can sól fa and síng it.

The doggerel in *Love's Labour's Lost*, *Comedy of Errors*, &c., has either five or six measures in each line; and lines like these of four measures occur nowhere else in Shakespeare.

6. There are many rhymes of one or two measures in each line introduced in the midst of the dialogue.

Examples :—

i. 1, 79. Put ginger in the eye,
An she knew why.
iii. 1, 83. Nay, by S. Jamy,
I hold you a penny,
A horse and a mon
Is more than one,
And yet not many.

iv. 1, 6. Little pot,
And soon hot.
iv. 4, 101. And so may you, Sir;
And so adieu, Sir!

These peculiarities of metre are enough of themselves to show that the greater part of this play is not Shakespeare's. On the lines that are deficient by a syllable or a measure I do not lay great stress, since similar instances occur, though in much smaller number and in corrupted passages only, in Shakespeare's undoubted plays. But when we find over 20 lines in which the first measure consists of one syllable; and, on looking into the other plays, find that 12 instances at most can be alleged from the whole of them, and that these 12 are in every instance explicable on other principles, then the fact that the metrical scheme of this play differs entirely from the Shakespearian, becomes manifest. In fact, the average of such lines in Shakespeare is (if none of them be corrupt, which is extremely unlikely) less than one in two plays.

The peculiar anapæstic doggerel lines with four measures, and the frequent occurrence of short rhymes in proverbial or quasi-proverbial sayings in the dialogue, confirm the conclusion reached above. Still more does the occurrence of lines of six measures, the first one being monosyllabic: not one instance of such a line can be adduced from the undoubted plays.

The frequent contraction of the word "Gentlemen" into "Gent'-men" in this play is also noticeable; it occurs,

i. 2, 219. Gent'men, God save you! If I may be bold.
ii. 1, 47. I am a gent'man of Verona, Sir.
ii. 1, 328. Faith, gent'men, now I play a merchant's part.
ii. 1, 343. Content you, gent'men: I'll compound this strife.
iii. 1, 185. Gent'men and friends, I thank you for your pains.
i. 2, 247. What! this gent'man will out-talk us all.
ii. 1, 109. Sirrah, lead these gent'men to my daughters!

II.—*Argument from the use of Latin quotations and classical allusions.*

Latin quotations are introduced in *Henry VI.*, *Titus Andronicus*, the first two acts of *Pericles*, the parts of *Timon* which I have shown elsewhere not to be Shakespeare's, and in this play. In the whole 34 of Shakespeare's undoubted plays, only one Latin *quotation* occurs, namely, that in *Love's Labour's Lost*, *Fauste precor*, &c. There are 18 in the spurious plays.

The manner of introducing classical allusions is not Shakespearian.

Compare

i. 1, 173. " I saw sweet beauty in her face,
   Such as the daughter of Agenor had,
   That made great Jove to humble him," &c.

with

M. V., iii. 2, 244. "We are the Jasons, we have won the fleece."

as fair typical instances.

So,

i. 1, 159.   " as secret and as dear
   As Anna to the Queen of Carthage was."

This manner of introducing such comparisons is found in *Henry VI.*, 3rd part, often; but never in Shakespeare's undoubted plays. For example, *Henry VI.*, (3) v. 2, 19 :—

" As Ulysses and stout Diomede,
   With slight and manhood stole to Rhesus tents,
   And brought from thence the fatal Thracian steed,
   So we," &c.

N.B. "Lying'st knave in Christendom," Induction, 2, 25, is taken from 2 *Henry VI.*, ii. 1.

But the most remarkable and conclusive phenomenon has yet to be noticed: all the above peculiarities—the lines with monosyllabic initial measures, the classical allusions, the doggerel rhymes,—all alike disappear in certain portions of the play, notably in the last scenes of the 4th and 5th acts, and in portions of previous scenes, *e.g.* of iv. 3; ii. 1. But these parts of the play are those in which Katherine and Petruchio are on the stage together: they are just the parts which any critical reader would pick out as far superior to the rest; they are, in fact, the very salt of the whole. I feel justified therefore in concluding that the only characters in this play which have Shakespeare's handiwork in them are the two principal ones, Katherine and Petruchio; and that to quote this play in proof or illustration of any peculiarities of Shakespeare's metrical system, or otherwise, is decidedly unsafe. Dr. Abbott, for instance, seems to have formed some erroneous notions of the metrical system of Shakespeare, from relying too much on the doubtful plays, if one may judge by the number of times he quotes them to support his theories.[1] It also follows that the early date assigned to this play, chiefly founded on its inferiority, need not be, and, as I think, is not accurate. In fact, nothing is more dangerous than assigning dates to authors' works by their supposed excellence of execution, or the contrary. Nothing is more safe than a conclusion founded on the *manner* of work, where the author shows development of style in his productions; nothing less sure than inferences from the *matter*, or the relative value of it.

Thus far, then, our work has been destructive; but I feel bound to give a theory (at any rate) plausible as to the composition of the play. Now, first I would notice, that although it is certainly inferior to Shakespeare's comedies of the Second Period, the inferiority does not consist in immaturity, but in comparative want of genius. It is the work of a second-rate author at his best, not of our greatest author in his youth. Any one who reads it without a preconceived notion that it is Shakespeare's, will, I am certain, agree as to this point. Now, remembering how this notion of inferiority being necessarily associated with early date has led critics astray, inducing them to group *Titus Andronicus*, *Pericles*, and *Two Gentlemen of Verona*, as productions of the same period, although three plays more different in style, in handling, and in metre could not be found, I will not say in Shakespeare, but in all the Elizabethan drama; remembering this, let us throw aside all prejudice, and look into the metre of the scenes that I believe are Shakespeare's, especially the last in the play. We shall find that the percentage of double endings in these scenes, the number of rhymes, and the general tone of the rhythm as to cæsura and stopped lines, coincide with

---

[1] Since I wrote the above, my attention has been called to the following words in Dr. Abbott's *Shakespearian Grammar*, Par. 505: "the frequent recurrence of these lines in the *Taming of the Shrew* will not escape notice," recognising the difference between this play and Shakespeare's general style.

the plays at the end of the **Second Period**, with *As You Like It* and *Much Ado about Nothing:* and point to a date of 1602. Now, in the *Taming of the Shrew* there is a line

"**This is the way to kill a wife with kindness,**"

which distinctly refers to Heywood's play of *A Woman Killed with Kindness*, which dates **1602**. I would therefore assign the *Taming of the Shrew* to 1602, and explain its form in some such way as this. It was written by some one[1] on the model of the older play, and generally in a satisfactory manner; but the ending being found unsatisfactory, Shakespeare was desired to furnish some alterations, which he did; but the playwright who interwove these in the drama cut out the ending of the play as it stood, together with the end of the Induction, not noticing that Sly was then left undisposed of; and the ending in Shakespeare's scene was so satisfactory, that it was not found advisable to meddle with it afterwards. This will explain the absence from Meres's list, and all the other phenomena which appear at first so inexplicable. I might adduce other arguments to confirm the above; for instance, the extreme unlikelihood that Fletcher should in 1618, or thereabouts, choose a play to ridicule that had been published at least twenty-five years, if the ordinary theory is correct; or the much stronger argument, that if there is any truth in metrical tests, there is no place whatever in which this play can be introduced into any scheme of development of Shakespeare's metrical system. The number of rhymes would place it at the end of the First Period, after *Midsummer Night's Dream* and *Romeo and Juliet;* but its other metrical peculiarities, as noticed above, would not fit into any part of the plays of any period.

I may add that if this theory be the right one—and I feel rather confident it is—it brings the date of the play just to the time when Shakespeare's mind was busied in re-organizing his *Twelfth Night*, and other works, previously to his turning his attention from Comedy to Tragedy, to which he devoted all his energy up to the last year of his dramatic life.

[1 In my opinion, Thomas Lodge.—F. G. F., Jan. 1876.]

In order finally to impress on the memory the differences of style in the Shakespeare parts of this play and in the other portions, compare the following passages, the most characteristic I can find in the play:—

> " Fie, fie, unknit that threat'ning unkinde brow,
> And dart not scornfull glances from those eies,
> To wound thy Lord, thy King, thy Governour.
> It blots thy beautie as frosts doe bite the mead,
> Confounds thy fame, as whirlewinds shake faire budds,
> And in no sence is meete or amiable.
> A woman mou'd is like a fountaine troubled,
> Muddie, ill-seeming, thicke, bereft of beautie,
> And while it is so, none so dry or thirstie,
> Will daigne to sip, or touch one drop of it."
> Act v. Sc. 1. (SHAKESPEARE.)

> " Tranio, since for the great desire I had
> To see faire Padua, nurserie of Arts,
> I am arriu'd from fruitfull Lombardie,
> The pleasant garden of great Italy,
> And by my father's loue and leaue am arm'd
> With his good will and thy good companie,
> My trustie seruant, well approu'd in all,
> Here let us breath and haply institute
> A course of learning and ingenious studies."
> Act i. Sc. 1. (*Not* SHAKESPEARE.)

> " Oh, monstrous arrogance :
> Thou lyest, thou thred, thou thimble,
> Thou yard, three-quarter, half-yard, quarter, naile,
> Thou Flea, thou Nit, thou winter cricket thou :
> Brau'd in mine owne house with a skeine of thred :
> Away, thou rag, thou quantitie, thou remnant,
> Or I shall so bemete thee with thy yard
> As thou shalt think on prating while thou liu'st."
> Act iv. Sc. 3. (? SHAKESPEARE.)

"*Hor.*   Sir, a word ere you go.
Are you a sutor to the Maid you talke of, yea or no?
  Tra. And if I be, **Sir, is** it any offence?
  Gre. No : if without more words you will **get you hence**.
  Tra. Why, Sir, I pray, are not the streets as **free**
For me as for you?
  Gre.   But so is not she.
  Tra. For what reason, I beseech you?
  Gre.   For this, Sir, if you'll know,
That she's the choise loue of Signior Gremio."
Act i. Sc. 2. (*Not* SHAKESPEARE.)

"**For 'tis the minde that** makes the bodie rich,
And as the sunne breakes through the darkest clouds,
So honor peereth in the meanest habit.
What, **is the Jay** more precious than the **Larke,**
Because his feathers are more beautifull?
Or is the Adder better than the Eele,
Because his painted skin contents the eye?
Oh no, good Kate ; neither art thou the worse
For this poore furniture and meane array."
Act iv. Sc. 3. (*Not* SHAKESPEARE.)

"**Be she as foul as** was Florentius loue,
As old as Sibell, and **as curst** and shrow'd
As Socrates' Zentippe, or a worse ;
She moues **me not,** or not remoues at least
Affections edge **me in.** Were she as rough
As are the swelling Adriaticke seas,
I come to wiue **it** wealthily in Padua.
If wealthily, then happily in Padua."
Act i. Sc. 2. (*Not* SHAKESPEARE.)

"**Such** dutie as the subject owes the **Prince,**
E'en **such a** woman oweth **to** her husband :
And when she is froward, peeuish, sullen, soure,
And not obedient **to** his **honest** will,

> What is she but a foul, unbending Rebell,
> And gracelesse Traitor to her louing Lord?
> I am ashamed that women are so simple
> To offer warre when they should kneele for peace,
> Or seek for rule, supremacie, and sway,
> When they are bound to serue, loue, and obay."
>
>   Act v. Sc. 2. (SHAKESPEARE.)

[P.S. The lists formerly given in this paper of peculiar words were only preliminary to my edition of *Henry VI.;* in which the whole question of "once-used" words will be thoroughly discussed, and the method of using them in discriminating authorship laid down in detail.]

Hereupon follows my division of *The Taming of the Shrew* into Shakespearian and non-Shakespearian portions, with the results of the rhyme-test as applied to each. Nothing more is, I think, needful to confirm Dr. Farmer's theory as to the authorship, and Mr. Collier's as to the date, of this play.

METRICAL TABLE.

SHAKESPEARE.	Total Lines.	Verse Lines.	Rhyme Lines.	Ratio of Rhyme to Verse.
ii. 1, 168—326	156	156	2	78
iii. 2, *a. c.*	233	187	7	27
iv. 1, ...	224	102	6	17
3, ...	198	159	6	26·5
5, ...	78	78	4	19·5
v. 2, 1—175	175	175	10	17·5
Total..........	1064	857	35	24

Second Author.	Total Lines.	Verse Lines.	Rhyme Lines.	Ratio of Rhyme to Verse.
i. 1.	253	227	18	12·6
2.	282	250	51	5
ii. 1. a. c.	413	247	14	17·6
iii. 1.	92	74	12	6·1
2, 129—150 ...	21	21	2	10·5
iv. 2.	120	120	8	15
4.	109	79	6	13·1
v. 1.	155	33	18	1·8
2, 176—189....	14	14	14	1
Total..........	1449	1065	143	7·4

The *Induction* (not Shakespeare's) is rhymeless, evidently with intention, just as the play in *Hamlet* is rhymed : to distinguish the play within the play. The rhyme-ratio of rhyme to verse, 1 to 24 ; that is, of rhyme to blank, 1 to 23; places this play in 1602 : exactly where I anticipated it would come, for other reasons : it comes at the extreme end of the Second Period along with *Twelfth Night* and *As You Like It.* (See my paper on *Twelfth Night*.) The difference of the ratios in the Shakespeare and other parts of the play (7·4 and 24) is so great as to distinctly show the value of the rhyme-test in determining authorship when properly used.

[P.S. Since this paper was written, I have seen reason to enlarge the hypothesis I proposed in it to the following purport :—The original *Taming of a Shrew* was written by Shakespeare and Marlowe in conjunction for L. Pembroke's company ; Shakespeare writing the prose scenes and Marlowe the verse. In 1600 *The Whole Contention, Hamlet, Titus Andronicus,* and *The Taming of a Shrew,* became the property of the Chamberlain's men, all having formerly belonged to Pembroke's. Shakespeare re-wrote his own part of the *Taming of a Shrew,* and Lodge re-wrote Marlowe's ; hence our present play *The Taming of the Shrew.* Shakespeare also re-wrote *Hamlet* (perhaps his own part only at first, Lodge helping him by re-writing Marlowe's for the first Quarto) ; he also touched (slightly) the other plays. All this was done in 1601-2. See my paper on *Henry VI.,* "Macmillan's Magazine," Nov. 1875.— F. G. F., Jan. 1876.]

CHAPTER V.

ON "TIMON OF ATHENS."

PART I. (1874.)

(Read May 8, 1874.)

SYMPSON, Knight, and others have held that this play is not entirely the work of Shakespeare : but they have, so far as I know, all proceeded on the hypothesis that Shakespeare took up an older work of an inferior writer, and founded on it our present play, by retouching, rewriting, and interpolating new scenes. The object of the present paper is to show that the nucleus, the original and only valuable part of the play, is Shakespeare's ; and that it was completed for the stage by a second and inferior hand.

Before going into details as to metre, &c., I will examine the scenes of the play in order : In Act i. Sc. 1, I find nothing that we can reject except the prose parts, l. 186—248, and l. 266—283. The former of these is exactly in the same style as other prose talk with Apemantus, which we shall presently see must be rejected : it is bald, cut up, and utterly unlike the speeches of the same personages in the other parts of the same scene ; and above all, it has nothing to do with the plot, and does not advance the story a step : the latter bit is clearly parenthetical : after Timon has said, "Let us in !" one of *the rest* who entered with Alcibiades says, "Come, shall we in? and taste L. Timon's bountie?" and after a little conversation, he and his friend, another of *the rest*, go in together. So I think Shakespeare arranged it : his alterer

empties the stage of all but Apemantus, who stays in order to
"drop after all discontentedly like himself" in the next scene: but
as there was a bit of Shakespeare to be used up (and we shall see
that he could not afford to lose a line, for reasons to be given
hereafter), the alterer brings in two extra Lords to talk to Apemantus,
so that, after all, Apemantus has no opportunity of leaving the stage
discontentedly like himself. This is too clumsy for Shakespeare,
whether doing his own work, or vamping another man's. The
prose therefore in this scene I reject: the verse, which all hangs
together, I retain: it is Shakespeare's certainly; for instance—

> "All those which were his fellowes but of late,
> Some better than his valew, on the moment
> Follow his strides, his Lobbies fill with tendance,
> Raine Sacrificiall whisperings in his eaer,
> Make Sacred euen his styrrop, and through him
> Drinke the free Ayre."

Act i. Sc. 2, on the other hand, has not a trace of Shakespeare
in it. Ventigius (who is called Ventidius in the Shakespeare part
of the play) offers to repay the 5 talents advanced by Timon, and
tells of the death of his father. This is certainly not known to
the author of the last part of Act ii. Sc. 2, where the information
as to Ventidius's father is given again, but no allusion is made to
Ventidius's offer. Timon quotes hackneyed Latin: the whole
scene is inferior, and leaves the story unadvanced, and it contains
the first mention of Lords Lucius and Lucullus, of whom, with
their worthy colleague Sempronius, there is no notice in the
original part of the play. The steward also, or at any rate some
one who talks very like the steward of the second author's scenes,
is here called Flavius, and here only. But in Act ii. Sc. 2, Flavius
is given by Shakespeare as the name of one of Timon's servants
who is not the steward. As to the poor humour, poorer metre,
and wretched general style of this scene, I need say nothing: it
is manifest on a mere cursory reading, but I give a specimen of
the *poetry*, the best I can find.

> "He commands vs to prowide, and giue great guifts,
> and all out of an empty Coffer:

Nor will he know his Purse, or yeeld me this,
To shew him what a Begger his heart is,
Being of no power to make his wishes good.
His promises flye so beyond his state,
That what he speaks is all in debt; he owis for every word;
He is so kind that he now pays interest for 't,
His Land's put to their Bookes."

However **fine this may be, it is** certainly **not in the** style of Shakespeare, **or of the** preceding scene.

But in Act ii. Sc. 1 we come on the genuine play again :—

"For I do feare,
When every Feather stickes in his own wing,
Lord Timon will be left a naked gull,
Which flashes now a Phœnix."

There is the true ring in this.

Act ii. Sc. 2 is also genuine, except the prose part, l. 46—131, and 195—204. When Timon has demanded an explanation of the steward, and the steward has desired the duns to cease their importunity till after dinner, he adds to them, "Pray you walk neere! I'le speak with you anon;" and straightway gives the explanation desired: but the playwright who improved the drama wanted Apemantus to talk nonsense to the Page and Fool of a harlot (unknown in the rest of the piece): so he makes the steward say, "Pray draw neere!" and go out with Timon, apparently to have out their explanation. Caphis and Co. do not *draw neere*, but stop to talk to Apemantus. When we've had enough of that, in come Timon and the steward, who again says, "Pray you walk neere," which the creditors do this time, and Timon and the steward go on with their talk as if they had never left the stage to say anything outside. This prose part must be accepted or rejected along with the prose in Act i. Sc. 1.

The other smaller bit is also evidently an insertion. Timon is going to try his friends: he calls for Flavius and Servilius, his servants; they come; he says he will despatch them severally: accordingly, he tells one to go to Sempronius the other to Ventidius. But the second author, having already in a previous scene introduced Lords Lucius and Lucullus by name, now adds Sempronius to them, increases the number of servants to three, sends them off to these three Lords, and leaves the messages to the Senators and Ventidius for the steward.

Note also that he sends to each of these friends for 50 talents a piece : but I do not enter on the question of the moneys in this part of my paper. It is sufficient here to mention that the verse part of the scene is pure Shakespeare. No one else could have written it. The "drunken spilth of wine," the "one cloud of Winter showres, These flyes are couch't," the "halfe-caps and cold mouing nods, They froze me into silence," bear the lawful stamp of his mintage.

But next come three short scenes in which we find the *three* servants, Flaminius, Servilius, and Anonymus, applying to Lords Lucius, Lucullus, and Sempronius, in detail; but the most dramatic situation of all, the application of the steward (Flavius, according to this writer) to Ventigius, is not given, only alluded to. In these scenes there is not a spark of Shakespeare's poetry, not a vestige of his style ; and they are inseparably tied up with the prose bit in Act ii. Sc. 2, which we have just rejected. As a specimen of style, take the following, arranged to show the monotony of the pauses :—

> " Why, this is the worlds soule ;
> And iust of the same peece
> Is euery Flatterers sport.
> Who can call him his Friend,
> That dips in the same dish ? "

And in Act iii. Sc. 4, where the creditors again dun Timon, there is no trace of Shakespeare. Timon gets in a vulgar passion ; he bids to a banquet the three apocryphal Lords, Lucius, Lucullus, and Sempronius ; the rest of the scene is taken up with the talk of the creditors' servants, who can rhyme much more easily than the best educated personages in the Shakespeare part of the play, and are thus far poetic, if not dramatic. I need give no specimen of their speeches : they speak the same dialect, and use the same rhetoric, as all the characters of the second author ; any speech of any one might be spoken by any other, so far as the language and form of expression are concerned. It will suffice to give a bit from the **Alcibiades of the** next scene, which is one wholly **by the** vamper :—

> "**Why do fond men** expose themselues to **Battell**
> **And not endure all** threats? **Sleepe vpon 't,**
> **And let the Foes** quietly cut their **Throats**
> **Without** repugnancy? If there be
> **Such** Valour in the bearing, **what make** wee abroad?"

I am **tired of reiterating** that **these** scenes by author the second add nothing to **the progress of the play.**

But I **must notice the difference in the enumeration** of the servants **here and in Act ii. Sc. 2. In the earlier scene** the only ones present **are Caphis and the** servants of Isidore and Varro; in the latter there **are Lucius, Titus,** Hortensis, **Philotus, and Varro's** *two* men **(unnecessary doubling, a sure** sign of inferiority); **and it is expressly stated in the stage direction** that *all* Timon's **creditors are present. This scene cannot have** emanated from the same hand **as the** former; but the former agrees with other portions of **the** Shakespeare part of the play, the latter scene **does not.** Compare, **for** instance, Act ii. Sc. 1. "**To Varro and to Isidore,**" and a little **further on,** "Caphis hoa!" which exhausts **the** Shakespearian list. But to pass on.

In Act iii. **Sc.** 6 Timon's speech **is certainly** Shakespeare's; for example :—

> "This is Timons last.
> **[He] Who** stucke and spangled you with Flatteries,
> **Washes it off, and sprinkles in** your faces
> Your reeking villany."

An inferior **author would not have** thought of the flattery Timon had used to his false friends, **but of** their adulations to **him, and** would have written

> "Spangled *with your* flatteries."

But the rest of the scene is certainly not Shakespeare's. It is a muddle. There seem to be two Lords on the stage at first (taken **from** the two in Act i. Sc. 1), whom Timon calls "gentlemen *both*": the other **Lords who** speak after must be part of his "attendants";

there are senators who don't speak at all. Timon throws warm water at them, which apparently freezes before it reaches them, so that they feel it on their bones, and are pelted with stones, like the guests in the old Timon play, which Shakespeare, I feel sure, never read.

From this point onward I shall notice only the added portions. The Shakespeare parts are not only his, but his of his best style; so distinctively his that any one with ears as good as an ordinary schoolboy's will recognise them at once. In Act iv. Sc. 2 the soliloquy of Flavius, lines 29—50, is not Shakespeare's. It is in the rhythm of the second playwright, and is inseparably connected with Act iv. Sc. 3, l. 463—543, which is certainly an added part. I am ashamed to say that I rejected most carelessly the whole of this scene in my original paper in 1868. My present opinion Mr. Tennyson has confirmed.

The next piece to be omitted is Act iv. Sc. 3, l. 292—362, which is written in the same chopt-up prose as the Apemantus-parts which we have omitted before; it also interferes with the sense. Timon says, "*Gold sleeps here*, and does no *hired harm*; here is the *truest use* for gold." Apemantus answers, "Thou art the cap of all the fools alive." But our cobbling playwright makes him answer, "Where liest o' nights, Timon?" and we are expected by the supporters of Mr. Knight's theory—or other similar theories—to believe that in this, and the many other instances pointed out above, Shakespeare, working up an old play, has left all these gross and clumsy sutures unclosed! But above all, in this bit Apemantus tells Timon—"Yonder comes a poet and a painter." They talk for 60 lines, and then enter—Banditti! more talk with Banditti 63 lines, and then enter—Steward! more talk (80 lines), and then at last enter "poet and painter!" To avoid this, modern editors make the curtain fall when the steward goes out; but this makes matters worse; the poet and painter must be then "coming yonder," not only while that interminable talk goes on, but while the curtain is down: imagine this to be Shakespeare's arrangement! But suppose the curtain does not fall? Then the poet and painter enter as the steward goes out: and one of the first things they tell us is that "'*tis said* he gave unto his steward a mighty sum." No, as the play stands, the curtain must fall in the middle of a scene, and the poet and painter wait yonder all the while. This point alone settles the question of the present arrangement being Shakespeare's.

But cut out the prose parts in these scenes, or this scene rather, and all is right. Omit l. 292—362; l. 398—413; l. 453—543; and Act v. Sc. 1, l. 1—57. In this scene we also omit the talk with the steward, which is æsthetically contrary to the whole drift of the play. Had Timon been convinced that there was one "just and comfortable man," he would have ceased to be *misanthropos*, and would not have concluded his interview with—

"Ne'er see thou man, and let me ne'er see thee."

In style also it agrees with our botcher.

"O you Gods!
Is yon'd despis'd and ruinous man my Lord?
Full of decay and fayling? Oh Monument
And wonder of good deeds euilly bestow'd!
What an alteration of Honor has desp'rate want made?"

This, and the like all through! Enough.

But I must warn the reader in comparing these passages with Shakespeare to take them as they stand in the Folio, before they have been Poped and Theobalded and Walkered, into somewhat of a pseudo-Shakespearian form. The only other bit I would reject is, Act v. Sc. 3, where the Soldier who can't read, reads an Epitaph which is not written, and gives us the most useless and superfluous information of his own afterwards. Thus much then for the division I make of the play between the writers. I spare the reader any comment of mine on the unity of the Shakespeare work so separated; it is printed by itself in The New Shakspere Society's *Transactions*: if he wants to feel the dislocated corduroy road one has to travel over in reading the other writer's work by itself, it is a slight task to mark his work in any edition of the play as generally printed, and read it separately.

But I have only done one part of my work. I have next to show how this curious treatment of a play of Shakespeare's came to be adopted. His share of the play was written undoubtedly about

1606. Delius places it with *Pericles* rightly. The rhyme test places it there also. But I believe that *Timon* differs from other plays in not being finished in Shakespeare's lifetime at all, though I do not advance this as *certain*, but as *probable* only. The play is printed in the Folio next to *Romeo and Juliet*, and is paged 80, 81, 82, and then 81, 82 over again; then 83, &c., to 98; then follow a leaf unpaged, with the actors' names printed on one side, and *Julius Cæsar*. Now the play of *Troylus and Cressida*, which is not mentioned at all in the Index ('Catalogue') of the Folio, is paged 79 and 80 in its 2nd and 3rd pages, and was evidently intended at first to follow in its proper place as the pendant or comparison play to *Romeo and Juliet*. But as this play was originally called "*The History of Troylus and Cressida*" (so in the Quarto Edition), and as there is really nothing tragical in the main bulk of it, it was doubted if it could be put with the Tragedies, so the editors of the Folio compromised the matter by putting it between the Histories and Tragedies, and not putting it at all in the Catalogue, though they still retained their first title for it as "*The Tragedie of Troylus and Cressida.*" This space, then, of pp. 80—108, which would have *just* held the *Troylus and Cressida*, being left unfilled, it became necessary to fill it. But if, as I conjecture, some of the following plays from *Julius Cæsar* to *Cymbeline* were already in type, and had been printed off, there was nothing to fall back on but *Pericles* and the unfinished *Timon*. I have given reasons in my paper on *Pericles* for believing that the editors would not have considered it respectful to Shakespeare's memory to publish the *Pericles;* they therefore took the incomplete *Timon*, put it into a playwright's hands, and told him to make it up to 30 pages. Hence the enormous amount of padding and bombast in his part of the work: hence the printing of prose cut up into short lines as if it were verse, which is a very common characteristic of spurious or otherwise irregular editions: hence the Dumas style of dialogue so frequent in the Apemantus parts: hence the hurry that left uncorrected so many contradictions, and unfilled so many omissions. The hypothesis is bold even to impudence; but it accounts for the phenomena, and no other can I find that will.

Having, then, laid down as certain the division of the play, and the assignment of the nucleus to Shakespeare; and, as probable, the manner in which the play came to be so composed, we come to the more difficult question still—Who was the second author? The ratio of rhyme to blank verse, the irregularities of length (lines with four accents and initial monosyllabic feet), number of double endings, &c., agree with only one play of all that I have analysed (over 200), viz. *The Revenger's Tragedy*. But I am doubtful as to pressing this argument very strongly, unless we give up (as I am quite ready to do) the notion of the play being finished in 1623, as *The Revenger's Tragedy* was written in 1607. The evidence of general style, however, appears to me strongly to confirm the conjecture that Cyril Tourneur was the second author. If we could find out the date of his death, it might help to determine the question as to when his part was written: but, so far as I know, there is no reason whatever why he should not have written it in either 1608 or in 1623.

This bit seems to me exactly in the metre of Shakespeare's recaster:—

"In the morning
When they are up and drest, and their mask on,
Who can perceive this save that eternal eye,
That sees thro' flesh and all. Well, if any thing be damn'd,
It will be twelve o'clock at night, that twelve will never 'scape."
Revenger's Tragedy, p. 322 (Dodsley's edition).

Tourneur quotes Latin too :—

"Curæ leves loquuntur, majores stupent."

He writes in the Dumas dialogue :—

"*Duke.* My teeth are eaten out.
Vind. Had'st any left?
Hip. I think but few.
Vind. Then those that did eat are eaten.
Duke. O my tongue!" &c. (p. 354.)

Sometimes there is a whole page like this.

Here again is a bit in the style of metre we want :—

"'Tis well he died; he was a witch.
And now, my lord, since we are in for ever,

> The work was ours which else might have been slipt,
> And, if **we list**, we could have nobles clipt,
> And **go** for less than beggars : but we hate
> To bleed so cowardly : we have enough,
> I' faith we're well, our mother turn'd, our sister **true,**
> We die after a nest of dukes, adieu." (P. 384.)

But **with less** than extracting **the whole** play, I cannot expect to produce conviction on this point ; and I have already taken as much space as **can** be afforded now. I subjoin the numerical data for **the** metrical examination of *The Revenger's Tragedy* as near as I **can** count them **in** such **a** badly printed edition as we yet have.

Total No. of lines, over 2400.

No. of rhyming lines exactly 460.

double endings　,,　443.

Alexandrines　,,　**22.**

Deficient and short lines **about 125.**

For the data of the metre of *Timon*, and other arguments derived from the sums mentioned (50 talents, &c.), and similar statistical matters, I refer to Part II. of this paper, which contains nothing opposed to my present views except that I have transferred since **three** prose bits from and **one** verse bit to, **Shakespeare.** This Part II. is reprinted as it stood in 1869, for reasons **given** in the note on its first page. The **additional** matter given in **this** Part I. formed **part** of my first essay on the subject, which was remodelled into **the present form of Part II.** at the request **of** Mr. P. A. Daniel **in** 1868.

I **have only to add that** the *essential* part of this paper is **the proof that the** Shakespeare part of this play was written *before* the **other part : the theory how** this came to be done is accessory and **unimportant.** If any one likes to believe as I did in 1869 that the unfinished play of Shakespeare was given to another theatre poet to finish **in** 1607, he is welcome **to his** belief : he avoids some difficulties **and** incurs others. But **that** Knight's theory as held by Delius, &c., is untenable, I hold to be proven : the un-Shakespearian parts were **certainly** the latest **written.**

ON "TIMON OF ATHENS."[1]

PART II. (1869.) [Reprinted *verbatim*.]

(*Read May* 8, 1874.)

THIS question is so intricate, and involves considerations of so many kinds, that I shall, for the purpose of making the argument clear, pursue a somewhat irregular course in its arrangement. I shall first submit to the reader, in a tabular form, the results that I have arrived at after a careful and prolonged investigation of the question. This Table is grounded on an examination of every line of the play, one by one, as regards the metre; on a specific analysis of the plot with regard to the bearing of each scene or portion of a scene on every other; and on a minute examination of the Folio of 1623 with regard to the printing and spelling of proper names, stage directions, &c., which have been altered by modern editors, without authority and on (I think) insufficient grounds. The first portion of the subjoined table shows in parallel columns the parts of the play which I believe to be undoubtedly Shakespeare's, and those which I assign to a second author: the other portion gives a metrical analysis of the lines assigned to each.

It will be observed that I have divided the Scenes into five distinct portions, other than the Act-and-Scene division; and have marked these **A, B, C D, E, F**. This arrangement I believe to be that which Shakespeare intended for his Act-divisions; but, at present, I wish it to be regarded only as a convenient arrangement for purposes of reference in this discussion.

[1] This paper was written in 1868 by Mr. Fleay, and sent in 1869 to Mr. W. G. Clark, of Trinity College, Cambridge, the senior of the joint-editors of the Cambridge *Shakspere*. In his rooms it remained till yesterday, when his friend, Mr. W. Aldis Wright, took it out and posted it to me. It reached me this morning, Wednesday, April 8, 1874, and I post it at once to Mr. Childs, to print for The New Shakspere Society's *Transactions*. This course is taken because Mr. Fleay heard in 1870 that a German critic had published a paper for the German Shakspere Society, in which he took a similar view of *Timon* to that which Mr. Fleay had before taken. The German critic's views may, after all, be very different from those expressed in the present paper; but Mr. Fleay wishes, in any case, to avoid the charge of plagiarism.—F. J. FURNIVALL.

198   SHAKESPEARE MANUAL.

		SHAKESPEARE.				UNKNOWN.	
	Act.	Scene.	Line.		Act.	Scene.	Line.
A	I.	1	1-293	A	I.	2	1-257
B	II.	1	1-35				
		2	1-193	B	II.	2	194-204
			205-242		III.	1	1-66
						2	1-94
						3	1-42
						4	1-119
C	III.	6	1-131	C		5	1-117
D	IV.	1	1-41	D	IV.	2	1-50
E		3	1-291	E		3	292-362
			363-398				
			414-453				399-413
							454-543
	V.	1	50-118		V.	1	1-50
F			119-231				
		2	1-17	F		3	1-10
		4	1-85				

METRICAL TABLE.

	Prose.	Blank.	Irregular.	Rhymes.		Prose.	Blank.	Irregular.	Rhymes.
I. 1	*58	208	25	2	I. 2	64	126	21	36
II. 1		31	2	2	II. 2	11			
2	*85	133	8	6	III. 1	49	11	3	2
III. 6	*111	12	2	6	2	58	30	2	4
IV. 1		33	2	6	3	8	19	9	6
IV. 3		339	28	2	4	18	78	12	8
V. 1		162	14	6	5		73	14	30
2		14	1	2	IV. 2		*36	4	10
4		77	4	4	3	85	53	9	18
					V. 1	46			4
					3		5	1	4
	254	1009	86	36		339	441	75	122

* But see Part I.—F. G. FLEAY.

It will conduce to ease of comprehension, if we begin with the latter divisions; as the difficulties in the end of the play are easier to examine than the early ones. We commence, therefore, with F.

In F, there is only one passage at all doubtful; the rest coheres, is in one style; and that style is certainly Shakespeare's. The doubtful piece is Act v. Sc. 3. The objections are:

F.—1. Lines 3, 4,

"Timon is dead, who hath out-lived his span:
Some beast *read* this! There does not live a man,"

must be—in spite of the alteration of *read* into *rear'd*, as proposed by Warburton—intended for Timon's epitaph. In this case we have a soldier, who "cannot read" (l. 6), first reading, and then taking, in wax, an inscription, which, in Sc. 4, turns out to be quite different.

F.—2. The "Soldier" of this scene is the "Messenger" of Sc. 4. This would be of little importance, but as it is (as we shall see) only one instance of several in this play of a like kind, the cumulative weight of the whole becomes considerable.

F.—3. The last four lines, telling us that Alcibiades ("our captain"), an aged interpreter, young in days, makes the fall of Athens the mark of his ambition, which fact we knew scenes ago, cannot be Shakespeare's.

E.—From Act iv. Sc. 3 to Act v. Sc. 1, l. 118, must be in one scene. There is no possibility of a break in the Acts, unless a very awkward one at "*Exit* Alcibiades" (as arranged by modern editors); for, as the text stands, Apemantus (iv. 3, l. 356) sees the poet and painter coming; and the curtain cannot be allowed to fall without their presenting themselves. In the Folio there is *no* division into Acts or Scenes. I imagine the inordinate length of the scene, and the extreme shortness of Act v., are the *chief* reasons for the modern division. In this division (E) the *omissions* fall into two sections: (1) The *Steward* part. ("Flavius" is an alteration of the editors.) (2) The *prose* portions with Apemantus, Banditti, and Poet and Painter.

(1) I leave till I treat of **D.**   (2) includes :—

iv. 3, l. 292, "where **liest,**" &c.,   to iv. 3, l. 362, "Apemantus."
iv. 3, l. 399, "where should," &c., to **iv. 3,** l. 413, "know him."
iv. 3, l. 454, "Has almost," &c., to iv. 3, l. 463, "true."
v. 1, l. 1, "As I."   to v. 3, l. 50, "the turn."

Now these are by no means to be **objected to** as *prose:* there is plenty of prose in the Shakespeare part **of this play** : though not, I think, **prose** so utterly different in feeling from all **the rest of the scene, as** in this instance. The objections are :

E.—1. iv. 3, 292, &c., is parenthetical. "Where liest o' nights?" is no answer to "here it [gold] sleeps and does no hirèd harm." But "thou art the cap of all the fools alive" fits well.

E.—2. l. 356. A poet and painter are announced as in sight; they do not come in for nearly 200 lines ; but Banditti and Flavius, who apparently are not in sight, come first.

E.—3. Timon's long prose speech, l. 329—349, is utterly unlike any other speech of his **in the** play, and bears strong marks of inferior writing.

E.—4. The Banditti have heard it **"noised"** that Timon has gold : not **from** Apemantus, who has only left the stage one line since ; therefore, from Alcibiades or the women. Apemantus threatens to **spread the** rumour, and does not ; the women do not threaten, and **do spread the** rumour. This is very clumsy.

E.—5. In **v. 1,** which is certainly a continuation of the same scene, **the poet and painter** have not only heard the rumour, but they know exactly all **Timon's** visitors : Alcibiades, the women, the "soldiers," **and the steward who has** just left the stage ; they only know "'tis said," however, **so they** did not see him go. We avoid Scylla, certainly, by allowing the curtain to fall at the end of iv. 3. But Charybdis is then inevitable. The poet and painter must have been coming, *and in sight*, all through Sc. 3, from l. 356 to the end, *and while the curtain is down.*

E.—6. Phrynia and Timandra are called Phry*nice* and Timan*dylo.* This is one among several instances, tending to show that the second author worked on a badly-written MS. of Shakespeare's portion.

E.—7. The whole style of these parts is mean and poor; reading E without them, and then any of these portions, the discrepancy is at once manifest. Note specially the couplets in v. 1, 43—49, which are thoroughly unlike Shakespeare.

Next, take the two Steward bits, **iv. 2,** and iv. 3, 463 to end. I shall **mark the objections to these, D.**

D.—1. The style of these, **and** especially the **metre, is** utterly unlike anything in the other plays of Shakespeare. It is marked by great irregularity, many passages refusing to **be orthodox,** even under torture; it **abounds in rhymes, in** emphatic and **unemphatic** passages alike; the **rhymes are often** preceded by incomplete lines; one of the rhyming **lines is** frequently imperfect or Alexandrine. This style **was introduced by** Webster, and followed by Tourneur, who are the chief **masters therein.** It has some considerable **power in** these authors' **own class of subjects—the** horrible—as in the *Dutchess of Malfy*, or *The Revenger's Tragedy;* but is utterly unsuitable here. Where the Steward enters in the genuine parts, viz. **ii. 2,** and **v. 1,** the style is very different.

D.—2. iv. 3, 476. *Has* for *he has.*
Exactly the same reasoning applies to **C (iii. 5).**

C. D, I reject on internal evidence **of style** and metre; see the Metrical Table, and also the general considerations at the end of this essay.
Our next batch **B (ii. 1—iii. 5)** is the most difficult of all.

B.—1. In the genuine parts of the play,

			£	s.	d.
i. 1, 95	Ventidius borrows 5 talents		1218	15	0
ii. 2, 235-8	Same amount is "instant due"				
i. 1, 141	Lucilius's dowry is 3 talents		722	5	0
ii. 1, 1–3	Timon owes 25,000 (pieces?)		4062	10	0(?)
ii. 2, 208	Proposes to borrow 1000 talents (?)	245,750	0	0
iii. 6, 23	Has asked of a Lord 1000 pieces		162	10	0(?)

In the other parts,

ii. 2, 201	Timon sends to Lords for 50 talents	12,187	10	0
iii. 1, 19	N.B. There 3 sums of this amount.			

iii. 2; **13,** 26, 41. "*So many*" talents are mentioned.

				£	s.	d.
iii.	2,	43	5500 talents (?)	1,340,625	0	0
			or if we read 50,500	121,875	0	0
iii.	4,	28	Due to Varro, 3000 crowns	487	10	0
iii.	4, 29,	96	Due to Lucius, 5000 crowns	812	10	0
iii.	4,	94	Due to Titus, 50 talents	12,187	10	0
iii.	1,	46	Lucullus offers Flaminius 3 solidares.			

The Attic talent is 243*l.* 15*s.* 0*d.*; the largest silver coin in Greece was the tetradrachm (3*s.* 3*d.*); I have taken this for the "crowns" and "pieces." The value of silver (Greek standard coinage) has, of course, much diminished; but 15 talents was reckoned a fair fortune for the elder Demosthenes to leave his son;—the sum of 150 talents, for which Timon sends to the Lords, viz. 36,562*l.* 10*s.* 0*d.*, is, of course, absurd: still more so is the simultaneous application of the creditors for such discrepant sums (iii. 4, 30). Five thousand crowns (800*l.*) is said to be "*much deep*," yet another creditor demands 12,000*l.* If it be said the sums are indefinite, and not Greek money at all, I answer that this may be true for the second writer, but not for Shakespeare; for he clearly drew part of his account from Lucian, who distinctly mentions all the Greek moneys—the drachma, the mina, and the talent.

The "so many" talents of iii. 2, and the "fifty-five hundred" in the same scene, look like the work of a man who had some misgivings as to his previous amount of 50 talents; but was finally too hurried to remember to alter it. Note, in iii. 2, no amount is given.

The thousand talents (more than a quarter of a million sterling) in ii. 2, is in any case absurd. I would read 1000 *pieces*, believing talents to have come in after the second writer had inserted ii. 2, 201, to make the amount demanded of the senators larger than that from a private lord. The senators, however, are mere usurers. Timon owes two of them 9000 in ii. 1, and usury is an accusation brought against them by Alcibiades in iii. 5, 108. Neither does the "joint and corporate voice" mean that they acted as *the senate;* but simply that they were unanimous in refusing Timon's request, viz. of 1000 pieces *each;* as we learn from iii. 6, 23. With this emendation, all in the genuine parts is clear, and the amounts are reasonable; in the other parts we have a mass of inconsistency.

B.—2. The only creditors of Timon in the Shakespeare part of the play, are, Caphis's master, Varro, and Isidore. In the other parts they are Varro, Lucius, Titus, Hortensius, and Philotus.

B.—3. The lords Lucullus, Lucius, and Sempronius occur in i. 2, ii. 2 (rejected part), iii. 1, 2, 3, and 4, but never in the genuine parts. They are not the same as the lords in i. 2 (who seem to be meant for the same as those in i. 1), but I imagine are intended to be three of the lords in iii. 5 (Ventidius being the other), seeing that they and "Ullorxa" (? Ventidius)[1] have been bidden by Timon, iii. 4, 112; and that they, as well as the lords in iii. 6, have been asked for loans. But this is incompatible with the supposition of these parts and iii. 6 being by one writer. He would certainly have given the names in iii. 6 as well as in *all* the other scenes.

B.—4. Ventidius in i. 1, and ii. 2, is spelled Ventidius or Ventiddius; in ii. 1, and iii. 3, Ventigius or Ventidgius. I think this points to the same conclusion as E 6.

B.—5. The servants of the dunning scene, ii. 2, agree with the names of the masters in ii. 1; but not with those of iii. 4. See B 2.

B.—6. Flaminius and Servilius, Timon's servants, occur only in connection with Lucius and Co.; never in the Shakespeare parts, where the servants are all anonymous—just as the senators, lords, or friends are.

B.—7. Great poverty of invention is shown in iii. 2, 38—41, which repeats iii. 1, 16—21.

B.—8. In ii. 2, 20, the writer knows the Greek days for paying debts, the νουμηνια, and surely he would know the Greek money too.

B.—9. In ii. 2, there is a servant called Flavius, who talks very like the steward in iii. 4, iv. 2, and iv. 3, though not so like the steward of ii. 2 and v. 1. He has however been identified with the steward by the modern editors, and perhaps by the second writer; but if so, it must have been an afterthought, as in ii. 2, 194, he

---

[1] [I have since tried to show that Ullorxa is a misprint for "all luxors," Tourneur's favourite expression.—F. G. F., January, 1876.]

is summoned by Timon "Within there! Flavius! Servilius!" The editors, against all metre, but determined to perform the impossible feat of making the play, as it stands, self-consistent, alter Flavius to Flaminius. I feel sure that the third servant in iii. 3, was originally meant to be Flavius. The stage direction in ii. 2, is "Enter 3 Servants." I fancy the original reading was "Within there! Flavius, Servilius, Flaminius!" but after the second writer had altered the Steward into Flavius, he struck out the name in iii. 3, and meant to do so in ii. 2, but, in his hurry, struck out the wrong name. He seems very fond of the number *three*; he has 3 strangers, **3 lords**, twice **3** creditors, &c.

A. I reject i. 2, on the same grounds as iii. 5, iv. **2**, &c. See D 1 also.

A.—1. The hack Latin quotation, "Ira furor brevis est," is not at all in Shakespeare's style. We find similar ones in *Henry VI.*, *Taming of the Shrew*, *Titus Andronicus*; but where in Shakespeare?

A.—2. Ventidius offers to return **the 5** talents lent by Timon (i. 2, 1—8) in consequence **of** coming **into his** inheritance; yet in the end of ii. 2, Timon tells us this latter fact **over** again, without any allusion to Ventidius's offer in i. **2**. This **is** not like Shakespeare's work.

A.—3. Apemantus, sometimes misprinted Aper̄mantus in other scenes, is so all through this one; this again looks as if the MS. of Shakespeare was badly written: it quite deceives the second writer, and occasionally the printer.

I have now given a number of reasons why each of the passages in the second column of our table is not by Shakespeare. Let us next consider some points which affect the whole play.

I. The play is, in its present state, unique among Shakespeare's for its languid, wearisome want of action. This renders it one of the least read of all his works. But this fault is due entirely to the passages which I assign to the second writer, not one of which adds anything to the development of the plot, for they are in every instance mere expansions of facts mentioned in the genuine parts of the play. Thus the germ of—

    i. 2 is in i. 1, 270, &c.,
   of iii. 1—3 ,, ii. 2, 192,
   of iii. 4 ,, ii. 2,
   of iii. 5 ,, iii. 6, 61,

and the added parts of iv. and v. are merely padding to fill out the deficiency in quantity. The Shakespeare part is complete in itself, and never flags at all.

II. The whole of the brief account in Plutarch is contained in the Shakespeare parts; which also have the two allusions to Lucian's dialogue, viz. the beating out the Poet and Painter, and "Plutus the god of gold is his steward," i. 1, 287.

III. The rhythm of the two portions of the play differs in every respect. The Shakespeare parts are in his third style (like *Lear*), with great freedom in the rhythm, some 4 and 6 syllable lines, some Alexandrines with proper cæsuras, and rhymes where the emphasis is great, at the end of scenes, and occasionally of speeches in other places. The other parts have irregularities, both in defect and excess, of every possible kind. There are lines of 8 and 9 syllables, Alexandrines without cæsura, imperfect lines in rhyming couplets, broken lines preceding rhymes, and other peculiarities, not one of all which is admitted in Shakespeare's rhythmical system. i. 2, end, is one of many instances of intolerably bad rhythm :—

> I'll lock thy heaven from thee.
> O that men's ears should be
> To counsel deaf, but not to flattery!

One point in the metre may appear clearer if expressed statistically. In the Shakespeare parts the proportion of blank verse to rhyme is as 280 to 10; in the other parts as 36 to 10; in other words, there are proportionally 8 times as many rhymes in the latter as in the former.

IV. If, as I suppose, the second writer worked on an unfinished play of Shakespeare's, his additions ought to be more or less fragmentary, and Shakespeare's should contain the main plot. If, as some have conjectured, the converse was the case, we ought to have converse results. Now our first column appears to me to contain the complete story, and to have been intended by Shakespeare to be read as follows:—

    I. Act. Timon's prosperity, i. 1 of **present play.**
   II. ,, Debts and Duns, ii. 1 **2, of** present play.
  III. ,, Farewell to Athens, iii. **6, iv. 1**, of present play.
  IV. ,, Cave life, iv. 3 (part), **v. 1 (1—118)**, of present play.
   V. ,, Death and indirect revenge **through** Alcibiades, **v. 1** (119—231); **v. 2; v. 4; of** present play.

In I. I have already pointed out on what portions of the genuine work the other is founded; the fragmentary nature of the spurious work can only be appreciated on continuous reading.

V. **In the** Cambridge edition the following notice is given:—

"*Timon of Athens* was printed for the first **time in** Folio, 1623." It "occupies 21 pages, from 80 to 98 inclusive, 81 and 82 being numbered twice over. After 98 the next page is filled with the actors' names, and **the** following page is blank. The next page, the first of *Julius Cæsar*, is numbered 109, and instead of beginning, as it should, signature ii., the signature is kk. From this it may be inferred that for some reason the printing of *Julius Cæsar* was commenced before that of *Timon* was finished. It may be that the MS. of *Timon* **was** imperfect, **and** that the printing was stayed **till** it could be completed by some playwright, engaged for the purpose. This **would** account for the manifest imperfections at the close of the play. But it is difficult to conceive how **the** printer came **to** miscalculate so widely the space required **to be left.**

"**The** well-known carelessness of the printers of the Folio, in respect of metre, will not suffice to account for the deficiencies of *Timon*. The original play, on which Shakespeare worked, must have been written, for **the** most part, either in prose or in very irregular verse."—CAMBRIDGE EDITORS.

On this I have to observe, that if there is, **in** supposing the printer miscalculated the space to be left, a difficulty on my hypothesis, the difficulty is certainly not lessened by supposing that the whole of the play was in the printer's hands from the first. In no other instance do the printers give a whole leaf to the actors' names; in only one other do they give a *whole* page; and they *never* insert the actors' names at all, except for the purpose of filling a blank space.[1] This looks as if the writer or printer were hard up for material; which is confirmed by the way in which the prose is printed (in the second writer's part only), as irregular verse; so as to fill a third more space than it would otherwise.

I append a List of the Actors for reference :—

IN SHAKESPEARE'S PART.	SECOND WRITER.
[2] Timon.	Lucius.
[2] Apemantus.	Lucullus.
[2] Alcibiades.	Sempronius.
[2] Ventidius.	Flaminius.
[2] Steward.	Flavius.
[3] Poet.	Servilius.
[3] Painter.	3 Strangers.
[3] Thieves.	Titus.
Jeweller.	Hortensius.
Merchant.	**Philotus.**
Athenian.	**Cupid.**
Lucilius.	**Amazons.**
Caphis.	**Soldier.**
Varro's servant.	
Isidore's servant.	
4 Lords.	
[4] Page.	
[4] Fool.	
Phyrnia.	
Timandra.	
Messenger.	

N.B.—The leaf with the actors' names in the Folio is not paged, so as to hide the fact of 10 pages being missed.

---

[1] But see Part I.—F G. FLEAY.
[2] These are common to both Shakespeare and the second writer.
[3] These have been touched up by the second writer.
[4] But see Part I.—F. G. FLEAY.

VI. Finally. On any one who really cares to form a well-grounded opinion as to this question, I would urge this practical test:—Read the parts of the play in our first column by themselves, and the other parts by themselves; and **see** whether the flavour left by them is the same in both cases. I abstain from any comparison of passages here, because any one who really is interested in the matter can easily make them for himself; and, moreover, I know by experience, that **if** I put passages side by side to compare the *rhythm*, some readers will immediately **fancy it is** the relative *excellence* of the quotations which **is in** question. And herein lies one of the greatest hindrances **to the advance of criticism in this** country. People look **at a** handwriting, and say, "*This* is **not Smith's; he** writes better than that." They read **a** play, and say, "This *must* be Shakespeare's, it is so good." The expert **knows that men** write sometimes well and sometimes **badly;** but that in the **handwriting and the** poem, alike, there is a character **or** style which **cannot deceive. In this** case I address myself **to the** expert, and **have no doubt,** whatever, **of** the verdict.

CHAPTER VI.

ON "PERICLES."

(Read May 8, 1874.)

WITH regard to the authorship of this play, we may, I think, take it at once for granted, that the first two Acts are not by Shakespeare. It has been so long admitted by all critics of note that this is the case, that it cannot be worth while to go over the evidence again in detail. In order, however, to extinguish any lingering doubt, I give the metrical evidence; which will, at the same time, show how much more easily and certainly this result would have been arrived at had this method of investigation been earlier adopted. The play consists of verse scenes, prose scenes, and the Gower chorus. Considering at present only the first of these three parts, we shall find so marked a difference between the first two, and last three, Acts, as to render it astonishing that they could ever have been supposed to be the work of one author.

COMPARATIVE TABLE.

	Acts i., ii.	Acts iii., iv., v.
Total No. of lines	835	827
No. of rhyme lines	195	14
No. of double endings	72	106
No. of Alexandrines	5	13
No. of short lines	71	98
No. of rhymes not dialogue	8	16

The differences in the other items are striking, and of themselves conclusive: but the difference of the numbers of rhymes, the proportion being 14 in the one part to 1 in the other, is such as the most careless critic ought to have long since noticed. With regard to this main question, then, there can be no doubt: the three last Acts alone can be Shakespeare's; the other part is by some one of a very different school. But we have minor questions of some interest to settle. The first of these is, Who wrote the scenes in the brothel, Act iv., Sc. 2, 5, 6? I say decidedly, not Shakespeare; for these reasons: These scenes are totally unlike Shakespeare's in feeling on such matters. He would not have indulged in the morbid anatomy of such loathsome characters; he would have covered the ulcerous sores with a film of humour, if it were a necessary part of his moral surgery to treat them at all—and, above all, he would not have married Marina to a man whose acquaintance she had first made in a public brothel, to which *his* motives of resort were not recommendatory, however involuntary *her* sojourn there may have been. A still stronger argument is the omission of any allusion in the after-scenes to these three. In one place, indeed, there seems to be a contradiction of them. The after-account of Marina, which is amply sufficient without the prose scenes for dramatic purposes, is given thus:—

"We haue a *maid* in Metiline
She *with her fellow maides* [is] now upon
The leauie shelter that abutts against
The Island's side."—Act v. Sc. 1.

I cannot reconcile this with

"Proclaim that I can sing, weave, sowe, and dance,
And [I] will undertake all these to teach."—Act iv. Sc. 6.

Nor with

"Pupils lacks she none of nobler race,
Who pour their bounty on her: and her gain
She gives the cursed bawd."—Act v., Gower.

But if these scenes are not Shakespeare's (and repeated examination only strengthens my conviction that they are not), the clumsy Gower chorus is not his either. And this brings us to the only hypothesis that explains all the difficulties of this play. The usual

ON PERICLES.

hypothesis has been that Shakespeare finished a play begun by some one else: that is, that he deliberately chose a story of incest, which, having no tragic horror in it, would have been rejected by Ford or Massinger; and grafted on to this a filthy story, which, being void of humour, would even have been rejected by Fletcher. This arises from the fallacy which I noted in a previous paper, caused by the inveterate habit of beginning criticism from the first pages of a book, instead of from the easiest and most central standpoint. The theory which I propose as certain, is this:—Shakespeare wrote the story of Marina, in the last three acts, minus the prose scenes and the Gower. This gives a perfect artistic and organic whole: and, in my opinion, ought to be printed as such in every edition of Shakespeare: the whole play, as it stands, might be printed in collections for the curious, and there only. But this story was not enough for filling the necessary five acts from which Shakespeare never deviated; he therefore left it unfinished: and used the arrangement of much of the later part in the end of *Winter's Tale*, which should be carefully compared with this play. The unfinished play was put into the hands of another of the "poets" attached to the same theatre, and the greater part of the present play was the result; this poet having used the whole story as given in Gower and elsewhere.

It is somewhat confirmatory of this theory that the play was not admitted into the first Folio; nor published before 1623, except in Quarto, first by Gosson, then by Pavier, whose dealings in *scarcely anything but* surreptitious editions are so conspicuous. It is difficult to understand how such poetry as is contained in the Shakespeare part of this play could have been neglected, had there not been some reason for the editors of the Folio to leave it out of their edition; either some tradition of Shakespeare's disgust at the way in which his work had been completed, or some strong feeling that its publication in their authorized edition would be no credit to its author. One thing is certain, that it was absolutely neglected by Shakespeare himself: no play of his, however carelessly printed, has its text in so wretched a condition; nor has the way in which modern editors have arranged its verse—which is for the most part printed as prose in the old editions—been much more creditable to them than the disarrangement of it was to the older editors.

14—2

In confirmation for the general conclusions arrived at above, I may add a few isolated considerations. In the list of the actors' names, Boult, Bawd, and **Pander** are omitted: now these, and these only, are the additional characters introduced in the brothel scenes in the fourth act. This looks very much as if these scenes had been an after-thought added when the rest of the play had been already arranged. Couple with this the fact that the Gower parts in Acts iv., v., in which these scenes are alluded to, are in lines of five measures, and not of four, as those in the earlier acts are: observe, also, that these scenes, though far from reaching to Shakespeare's excellence, are certainly superior to anything in the first two acts, so far as mere literature is concerned, and it will be almost certain that *three* authors were concerned in this play. The first author wrote the first two acts, and arranged the whole so as to incorporate the Shakespeare part. The second wrote the five-measure Gower parts and the brothel-scenes in Acts iv., v., in order to lengthen out the play to the legitimate five acts. Even as it stands the play is far shorter than any play of Shakespeare's; and it was probably in order to make up for the want of poetic invention that the long dumb-show performances were introduced into the Gower parts. It is scarcely possible to test the prose in the same way as we can the verse in these scenes; but even the little verse we have of the second writer's will, I think, be enough to confirm my theory. Not that the prose in Act iv. is like that in Acts i., ii.; but that the differences are not, by any test I have yet devised, capable of tabulation. I give specimens of the verse, for comparison.

I.—Shakespeare. His first piece in the play:—

"Thou God of this great vast, rebuke these surges,
Which wash both heauen and hell; and thou that hast
Upon the windes commaund, bind them in Brasse,
Hauing [re]call'd them from the deep. O still
Thy deafning, dreadfull thunders: gently quench
Thy nimble sulphirous flashes."—Act iii. Sc. 1.

II.—Author of brothel scenes:—

"Neither of these are so bad as thou art,
Since they do better thee in their command;

ON PERICLES. 213

Thou hold'st a place for which the painedst fiend
In hell would not in reputation change :
Thou art the damnèd doorkeeper to every
Cusherel that comes enquiring for his Tib :
To the cholerick fisting of every rogue
Thy ear is liable : thy food is such
As hath been belcht on by infectious lungs."—Act iv. Sc. 6.

III.—Arranger of whole piece :—

" Yet cease your ire, you angry Stars of heaven,
Wind, Rain, and Thunder : Remember earthly man
Is but a substance that must yield to you :
And I, (as fits my nature,) do obey you.
Alas, the Seas hath cast me on the Rocks,
Washt me from shore to shore, and left my breath
Nothing to think on but ensuing death :
Let it suffice the greatnesse of your powers
To have bereft a Prince of all his fortunes,
And having thrown him from your wat'ry grave,
Here to have death in peace is all he'll crave."—Act ii. Sc. 1.

These three styles are about as different as any can be ; but still further to distinguish the non-Shakespearian writers, let us compare their rhyming-verse.

I.—Writer of brothel scenes :—

" And Pericles, in sorrow all-devourd,
With sighes shot through, and biggest teares o'reshow'r'd,
Leaves Tharsus and again imbarks, he sweares
Never to wash his face nor cut his haires,
He puts on Sackcloth and to Sea he beares,
A tempest which his mortall Vessell teares.
And yet he rides it out. Now take we our way
To the Epitaph for Marina writ by Dionizia,
The fairest, sweetest, and best lies here,
Who withered in her spring of year :
She was of Tyrus the King's Daughter,
On whom foule death hath made this slaughter :

> *Marina* was she call'd, and at her birth
> *Thetis*, being proud, swallow'd some part of **th' earth :**
> **Therefore the earth,** fearing to be o'reflow'd
> Hath *Thetis* birth-childe on the heav'ns bestow'd,
> Wherefore she does & swears she'll never stint,
> Make raging Battry vpon shores of flint."—*Gower*, Act iv.

Before, however, comparing **this** with passages from Acts **i. and ii.,** consider the monstrous theory which all the best critics, except Sidney Walker, have hitherto held.[1] Delius, for instance, **in his preface to** his translation of *Pericles* (in Bodenstedt's edition), **says that "the original** Composer of this Drama, later **on withdrew in** favour of his co-worker Shakespeare—so to say, allowing **himself to be eclipsed."** Imagine Shakespeare in his best period allowing **this stuff to** stand in a play over which he had the full control! It is impossible. Shakespeare certainly never had any management or arrangement **of the play:** he only contributed the Marina story, which I **have** tried to separate and restore **to** him. **Read that by itself :** then turn to any of the other portions, and see **how you like the flavour !** But to return **to** our comparison. **Take from Act** ii., Gower, this bit ; note its affected and obsolete **form,** and see whether **it is** by the same hand as the last-quoted **bit,** which is almost modern **in form** and arrangement :—

> " **By many** a dearne and painfull pearch
> Of Pericles, the carefull search,
> **By the** four opposing Coignes,
> **Which the world** together joynes,
> Is made with all due diligence,
> **That horse** and saile, and high expence,
> Can steed the quest. At last from Tyre,
> Fame answering the **most** strange enquire,
> To th' Court of King Simonides,
> Are Letters brought, **the** tenour these."

---

[1] Walker held **the** theory of three authors, and rightly divided the play; but was certainly wrong in fixing on Dekker as the third man. I did not know this when I wrote the text.

And with the Epitaph compare

The Riddle (Act i. Sc. 1).

" I am no Viper, yet I feed
On mother's flesh which did me breed:
I sought a husband, in which labour
I found that kindnesse in a father.
Hee's father, sonne, and husbande mild,
I Mother, Wife, and yet his child.
How they may be, and yet in two,
As you will live, resolve it you."

Surely, we may conclude that there were three authors. But who were they?

The original manager and supervisor of the whole work was, as Delius says, George Wilkins: he made the play as far as he *wrote* it, from Twine's novel: he calls it " a poore infant of my braine;" he plumes himself on the arrangement of the Gower choruses as his own invention. In this, Delius is undoubtedly right; and to his preface I refer for further information on the matter. In confirmation, however, of this theory, I give an analysis of the metre of the only play of G. Wilkins which we possess— *The Miseries of Inforced Marriage*,—which will be found to coincide very closely with that of Acts i., ii., of *Pericles* given above, and which is more like it than that of any other play among the hundreds I have tabulated. There are in that play 526 rhyming lines, 155 double endings, 15 Alexandrines, 102 short lines, 14 rhyming lines of less than five measures, and a good deal of prose, which, seeing that the play is about three times the length of the first two acts of *Pericles*, gives a marvellously close agreement in percentage.

The second author was, I think, unquestionably W. Rowley. I have not just now access to complete plays of this author in verse, but comparison of the prose with that of *A Match at Midnight*, and of the verse with that of the plays he wrote in conjunction with Fletcher and Massinger, assures me absolutely of the truth of this conjecture. Indeed, if I had complete plays of his in verse here, the quantity of verse in the *Pericles* by Rowley is too small to build a tabulation on. One peculiarity of his work, however, gives us a strong confirmation; it is always detached, and splits off from his conjuncts' with a clean cleavage.

In Fletcher's *Maid of the Mill*, the work of the two men might be published as two separate plays: so it is here. Rowley's scenes are useful for no dramatic purpose, and might be cut out as cleanly as his characters have been from the list of the actors' names.

Since writing the above, I find that, just about the time that *Pericles* was written, GEORGE WILKINS was joined with John Day and W. ROWLEY in writing "*The Travels of the Three English brothers, Sir Thomas, Sir Anthony, and Sir Robert Sherley, an Historicall Play, printed in Quarto*, 1607." This makes assurance doubly sure, that ROWLEY and WILKINS were also joint-writers in the *Pericles*. Moreover, the impudent use of Shakespeare's name in 1653 on the title-page of *The Birth of Merlin*, in conjunction with Rowley's, indicates a tradition that Shakespeare and Rowley had worked on the same piece or pieces at some period. A specimen of Rowley's style is given in my second paper. Here is a bit of Wilkins:—

"That man undid me: he did blossoms blow
Whose fruit proved poison, tho' 'twas good in show:
With him I'll parley and disrobe my thoughts
Of this wild frenzy that becomes me not.
A table, candle, stools, and all things fit!
I know he comes to chide me, and I'll hear him:
With our sad conference we will call up tears,
Teach doctors rules, instruct succeeding years."
Miseries of Inforced Marriage, Act v. Sc. 3.

I have also had an opportunity of examining Wilkins's novel: and although to my surprise I find that Delius has strained Wilkins's expressions to a meaning that I think they will scarcely bear, I am much pleased that the structure of the novel confirms my own conclusions in all respects. It is, I think, quite worth while to give a somewhat full account of it here.

In the first place the story closely coincides with that of the drama, but the novel does not, as Collier says, "very much adopt the language of the play," nor is there the slightest probability of "recovering a lost portion of the language of Shakespeare" from it. Excepting the two passages following, I can find no portions of the play *accurately* reproduced in the novel.

"A gentleman of Tyre, his name Pericles, his education been in arts and arms, who, looking for adventures in the world, was, by the rough and unconstant seas, most unfortunately bereft both of ships and men, and after shipwreck thrown upon that shore." (p. 32.) Compare Act ii. **Sc. 3, l. 81, &c.**

"Poor inch of nature!
Thou art as rudely welcome to the world
As ever princess' babe was,
And hast as chiding a nativity,
As fire, air, earth, **and water** can afford thee." (p. 44.)

Compare **Act** iii. Sc. 1, l. **31, &c.**

Mr. Collier says, "though it would be easy to multiply proofs, I shall pursue this point no farther." He quotes every syllable in favour of his theories, and then insinuates that his quotations are only samples of a large stock kept behind in reserve. So, **in his** endeavour to show that *Edward III.* is *entirely* **written** by Shakespeare, he gives a few quotations without references, all from the small portion (2½ scenes) that Shakespeare did really write in that drama, and then tells us that the whole play is Shakespeare's, that he (Mr. Collier) might "quote the whole Quarto," that "the three last acts are **all** conducted with true Shakespearian energy and vigour," &c. &c. In the same way Mr. Collier quotes from Wilkins, "If, as you say, my lord, you are the governor, let not your authority, which should teach you to rule others, be the means to make you misgovern yourself. If the eminence of your place came unto you by descent, and the royalty of your blood, let not your life prove your birth a bastard: If it were thrown upon you by opinion, make good that opinion was the cause to make you great," **and the next** seven lines which continue in the same style, and **adds,** "If these thoughts and this language be not the thoughts and the language of Shakespeare, I am much mistaken, and I have read him to little purpose." I should be sorry to say Mr. Collier had read Shakespeare **to** little purpose, as he (above most critics) has done for us excellent service; but I reckon this view of Wilkins's novel as one **of** the mistakes he has fallen into.

The fact is, that Wilkins in his novel and in his play (*Miseries of Inforced Marriage*) has many blank-verse lines in the midst of his prose, and not lines only, but passages. I here give some from his novel :—

1. " He did not well so to abuse himself,
    To waste his body there with pining sorrow." (p. 19.)

2. " That this their city, who not two summers younger
    Did so excel in pomp and bore a state
    Whom all her neighbours envied for her greatness." (p. 21.)

3. " Before help came, up came the fish expected,
    But proved indeed to be a rusty armour." (p. 28.)

4. " Begging this armour of the fishermen,
    And telling them, that with it he could show
    The virtue he had learn'd in arms, and tried
    His chivalry for their princess Thaisa." (p. 29.)

5. " Vengeance, with a deadly arrow, drawn
    From forth the quiver of his wrath,
    Prepared by lightning, and shot on by thunder,
    Hit, and struck dead
    These proud incestuous creatures where they sat,
    Leaving their faces blasted, and their bodies
    Such a contemptful object on the earth
    That all
    Those eyes but now with reverence lookt upon them,
    All hands that served them, and all knees adored them,
    Scorn'd now to touch them, loath'd now to look upon them,
    And disdained now to give them burial." (p. 33.)

6. " Ay, traitor,
    That thus disguised art stolen into my court
    With witchcraft of thy actions to bewitch
    The yielding spirit of my tender child.
    Which name of traitor being again redoubled
    Pericles then instead of humbleness
    Seemed not to forget his ancient courage." (p. 38).

ON PERICLES.

7. " Equals to equals, good to good is joined,
    This not being so, the **barrin of your mind**
    In rashness kindled **must** again be quenched
    Or purchase our displeasure." (p. 40.)

8.   "**I have** read of some Egyptians
    Who after four hours' death (**if** man may call it so)
    Have raised impoverisht bodies like to this
    Unto their former health." (p. 48.)

9. " First what **offence** her ignorance **had done**
    (For wittingly she knew she could do **none**)
    Either to **him that** came to murder her
    Or her that **hired him.**" (p. 57.)

10. " Lady, for such your virtues **are, a far**
    More worthy style your **beauty** challenges.
    I hither came with thoughts intemperate,
    Foul and deform'd **the which** your pains
    So well hath lavèd **that they are** now white,
    Continue still to **all so, and for** my part
    Who hither came **but to have paid the** price,
    A piece of gold **for your** virginity,
    Now give you twenty to relieve **your honesty.**
    It shall become you still
    To be even as you are a piece of goodness,
    The best wrought up that ever Nature made,
    And if that any **shall enforce you ill**
    If you but send for me **I am your** friend." (p. 66.)

11. " But sorrows' pipes will burst have they not rest." (p. 71.)

These passages occur in *all* parts of the story, and quotations can be multiplied of them: but these already given would be too numerous, were it not that I wished to show that they not only occur in the parts of the novel corresponding to the Wilkins, Rowley, and Shakespeare parts of the play indiscriminately, but also in passages of pure narrative, as well as in the speeches of the characters. In fact they are inseparable from Wilkins's style, **and** very often his prose is in better iambic rhythm than his verse is. This entirely upsets Mr. Collier's argument on the passage,

> " His blood was yet untainted, but with the heat
> Got by the wrong the king had offered him,
> And that he boldly durst, and did defy himself,
> His subjects, and the proudest danger that
> Either tyranny or treason could inflict upon her."

As to which Mr. Collier says,

" Would the above have got so readily into blank verse if it had not in fact been so originally written, and recited by the actor when *Pericles* was first performed ?"

I should not indeed have thought it necessary to have noticed these views of Mr. Collier's, were it not that both Mommsen and Delius have been misled by them: which is surprising, as both of them have excellent ears for rhythm.

There are, however, other more important points in this Wilkins novel that demand our attention ; for instance, the difference in his treatment of the rhyming documents in the play. The riddle which occurs in the part he wrote himself he quotes in exactly the same form: but the inscription on Thaisa's coffin he alters thus :—

> " If ere it hap this chest be driven
> On any shore or coast or haven,
> I, Pericles, the prince of Tyre
> (That, losing her, lost all desire),
> Intreat you give her burying,
> Since she was daughter to a king,
> This gold I give you as a fee ;
> The gods requite your charity !"

As he has put in his novel the four lines of undoubted Shakespeare quoted above,—"Thou art as rudely welcome," &c.,—he must have had Shakespeare's work before him when he wrote the novel, and this inscription must therefore have been altered to show how much better he could do it himself. I do not think his attempt a success. In like manner he has altered Rowley's epitaph on Marina into

> "The fairest, sweetest, and most best, lies here,
>   Who wither'd in her spring of year.
>   In Nature's garden, though by growth a bud,
>   She was the chiefest flower, she was good."

Had he written this himself originally, he would have done it, as he has all the rhymes in his part that are not dialogue, in octosyllabics.

But his crowning achievement is the song he quotes from Twine, given to Marina, and which Delius—if I understand him rightly—takes to be the same that Shakespeare intends her to sing:—

> "Among the harlots foul I walk,
>   Yet harlot none am I;
> The Rose among the thorns doth grow,
>   And is not hurt thereby:
> The thief that stole me sure I think
>   Is slain before this time;
> A Bawd me bought, yet am I not
>   Defiled by fleshly crime.
> Nothing were pleasanter to me,
>   Than parents mine to know;
> I am the issue of a king,
>   My blood from kings doth flow.
> In time the Heavens may mend my state,
>   And send a better day;
> For sorrow adds unto our griefs,
>   But helps not any way.
> Shew gladness in your countenance,
>   Cast up your cheerful eyes,
> That God remains that once of nought
>   Created earth and skies."

The treatment, then, of these lyrics strongly confirms our conclusion as to the share Wilkins had in writing the play, and so does the exact similarity of the style of his verse-prose to that of the prosaic verse of the drama: that he should have expanded and given more detail in the prose work is only natural; as, for instance, in giving Thaisa's letter to her father in full: there is not, however, the slightest pretext for foisting any of the novel into the play. On the contrary, some of the alterations are essentially undramatic. For example, the following passage, which Delius praises, is very inferior to the treatment in the play (Act ii. Sc. 2, end): "But Cerimon, who best knew that now, with anything to discomfort her, might breed a relapse which would be unrecoverable, intreated her to be cheer'd; for her Lord was well, and that anon when the time was more fitting, and that her decayed spirits were repaired, he would gladly speak with her." Is Thaisa a petulant baby, then, to be coaxed and petted into reason? And again: in Act v. Sc. 1, Pericles, according to Wilkins, **strikes** Marina on the face! His Marina certainly deserves any punishment for her detestable song; but Shakespeare's Pericles is a **gentleman and a** father.

A much more important matter, however, **is**, that when Pericles in the novel, in obedience to Diana, **tells the** story of his life, he gives **all the events that happened** at Antioch and Pentapolis **in full, the riddle and** the tournament, **and all the rest of** it. None of this occurs in the play: Shakespeare **carefully confines Pericles's speech to the** events that concerned his sole subject, the life of Marina. A stronger argument that his work was not founded on Wilkins's **play, but done** previously and independently, one cannot **well have: and in** like manner afterwards in the same **scene in the novel, Thaisa** aludes to Pericles having been her schoolmaster; **Shakespeare has not** this allusion: and finally, the novel ends with Pericles burning **the Bawd, Marina** rewarding the Pander, Pericles rewarding **the fisherman, stoning Cleomenes** and Dion, and succeeding to **the kingdom of** *Antioch*, all of which is foreign to the Shakespeare play. In fact, the shifts that critics who hold the common opinions **as to this play are** reduced **to, are** strong arguments in favour of **my views.** Delius, for instance, is obliged to make such assumptions **as these:**
1. That the abundance of material compelled the author of the play to introduce Gower and the dumb-show business:—the fact being, that the play is an unusually short one, and that there was abundance of space for all that Wilkins wanted to introduce: his poverty of invention was the only drawback to his doing so. 2. That in Act v.

Sc. 3, some of Wilkins's work is retained and patched up by Shake-speare: why, he could have re-written it with half the trouble of cobbling up Wilkins. 3. That in the Epilogue and five-foot Gower part, Shakespeare imitated Wilkins! The author of *Lear* imitated the author of the *Miseries of Inforced Marriage!* It is true he couldn't keep up the imitation, and the real Shakespeare shows in the dialogue. 4. Finally, that the Gower in Act v. is like Prosper's Epilogue: and that Wilkins wrote the parts of *Timon* that are not Shakespeare's. I say nothing in reply to this: I can only admire, and conclude with one little piece of lower criticism, that the author of "she was rather a deserving bed-fellow for a prince, than a play-fellow for so rascally an assembly" (p. 62 in the novel), was probably author also of the first chorus in the play,

"To seek her as a bed-fellow,
In marriage pleasures play-fellow."

CHAPTER VII.

ON "ALL'S WELL THAT ENDS WELL."

WHETHER this be the same play as *Love's Labour's Won* is doubtful: that it has a better title to be considered so than any other extant play of Shakespeare is certain, and has been abundantly shown by others. I confess that I feel little interest in the question, as it cannot from any data at present in our possession be settled satisfactorily. All that we are here concerned with is the demonstrable fact that it contains portions written at a much earlier date than the completed work. At the time of its completion Shakespeare had introduced the free manner of his third period—that of the Tragedies; was using many Alexandrines and short lines; was indulging freely in double endings; and *in the greater part of this play* was comparatively sparing in the use of rhymes. There are however portions of the play which are quite in his earliest style; *i.e.* in the continuous rhyming manner of *Love's Labour's Lost*, and in a few instances we find also *alternate rhymes and even stanzas*. These parts are indubitably of a much less matured time; and indicate that the play is founded on an earlier draft. I now proceed to give a list of these portions.

I.—Act i. Sc. 1, last 14 lines in rhyme, forming a speech of Helen's, perfectly appropriate to her position and feeling at the moment, but in no way connected with or necessitated by the context.

II.—Act i. Sc. 3, l. 134—142; an eight-line stanza, spoken by the Countess; pure youthful poetry, not dramatic; not required in the scene or connected with the context.

III.—Act ii. Sc. 1. l. 132—end; 71 lines in continuous rhyme, quite different in general tone from the rest of the play, but forming an essential part of the action.

IV.—Act. ii. Sc. 3, l. 78—111, **contains 20** lines in rhyme exactly like III., with some prose bits of Lafeu's introduced at a later date in the completed play.

V.—Same scene, l. 131—151, in rhyme; **20 lines exactly of** the same character as the preceding.

VI.—Act iii. Sc. 4. Helen's letter in form of sonnet. This sort of composition does **not** quite die **out** till the **end** of Shakespeare's Second **Period, but it** is very rare in that period and never appears in the Third; I assign this therefore to the early play.

VII.—Act iv. Sc. 3. The same remarks apply to Parolles' letter.

VIII.—Act v. Sc. 3. l. 60—72, a rhyming passage of the same character as III. IV. V. So lines 291—294; 301—304; 314—319; 325—340, indicate by frequent rhymes that they are *débris* **of former play used in** the rebuilding.

To my mind this metrical evidence of itself is conclusive; but if any one doubts let him read the passages tabulated above and notice the total difference of manner and feeling in them from the rest of the play; the way in which the sense is concluded in each couplet, often in each line; the grammatical structure of the sentences; and I think that his poetic feeling will **convince him if** his judgment on the evidence do not.

I need only notice further that, of the above passages, I. II. VI. VII. are clearly poetic bits retained in the complete play for the sake of their *poetic* worth; III. IV. V. VIII., the dramatic bits are almost entirely from the speeches of Helen and the King; whose characters appear to have been more completely conceived in the original play than the minor personages, and to have required less alteration.

There are **no** doubt many **other boulders** from the old strata imbedded in the later deposits, *e.g.* the end of Act iv. Sc. 2, &c. ; but only in a special consideraion of this play would it be possible to trace out every line of this character. Enough has, I hope, been given to show the truth of our main proposition, and I now leave the further prosecution of the question to those who are investigating the problem, What was the original form of *Love's Labour's Won?* or if needful to some future paper of my own.

CHAPTER VIII.

ON "TWELFTH NIGHT."

IN order to examine into the question of the date of *Twelfth Night* it is first necessary to consider the structure of the plot. There are two distinct plots in it, as in *Troylus and Cressida* there are three. In Shakespeare's usual practice, where there are two plots in a play, as in *Lear*, they are, even when derived from distinct sources, so interwoven that it is impossible to disentangle one of them and present it separately. But this is not the case in the two plays mentioned above. Just as the story of Troylus' love is separable from that of Ajax's pride and Achilles' wrath, so is the story of Viola, the Duke and Olivia, separable from that of Malvolio, Sir Toby and Maria. Wherever this is the case, one of three conclusions must be drawn: either the play has been written at two periods (as I think is the case here); or by two authors, which is not the case here; or it is an inferior piece of work, which is also not the case here. The characters that belong to what I consider the early part of the play are, the Duke, Sebastian, Antonio, Viola, Olivia, Curio, Valentine, and the Captain. The part of the play in which they enter is I. i. ii. iv. v. (part); II. i. ii. iv.; III. i. (part), iii. iv. (part); IV. i. (part), iii.; V. i. This can be cut out so as to make a play of itself entirely independent of the other characters, which is the infallible sign of priority of composition.

This part of the play is full of the young, fresh, clear poetry of Shakespeare's early time, the time of *Midsummer Night's Dream*, his first period. The other part is that of the man of the world, the satirist; kindly and good humoured, but still the satirist.

15—2

All this latter part is added by Shakespeare himself; it is from the same mint as Falstaff and his companions, the same as Pistol and Parolles. For the play of *All's Well that Ends Well* in like manner divides into two parts. The part taken from the novel is early, and perhaps contains in it all that remains of *Love's Labour's Won*. The characters of the Countess, Parolles, and the Clown, are Shakespeare's additions, like Sir Toby Belch, Sir Andrew Aguecheek, Fabian, Maria, Feste, and Malvolio; and as I have stated in the examination of that play, they are additions of a later time. In both these plays, too, the early part has been revised; and *All's Well* has been nearly rewritten, so that the old play has been broken up, and only pieces of it can be recognised as boulders embedded in the later strata; in *Twelfth Night*, the stratification has not been disturbed; only the surface has been denuded and scratched a little, and some new material has been deposited here and there.

The first indication I have found of this date is in II. iv.

"Now, *good Cesario*, but that piece of song,
That old and antique song, &c.
Come, but one verse;"

where Viola was evidently intended to be the singer: (compare I. ii. 56:

"Thou shalt present me as a *eunuch* to him:
It may be worth thy pains: *for I can sing
And speak to him in many sorts of music.*)"

This is from the first draft; but in the revised play Curio makes the strange answer (in prose, as all, or nearly all, the latter work is in this drama), "He is not here that should sing it;" and the Duke says, "Who was it?" forgetting the singer he had heard the night before. He afterwards points out the special character of the song (l. 44—48) to Cesario, who had also heard it, and who had just been asked to sing it; all this I think could not have been written at one time.

But external proof as to the date of this play we unfortunately have none, except as to its final completion and production before 1602; and its character in style is not pronounced enough to fix the date of any portion. I feel certain myself that the prose part is of the same time as *As You Like It* and *Much Ado about Nothing*: and that the verse part is a **revision of earlier** work done quite at the beginning of the Second **Period**; but for this I rely rather on the many subtle undefinable links between it and the other plays of that **date** than on **such** broad facts as **we have here room for.** The community of origin with *The Two Gentlemen of Verona* pointed out by Karl Simrock in 1833 is, however, a **strong** ground for presumption, and we shall find that the **metrical** evidence gives important confirmation.

We have next to assign some plausible **theory why just at** this period, 1594-5, **Shakespeare** should have written nothing but unfinished fragments **of plays if my** theory be true, and that too in so many instances: *Troylus and Cressida*, *The Two Gentlemen*, *Twelfth Night*, being all begun **and left** unfinished at this date, just **at the** end of **his First** Period, after **which a great** and important **change takes place in his** style. Exactly the same thing takes **place at the end** of his Third Period, **when he** begins and leaves unfinished the plays of *Pericles* and *Timon*; at **the** end of his Fourth **Period**, **when** he begins and leaves unfinished *The Two Noble Kinsmen* and *Henry VIII*. At the end **of** his Second **Period, it is** true, we have not a like phenomenon, **no** plays having **been begun and left** unfinished at that time; **but on** the other hand, the plays of *Twelfth Night*, *The Taming of the Shrew*, and *All's* **Well that** *Ends Well* were either revised or completed in **1601-2.**

There are periods in all organic growth when secretion is lessened for a time, and all the forces of the organism are busy in assimilation: there **are** also periods when assimilation ceases for a time, and all the forces are occupied in laying up new stores for future development. Such periods **I** hold these dividing epochs in Shakespeare's style to have been. **From his** external life **we are, as it** seems to me, able to connect these epochs with some of those **great joys and sorrows which leave their permanent** marks on **men for good or evil.** Hallam has noticed the **cynical turn of his mind during his** Third Period; others have conjectured **that the plays of the** Fourth **Period** were produced in rest **and** retirement; **and I think** in passing from the First to **the** Second Period **we may see a change** from the dreams of **youth to the** sad realities of the world. **The sorrows of** *Love's Labour's Lost*, *Midsummer Night's Dream*, and *The Comedy of Errors* are unreal, and **excite no** deep feeling in us; even *Romeo and Juliet*[1] and *Richard II.*, **though** they move our pity, **do** so only because in them passion is disappointed or calamity rashly incurred. We are sorry for **the** events, and wish they had been otherwise; but with **the** actors in the dramas we have no deep individual sympathy such **as** we feel at **the very** beginning of the Second Period with the passionate agony of Constance, the Christian resignation of Antonio, or the logical **though** extreme vengeance of Shylock. We have passed from the **youthful land of** dreams, from **the** youthful impulses of passion, **from the** youthful view of history as a spectacle **or** a romance, **to a world in** which men **and women have duties to** perform and tasks to accomplish. Romeo and Juliet are **severed by** remorseless fate, but Portia and Bassanio by **the stern call of duty**; Richard **II.** suffers **for** making a mistake in banishing **Bolingbroke, but** John for his crimes towards his nephew and his **country. Between** these periods come the unfinished plays in which **the first** unfaithfulness in friendship (Proteus), the first infidelity **in** woman **(Cressida)**, the first uncomplaining submission to unknown and therefore unrequited love (Viola), are to be found in Shakespeare's plays. And **just at this period** there **are** in his outward **life** enough of sorrows yet visible to us to account for this. In **1593** Marlowe, with whom he had certainly **been** closely connected, was taken away by death; in 1595 **Hamnet,** his only son, **was** most likely sickening, to die in the early part of the next year. Henceforth his method of work changed, his poetry is mingled with **prose to an** extent previously unknown; the jingle of rhyme is **for the most part** abandoned for the sterner cadence of a rhymeless rhythm; **a change** of style is initiated which ceased not till the end of work came **with** the night in which no man can work. During this anxious time no wonder that he could finish nothing. He could publish the already finished *Lucreece*; but the realities of life would **allow no** completeness to the fevered incoherent creations of the **fancy.** After his son had been taken away from him, then he could **buckle** himself to the work before him, and do **it with** his might. **It may be** that without this sorrow we should have had no Cordelia.

In the same way I connect the ends of his Second and Third

---

[1] But this play I now think is founded on one by George Peele. (Sept. 1875.)

Periods with the deaths of his father and of his youngest brother, Edmund, the actor.

But if I say all that I wish to say on this subject this paper will be interminable. I must come to the metrical tests, and see if they confirm or refute my theory. I much regret that in these early plays we have to depend on the rhyme-test almost alone; the weak-ending test, by which I separated all Massinger's work from Fletcher's, and which I have used for all the Third and Fourth Periods for Shakespeare, is inapplicable to his first two periods, and the cæsura-test is not yet worked out. I have no doubt that nearly all the peculiarities of the secondary dramatists can ultimately be traced to Shakespeare, and their rank may almost be assigned by the peculiarity of metre that each assimilated from his storehouse: that, for instance, Jonson's use of the extra-middle syllable at a pause, Fletcher's double-ending, and Massinger's weak-ending, were all adopted from Shakespeare's later time; while Dekker's, Tourneur's, and Webster's rhymes are all reproductions of his early system though in a comparatively awkward and mistaken manner. Will some one volunteer to count the cæsuras? I have done one man's share of counting.

The part of *Twelfth Night* that contains the Viola story comprehends nearly all the verse part; and as there is none of the Malvolio and Aguecheek part in verse except 17 lines of V. i. 280—323, we may take the rhyme-ratio of the whole play (minus these 17 lines) or 112 : 876—17, or 112 : 859, or 1 : 7·5, as that required for our purpose. But it is impossible in those cases when an author has partly rewritten his early sketch, as is clearly the case in these two plays, to ascertain what part of the early work has been *cancelled*; and therefore we must not press the rhyme-ratio too strictly. This will apply still more to *All's Well that Ends Well*. In *Troylus and Cressida*, on the other hand, the old work was almost untouched, and we can draw more exact conclusions. In the present plays I am quite content to find that the results I arrive at from totally different reasoning are entirely confirmed by the rhyme-test: and on all grounds alike I conclude that the original draft of the story of Viola was made about the date of 1594.

CHAPTER IX.

ON "TROYLUS AND CRESSIDA."

THIS play of *Troylus and Cressida* differs from all others of which I have as yet made special analyses, in having been composed at three distinct periods: begun in 1594-6; continued shortly after; finished about 1606-7. And here I desire again to repeat that I by no means wish my inferences as to any date to be regarded as final until each play has been separately studied: my table is only a first approximation, which will aid in obtaining a second and I hope a truer one. I also wish that any use of exact dates may not be looked on as meant to serve any further purposes than distinctness and brevity: thus, when I say this play was begun in 1594, &c., what I mean is this, that it was begun at the end of Shakespeare's First Period, as I arrange his plays, after *Richard II.* and before *The Merchant of Venice;* that it was continued a year or two later; that it was finished after the great Tragedies and before the Roman plays: but I by no means pretend that any play, or group of plays, may not be slipped up or down in the scale a year or two, provided the relative order be retained.

This being premised, I proceed with the exposition of my theory as to this play. I hold, then, that there are three plots interwoven, each of which is distinct in manner of treatment, and was composed at a different time from the other two. There is first the story of *Troylus and Cressida* which was earliest written, on the basis of Chaucer's poem: next comes the story of the challenge of Hector to Ajax, their combat, and the slaying of Hector by Achilles, on the basis of Caxton's *Three Destructions of Troy:* and finally, the story of Ulysses' stratagem to induce Achilles to return to the battle-field by setting up Ajax as his rival, which was written after the publication of Chapman's *Homer*, from whom Thersites, a chief character in this part, was taken. If this theory be true, the Troylus story ought to split off tolerably clean from the other two, and unless in passages interpolated at the same time as the after-additions were made, not to contain any allusions to them: the second story in like manner should contain no allusions to the third; but it may or may not to the first. Let us examine the play as to its arrangements. The passages containing the Troylus story are :—

Act. Scene. Line.	
I. 1, 1-107.	(Troylus and Pandarus.)
I. 2, 1-321.	(Pandarus and Cressid.)
III. 1, 1-160.	(Pandarus, Paris, and Helen.)
III. 2, all.	(Pandarus, Troylus, and Cressid.)
III. 3, 1-33.	(Calchas, Agamemnon.)
IV. 1, all.	(Æneas, Paris, Diomed.)
IV. 2, all.	(Troylus, Cressid, Pandarus, Æneas.)
IV. 3, all.	(Paris, Troylus.)
IV. 4, 1-141.	(Pandarus, Cressid, Troylus, Diomed.)
IV. 5, 12-53.	(Cressid, Diomed, Grecian Generals.)
*V. 2, ?	(Cressid, Diomed, Troylus, Ulysses.)
V. 3, 97-115	(Troylus, Pandarus.)

In no part of this story is there the slightest overlapping of the other stories, except in the asterised scene where Ulysses enters, and in IV. v. 277-293; V. i. 89-93; V. iv. 20-24; V. v. 1-5; V. vi. 1-11; which bits also involve Ulysses, Diomed, and Troylus.

We shall treat of these presently: but putting them aside for a moment, I would ask any one who wishes to analyse the play to examine this story by itself, and see whether he thinks it written in Shakespeare's best style. I will give the metrical evidence in tables for all three parts at the end of this paper: but, apart from all statistics, is there not something about such a passage as this quite inconsistent with the hitherto usually-received theory of the play

—that it belongs (except a doubtful passage or two at the end) altogether to Shakespeare's **Third or Fourth Period?**

> "**Tell me,** Apollo, for thy Daphne's **love**
> What Cressid is, **what** Pandar, **and what we?**
> Her **bed is** India, **there** she lies a **pearl;**
> Between **our Ilium, and** where she **resides,**
> **Let it be** called **the wild and wandering flood;**
> **Ourself** the merchant; and **this sailing Pandar**
> Our doubtful hope, our convoy, and our bark."—Act i. Sc. 1.

Is it **not** written just in the same **mode as—**

> "**In one little body**
> **Thou counterfeitst a** bark, a sea, a **wind:**
> **For still thy eyes** which I may call the sea
> **Do ebb and flow with** tears; the bark **thy body is**
> **Sailing in this salt flood;** the winds, **thy sighs,**" &c.
> *Romeo and Juliet.* Act iii. Sc. 5?

or the passage in *Richard II.*, Act **v. Sc. 5, which is too** well known to need quoting at length, **beginning,**

> "For now hath Time **made me his numb'ring clock."**

or,

> "**her sunny locks**
> **Hang on her** temples like a golden fleece;
> **Which makes** her seat of Belmont Colchos' strand,
> **And many** Jasons come in quest **of her.**"
> *Merchant of Venice,* Act i. Sc. **2.**

This **is not the** style of **the** later plays; nor **is**

> "**Buried this** sigh **in** wrinkle of a smile."—I. 1, 38;

nor the prose of **Pandarus's** speeches: but **I** need not multiply quotations, the book is in everyone's hands.

For my own part, I **cannot** read this **Troylus** part without being reminded—**in its conceits, its** dirty jokes, **the** peculiar turn of its comparisons, the flow **of its** metre, the **unstayed** youthfulness of **its** ideas, and the **sensuous** passionateness of its love—of the companion play of *Romeo and Juliet.* For whatever may be thought of the other plays of Shakespeare that I would class together as twin productions of his genius, I hold that nothing can be more certain than that the two plays of Friendship which contain the stories of faithful Antonio and faithless Proteus were meant as pendants to each other; and that the two plays of youthful passion, with the stories of "True and Faithful Juliet" and "False and Faithless Cressid," were also meant as pendants. Try the experiment; prepare your ear by reading straight off a couple of Acts of *Romeo and Juliet*, and then read this Troylus story without a word of the other parts of the play, as far as Act iv. Sc. 4, and I confidently await the verdict.

But we must pass on to the second story, that of Hector. This is contained in the following parts:—

Act. Scene. Line.

I. 1, 108-119.   (Æneas and Troylus.)
I. 3, 213-309.   (Æneas and Agamemnon.)
II. 2, all.   (Priam, Hector, Troylus, Paris, Helenus, Cassandra.)
III. 1, 161-172. (Paris, Helen.)
IV. 4, 142-150. (Paris, Æneas.)
IV. 5, 1.11.   (Grecian Generals.)
IV. 5, 54-276.   (Hector, Æneas, Greeks, &c.)
*V. 1, all.   (except Thersites and Patroclus part.)
V. 3, 1-97.   (Hector, Andromache, Cassandra, Priam, Troylus.)
V. 5, 1—end of play—(Troylus's last speech, &c.)
(But Sc. 7, 8, 9, and perhaps Epilogue, probably spurious.)[1]

[1] The spurious part of the last Act is probably *débris* from Dekker and Chettle's *Troylus and Cressida*, written in 1592, and reproduced in a revised form as *Agamemnon* in 1599. If any one doubts that such an amalgamation of plays by different authors could take place let him refer to *The Tragedy of Cæsar and Pompey*, by Chapman, Act ii. Scene 1, which is clearly not a piece of the play, but the remains of an old play of the same title acted in 1594 at the Rose. It alludes to the *Knack to Know a Knave*, published in the same year, 1594, and acted two years earlier. There are other instances of this: I hope the French scene in *Henry V*. between Alice and Katharine is one of them. At any rate, no play should be edited without careful consideration of all evidence obtainable as to other plays on the same subject. The play entered in the Stationers' books in 1602 for publication was probably Shakespeare's, not including the Achilles' story; it could not have been Dekker and Chettle's, as they did not write for the Chamberlain's company. It may have been, however, partly made up from their play in the catastrophe, as the Quarto *Hamlet* was from the early *Hamlet* of 1588-9. Editors have been misled in this matter by not noticing that the 1602 entry was of a play belonging to the Chamberlain's men.

This part of the play, which contains everything connected with the war, with Hector's challenge to Ajax, with his combat with him, with his final encounter with Achilles, and his death, was, in my opinion, added to the early sketch of Troylus' loves (which was not enough to make a five-act play), not long after the writing of the first part.

The style of this second part is more advanced than the first; but not so much so as many of the Second Period plays. It reminds us most of *The Merchant of Venice* or *John*. It also in parts has an echo of Marlowe, just as we might expect, if I am right as to its date of composition. See my edition of *Henry VI.*[1]

For instance:—

"*Is she worth keeping? why she is a pearl
Whose price hath launch'd above a thousand ships
And turn'd crown'd kings to merchants.*
If you'll avouch 'twas wisdom Paris went,
As you must needs, for you all cried 'Go, go:'
If you'll confess he brought some noble prize,
As you must needs, for you all clapt your hands,
And cried 'Inestimable,' why do you now
The issue of your proper wisdoms rate?" &c.—Act ii. Sc. 2.

Compare with the first three of these lines Marlowe, *Faust*—

"*Was this the face that launch'd a thousand ships
And burnt the topless towers of Ilium?*"

I must also notice that, according to Theobald, the Margarelon of Act v. Sc. 5 and Act v. Sc. 7, with the Sagittary of Act v. Sc. 5, are derived from Caxton's *Three Destructions of Troy:* according to Malone, the Knights, Act iv. Sc. 5, l. 158, are from the same source. All these references are from the Hector story: which confirms my opinion that that is an integral and separable part of the play. I have not seen the above-named story-book, nor Lydgate's poem on this subject: had I had an opportunity of doing so, I should probably have had something to add to what I have here stated: as it is, I must be content at present to give the evidence derivable from the materials at my command. I cannot

[1] Unfortunately still in MS. (Sept. 1875).

omit, however, one little confirmation of my theory that lies on
the surface. In Act i. Sc. 2, Hector goes to the field and fighıs.
In Act i. Sc. 3, after this, we find him "grown rusty in the long-
continued truce." Surely these passages were not written at the
same period.

Of course this Hector part will not read as complete in itself as
the Troylus story does, inasmuch as it had to be fitted on to it : it
is, however, wonderfully near completeness, taking all circumstances
into account.

The third story is contained in

Act. Scene. Line.
 I. 3, 1-212.   (Ulysses, Nestor, Agamemnon.)
 I. 3, 310-392.   (Ulysses, Nestor.)
II. 1, all.   (Ajax, Thersites, Achilles, Patroclus.)
II. 3, all.   (Ditto ditto and Greek Generals.)
III. 3, 34-316.   (Ulysses, Achilles, Thersites, Patroclus, &c.)
IV. 5, 277-293.   (Ulysses, Troylus.)
 V. 1, all.   (Thersites and Patroclus.)
 V. 2, all.   (Ditto   ditto.)
 V. 4, all.   (Thersites, &c.)

In this part, and this only, we have the style of Shakespeare's
third-fourth manner in metre ; in word-coining ; in metaphor, in
development of character. I need not dwell on this, it is the
extreme palpability of this fact that has caused all this play to be
usually assigned to the date of 1608, or thereabouts : what has not
been seen is, that these characters do not run through the whole
play, but only this Achilles and Thersites part. I must, however, say
a few words on the alterations Shakespeare must have made, if he
wrote this play in the way I say he did.

It will have been noticed that I asterised some parts of the
Troylus story. This is the reason. These parts are in their present
shape evidently remodelled in the last revision. Ulysses's speeches
are clearly in the latest manner. The scene between Diomed and
Cressida, however, if Troylus, Ulysses, and Thersites are cut out,
falls into regular metre rather more than the scene as it stands does :
and is in the earliest style. I *think* it is part of the first Troylus
sketch : I am sure that Cressida's rhymed soliloquy is. Readers of

Chaucer will remember, that Troylus in his version discovers Cressida's faithlessness by finding a brooch in a cloak he wins from Diomed in battle. I believe that Shakespeare followed Chaucer, as his only authority, in his first sketch, and so did not take Troylus to the Greek tents at all: this scene being given between Diomed and Cressida only to show that Troylus's suspicion from the brooch was a true one. But finding afterwards how easily he could make him *see* instead of *suspect* by sending him with Hector to the Greek tents, he cut out the fighting scene and the brooch, and put in the additions to this scene. So we explain all the difficulty under this head. The other asterised bits are all of the Third Period, put in to match the new version of this scene. There are other little links too minute to note here, which I should point out in editing the play.

But there is one point noticed by the Cambridge Editors that so strongly confirms my theory, that I must give it in full. It will be seen from the tables given above that the Troylus story ends at Act v. Sc. 3, the Hector story at the end of the present play: while the final additions as to Ajax, Ulysses, &c., are all inserted in the previously existing parts, and do not reach to the end; either as we have it now, or as it existed in either of the two earlier stages. Now Shakespeare would not in all probability write even so incomplete a sketch as the Troylus story without contriving an end for it and writing this end. This is the practice of all great writers, as far as we can trace their manner of work: and we find it exemplified in *Twelfth Night*, the only other play of Shakespeare composed in the same way as this one, at two distinct periods: the end there is clearly of the early work. We ought, therefore, to find some trace of the first ending of the Troylus story, if anywhere, at the close of Act v. Sc. 3. Of course Shakespeare may have obliterated it, but if he has not, it can be only looked for where the love story is closed. Now exactly at that point we read in the Folio three lines,

> "*Pan.* Why but hear you?
> *Troy.* Hence, brother lackey, ignomy and shame,
>   Pursue thy life and live aye with thy name;"

which three lines are evidently meant for the original end of the play, as they occur again just before Pandarus's final epilogue. The occurrence of these lines in **both these places cannot be explained by** supposing a second author **for** the last scenes; for Act **v. Sc. 5,** and **Act v.** Sc. 10, which occur *after* the first **insertions of them in Act v. Sc. 3, are** undoubtedly Shakespeare's, although **the piece** from the entrance of "one in sumptuous armour" (Act v. Sc. 6), to the end of Act v. Sc. 9, is of dubious authenticity, and perhaps the Pandar epilogue. I do not, however, discuss this question here. It is of more importance to our present subject to see if the metrical tests will bear **out our** previous conclusions. And before giving statistics, I must observe that the **use of these** tests seems to be misunderstood even by those who **have used** them as supporting their views; or are using them **to obtain conclusions** on disputed points. I lay **down, therefore, some** canons of method relating to them.

I.—**No** conclusion can **be drawn from an** insufficient **number of** instances. This number varies **with the test.** A dozen **instances of** weak-ending in a page of **ordinary 8vo.** would stamp **a play at once as** Massinger's; but to **any conclusion** drawn from **less** than **1,000** lines **as to** number of **rhymes or** double-endings **I should attach** very little value.

II.—**Tables of ratios must not be used without considering** the **positive amounts of the numbers** from which the ratios are calculated: thus, in comparing *The Tempest* with *Winter's Tale*, **the** ratios of **rhymes to blank verse lines come out as 1 : 729 and 1 :** infinity respectively. **This looks like an enormous** difference, but it means only that there **is one rhyming** couplet in *The Tempest* and none in *Winter's Tale*. **No** conclusion could be based on such a ground. Again, in *The Merry Wives of Windsor* the addition of one **rhyme** would alter the proportion from 1 : 22 to 1 : 20, so that if **anyone** unacquainted with Shakespeare's metre were to **count**

> " Fear you not that! Go, get us properties
> And tricking for our fairies,"

as a rhyme, **he would** displace the position **of the play** considerably in the table. **It is** clear that, **in plays chiefly** prose, conclusions cannot be drawn from these tests in cases where the numbers are close together.

III.—Cases where the author adopts a manner or metre quite contrary to his usual custom cannot be determined by them. Thus Fletcher's *Faithful Shepherdess* can no more be compared with his other plays than Beaumont's *Masque* can with his: nor can Ben Jonson's *Masques* or even his *Sad Shepherd* be included in any argument as to his general metrical peculiarities. *Midsummer Night's Dream*, on the other hand, which is *not* different in any respect of handling from Shakespeare's other early plays, cannot be so excepted.

IV.—No conclusion can be drawn from any peculiarity of style that was consciously or deliberately adopted by an author, so far as the chronology of his works is concerned: thus, no result could be gathered from the number of lines with double-endings in Fletcher, as he clearly from the very first *chose this manner* of style. That he chose it is clear from its entire absence in the *Faithful Shepherdess*, although never missing for a moment in the succeeding plays, as far as they are Fletcher's.

On the other hand, this kind of peculiarity is the most valuable for determining authorship. Hence the extreme ease of separating the Fletcher parts of *Henry VIII.* and *The Two Noble Kinsmen:* the Wilkins or Tourneur parts of *Timon*, the Wilkins parts of *Pericles*. Hence also the enormous difficulty of separating the different authors in the three parts of *Henry VI.* That this problem can be solved I hope to show; but I say confidently that, though I believe I have fully solved it, yet any attempt at solution by metrical tests alone, as far as such methods are yet published, must utterly fail. In fact, all the men after Shakespeare clearly adopted deliberately what I may call a metrical *humour:* Fletcher, his double-endings; Massinger, his weak ones, and his full-complement lines; Dekker, his numerous rhymes *scattered* in the dialogue; Middleton, his triple endings, such as—

"As wild and merry as the heart of *innocence*,"

(which must be carefully distinguished from Alexandrines); and so on for the rest. But the earlier men, Marlowe, Greene, Peele, &c., who formed the first blank-verse school, all wrote in the same hard, inflexible monotone, that deterred Shakespeare from at first giving up rhyme, which he dropped only when, and in exact proportion as, his blank-verse became freer, less subject to such arbitrary rules as Puttenham's, and consequently more dramatic. That he did this unconsciously I am certain : for whenever a piece of his old work was good enough in other respects, he never altered it for metrical reasons in his subsequent revises : hence the possibility of such a paper as this present, in which we shall presently see that one can recognise his early work by the glitter of the early rhymes.

This same principle compels us to exclude from calculations for determining the date of Shakespeare's plays all such cases as the inner play in *Hamlet*, the masque in *The Tempest*, the fairy scene in *The Merry Wives* (which is really an inserted play as much as the *Hamlet* one), for in all these the different rhyming treatment was clearly adopted deliberately beforehand, in order to differentiate this part of the work from the rest ; it did not grow up in the author's mind spontaneously, while the actual writing was going on, as an emphatic rhyme in the middle or even at the end of a scene did : it was a preconceived limitation, not an unforeseen development. Similar remarks apply to Pistol's iambics, which are an essential part of his original conception.

V.—The test chosen must be suited to the special author or special case treated of. Thus the weak-ending test is infallible for separating Fletcher's work from Massinger's. It is only of use in Shakespeare for the later periods of his plays. The *number* of rhymes will separate Dekker from late Shakespeare ; but the *manner* of their introduction would have to be noted in separating Dekker from early Shakespeare. To use rhymes as a test in any of Ben Jonson's work would be a waste of labour, while his triple endings, the one characteristic which distinguishes him from all dramatists but Middleton, should be carefully worked out in any question concerning his metre.

VI.—Metrical tests should, unless in special cases, not be used in the initiatory stages of investigation. The chemist will understand me at once when I say they are to be used as *characteristic* and not as *class* tests. All questions as to authorship, date, &c., should be approximately determined **on other** grounds, and then the metrical test should be applied to **each** portion to see if **the** separation **of** unlike **parts is** complete. Thus in dividing *The **Witch** of Edmonton* **amongst its three authors, I** first examined the plots and separated the scenes belonging to each; then I **looked to the** treatment **of** character, the style, and what are called the æsthetic tests : I found these agree with the former division; then applied **my** metrical tests to each portion, and found my conclusions in all respects confirmed and finally approved. **But** in dividing *The **Maid in the** Mill* between Fletcher and Rowley, after separating the **plots, I** found **the** metrical **tests distinctly** contradicting the division for **the first Act :** I had **to try back, and make a** new hypothesis of change **of work between the contributors, and** then all agreed with the metrical tests—and **the work was done.** So, again, in Shakespeare, I put forth **in the** year 1874 **a** chronological table of Shakespeare's plays. This **was** founded **on such** knowledge as I then had of other evidences as confirmed by my **test of** proportion of rhymes in verse scenes to number of blank-verse lines **; since** that time I have **seen** occasion, as this chapter shows, to **change the** place of *Troylus and Cressida* by assigning it to three periods **instead of two.** **This division** is not *based* on **metrical** grounds : I **only** use the metre to confirm my conclusions **;** but if the metre were to *contradict* my conclusions drawn from other **grounds,** I should throw up the whole theory **and try** again. So I **have found** occasion to transfer the place of *Cymbeline* from before *Lear, Hamlet,* and *Othello,* to after them **; and to** leave a much greater margin for **the date of** *Macbeth :* but **in** neither case do the **metrical tests** contradict these changes, for the proportions for the **first-named plays** are so close, **1 : 30,** and **1 : 31, that I cannot** attach **importance to** them, and **the place** of *Macbeth* **must** stand undetermined by **me** till we come to the chapter **on that** subject.

These tests are infallible when used with due precaution, but **useless** otherwise. The **chemist will** understand me **again** when I say that disturbing elements **must** be eliminated before characteristic tests are applied **; and that specific** results are **not** to be expected from tests not characteristic. **I may** some **day** make a tabular scheme **of** my tests drawn up **in** the same **form as** chemical tables for the laboratory, as a guide for future inquirers in these matters.

VII.—Tests must be applied **singly**, but interpreted jointly. Descriptions of *all* peculiarities of any author **or any work**, given together, are comparatively **useless. The dividing tests** must first be carefully determined for each case, and used **one at** a time. If they give the same results, then the characteristic tests should **be** applied one by one till all have been tried; and if any one **fails**, the whole analysis must be repeated **on** a different arrangement. **In fact**, whatever **is true of** chemical testing is true *mutatis mutandis* **in this** kind of testing also.

VIII.—Mathematical deductions from **the doctrine of** chances and inferences from **one set of numerical results to another are** most valuable, **and to** be applied whenever possible. For instance, Dr. Abbott's deduction from **Mr.** Simpson's numerical statement, that **2,700** words in Shakespeare occur **in two** plays each and in no others —to the effect that four words **only are to be** expected as peculiar to any given pair of plays—is most valuable **as** well as ingenious. I found it of the greatest use **in dividing** *Henry VI*.

IX.—The accuracy of **our** present **texts must be** considered. Some of **Fletcher's plays are in** such a mutilated **and incorrect state that it is impossible** to determine how many **Alexandrines, &c.,** are **in them.** A great part of *The Scornful Lady*, **printed as prose** even in Mr. **Dyce's edition,** is distinctly verse. Much Shakespeare verse in *Pericles* is printed **as prose in the early editions.** It is clear that **any tabulations, or** deductions of numerical character in such cases **as these, depend** entirely **for their value, in the** first place, on the **editor's arrangement** of the text. Thus, any *exact* critical conclusions from stopped lines or weak-endings derived from the received **text in** *Pericles*, I assert *meo periculo* to be worthless.

X.—We must adopt **every scientific method from other sciences** applicable to our **ends.** From the mineralogist we must learn by long study **to recognise a chip of rock at once from its general** appearance; **from the chemist, to apply** systematic tabulated tests to confirm our **conclusions;** from **both, to** use varied tests—tests as to form, as for crystals,—tests **as to material, as for** compounds; from the botanist we must learn to classify, **not in an** empirical way, **but** by essential characters arranged in due subordination; finally, from the biologist we must learn to take into account, not only the state of any writer's mind at some one epoch, but to trace its organic growth from beginning to end of his period of work: remembering that we have often only fossils, and even fragments of fossils, to work from, when our object is to restore the whole living animal. When these things are done systematically and thoroughly, then, and then only, may we expect to have a criticism that shall be free from shallow notions taken up to please individual eccentricities: a criticism that shall differ from what now too often goes under that name, as much as the notions on the determining causes of the relations between wages and capital differ in the mind of a Stuart Mill and that of a Trades-Union delegate.

METRICAL TABLE.[1]

(1) Troylus Story.	(2) Hector Story.	(3) Ajax Story.	
72	58	16	Rhyme lines.
607	798	873	Verse lines.
1 : 8·4	1 : 13·6	1 : 54·5	Ratio.

If, then, our rhyme-test is true,

(1) was written between first and second periods, nearer the first than the second;

(2) between first and second periods, nearer the second than the first;

(3) between third and fourth periods, nearer the fourth than the third.[2]

But these are exactly our conclusions from æsthetic and other grounds. The rhyme-test gives reliable results as usual when used as a characteristic test.

[1] This division in no way contradicts that published by me in *The Academy*. It only carries the analysis a step further. I first separated the Troylus story; this separation I published in that paper. I now separate the Hector story. The arguments that prove one prove the other.

[2] No, nearer the third than the fourth. See Professor Ingram's excellent paper (Sept. 1875).

CHAPTER X.

ON "MACBETH."

WERE it not that I have the high authority of the Cambridge editors to countenance me in my main theory of this play, I should almost fear to produce it : the popular idea that this is not only one of the most powerful, but also one of the most perfect works of Shakespeare, must necessarily raise so strong a prejudice in the minds of my readers against so bold a hypothesis as I shall have to lay before them, that it will be in most cases difficult even to obtain a hearing, much more a candid consideration of it. And if difficult, as I know by several years' experience it is, to get a hearing for their hypothesis as they present it, it will be far more so when pushed to the greater extent that appears to me inevitable. The general statement is this : *Macbeth* in its present state is an altered copy of the original drama, and the alterations were made by Middleton. I commence by a condensed statement of the arguments of Messrs Clark and Wright.

1. The stage directions in **III. v.** 33, *Sing within, Come away, Come away, &c.;* and IV. i. 43, *Musicke and a Song, Black Spirits, &c.*, refer to two songs given in full in Middleton's *Witch*.

2. The *Witch* and *Macbeth* have points of resemblance. (*a*) As Hecate says of Sebastian, "I know he loves me not," so Hecate says of Macbeth, "He loves for his own ends, not for you." (*b*) In the *Witch*, "For the maid-servants and the girls o' th' house, I spiced them lately with a drowsy posset :" in *Macbeth*, "I have drugged

their possets." (c) In the *Witch*, Hec., "Come, my sweet sisters, let the air strike our tune:" in *Macbeth*, "I'll charm the air to give a sound." (d) In the *Witch*, "The innocence of sleep:" in *Macbeth*, "The innocent sleep." (e) In the *Witch*, "There's no such thing:" in *Macbeth* the same words. (f) In the *Witch*, "I'll rip thee down from neck to navel:" in *Macbeth*, "He unseamed him from the nave to the chaps." And, they add, there are other passages.

3. The witches in the two plays are strongly alike, though Hecate in one is a spirit,[1] and in the other an old woman.

4. There are parts of *Macbeth* not in Shakespeare's manner: namely—

(a) I. ii. **Slovenly in** metre, bombastic; l. **52, 53,** not consistent with I. iii. **72, 73, 112,** &c. Shakespeare **would** not send a severely wounded **soldier with** news of victory.

I. iii. **1—37.** Not in **Shakespeare's style.**

II. i. 61. "Words **to the heat of deeds too cold breath gives."** Too feeble for Shakespeare.

II. iii. Porter's part. **"Low, written for the mob** by another hand."—Coleridge.[1]

III. v. Not in Shakespeare's manner.

IV. i. **1—38.** Masterly, but doubtful: falls **off in l.** 39—47.

III. v. 13. "**Loves** for his own ends." But Macbeth hates them: calls them "secret, black, and midnight hags."

III. v. **125—152. Cannot be Shakespeare's.**

IV. iii. **140—159.** Interpolation: probably before a Court-representation.

V. ii. Doubtful.

V. v. 47—50. Weak tag: unskilful **imitation.**

V. viii. 32. "Before **my body I** throw my war-like shield." Interpolation.

[1] I do not agree with this.

V. viii. last 40 lines.   Two hands clearly.   Double-stage direction.   "Fiend-like queen" dispels the pity excited for Lady Macbeth:[1] "by self and violent hands" raises the veil dropped over her fate with Shakespeare's fine tact.

III. ii. 54, 55.   Interpolation.
Play probably interpolated after Shakespeare's withdrawal from theatre [not earlier than 1613].

Their opinion as to I. i. is doubtful. They also decline giving opinion as to date of the *Witch*.

The above is, I hope, a fair abstract of their views : what I shall try to do is to carry them out still farther, and to support them with new arguments.

[Here followed in the first issue of this chapter a discussion on the Porter's speech in Act ii. Sc. 3.   As this rough and incorrect draft was never intended for publication, I have withdrawn it. There was in it one blunder which even now I wish to set right.

The singular words "everlasting bonfire" have been misunderstood by the commentators. A bonfire at that date is invariably given in the Latin Dictionaries as equivalent to *pyra* or *rogus;* it was the fire for consuming the human body after death : and the hell-fire differed from the earth-fire only in being everlasting. This use of a word so remarkably descriptive in a double meaning (for it also meant *feu de joie:* see Cotgrave) is intensely Shakespearian.[2]   I do not however say that this speech is *unaltered* Shakespeare : I only leave out all discussion of it as not bearing on my main argument, and coming into unnecessary collision with opinions worthy of great respect even if one differs from them.][3]

Taking, then, for granted that one of the two plays, the *Witch* and *Macbeth*, was copied from the other in certain parts, it is important to consider if there is any evidence which was the earlier. Some external evidence that we have favours the view that the *Witch* was. Middleton says in his dedication, "Witches are *ipso facto* by the law condemned : and that only, I think, hath made her lie so

---

[1] I do not agree with this.
[2] Compare also *All's Well that Ends Well*, iv. 5, "They'll be for the flowery way that leads to the broad gate and the great fire."
[3] This passage between brackets was inserted in September 1874.

long in an imprisoned obscurity." It seems from this at first sight as if the play had been written long before the dedication, and the dedication had been written soon after—(in King James the First's first year, 1603)—the laws against witches had been confirmed. But the words will bear another interpretation, and we cannot build on this. Malone gave up this opinion in favour of the other, that *Macbeth* was the earlier: nor do I see how the coincidences of expression pointed out by Clark and Wright are to be explained otherwise, as several of these occur in parts undoubtedly Shakespeare's: and he would not imitate Middleton. In this view the Cambridge editors coincide. This point being, then, probably determined, the question arises, Could Middleton have altered this play after 1613, and yet have written the *Witch* after that? Certainly; for he continued writing till 1624; and there is good reason to believe that all his plays written for the King's company date between 1615 and 1624.

I next pass to the consideration of the nature of these witches. In Holinshed we find that "Macbeth and Banquo were met by iij women in straunge and ferly apparell resembling creatures of an elder world:" that they vanished: that at first by Macbeth and Banquo "they were reputed but some vayne fantasticall illusion," but afterwards the common opinion was that they were "eyther the weird sisters that is *ye Goddesses of destinie*, or else some Nimphes or Feiries endewed with knowledge of prophesie by their Nicromanticall science." (Act ii. Sc. 2.) But in the part corresponding to IV. i. Macbeth is warned by "certain wysardes" to take heed of Macduff: but he does not kill him, because "a certain witch whom he had in great trust" had given him the two other equivocal predictions. Now it is to me incredible that Shakespeare, who in the parts of the play not rejected by the Cambridge editors never uses the word, or alludes to witches in any way, should have degraded "ye Goddesses of destinie" to three old women, who are *called* by Paddock and Grimalkin (their incubi or familiars), sail in sieves, kill swine, serve Hecate, and deal in all the common charms, illusions, and incantations of vulgar witches. The three who "look not like the inhabitants o' th' Earth and yet are on't;" they who "can look into the seeds of Time and say which grain will grow;" they who "seem corporal," but "melt into the air" like "bubbles of the Earth:"

the "weyward sisters" who "make themselves air" and have "more than mortal knowledge" are not beings of this stamp. Were it for this reason only, Act I. Sc. i, Sc. iii l. 1—37, and III. v. (in which the servants of Hecate are identified with the three beings who meet Macbeth in I. ii.) must be rejected. Shakespeare may have raised the wizard and witches of the latter parts of Holinshed into the weird sisters of the former parts; but the converse process is impossible. I shall recur to this, but want first to dispose of Hecate. The Hecate of III. v. and IV. i. occurs nowhere else in Shakespeare. Even in this play the "pale Hecate" whose "offerings witchcraft celebrates," the "black Hecate who summons the beetle to ring night's yawning peal," is the classical Hecate, the mistress of the lower world, arbiter of departed souls, patroness of magic, the threefold dreadful Goddess: so she is in *Midsummer Night's Dream*, in *Lear*, in *Hamlet*. "Triple Hecate's team," "The mysteries of Hecate and the night," "with Hecate's ban thrice blasted," are the phrases we meet with there: in this play she is a common witch, as in Middleton's play (not a spirit, as the Cambridge editors say); the chief witch: who sails in the air indeed; all witches do that: but a witch; rightly described in the stage direction: *Enter Hecate and the other three witches*.

I must here in parenthesis ask how the usual theory can be made consistent with this stage direction? The three *witches* are already on the stage; the *other three* must mean the weird sisters who appear in I. iii. to Macbeth in the Shakespeare part of the play, and are identified with the Middleton witches in I. iii. 32. They are quite distinct from the Shakespeare witches of IV. i. The attempts made to evade the evidence of this stage direction as being a blunder should be supported by instances of similar blunders: instances where characters already on the stage are described as entering: omissions of such directions are easy to understand: their insertion without cause is unexplained, and I think inexplicable. Then this un-Shakespearian Hecate does not use Shakespearian language: there is not a line in her part that is not in Middleton's worst style: her metre is a jumble of tens and eights (iambic, not trochaic like Shakespeare's short lines) like some of the Gower choruses in *Pericles*, a sure sign of inferior work; and what is of most importance, she is not of the least use in the play in any way: the only effect she produces is, that the three fate-goddesses who in the introduction of the play were already brought **down to** ordinary witches, **are** lowered still further to **witches of an inferior** grade **with a mistress who "contrives their charms"** and is jealous if any "trafficking" goes on in which she does **not** bear **her part.** She and her songs, and the speech in IV. i. 125—132, which is certainly hers, although all the editors assign it to *First Witch*, **are all alike not** only **of the earth earthy, but of the mud muddy. They are the sediment of** Middleton's puddle, not **the** sparkling foam of the living waters of Shakespeare.

Thus far, then, my results coincide with the Cambridge editors': **I reject I. i. and I. iii.** 1—37; III. v. and IV. i. **39—44.** But now **we must face** the real difficulty. What are the witches of **IV. i.?** are they the "weird sisters," fairies, nymphs, or goddesses? or **are** they ordinary witches or wizards, as we should expect from the narrative in Holinshed, **and** entirely distinct **from** the three mysterious beings in I. iii.? I hold the latter view. In order to support it, it will be necessary to show that they are not weird sisters in the higher sense : **to** give a hypothesis as to how they got confused with them : **to try** to present some **idea of** Shakespeare's intentions regarding **them.** Now Act IV. Sc. i. 1—47 is **admitted by all** critics to be greatly superior to the corresponding passage in I. iii. 1—37. Clark **and** Wright hold it to be Shakespeare, except **the Hecate** bit. I **agree with them ;** but then I cannot identify these witches with the **Nornæ of I. iii.** 38—80. The witches in Act IV. are just like **Middleton's** witches, only superior in quality. They are clearly **the originals from** whom his imitations were taken. Their charms **are of the sort** popularly believed in. Their powers are to untie the winds, **lodge** corn, create storms, raise spirits, but of themselves they have not **the** prophetic knowledge of the weird sisters, the all-knowers **of Past,** Present, Future ; they must get their knowledge from their *masters*, or call them up to communicate it themselves. **Nor do** they call themselves weird sisters, although the three in I. iii. **(early** rejected part) do so ; their knowledge is from the pricking of **their** thumbs ; they are submissive to the *great King* who calls them *filthy hags*, *secret, black, and midnight hags;* the oracles their masters are ambiguous, delusive : those of the weird sisters were pithy, inevitable ; the witches are of the middle ages, a growth of the popular superstitions; the Nornæ are of the old Aryan mythology, and worthy of their parentage. But however strongly I may feel this difference between the supernatural beings of I. iii. (latter part) and IV. i.;—and I think that anyone who can read these two scenes divested of old associations and prejudice will agree with me; —however sure I may feel that Shakespeare could not have given up the "destiny goddesses" of his authority for this play so as to lower them to the wizards and witches of Macbeth's later time, there is a great stumbling-block in our way. In III. iv. 133, and IV. i. 136, Macbeth calls the witches of IV. i. "the weird sisters." It is true that he has called them *filthy hags*, that he describes them as *riding on the air*, that he is surprised that Lennox did not see them pass by him, that they may have[1] left the stage in the ordinary way, while Macbeth was in a reverie: that he never alludes to them afterwards as he so often does to the real "weird sisters," but only mentions "the spirits" or "the fiend." All this is true; but if my theory be true also, those two passages must be explained. This is a real difficulty, and I cannot satisfactorily solve it at present. III. iv. 133 I *think* is an insertion of Middleton's, and in IV. i. 136 the original reading may have been, *Saw you the sister witches?* or something like this: but I don't think the text has here been tampered with: I can only conjecture that Shakespeare made a slip, or intended Macbeth, who was thinking of the original prophecy, to make one. I do not think the difficulty weighty enough to support the common view *of itself*, but I admit its importance.

I next pass to a matter of an entirely different nature. The Cambridge editors have pointed out some instances of rhyming tags so weak in this play that they cannot admit them as Shakespeare's work. I desire to add to the number of such exceptionable rhymes. For instance, I. iv. 48—53. Macbeth has "humbly taken his leave," and been dismissed by the king. While going out he soliloquizes thus:—

> " The Prince of Cumberland! That is a step
> On which I must fall down, or else o'er-leap:
> *For in my way it lies.* Stars, hide your fires!
> Let not light see my black and deep desires:

[1] I feel certain on this point. The stage direction, *vanish with* HECATE, is Middleton's.

> The eye wink at **the hand**: yet let that **be**
> Which the eye **fears**, when it is done, **to see**."

During this, Banquo has been praising him to Duncan in words not reported to **us**. Then Duncan goes on, "True, worthy Banquo," &c. This is not like Shakespeare: **but is just such** an attempt **at** being like Shakespe*re as I should expect Middleton to write. **Note** specially the weakness of the italicized **words**, and of the **next line**. The play has evidently been cut down at this point.

In II. iii. end :

> "there's warrant **in that theft**
> Which steals itself, when there's **no mercy left**."

This **is too weak and** thin for Shakespeare to emphasize, and the ending of II. **iv. is worse** :

> "Ross.   **Well**, I will thither.
> Macd.   **Well**, may you **see** things *well* done there! Adieu!
>   Lest our old robes sit easier than **our new**.
> Ross.   Farewell, father.
> Old M. God's benison go **with** you, and with those
>   That would make good of bad, and friends of foes."

Delete both couplets, which **are** bad, especially the last.

IV. i. end :

> "No boasting like **a fool**;
> This deed I'll do before this purpose cool,"

is wretched. See how the passage reads without it :

> "give to the edge of the sword
> His wife, his babes, and all unfortunate souls
> That trace him in his line. But no more sights!
> Where are these gentlemen ?"

In V. i. end :

> "*Doctor*.   **So**, good-night :
>   My mind she **has** mated, and *amazed my sight*.
>   I think, but dare **not** speak."

Omit second **line** of couplet.

In V. ii. the invitation "to pour in our country's purge as many drops of us as are needed to dew the sovereign flower and kill the weeds" is unlike Shakespeare.

V. iii. end, after Macbeth's emphatic declaration:

" I will not be afraid of death and bane,
Till Birnam forest come to Dunsinane,"

the Doctor's washy sentiment,

" Were I from Dunsinane away and clear,
Profit again should hardly draw me here,"

is surely out of place. Why should our sympathy with Macbeth be interrupted by the Doctor's private sentiments?

V. iv, end:

"The time approaches,
That will with due decision make us know
What we shall say we have, and what we owe:
Thoughts speculative their unsure hopes relate;
But certain issue strokes must arbitrate."

cannot surely be Shakespeare's.

V. vi. end:

" *Make* all our trumpets *speak; give* them all *breath*,
Those *clamorous* harbingers of blood and death."

This tautology cannot be Shakespeare's; besides, the whole sentiment is too weak for the situation.

In a few of these I may have missed some inner æsthetic meaning which is too deep for my comprehension; but the number of them is far too great for me to be wrong in all. I conclude therefore that Middleton altered the endings of many scenes by inserting rhyming tags: whether he cut anything out remains to be seen.

The next point I notice is, that the account of young Siward's death and the unnatural patriotism of his father, which is derived from Holinshed's history of England, and not of Scotland like the rest of the play, is a bit of padding put in by Shakespeare after finishing the whole tragedy; this shows great haste in its composition: to my mind the story is not nearly so well told as in Henry of Huntingdon, and spoils the *dénouement*, which would be decidedly better if the first whom Macbeth combated turned out to be the fated warrior not born of woman. But this leads us to a much larger and more important point: the number of characters in this play who only appear for a scene or two and then are heard of no more. In the 27 scenes (20 in Folio, 28 in modern editions) there are only 8 in which new characters are not introduced; a phenomenon unexampled in all the dramas I have read. Some of these—Fleance, Donalbain, Macduff's wife, the Scotch Doctor— are real aids to the story; but others are not as it now stands. For example:—

The severely-wounded captain in I. ii., who mangles his metre so painfully, I surrender at once to the Cambridge editors as Middleton's. In all probability, however, this scene replaces one of Shakespeare's; one of whose lines, at least,

"The multiplying villanies of nature,"

seems to be still left in it as it now stands. In this scene Ross comes in afterwards, and is sent to Macbeth to greet him with his new title; he says, "*I'*ll see it done." Lennox also is present, not Angus. Ross and Angus take the message to Macbeth in I. iii. where Angus speaks 10 lines, and then disappears till V. ii.; he there has 7 lines to repeat; so that he has 17 in all. He is not of the slightest use in the play. Lennox could have done his work better in I. iii. on account of his after connection with Macbeth: V. ii. is not wanted at all. I think, therefore, that Middleton has cut down Angus's part in the original play by omitting scenes in which he appeared.

This shows that the play has been greatly abridged for acting purposes.

Hecate we have already discussed.

The Cambridge editors have pointed out the double stage-direction, *Exeunt fighting;* and *Enter fighting, Macbeth dead*. (Compare the double-ending of *Troylus and Cressida*.)

We have yet to consider III. iv. 130—to end. The metre of

"And betimes I will to the weird sisters;"

the poverty of thought in

"For mine own good
All causes shall give way: I am in blood
Stept in so far, that, should I wade no more,
Returning were as tedious as go o'er:
Strange things I have in head that will to hand,
Which must be acted ere they will be scann'd;"

the putting this long tag in Macbeth's mouth when he is so bewildered that he answers Lady Macbeth's—

"You lack the season of all natures, sleep"—

by

"Come, we'll to sleep,"

are all marks of inferior work, and make me sure that this part has been worked over by Middleton.

There is a passage in IV. i. that has been worked over in a similar way. After the speech of the third apparition Macbeth says,

"That will never be.
Who can impress the forest, bid the tree
Unfix his earth-bound root? Sweet bodements, good!
Rebellious dead, rise never till the wood
Of Birnam rise, and *our* high-placed Macbeth
Shall live the lease of nature, pay his breath
To time and mortal custom."

"Our high-placed Macbeth" cannot be said by Macbeth himself: it must be part of a speech of a witch. "Sweet bodements!" looks also like Middleton, and the whole bit is, in my opinion, a fragment of *Hecate's* inserted by him. "Rebellious dead" seems to me an allusion to Banquo's ghost, misplaced by Middleton. If we read "Rebellion's head" it seems a mistaken interpretation of the armed-head apparition: in any case, it is not Shakespeare. And I have no doubt a minute examination may detect still more traces of Middleton; but in an essay of this kind more detail would be wearisome.

Enough is given for my purpose to make it likely that Middleton was a recaster of the play, not a joint author.

Before giving my theory as to this play, and the metrical confirmations of it, I had better perhaps add a Table of the parts I do believe to be Shakespeare's.

SHAKESPEARE.	MIDDLETON.[1]
	I. i. (Witches).
I. ii. (altered)	
	iii. 1—37. (Witches).
iii. 38—146.	
iv.	* rhyme-tag.
v.	
vi.	
vii.	
II. i.	rhyme-tag.
ii.	
iii.	* rhyme-tag.
iv.	* rhyme-tag.
III. i.	
ii.	rhyme-tag.
iii.	
iv.	bit at end.
	III. v. (Hecate).
vi.	
IV. i.	Hecate and *6-line bit and *tag.
ii.	
iii.	140—158 (touching for evil).
V. i.	* one line.
ii. (altered)	rhyme-tag.
iii.	* rhyme-tag.
iv.	* rhyme-tag.
v.	rhyme-tag.
vi.	* rhyme-tag.
vii.	* rhyme-tag. —(l. 12 & 13).
viii. (altered)	

[1] The part assigned by me to Middleton, but not by the Cambridge editors, is not 30 lines in all; I have asterised it in the table.—F. G. F.

This is an instance in **which** such editions as I have given in the *Transactions* of the New Shakspere Society of *Marina* (*Pericles*) and *Timon* would be worthless. Middleton certainly did **not** confine himself to adding to Shakespeare's work: he also re-modelled, re-wrote, and made large excisions. We ought to have an edition of this play in two types: the presumed alterations, and additions of Middleton's being in a smaller type than the rest, so that the better and more important portion might be read by itself.

I now give my theory as to the composition of the play. It was written by Shakespeare during his Third period: I think after *Hamlet* and *Lear* (see Malone); so **that its date** was probably 1606. Metrical evidence is of no use in determining the date: as we cannot tell how Middleton altered the play, or *how much he omitted*, except that the weak-ending **test is** not opposed to Malone's date. At some time after this, Middleton revised and abridged it: I agree with the Cambridge editors in saying not earlier than 1613. **There is a decisive** argument that **he did** so after he wrote the ***Witch*, namely,** that he borrows the songs from the latter play, **and repeats himself** a good deal. It is to me very likely that he should repeat himself in *Macbeth*, and somewhat improve on his original conception, as he has done **in** the corresponding passages: and yet be unable to do a couple **of** new songs, or to avoid the monotony of introducing Hecate in both plays (Hecate being a witch in both, re**member**). I can quite understand a third-rate man, who in all his **work** shows reminiscences of others, and repetitions of Shakespeare, being unable to vary such conceptions as he had formed on the subject. I believe that Middleton, having found the groundlings more taken with the witches, and the cauldron, and the visions in **IV. i.** than **with** the grander art displayed in the Fate goddesses of **I. iii.**, determined **to** amalgamate **these, and** to give us plenty of them. Hence the **witches** call themselves weird sisters in the lyric part of I. iii.: hence **the** speech of Macbeth, "I will to-morrow to the weird sisters," &c. I believe also the extra fighting **in the last scenes was inserted** for the same reason. But finding that the magic and **the** singing **and the fighting made** the play too long—for a play of that kind **cannot be endured to the** length **of an** ordinary tragedy **of Shakespeare's—he** cut out large portions of the psychological Shakespeare **work, in** which, as far as quantity is concerned, this play is very deficient compared with the **three other masterpieces of** world-poetry, and left **us the torso we now have.** That the taste of the mob is of the nature **I** assign to it, is evident enough from **the** way **this play** is put on the stage now. I am not play-goer enough to say **how** often it has **been** represented in my time without still further additions from Middleton's lyrics and Locke's music, but I think it cannot be very **often.** To hide the excisions, Middleton **put** on tags at the places where he made the scenes end : and to my thinking, **if any** one will compare the endings of the **scenes** where Shakespeare has left them without tags with those **where I have** tried to **show** that Middleton put them in, **he** will find that **there is a** great difference in the completeness **of the scenes.** Or try another experiment : cut off **the tags** from the scenes where **Shakespeare put them and** those where Middleton put them ; **a** similarly decisive result will **be felt.** **It is** impossible to show this **in a** paper : **if** I were doing an edition **of the play** with the opportunity **of summing up** the æsthetic of each scene at the end of it as I went **on, I** am certain I could make it manifest : not to mention many smaller details I cannot stay to **discuss here,** such as the **stage** direction in IV. i. **about** Banquo's **carrying the** glass. But I must stay to protest **against** the modern way **of altering and** inserting stage directions *ad libitum ;* it has thrown back **our** criticism **twenty** years. I could not myself stir in this matter till I obtained reprints of Folio and Quartos, which **I could not for many** years, for reasons I need not dwell **on here.** **I do not think we** should do well in issuing mere reprints only, **but no** alteration even in popular editions should be made without being marked by brackets **or** italics, **or** some warning that there is an alteration : unless in correction of mere printers' errors, **or in** arranging the lines, **or** in punctuation.

We now come to the metrical evidence. **From the nature of the** interpolations in the rhymes, **&c., our usual tests are not** attainable. Fortunately there are others **that are.** I give first, then,

TABLE OF SHAKESPEARE'S PLAYS ARRANGED ACCORDING TO THEIR LENGTH.

Anthony and Cleopatra,	3964	Winter's Tale,	2758
Hamlet,	3924	(Henry VIII.,	2754
Richard III.,	3599	(Two Noble Kinsmen,	2734
Cymbeline,	3448	Merchant of Venice,	2705
2 Henry IV.,	3437	1 Henry VI.,	2693
Troylus and Cressida,	3423	Twelfth Night,	2684
Coriolanus,	3392	Taming of Shrew,	2671
Othello,	3324	Richard II.,	2644
Henry V.,	3320	King John,	2553
Lear,	3298	Titus Andronicus,	2525
1 Henry IV.,	3170	*Julius Cæsar,	2440
2 Henry VI.,	3032	*Pericles,	2386
Merry Wives,	3018	*Timon,	2358
Romeo and Juliet,	3002	Mid. Night's Dream,	2217
All's Well, &c.,	2981	*Tempest,	2068
As You Like It,	2904	Two Gent. of Verona,	2060
3 Henry VI.,	2904	*Macbeth,	1993
Much Ado, &c.,	2823	Comedy of Errors,	1770
Measure for Measure,	2809	Average,	2857·5
Love's Labour's Lost,	2789	Average to the dark line,	3000

From this table we see that all the last eight plays fall into two classes. One class consists of three early plays which were produced before Shakespeare had learnt his work as a playwright, however much he excelled already as a poet. The other is composed of five plays, four of which were finished or altered by some other poet, as I have myself tried to show, and Mr. Staunton has satisfactorily accounted for the fifth (*The Tempest*). It cannot be accident that five plays[1] thus altered should fall among the eight shortest of the total series of 38.

The chance of such an event is 1 in 8962¼ : there must be a cause. One possible cause is assignable. We know from comparing the Quartos and Folio of *Lear*, *Hamlet*, *Othello*, *Richard III.*, &c., that

[1] The two plays finished by Fletcher do not fall under this category. They are of Fletcher's average length.

the acting plays were often shorter than the written ones : we know also that many of Shakespeare's plays as we have them could not well be performed in the customary *two hours* (see Prologues to *Henry VIII.*, and *Romeo and Juliet*) : we know also that in modern times his plays are invariably shortened for representation. What then more likely than that *Macbeth* and *Julius Cæsar* should have been shortened on account of their prolixity, and that the alterer should have overshot his mark? This is, however, merely conjecture : whatever the cause, the fact remains the same : the guess is merely offered till a better be proposed or further evidence obtained.

Next I give

TABLE OF RHYME-TAGS IN SHAKESPEARE.

	No. Scenes in play.	No. Scenes with tags.	No. tag rhymes.
Love's Labour's Lost,	9	4	8
Mids. Night's Dream, (cannot be calculated : whole scenes rhyme).			
Comedy of Errors,	11	9	19
Romeo and Juliet,	24	12	29
Richard II.,	19	13	28
Two Gent. of Verona, *a*.	10	4	7
,, ,, *b*.	10	1	1
Troylus and Cressida,	24	15	27
Twelfth Night,	18	12	26
Richard III.,	25	11	13
Merchant of Venice,	20	13	19
John,	16	11	14
1 Henry IV.,	19	9	12
2 Henry IV.,	19	8	12
Henry V.,	23	13	14
Much Ado,	17	3	13
Merry Wives,	23	3	3
As You Like It,	22	8	16
Taming of Shrew,	12	8	16
All's Well,	23	14	22
Measure for Measure,	17	7	10
Hamlet,	20	14	15
Othello,	15	7	8

	No. Scenes in play.	No. Scenes with tags.	No. tag rhymes
Lear,	26	9	13
Macbeth,	28	21	33
Cymbeline,	27	11	16
Pericles, a.	9	8	8
,, b.	11	4	4
Timon, a.	7	6	6
,, b.	10	8	12
Coriolanus,	29	2	4
Julius Cæsar,	18	4	5
Anthony and Cleopatra,	42	4	6
Two Noble Kinsmen, a.	11	1	1
,, ,, b.	11	1	1
Tempest,	9	1	1
Winter's Tale,	15	0	0
Hen. VIII. (all Fletcher's tags),	17	4	5
Titus Andronicus,	14	3	3
1 Henry VI.,	27	13	14
2 Henry VI.,	24	8	9
3 Henry VI.,	28	10	14

On the other uses to be made of this table this is not the place to dwell: I wish only to call attention to the fact that in this play more scenes end with tags than in any other play in Shakespeare: that the number of tag-rhymes is also greater than in any other play, including his very earliest. In other words, that at a time when he had given up the use of rhyme in great measure (for all critics admit this for his Third period), in that part of the play where the supernatural is not introduced, he has on the common theory used more than twice as many tag-rhymes as he has used in any play subsequent to *The Merchant of Venice*: and these for the most part, as Clark and Wright have so justly pointed out, of the baldest and most feeble description. If the difference were small, it might be explained perhaps from the nature of the play; but such a difference is only explicable on the hypothesis of a second writer: the conclusion we have reached on other grounds.

CHAPTER XI.

ON "JULIUS CÆSAR."

MY theory as to this play is so unlike anything hitherto advanced that I shall begin by stating it; so that the startled reader may have it in his power to shut the book at once, if the hypothesis seems to him too absurd to be entertained. I believe that this play as we have it is an abridgment of Shakespeare's play, made by Ben Jonson. I will first give a number of reasons for my belief that the common theory cannot be true, and then enter into details as to my own.

1. The name Anthony is a very favourite one with Shakespeare: it occurs in *Much Ado about Nothing*, *Love's Labour's Lost*, *Macbeth*, *Henry V.*, *Richard III.*, *Romeo and Juliet*, and *Anthony and Cleopatra*: in all these seven plays it is *always* spelt Anthony, or Anthonie, with an h; but in this play invariably Antony or Antonie, without one. So Ben Jonson always rejects the h; see *Catiline*, especially, *passim*.

2. The number of participles in -èd, with the final syllable pronounced, is out of all proportion to the other plays, especially the latter ones. I have not had time to count them, but it is clear on merely reading the play. Examples: plungèd, vexèd, transformèd.

3. I. ii. "To-morrow, if you please to speak with me
I will *come home to you*: or if you will
Come home to me, and I will wait for you."

Home = to thy house, **chez toi** : never used by Shakespeare where the **subject** of the sentence **is in the first person;** but Jonson, *Catiline,* III. i.:

> "I'll *come home to you.* Crassus would not have you
> To speak to him fore Quintus **Catulus.**"

4. **II. iii.** " Quality and kind " not found elsewhere in Shakespeare. He **has** " quality and brain," " quality and name," **not** " kind." Jonson, *Every Man in his Humour,* II. i.:

> " Spirits of our kind and quality."

5. The **phrase " bear me hard,"** occurs three **times in this play;** in I. ii.; II. i.; III. i., not elsewhere in Shakespeare. But Jonson, *Catiline,* **IV. v.**:

> "Ay, though he *bear me hard,*
> I yet must do him right."

Bear hard occurs in 1 *Henry IV.,* and *hard forbear* in *Othello,* but in a different sense from that in this place.

6. The number of short lines in this play, *where no pause is required,* is very great, and seems to point to the fact that it has been greatly **abridged for the** purpose of representation. Example:

II. i.   " He says he does, being then most flatterèd.
   Let me **work** !
   For I can give his humour the true bent."

II. i.   " Since Cassius **first had whet me against** Cæsar
   I have not slept.
   Between the acting of a dreadful thing," &c.

II. i.   " **And** by-and-by thy bosom shall **partake**
   The secrets of my heart.
   All my engagements I will **construe to thee,"** &c.

III. i.   " Thy master is a wise and valiant Roman,
   I never thought him worse.
   Tell him so please him come unto this place," &c.

III. ii. "Cassius, go you into the other street
And part the numbers.
. Those that **will hear me speak let 'em stay here!**"

These are exactly like the metrical forms assumed in the surreptitious **issues** of the first Quartos of *Hamlet* and *Romeo and Juliet*, **but** extremely unlike Shakespeare's **manner in his** complete works. I have intentionally taken the instances from the middle of continuous speeches; but the imperfection **more** usually occurs at the end of **a speech**, as excisions are more frequently made from ends **of** speeches than from the middle **of them.**

7. Mr. R. Simpson has noticed that this play bears the same relation to the tragedies that *The Two Gentlemen of Verona* does to the comedies as **to "once-used"** words (once-used in his sense). This is just what **would happen** if Jonson edited the play. For his dislike to **"strange words"** and his satire on Marston **for** inventing them, see Act **V.** Sc. **1** of *The Poetaster*, **where** Crispinus vomits his linguistic inventions **after** the emetic administered **by Horace.**

8. Shakespeare and Jonson **probably worked** together on *Sejanus* **in** 1602-3. He having helped Jonson then **in** a historical play, what more likely than that Jonson should **be chosen** to remodel Shakespeare's *Cæsar*, if it needed to be **reproduced in** a shorter **form than** he gave it originally? And for such reproduction (after Shakespeare's death, between 1616 and 1623), **to** what author would **such work of** abridgment have been entrusted except Shakespeare's critical friend Jonson? Fletcher would have enlarged, not shortened.

9. We know **that** rival theatres and rival publishers in the Elizabethan times frequently brought **out** plays on the same subject close on each other's heels. Thus the old play of *Leir* was republished when Shakespeare's *Lear* was produced: *The Danish Tragedy* and *Hoffman's Tragedy* were run in opposition to *Hamlet*: *The Taming of the Shrew* was **a** rival piece to *Patient Grissel*, *The Woman Killed with Kindness*, and probably Dekker's *Medicine for a Curst Wife*: *Grissel*, and the *Woman Killed* having come out first, **the *Shrew* being** then set up in rivalry, and the last-named piece being a retaliation for this opposition. But this practice is too well known to require illustration. Is it not, then, highly probable that this play, produced about 1601 originally, should be revived in 1607, the date of L. Stirling's *Julius Cæsar* and of *"Cesar's Revenge, or the Tragedy of Cesar and Pompey,"* called in the running title " *The Tragedy of Julius Cesar*," or if it were produced in 1607, as Malone believes it was, that the other play was then published in rivalry to it? In any case, I think it likely that *some* production or reproduction was at that date, and another after Shakespeare's death with Jonson's alterations.

10. There is a strange feeling about the general style of this play; which is not the style of Jonson: but just what one would fancy Shakespeare would become with an infusion of Jonson. I do not give passages here; as I look on the printing of long extracts from books in every one's hands, except for cases for comparison, as useless and wasteful. I prefer relying on the taste and judgment of those who will take the trouble to read the play and judge for themselves.

11. There is a quarrelling scene in the *Maid's Tragedy* imitated from the celebrated one between Brutus and Cassius; just in the same way as *Philaster* is imitated from *Cymbeline.* The *Maid's Tragedy* was probably produced in 1608-9, the year before *Philaster*. It is therefore not improbable that *Julius Cæsar* was reproduced a year or two before 1609, or at any rate some three years earlier than *Cymbeline*, that is, in 1607, just as Shakespeare's Fourth period began.

12. Act I. Sc. 2. "Chew upon this;" no such expression elsewhere in Shakespeare. Compare the use of "work upon that now" *passim* in *Eastward Ho*, of which Jonson was one of the authors.

13. Act II. Sc. 1. " Scorning the base *degrees*
                By which he did ascend."

The word *degrees* never used by Shakespeare, as meaning "stairs," but always of "steps," metaphorical ; as we use " gradually " now. But in *Sejanus* we have :

"Whom when he says lie spread on the *degrees*."

14. "And turn pre-ordinance and first decree
    Into the *lane* of children," (Act III. Sc. 1.)

where *lane* means narrow conceits. Compare *Staple of News*:

"A narrow-minded man! **my thoughts do** dwell
All in a *lane*."

I do not know an instance of such a usage in any other author.

15. V. v. "His life was gentle, and the elements
    So mixt in him that Nature might stand up
    And say to all the world, 'This was a man.'"

Compare *Cynthia's Revels*, II. iii. "A creature of a most perfect and divine temper: one in whom the humours and elements are peaceably met without emulation of precedency" (acted in 1600). Surely Shakespeare did not deliberately copy Jonson: but if he wrote before him, *Julius Cæsar* must come before 1601 into the time of the historical plays.[1]

16. Jonson was in the habit of altering plays, *e.g.* he altered and adapted *Jeronymo* by Kyd; and his share of work in *The Widow, Eastward Ho*, and other plays, was evidently of the supervising and trimming kind, as the main execution of nearly every scene is clearly traceable to the other writers.

We now come to an important argument:

In a celebrated passage in the *Discoveries* of Ben Jonson, we read: "I remember, the players have often mentioned it as an honour to Shakespeare, that in his writing (whatsoever he penned) he never blotted out a line. My answer hath been, Would he had blotted a thousand. Which they thought a malevolent speech. I had not told posterity this but for their ignorance who chose that circumstance to commend their friend by, wherein he most faulted, and to justify mine own candour: for I loved the man and do honour his memory on this side idolatry as much as any. He was,

---

[1] This agrees with the date of allusion discovered by Mr. Halliwell; but the paucity of rhymes, number of short lines, and brevity of the play are conclusive as to its not having been produced in its present state at that date. It has been abridged by some one for theatrical representation: if not by Jonson, then by some one else.—F. G. F.

indeed, honest, and of an open and free nature ; had an excellent
phantasy, brave notions, and gentle expressions : wherein he flowed
with that facility, that sometimes it was necessary he should be
stopped : *Sufflaminandus erat*, as Augustus said of Haterius. His
wit was in his own power, would the rule of it had been so too.
Many times he fell into those things, could not escape laughter : as
when he said in the person of Cæsar, one speaking to him, ' Cæsar,
thou dost me wrong.' He replied, ' Cæsar did never wrong, but
with just cause,' and such like ; which were ridiculous. But he
redeemed his vices with his virtues. There was even more in him
to be praised than to be pardoned."

It is clear from this passage (1) that a line in *Julius Cæsar*, as it
originally stood, has been altered from its first form as quoted by
Jonson into ("Cæsar, thou dost me wrong," being omitted !)

"Know, Cæsar doth not wrong, nor without cause
  Will he be satisfied."

(2) That this alteration had been made in the acting copy, published in Folio in 1623 ; though Jonson's statement of its being an
alteration was not published till after his death in 1637.

(3) That Jonson gives this as one of "many" instances. We
cannot now find these in Shakespeare's works : but it is a fair
inference that other similar corrections have been made.

(4) These alterations were not commonly known :[1] such an
opportunity for what our forefathers called "merry jests" would
never have been lost : we should have had traces of them in contemporary writing.

We have, then, a play in which one error at least (perhaps many)
has been corrected ; and an author to whom this correction (or
these corrections) was privately known : a play in which there is a
deficiency of some thousand lines as compared with the others of
the same class by the same author ; and a critic who desired that the
author in his writing had blotted a thousand : a play remarkable
for speeches ending on the second or third beat of an incomplete

---

[1] Yet the distinct allusion in *The Staple of News* (Induction), "Cry you
mercy, you never did wrong but with just cause," shows that in 1625 an allusion
to this alteration at any rate was well understood.—F. G. F.

line, and one known alteration, with others to be presumed, which introduces this peculiarity contrary to the author's usual manner : a play with various peculiar phrases and usages of words ; and the same critic-author in whose works these peculiar words and phrases are found. Add to these considerations the spelling of Antony, the use of words in -èd, the small number of once-used words, and the probability that these two writers had worked together in *Sejanus*, and I think there is a case made out that the play of *Julius Cæsar* as we have it was corrected by Ben Jonson : whether it had been produced by Shakespeare in 1600 in a different form or not. If it had, all questions of early allusion are accounted for : and it would be written by him as a continuation of the series of Histories immediately after *Henry V.*, to which play the general style of *Julius Cæsar* seems to me more like than to any other work of Shakespeare : also the pronunciation of the final -èds would be accounted for, as this is more frequent in *Henry IV.* and *V.* than in any other plays next to *Cæsar*.

It is fair also to consider what would probably have been Ben Jonson's conduct supposing he had revised this play. Would he have made any allusion to it such as that in *The Staple of News* quoted in the note on the preceding page ? We may judge of this by a parallel instance. We know that he made alterations in Kyd's *Hieronymo is Mad again*, or *Spanish Tragedy*. Accordingly, in the Induction to *Cynthia's Revels* Jonson alludes indirectly to the alterations he had made. Another, he says, swears down all that sit about him "that the old *Hieronymo, as it was first acted*, was the only, best, and judiciously penned play of Europe." This is just such an indirect allusion as I have pointed out to the passage in *Julius Cæsar* in *The Staple of News ;* and so far agrees with what may be expected on my theory.

Again, the speech of Polonius (*Hamlet*, iii. 2), "I did enact Julius Cæsar : I was killed in the Capitol : Brutus killed me," seems to me to allude to Shakespeare's play : "played once in the University," it may be : but if so, by a regular company, not by the students. But if this allusion is to Shakespeare's play, it distinctly points to an acting of Cæsar's part by an inferior player : which would give us a reason for the ill success of the piece at its first production. Hamlet's speech, "It was a brute part of him to kill so capital a calf there. Be the *players* ready?" so strongly contrasts Polonius with the good actors, that he must, I think, be referring to some actual performer. May not the play that was "caviare to the general, that pleased not the million" allude to the same failure? It can hardly refer to *Sejanus* acted in 1603, as it occurs in the first draft of *Hamlet*, which was acted probably in 1602, and printed certainly in 1603.

Of course, as I hold the alterations in this play, like those in *Macbeth*, to have taken place principally at the ends of speeches, and specially at the ends of scenes, the proportion of rhymes has been too seriously interfered with for our tables to be of any use by way of comparison with other plays of Shakespeare. The increased number of tags in the Middleton part of *Macbeth* put in to hide the alterations, and the diminished number of rhymes in *Julius Cæsar* caused by Jonson's abbreviations, alike interfere with the direct application of the rhyme-test. But to it indirectly I owe the fact of my attention being called to the very unusual characteristics of both these plays.

It may be well here to say a few words on the relation of metrical tests to "higher" criticism. If the peculiarities of a writer are regarded as matters of chance or arbitrary choice, it is absurd to take them as a basis of investigation: but they are not so: in every writer there are tricks of style and of metre which *unknown to himself* pervade all his work: the skill of the critic lies, first in selecting those which are really characteristic, and establishing their existence by adequate proof: then in tracing their gradual development or decay: and finally in showing their connection with each other and with the higher mental characters out of which they spring, and to which they are inseparably attached. The first part of this task I have approximately accomplished for Shakespeare; the latter, and far more difficult one, I have also attempted and shall publish in due course. I only here desire to record that I have not worked mechanically in this matter: and that I have studied the psychology of Shakespeare quite as diligently, and I hope as accurately, as I have the statistical phenomena which are its outcome and indication. As yet I have given only a *diagnosis* for individual authors and for individual plays, so as to classify and form a basis for higher investigations. The anatomy of each, and the comparative physiology of dramatic authors as a class, have yet to be given, and then the crowning work, the life history of our greatest men, as shown in their writings, their dynamical psychology, will become possible, which (with all deference to the metaphysical critics who have wasted their great acumen by beginning at the wrong end) it has not yet been and could not yet be.

NOTE ON "TWO GENTLEMEN OF VERONA."

[No result of my investigations appears to have been so unfavourably received as the date I have assigned to *The Two Gentlemen of Verona*. Professor Ward, for instance (a most judicious and accurate critic), expresses himself strongly adverse to it. Yet on carefully examining his own views he seems substantially to agree with me. I as well as he believe that *The Two Gentlemen* was anterior to our present versions of *Love's Labour's Lost*, *Midsummer Night's Dream*, and *Richard II*.—that is to say, to the revised, emended, altered, augmented versions published by Shakespeare; just as I believe *King John*, as we have it, to have been anterior to the revised *Richard II*. But in speaking of the dates of production of plays, I speak of their original performance, not their subsequent alteration for the press or for a second run at the theatres. No one, as far as I know, when discussing the date of *The Merry Wives of Windsor* ever speaks of the Folio version (probably made 1605), but of the first sketch as in the Quarto (probably made 1598). There is little doubt that all Shakespeare's plays were amended in this way. We know it to be true of a large proportion of them.

It may be well, however, in order to clear up this point, to show here the relation that his alterations bear to the Quarto editions, All Quartos (with the possible exception of Quarto 1 of *Romeo and Juliet*) issued up to the date of 1600 were authorized, and in my opinion superintended, by Shakespeare himself. All after 1600 were unquestionably surreptitious. The dividing point is found in the entry of August 4, where *As You Like It*, *Henry V.*, and *Much Ado*

NOTE ON TWO GENTLEMEN OF VERONA.

about Nothing, appear without name of enterer. At the beginning of the register is a rough note that these three plays were " to be stayed;" *As You Like It* was apparently stayed accordingly. *Henry V.* appeared afterwards in a surreptitious edition of Pavier's; but *Much Ado* was allowed and published by the firm who had hitherto published all the other authorized Quartos of the histories. For what reason they did not also publish the other comedies does not appear. But this we know : that excepting the surreptitious *Henry V.* every play printed in Quarto before 1600 was admitted as an authentic copy by the Folio editors. For even in the case of *Richard III.*, whoever made the Folio alterations made them on a copy of the third Quarto, and in all other cases they used this Quarto as copy to reprint from. In every case then of Quartos issued up to 1600 we may depend on having Shakespeare's authorized version of the play. Now it is very singular that the list of such authorized Quartos coincides in extent of time precisely with Meres' list of plays up to 1598, if we admit Mr. Brae's identification of *Much Ado* with *Love's Labour's Won;* and had *The Comedy of Errors*,[1] *The Two Gentlemen of Verona*,[1] and *King John*,[1] been edited, the two lists would have been identical, play for play. But as these were not re-written, we must expect them to appear immature and out of chronological position when compared with the other plays that had the advantage of adaptation in accordance with Shakespeare's more matured experience.

F. G. FLEAY, *January* 1, 1876.]

[1] These three plays, it will be observed, fall among the last nine in the Table, p. 259.

CHAPTER XII.

PERSONAL SATIRE COMMON ON THE OLD ENGLISH STAGE.

It has long been known that in certain instances, such as the quarrel between Jonson, Marston, and Dekker, the Elizabethan playwrights represented individual characters on the stage under fictitious names. Thus Jonson in his *Poetaster* ridiculed Marston as Crispinus and Dekker as Demetrius; Marston in his *What You Will* indicated himself by Lampatho Doria, and Jonson by Quadratus; Dekker in his *Satiromastix* retaliated on Jonson under the character of Horace. But the extent to which this "taxing of private parties" was carried has never yet been fully recognised. It has always been supposed that such instances as are mentioned above are exceptional: that the absence of private satire is as marked as that of political allusions; that just as any hint, however slight, to the effect that the government of the country was mismanaged was instantly repressed, and the players of the obnoxious drama silenced, so abuse directed towards individuals was, either by the authority of the Chamberlain or the influence of public opinion, generally banished from the stage. I am however prepared to show that in various plays the characters of private persons were attacked, their works ridiculed, incidents of their career, true, or supposed to be so, held up for animadversion, and personalities generally indulged in that could hardly be rivalled on the Athenian stage or in the lowest class of modern newspapers.

Among these plays one is conspicuous; and as it has lately been introduced into Dodsley's Collection, and has been prolific in errors through the prevalent habit of taking Malone's dicta as proven without further investigation, it specially commends itself to our notice. This play is called *Wily Beguiled*. Its plot is very simple. The hand of Lelia the heroine, daughter of Gripe the usurer, is sought by three suitors, Sophos a scholar, Churms a lawyer, and Peter Plodall a farmer's son. The last of these is favoured by Gripe because he has land and is rich; the scholar is forbidden his house on account of his poverty : and the lawyer seeks to further his own ends while pretending to assist Gripe in his. Fortunatus, Lelia's brother, who has been away in the wars, returns in the nick of time to frustrate Churm's plans and procure the marriage of Sophos with Lelia. Peter Plodall is discomfited as well as Churms, and his hireling Robin Goodfellow, who has attempted to frighten Sophos in a devil's accoutrements, comes in for a good thrashing. There is also an underplot, in which a match takes place between Peg Pudding the daughter of Lelia's nurse, and Will Cricket the son of one of old Plodall's tenants. I will now try to show that these characters have all special satirical significations, and that under this plot events then recent are figured and caricatured. First then, who is Churms the " Wily " lawyer who is " Beguiled " in this play ? He describes himself thus. " I have been at Cambridge a scholar, at Cales a soldier, and now in the country a lawyer, and the next degree shall be a coney catcher." This at once points to Thomas Lodge, who after taking his degree served in the army, travelled, and became a member of Gray's Inn. But on looking into the Prologue all uncertainty is removed : for in it " Prologue " having ascertained from the placard on the curtain that the play to be performed is *Spectrum*, "a looking-glass," which he characterises as a history

> " Of base conceits and damned roguery,
> The very sink of hell-bred villany,"

bids a "Juggler" tell the players' fiery poet that "before I have done with him I'll make him do penance on a stage in a calf-skin." The Juggler then "conveys" *Spectrum* away, and *Wily Beguiled* stands in its place. Prologue then says,

> "Go to that barm-froth poet and to him say,
> He quite hath lost the title of his play ;

18

His calf-skin jests from hence are quite exiled :
Thus once you see that *Wily is Beguiled.*"

This identifies Wily with the author of *The Looking Glass for London* which was chiefly written by Lodge, Robert Greene having also a hand in it, and at the same time prepares us to find in *Wily Beguiled* a mirror held up if not to Nature, yet to the theatrical events of the time. The "calf-skin jests" allude to the 14th scene of the *Looking Glass*, where "a man in devil's attire" is beaten by Adam : a wretched scene. This is parodied in the beating of Robin in our play, while he is in like manner dressed in calf-skin to represent a fiend.

Having then identified the knavish lawyer with Lodge, we naturally expect to find other dramatic authors among the characters. Some of these are easy to identify : for example, this passage,

"For Sophos let him wear the willow garland,
And *play the melancholy malcontent,*
And pluck his hat down in his sullen eyes,"

at once shows that Sophos is Marston the author of the *Malcontent :* the very name Robin Goodfellow identifies that character with Henry Chettle, whose play under that title was produced in 1602. Fortunatus in like manner is Dekker, the author of *Old Fortunatus,* 1595. The Dutch cobbler mentioned in the play I shall show by and by to be Michael Drayton : Tom Shoemaker, "who was constable of the town," is I think Thomas Middleton ; the gentleman-usher similarly alluded to must of course be Chapman ; and young Plodall the low-born peasant, the slow lout, is I fear Ben Jonson, whose tardiness in producing the promised Apology for the *Poetaster* is also alluded to in the words "as long as Hunks with the great head has been about to show his little wit in the second part of his paltry poetry."

Next as to the female characters. I have ascertained by induction from several plays of this class, that when a lover indicates a dramatic author, his mistress signifies the company of players for whom he writes, her father is the manager of the company, and marriage signifies his binding himself to write for them. Lelia in this instance must be the Prince's (or Admiral's if before 1602) company acting at the Fortune: this is confirmed by **such** allusions as when the Nurse says of Lelia's favour to Sophos,

"Sir, you may see that Fortune is your friend."

Old Gripe will consequently be Henslow (or Alleyn) the manager.

Before proceeding further in the identification of these characters, it will be necessary to ascertain the date of the play. Now, whether I am right or not in my interpretation of the plot, some of the allusions are certain, and fix a limit of date before which the play could not have been written. *Old Fortunatus* was written in 1595, published in 1600; *The Shoemaker's Holiday*, in which the character of the "Dutch cobbler" occurs, was produced **in 1600**; the *Poetaster* was acted in 1601, printed in 1602; *Robin Goodfellow* was written in 1602; the *Gentleman Usher* was printed in 1606, probably written in 1602; and the additions to the *Malcontent* as acted by the King's company were published in 1604 and acted probably in 1603; for **in the** Introduction there is distinct **allusion to** the reproduction of *Jeronymo* by the Admiral's company in 1601-2. **I fix** the date of *Wily Beguiled* then in 1602-3; for as it treats of the engagement of Marston by **the Admiral's or Prince's** company, it must have been **anterior** to the production of his *Malcontent* by **the** King's; and it must have been subsequent to the dates of the plays just mentioned that were produced in 1602. The most likely date is the establishment of the Prince's company in 1603. Jonson, who **is** ridiculed in the play, finally left the Admiral's company in the latter part of 1602, and his *Sejanus* was produced at the King's in 1603.

Now we can explain the underplot. As old Plodall must be the manager of **the** Globe company (Burbage), his tenants will be the occupiers **of the** Blackfriars theatre—viz. the Children of the Chapel who rented that theatre of him till 1601-2: they were then turned out, and the house afterwards let **at a** higher rent, probably to the Children of the Revels. But this is just the story of the play. Old Cricket (the manager of the Chapel Children) is turned out by old Plodall, and Will Cricket marries Gripe's nurse's **daughter.** This I take to mean that on the dissolution of the company of the Children **of the** Chapel, Will is engaged by the Children of Paul's (Peg **Pudding).** This latter company's manager may well be called **the** Nurse. Chapman, Dekker, Webster, Marston, Middleton, all

tried their prentice hands at it, and sometimes simultaneously at
the Admiral's before finally settling down to other companies. I do
not, however, find Will Cricket himself so easy to identify : the most
likely person is John Lyly : he wrote for the Chapel Children and
for the Paul's Children in 1600-1 ; he is (I think unquestionably)
called " Willy " by Spenser ; and in the play we have " I Peg
Pudding promise thee, William Cricket, that I'll hold thee for mine
own sweet *lilly.*" Again, Cricket's dancing is praised, and in Lyly's
Maid's Metamorphosis Cricket is one of the fairies who come in
dancing. Names of characters in their works can be more often
taken to indicate authors in these plays, and especially in this one,
than any other means of identification.

On the whole, then, the general meaning of the play is
clear. It is a celebration of the good luck of the Fortune
company in getting Marston to write the *Malcontent* for them ;
a high eulogy on Dekker, who had just returned from the
wars (on the stage) against the mighty potentate Ben Jonson : a
general abuse of the Globe company, its manager and its writers,
especially Jonson and Lodge ; an exposure of the knavery of Lodge
(real or pretended), and of the bullying propensities of Jonson and
his hireling Chettle :[1] a caricature of the style and plot of Lodge's
Looking Glass and other plays. (Note by the way that Chettle died
in May 1603, which confirms our limit of date.) Under the guise of
a love story nearly every dramatist of importance at that time is
either introduced as a character or alluded to in the dialogue. To
this, however, there is one important exception. There is no mention
of William Shakespeare. But if he is not mentioned, the whole
play is almost a continuous parody of his writings. Old Capulet is
the model on which Gripe has been pourtrayed. The Nurse is
closely imitated from the Nurse of Juliet. In the 15th scene there
is a dialogue between Lelia and Sophos taken from that between
Lorenzo and Jessica in *The Merchant of Venice*, Act. v. Sc. i. and
Gripe's grief for the loss of his daughter and his money is imitated
from Shylock's. There are also less strongly marked allusions to other
plays, but not to any that I can trace published later than 1600. I
have found in plays of this nature that Shakespeare is very seldom

[1] Chettle assisted Jonson in two plays, *Hot Anger soon Cold*, and *Robert II.
King of Scotland*.

introduced on the stage; only his plays, and not he himself, are generally alluded to. I believe the reason of this to be that he scarcely ever, if at all, alluded to others, or introduced them as personages in his own plays.

In several plays of this satirical description produced by the Admiral's company, or in early years by Lord Strange's, a recognised system of allegorical language was used. Thus a servant often meant an actor; a marriageable young lady indicated a theatrical company; the father of the said lady represented the company's manager; her suitors were poets who were seeking engagements to write for the company; brothers were other poets already in connection with the theatre; marriage was the agreement or hiring of the poet to produce plays; and so on. The converse however is not always true. These engagements and characters are not always represented by the same symbols: for instance, a poet is not always a suitor or brother—he is sometimes a cobbler; an actor is occasionally a juggler instead of a servant; and the like. It may be worth while to explain the term "cobbler," as an instance of the mode in which this symbolical language arose. One name, or rather synonym, for a mender of old shoes was "translator;" the same word "translator" is also used for an adapter or patcher, or piratical reproducer of other men's plays: hence "cobbler" easily suggests this latter character and is used for it.

It would be inconsistent with my plan to give here a detailed examination of more than one play: but on account of their connection with the quarrel between Jonson and Dekker and Marston, of which *Wily Beguiled* is a sequel, it may be not out of place to mention that Dekker's *Shoemaker's Holiday* and *Old Fortunatus* also belong to the series of attacks to which Jonson was (as he tells us) subject for three years before he made any retaliation. In the former of these two plays Hans, the Dutch shoemaker, otherwise Sir *Rowland* Lacy in disguise, is almost certainly Michael Drayton, whose *nom de plume* was Rowland, who was in the latter years of Queen Elizabeth one of the poets attached to the Admiral's company, for which he and others wrote the play of *Sir John Oldcastle* to be run in opposition to Shakespeare's *Henry IV*. Dodger in this same play is Thomas Lodge, and the other characters can also be identified. Dekker distinctly points out to us in *Old Fortunatus*, that the scene which is laid in Cyprus is intended to treat of theatrical affairs, and that the *dramatis personæ* are actors, **poets**, &c., disguised under fictitious names, by speaking in his own character of "other Cyprists, my poor countrymen." Accordingly, an examination of the play shows us that Fortunatus is Christopher Marlowe : his **two** sons, Ampedo the good son and Andolucio **the bad** one, are George Peele and Thomas Lodge: Shadow the servant **is** Shakespeare, who in 1595, the date of this play, had not yet printed any of his works, had not probably produced anything greater than his *Richard II.*, and had not corrected his *Love's Labour's Lost* or *Midsummer Night's Dream* into their present shape, which no doubt **is** far superior to that of their earliest production. He was certainly then, if not as Dekker represents him, merely a shadow of his predecessors, yet nothing **more** than **a** shadow of what he afterwards was **to** become.

> "No, **no**; I am but shadow of myself.
> You are deceived : my substance is not here :
> For what you see is but the smallest part
> And least proportion of humanity."
>
> 1 *Henry VI.*

The "wishing cap," which enables Fortunatus (Marlowe) to transport himself to any place, is the power of imagination; the magic purse, which produces ten pieces whenever the hand is put in it, shows the payments made for the writing a new play, namely ten marks, or 6*l.* 13*s.* 4*d.* With this clue to the meaning of the play the allusions to Lyly, Falstaff, Lodge, &c., as Endymion, the wandering knight, the French doctor, &c., grow clear, and **the** double meaning of the whole plot becomes manifest.

These plays then, along with Jonson's *Cynthia's Revels* and *Poetaster*, Marston's *What You Will*, Dekker's *Satiromastix*, and others that might be used to increase the list, may be taken as fair samples of the satirical and personally abusive comedies of the Elizabethan time. I **say** samples, because it is plain that the practice of thus assailing individuals on the stage must have been very common for several reasons. In the first place, **we** have a large number of such plays still in **existence.** I am prepared to show that between 1589 and 1607 there are still remaining at least a dozen of this personal character. Moreover, we must allow for the transient and ephemeral character of such productions. Unless they were remarkable for the great ability displayed in them, or were particularly interesting from the nature of the persons attacked, they would be unlikely to survive a very few years. Consequently we have probably now in existence a much smaller proportion of such plays than of those of deeper and more universal interest.

Another reason for believing them abundant is the great anxiety shown by playwrights to defend themselves against the imputation that they ever attack anybody. Prologues, Addresses to the Reader, statements in the body of the dramas themselves, are continually pressed into the author's service to show that he is free from blame, whatever strange constructions Hydra-headed Envy may put upon his work. *Qui s'excuse s'accuse.* In every instance of an apology of this kind being prefixed to a play, I have found that careful examination shows that invidious accusations are made against some person or persons in the work itself.

If then we can ascertain from these " Envy-plays " (I call them envy plays because Envy is invariably assigned in their Prologues, &c, as the cause of their production) a series of chronologically arranged facts determining the dates at which authors began or ceased to write for specific theatrical companies, we shall be able to settle many disputed points as to the dates of production of their works, to supply many gaps in their biographies, to throw additional light on their personal characters, to add in some respects to our knowledge of their manners and customs, and above all to ascertain more accurately than from Commendatory Verses or Dedications, the popular estimate that was formed of our greatest men by their contemporaries, and the amount of influence exercised by them.

One little link in this chain I have endeavoured to supply in this chapter. Many more such links I am ready to weld on to it. The one chosen to be here put forth as sample is selected merely because it is the easiest to detach, and being connected with well-known other links in the Jonson quarrel, is one not difficult to recognise as like to them in structure and purpose. *Wily Beguiled* is not however, in subject matter, one of the most important of the Envy plays : which fact perhaps accounts for its allegory never having been suspected, in spite of its grossly personal character being manifest on the surface in its allusion to Jonson as " Hunks with the big head."

CHAPTER XIII.

ON THE ANNALS OF THE STAGE FROM 1584 TO 1595.

[I WISH to specially acknowledge the great advantage that I have derived from Mr. R. Simpson's papers in writing this chapter. Although I differ from most of his conclusions, it is not too much to say that but for his previous work I should not have been able to make this investigation.—F. G. F.]

The theatrical companies known to have been regularly acting in London from 1584 to 1589 are—1, The Lord Admiral's; 2, The Queen's; 3, The Lord Strange's; 4, The Children of the Chapel; 5, The Children of Paul's. Neither of the Chamberlain's companies, that is, the Earl of Sussex's (1576-1582) and the later one of the same name, that is, Lord Hunsdon's (1594-1603), have been traced in the period we are at first concerned with (1584-1589). But in 1589 two companies, 6, The Earl of Sussex's; 7, The Earl of Pembroke's, began to attract their share of public attention. These dates are important in our inquiry. The writers of plays who are chiefly remarkable were—1, George Peele, who began to write at least as early as 1584, and died in 1596-7; 2, Robert Greene, who died in 1592, and who, as I shall try to show, began to write about 1585; 3, Christopher Marlowe, whose active career began with Greene's, and lasted only one year longer; 4, Thomas Nash, who came to London in 1589; 5, Thomas Lodge, who wrote with Greene about 1589; 6, Thomas Kyd, whose *Jeronymo* dates at latest 1588; 7, William Shakespeare. These dates are also important to us.

Having laid down then these data for reference, let us proceed at once to examine the plays of *The London Prodigal* and *Fair Emm*. In the latter of these plays two stories are combined. Firstly, William the Conqueror accompanied by the Marquis Lubeck, a Danish knight, visits Denmark under the name of Robert of Windsor, having appointed two co-regents to manage his kingdom during his absence. His intention at first is to woo Blanche, the daughter of the Danish king; but he falls in love with Mariana, a captive from Sweden, who is betrothed to Lubeck. He endeavours to carry her off; but Blanche is substituted for her, masked and disguised, and he fails in his attempt to deprive the Marquis of his bride. Sweno's invasion of England (which is the only historical fact in the play) is attributed to his anger at the loss of his daughter. William in the last act suddenly, and without explanation, becomes "the Duke of Saxon." All this is admirably explained by Mr. Simpson. William the Conqueror is William Kempe the actor, who with a troop of comedians visited the Danish Court in 1586; (three of these, by the bye, were afterwards actors in Shakespeare's plays in the Chamberlain's company, namely, Kempe, Brian, and Pope!) Kempe and one other, left Denmark in the autumn; but five of the company went to Saxony. The allegory is transparent enough; it is certain that William here is not the historical Conqueror; he is king over a troop of players, at first in England, afterwards in Saxony. But I cannot further than this agree with Mr. Simpson; his interpretation of Fair Emm as the Manchester public seems to me peculiarly unhappy. Kempe was the head of the Queen's company, and in 1587, the year after he left England, we find J. Dutton and J. Lanham acting as managers of that company : surely these are the two regents left in authority by the conquering Gullielmo. They have nothing to do with Manchester, nor indeed with the public. Fair Emm is the company of the Queen's players, with whom, as we shall see, the poets are seeking connection. We must not look for exact consistency in an allegory of this kind. But before explaining the second plot of the play, I would draw attention to the way in which this "marriage" of an author to a company or manager to his troop illustrates the allegory of the "marriage" of an author to his patron as exemplified in Shakespeare's *Sonnets*. Lubeck is pleading William's passion to Mariana.

"*Mar.* But Lubeck now **regards not Mariana.**
Lub. Even as my life, so love I Mariana.
Mar. Why do you post me to **another** then?
Lub. He is my friend, and I do **love the man.**
Mar. Then will Duke William **rob me of my love.**
Lub. No; as his life **Mariana he doth love.**
Mar. Speak for yourself, my lord; **let him alone.**
Lub. So do I, madam; **for he and I are one.**
Mar. Then loving you I do **content you** both.
Lub. In loving him you shall **content us both.**"

Compare with this Shakespeare's 42nd *Sonnet*, which seems to give many critics so much **difficulty** to explain allegorically.

" **If I lose thee my loss is** my love's gain;
    And losing **her my** friend hath found **that loss**;
Both find each other, and I lose both **twain**;
    And both for **my sake lay on me this cross.**
But here's the joy: **my** friend and **I are one.**
Sweet flattery: then **she** loves but **me alone.**"

Surely these two extracts will **bear a similar** interpretation. **And** nothing can be more certain **than** Mr. Simpson's explanation of **the** former of the two.

We must now consider the second plot. **In** this **Fair Emm is** wooed by three suitors, Manville, Vallingford, and Mounteney; by pretending blindness and deafness she hopes to drive away the two latter and be married to Manville her betrothed. Vallingford, however, is **not** deceived, and on **her** hearing of Manville's falseness **in** carrying on **a** second flirtation with Elinor of Chester, ultimately wins Fair Emm. There is also a scene of coarse levity between her and Trotter, a serving-man, of whom more hereafter. Mr. Simpson has rightly stated that Manville is Greene; but he is certainly wrong **in** identifying Vallingford **with** Shakespeare. **Camden** says that Wallingford is Gualt-hen, "The old **rampire or fort."** But an old **fort** is a *Peel*, and under this name **that of George** Peele is as certainly indicated as it is under **that of Pyeboard in** *The Puritan*. The remaining suitor, Mounteney, is Marley **or** Marlowe. Fair Emm is some theatre with which these rival poets sought to be connected during Kempe's **absence.** But the only theatrical company that Greene ever was connected with, as far as we know, was the Queen's, for which he wrote *Orlando, Friar Bacon and Friar Bungay,* and *James the Fourth.* These **were all** written before 1589. But in 1589 Kempe had returned to England and joined Lord Strange's company, with Pope, Brian, &c. In 1589 at latest, then, we must look for the dissolution of Greene's connection with the Queen's company, and the formation of a new engagement between it and George Peele. We shall see ultimately how exactly these dates coincide with what we know from other sources.

But there **is another** play, *The London Prodigal,* which is undoubtedly by the same hand as *Fair Emm.* It contains a line which occurs also **in the latter play,**

"**Pardon,** dear **father,** my follies that are past,"

and is exactly of the same tone throughout in metre, style, and general handling. In it the allegory **is still clearer.** Flowerdale, Oliver, and Sir Arthur Greenshield are suitors **for the hand of Luce** Spurcock; Flowerdale obtains her by a **trick**; Oliver, to whom she had been betrothed, is discarded, as well as Sir Arthur whom **she** really prefers. Her sister Frances, who is **determined to have** a husband named Tom, marries Tom Civet; her eldest sister Delia refuses all offers and remains unmarried. There is a scene between Daffodil and Luce exactly similar to, though still plainer than, that between Trotter and Emm in the former play. Flowerdale after his marriage with Luce ill-uses her, robs Delia, the eldest sister, and after a short career of debauchery is brought to express a repentance, evidently insincere, **at the** close of the play.

In this case there is no difficulty in deciphering the personages. Flowerdale's life combines the facts of Greene's public acts in con**nection with the** theatre, and of his private ones in forsaking his wife and living in open adultery with a common prostitute; his trickery, his gambling, and **his other** vices are unsparingly exposed. Oliver, "the Devonshire man," **is certainly George Peele, who** came from that **county.** Under the odoriferous agnomen of Tom Civet we can easily recognise Tom Kyd. Daffodil clearly means Lyly, and thus identifies the Trotter of the other play. Luce is the Queen's company; Delia, the eldest sister, is the Admiral's; and the foolish

Frances that of the Chapel Children. These Children, by the bye, had been incorporated longer than the Admiral's company; but this slight discrepancy is of no consequence in so loose an allegory, and may not even be a discrepancy at all; as their existence may be dated by the author from the time of their having a fixed place for their performances. Sir Arthur Greenshield, "the military officer," is Marlowe, of whom Lieutenant-Colonel Cunningham says, "His familiarity with military terms and his fondness for using them are most remarkable; and I make no doubt myself that he was trailing a pike or managing a charger with the English force a few months after *that strange engine for the brunt of war, the fiery keel*, had been hurled against Antwerp bridge." So much for the characters.

The plot tells the story of a rivalship between Marlowe, Greene, and Peele for the office of poet to the Queen's theatre; of Greene's success; of his subsequent forsaking of his engagement and defrauding the Admiral's theatre [*Defence of Cony-Catching*, 1592: "Master R. G., would it not make you blush if you sold *Orlando Furioso* to the Queen's players for 20 nobles, and when they were in the country sold the same play to Lord Admiral's men for as much more? Was not this plain cony-catching, M. G.?"]. It tells also of Kyd's engagement with the Chapel Children, for whom he wrote *Jeronymo;* of a half-serious proposition of Lyly to engage with the Queen's company; of the determination of the Admiral's not to employ a regular poet at all, but to accept the best plays they could get from anyone. Another character in this play is easily identified, namely, Weathercock, that is, Thomas Lodge. He was an actor, a play-writer of tragedy and comedy, a writer of prose tracts, a student of Lincoln's Inn, a soldier (?) in the expeditions of Clarke and Cavendish; a translator from Greek and Latin, a novelist, and finally, a physician. Rightly is he called Weathercock. He has, however, little to do with the plot. He is an early suitor of Delia's, but rejected by her; he makes no proposal to any other lady in this play. Here, then, we have the account of Greene's original engagement with the Queen's company; in *Fair Emm* that of his rupture and the engagement of George Peele in his stead.

We now turn to Greene's prose works for further information. As dates are all-important in this part of our investigation, I must say a few words on their chronology, which has never yet been entirely settled. From 1587 onwards Greene adopted the fashion of placing on his title-pages or elsewhere in his books a motto; which motto having once discarded, he did not again make use of. Thus he prefixed successively in

1587*a*. Ea habentur optima quæ et jucunda honesta et utilia.
1587*b*-1589*a*. Omne tulit punctum qui miscuit utile dulci.
1589*b*-1590*a*. Omne tulit punctum.
1590*b*-1591*a*. Sero sed serio.
1591*b*-1592*a*. Nascimur pro patria.
1592*b*. Mallem non esse quam non prodesse patria.
,, Felicem fuisse infaustum.[1]

Any apparent exception to this rule occurs only in books issued or reprinted after Greene's death.

Let us see if from these prose writings we can fix the date of *Fair Emm* and the *London Prodigal*. The latter play referring to Flowerdale (Greene) has the line

"If e'er his heart doth turn, 'tis *ne'er too late*,"

a distinct allusion to Greene's *Never Too Late*, published in 1590*a* (earlier part of the year 1590), with the motto *Omne tulit punctum*. Hence this play cannot be earlier than 1590*b*. Mr. Simpson has pointed out that in Greene's *Farewell to Folly* (1591*b*, motto *Sero sed serio*) *Fair Emm* is railed at as containing "blasphemous rhetoric, abusing of Scripture," &c. Hence that play cannot be later than 1591*a*. I have no doubt that the plays were produced at these dates respectively.

Now we are able to settle very nearly the dates of Greene's plays; hitherto a desideratum in dramatic history: *James IV.* is fixed in 1589*b*-1590*a* by its motto *Omne tulit punctum*; *Friar Bacon* in 1588*b*-1589*a*, by its motto *Omne tulit punctum qui miscuit utile dulci*; *The Looking Glass for London* has been assigned to 1589 by Mr. Simpson; and the only two remaining plays extant, *Orlando* and

[1] Mr. Simpson appears to have been misled by the date often erroneously given to *Menaphon* as 1587, when he says: "In this year 1587, Greene adopted a fresh motto or posy. His old one was OMNE TULIT PUNCTUM." Greene certainly does not use this motto till 1588, and Mr. Petherham has shown that the date of *Menaphon* is 1589, not 1587.

Alphonsus, must have been, from their immaturity and metrical peculiarities, written before these: one other, *The History of Job*, is lost. Hence we get our table:—

Alphonsus	. .	1585
Orlando	. .	1586
Friar Bacon	.	1587-8
James IV.	. .	1589
Looking Glass		1589-90

For the Queen's Company. (bracketing Orlando, Friar Bacon, James IV.)

These dates are confirmed by the following facts:—*The London Prodigal*, which was written in 1590, speaks of Greene's engagement as having been broken, but yet open to renewal. *Fair Emm* fixes the date of the original engagement in 1586, the year of Kempe's visiting Denmark; and that of George Peele's engagement as settled in 1591 early in the year. Greene never wrote for the Queen's players after 1589. Again, the play of *Locrine*, written by Charles Tilney in 1586 (he was executed in September 1586) with the help of George Peele, or edited and finished by Peele after Tilney's death, contains quotations from *Orlando* as well as from *Alphonsus*. Hence, as Bernhardt has shown, 1586 is the latest date for *Orlando*. The lines in *Locrine* coincident with those in Peele's *Farewell to Sir John Norris*, &c. (1589), only show that he repeated himself; a common trick with him, as Dyce has proved in his notice of *Alcazar*.

I now come to Greene's prose writings.[1] In 1587*b*, in his introductory epistle to *Penelope's Web*, he complains that his "toys at the *Theatre* in Rome (London) had been passed over with silence," and that "mislike was perhaps shrouded in such patience." In 1588, in his Introduction to *Perimedes the Blacksmith*, he writes: "I keep my old course still to palter up something in prose, using mine old posy still, *Omne tulit punctum;* although lately two gentlemen-poets made two madmen of Rome beat it out of their paper bucklers, and had it in derision for that I could not make my verses fit upon the stage in tragical buskins, every word filling the mouth like the fa-burden of Bow-bell, daring God out of heaven with that atheist

---

[1] For several of these references I am indebted to Mr. Simpson, who however interprets them very differently.

Tamburlane, or blaspheming with the Mad Priest of the Sun. But let me rather openly pocket up the ass at Diogenes' hand than wantonly set out such impious instances of intolerable poetry. Such mad and scoffing poets that have poetical spirits as bred of Merlin's race, if there be any in England that set the end of scholarism in an English blank verse, I think either it is the humour of a novice that tickles them with self-love, or too much frequenting the hot-house (to use the German proverb) hath sweat out all the greatest part of their wits." The two gentlemen of Rome are the two authors of *Locrine*, who derided Greene's mottos by prefixing a Latin motto in his style to each of the dumb-shows in that mock-heroic play presented by Até at the beginning of each of its five acts; the madmen of Rome are of course the actors who acted Phineus and Perseus in the combat in the second of these dumb-shows ; all of which are parodies of the similar performances as presented by Venus at the beginnings of the acts of Greene's *Alphonsus*. The allusion to Marlowe's *Tamberlane* (1585) our earliest play in good blank-verse, is palpable ; not so that to *The Priest of the Sun*. The only play known which contains such a character is *The Looking Glass for London*, and it occurs in the part written by Greene himself. This would incline one to place that play earlier than *Perimedes*, were it not that Greene in other instances, as we shall see, was in the habit of firstly abusing other people's writings and then copying them ; a practice not altogether obsolete. The play he speaks of is probably lost. His last sentence alludes to Peele's well-known profligacy, which ultimately caused his death ; and to Marlowe's innovation in discarding rhyme, which he had himself so miserably failed to imitate in that most stilted and topsy-turvy-sentenced play *Alphonsus of Arragon*. He calls it the humour of a novice, because in his next play, *James IV.*, he meant to recur to the use of rhyme ; as he accordingly did. After 1589 he wrote no plays. *The Looking Glass* was the play in which "young Juvenall (Lodge) *lastly* with him writ a comedy." This intention of abandoning the stage was probably caused by his being replaced by Peele in this year with the Queen's company, as we have seen above. It is distinctly announced in his *Menaphon* written in that year.

And now, after this long but necessary introduction, we come to the notices of Shakespeare. I must just recapitulate the state of stage matters in 1589. Greene had retired from the stage; so had Lyly (as shown by Malone in vol. ii. of the *Variorum Shakespeare*); Nash is just arriving in London; Kempe has taken a post as manager for Lord Strange's players; this company (just attracting notice) and that of the Admiral's are prohibited from playing for a brief space, in consequence of the license they had indulged in; Marlowe (as I shall prove) is in consequence leaving the Admiral's company to join that of Sussex or that of Pembroke; Lodge goes abroad; and what Shakespeare is doing I hope to show. A most eventful year for the drama; probably the most important of any except 1585.

In order to understand the relations of these poets to each other, it is necessary to bear in mind that the anti-Martinist writers were Greene, Nash, Lyly, and Kempe; of these Nash and Kempe are, so to say, new-comers; Greene and Lyly are quondam poets, but these four form a distinct clique of their own: there has not been a more fertile error than that common classification of Greene, Peele, and Marlowe in one group, and Shakespeare in another; their relative merit as poets has blinded critics as to their private relations. Neither Peele, Marlowe, nor Lodge belong to the same group as Greene; they are all addressed by him as "quondam acquaintance" in the well-known passage of *The Groatsworth of Wit* (1592). Greene had quarrelled with Marlowe and Peele before 1589; perhaps also with Lodge, for the date of *The Looking Glass* may be earlier than that usually assigned to it; and from this date we shall find that there is no friendship between him and Shakespeare. So far from Shakespeare's being on such terms with him as to write plays in conjunction with him, we shall find distinct indications that this anti-Martinist set assumed also the most hostile attitude towards the band of friends which included Shakespeare, Marlowe, Peele, and Lodge. I have indicated some grounds for this opinion in my paper on Shakespeare's *Sonnets*. I now proceed to give others from Greene's writings.

The key to the position lies in the old play of *The Taming of a Shrew*. No sound critic can read this play without seeing that the scenes corresponding to Act iv. Sc. 1, 3, in the *The Taming of the Shrew*, are by the same author as the same parts of the later play. But Shakespeare undoubtedly wrote these later scenes. Hence he

wrote the earlier ones. The verse part of the early play is by
Marlowe. It contains many lines taken after his custom (for he
shared this habit with Peele, witness his using the celebrated line,
"Make me immortal with a kiss" in two separate plays) from his
other writings. It bears manifest marks of his work, but not his
best work. It is hurried and careless. Now this play contains a
line, "Icy hair that grows on Boreas' chin," which is distinctly
alluded to in Greene's *Menaphon* (1589), which has "White as the
hairs that grow on Father Boreas' chin," and cannot therefore be
later than that year; probably is not far in date from it. But in
1589 Marlowe was leaving the Admiral's company for the Earl of
Pembroke's; and *The Taming of a Shrew* belonged to the Earl of
Pembroke's company. It could not then be written before 1589,
while Marlowe belonged to the Admiral's. We have here then a
fixed date at which Shakespeare was writing; not an important play
certainly; only a few prose scenes of humorous comedy, composed
to oblige a friend who could write the serious parts, but had not a
particle of humour in him; not important in itself, but very important to us as giving us the earliest specimen extant of our great poet's
comic powers. But in the same year, 1589, and in another part of
the same volume, we find an allusion to another play. In Nash's
preface to *Menaphon* is an attack, too well known to quote, on those
who leave the trade of *noverint* to which they were born, and will
afford you whole *Hamlets* or handfuls of tragical speeches. In the
record of the performances at the Rose under Henslow these two
plays, *Hamlet* and *The Taming of a Shrew*, occur side by side. Is
it possible to avoid the inference that Shakespeare (in conjunction
with Marlowe or alone) wrote this play also, from which the first
Quarto of *Hamlet*, as we know it, was botched up with the help of
pirated notes taken at the theatre by that arch-thief T. Pavier?
Surely we have here the strongest presumptive evidence that Shakespeare wrote his first attempts at Tragedy as well as Comedy under
the tuition of his friend and predecessor Marlowe. The further
history of these plays confirms this suggestion. The plays that we
know of as having belonged to the Earl of Pembroke's company are
Titus Andronicus, 3 *Henry VI.* (*The True Tragedy*), *The Taming
of a Shrew, Edward II.*, and probably the early *Hamlet*. We know
that all these became the property of the Chamberlain's Company,

with the possible but **improbable** exception of *Edward II*. If, as is most likely, they all changed hands at **the same** time, **the date of** the change can be fixed. For at some **time in** 1600 *The True Tragedy* was in the possession of the Earl **of** Pembroke's men, being printed with their name on the title-page **in** that year. Had the Chamberlain's men acquired it their name would certainly **have** been inserted, as it **was in** the next **edition.** But at one time in the **same year,** 1600, *Titus Andronicus* **was in their** possession, and their name printed on the title-page, although on turning the leaf we find only the names of the players of Sussex, Pembroke, **and** Darby. The transfer took place then in 1600, and accordingly, **if** my metrical **tests be true,** in 1601 we find Shakespeare re-writing *Hamlet* and *The Taming of a Shrew*, **as** I stated in my papers of 1874, **then** knowing nothing of this external evidence. Again, the first fruit of Shakespeare's invention is expressly stated by him to have been his *Venus and Adonis*, **which** there is **independent** evidence for believing to have been written in 1588, **and** this evidence is confirmed by Greene's writing what **he** calls "Sonnets" **on** that subject in his *Perimedes* that same **year in** evident imitation **of** the metre and style of Shakespeare, after his usual fashion. Shakespeare having begun to write was not the man to give it up ; but the necessities of Fortune luckily drove him to writing for the stage ; and from the date of his writing for the stage, if not earlier, begins **the enmity** of Greene, **who saw** in him a dangerous rival with whom he dared not compete ; **and of** Nash, whose natural spite sought for a vent anywhere **on anybody ;** and of Lyly (our pleasant Willy dead of late), who **felt that for his** style of Comedy there was no chance of resurrection. **The master** had come ; the apprentice hands might give over working, only the makers possessed of genius akin to his own felt no jealousy, and worked **in** unison with him. Lodge, Peele, and Marlowe held by him to the last as great minds always do. It is only the plagiarist, the word-vendor, and the **satirist,** who carp at the creation which they have neither the power to parallel nor the wit to understand.

To return to Greene's **prose works.** Mr. **Simpson** has collected the passages referring to players in **several of** his works. We shall understand them best by taking **them in** inverse chronological order. In *The Groatsworth of Wit*, 1592, Shakespeare (for there is no doubt of his being meant **in** the well-known passage in which he is called a Shake-scene) is described as "an upstart crow beautified with our feathers." Mr. Simpson has wrongly identified with Shake-scene the Roscius in *Never Too Late*, 1590, who is asked by Tully (Greene), "Art thou proud with Æsop's crow being prankt with the glory of other's feathers?" and rightly with one of "The upstart reformers of arts" in Nash's Introduction to *Menaphon*. These upstarts and Roscius again occur in *The Groatsworth of Wit*. Roscius is the author of *The Moral of Man's Wit* and *The Dialogue of Dives*; acts in *Delfrigus* and *The King of the Fairies*; and "for seven years has been absolute master of the puppets." The "bombasting of bragging blank verse" is also alluded to in Nash's introduction to *Menaphon*, where it clearly applies to Shakespeare (an "idiot art-master," or self-instructed gradeless student), and in *The Groatsworth of Wit*, where it also applies to him; and in *Perimedes*, where it refers to the authors of *Locrine*. Mr. Simpson has also tried to show that the "vain-glorious tragedian" Roscius (Kempe), in Nash's introduction to *Menaphon*, is the same person as Doron (Lodge)[1] in the novel itself; and consequently the same as Mullidor (Muiey d'or = Golde, Lodge's *nom de plume*) in *Never Too Late* (1590). The sum of these discoveries of Mr. Simpson's is that Shakespeare is distinctly introduced into various works of Greene's, all dating from 1589 to 1592. He has, however, as far as I can see, quite failed to discover any allusion to him by Greene as a writer[2] anterior to *Menaphon*. And this is just what I should have expected. Up to 1589 Greene had his hands full in quarrelling with Marlowe and Peele; it was not until Shakespeare began to write as well as act that he turned his attacks on the *novus homo*, and began to exclaim against uneducated upstarts and pilfering pirates. This was, no doubt, part of Nash's plan of the campaign, as was also the new tone assumed by both Greene and Nash towards Peele and Marlowe. Before Nash's appearance as an auxiliary, Greene attacked both these poets; afterwards "rare wits," "atlas of poetry," "*primus verborum artifex*," are among the phrases applied to them by this ingenuous brace of satirists.

Bearing in mind then that "mad actor" is probably a name for

[1] Roscius is Kempe and Doron Lodge; Mr. Simpson thinks they both mean Shakespeare. Note that the plays acted by Roscius are not tragedies but drolls.
[2] But Shakespeare may be one of the "madmen" actors in *Perimedes*.

Shakespeare, let us see if can find in this series of romances any traces of historical fact concerning him and his fellows, Kempe and Burbage. One fact is patent; the player who had been seven years the interpreter of the puppets in *Never Too Late* is certainly meant for Kempe; but date Greene's introduction to him when you will, he could not have been seven years previously to that in London; in fact, seven years is the extreme time we can give Greene between his leaving his living (in 1585 at the earliest, the date of residing on it being 1584) and his writing this treatise in 1592. And there can be little doubt that this period of time is so to be interpreted; it is frequent in old plays and novels also, thus to confuse the real writer with his fictitious hero, and real events with the imaginary ones of the poem. I believe then that this passage fixes the date of Greene's arrival in London in 1585. I do not think we are to look for any works of Shakespeare's as indicated by the list, *Delfrigus*, *King of Fairies*, *Moral of Man's Wit*, and *Dialogue of Dives* (*Devil and Dives*). These are rather to be sought for in Greene's own works. The player is accused by him, as I interpret the passage, of endeavouring to purloin other men's writings.[1] At any rate *The King of Fairies* occurs in Greene's *James IV.*, and the dialogue of the *Devil and Dives* is likely to be the scene where the evil angel tempts the usurer in *The Looking-Glass for London*. But on the other hand I hazard a conjecture that since the hatred of the actors, which Greene so often shows, is focussed and intensified in his hatred of Shakespeare, so that we can hardly separate the two in his later writings, we may believe it not unlikely that one of the "paper bucklerd madmen," who raised his wrath in acting *Locrine*, was Shakespeare himself. And this is the more likely seeing that in *Fair Emm* and *The London Prodigal*, one of which was certainly written for Lord Strange's men and the other probably, some part would almost inevitably be assigned to Shakespeare.

It may be interesting to the reader to see the kind of verse that this malignant writer puts in the mouth of the characters under whose names he hides his representations of a friend of the world's great poet, Lodge. In his *Menaphon* there is an eclogue called "Doron's joined with Carmela's," part of which is here subjoined.

---

[1] Lord Strange's Company seem to have acted plays belonging to the Queen's men, as well as others belonging to the Admiral, in 1592.

DORON.

"Sit down, Carmela; here are cobs for kings;
  Sloes black as jet, or like my Christmas shoes;
Sweet cider which my leathern bottle brings;
  Sit down, Carmela; let me kiss thy toes."

CARMELA.

"Ah, Doron, ah, my heart; thou art as white
  As is my mother's calf or brinded cow.
Thine eyes are like the slow-worms in the night;
  Thine hairs resemble thickets of the snow.
The lines within thy face are deep and clear,
  Like to the furrows of my father's wain;
The sweat upon thy face doth oft appear
  Like to my mother's fat and kitchen gain.
Ah, leave my toe and kiss my lips, my love," &c., &c.

This is about a quarter of the eclogue, of which the reader probably desires no more.

There are other specimens of Doron's verse; for instance, his jig:

"Through the shrubs as I can crack
  For my lambs, little ones,
    'Mongst many pretty ones,
  Nymphs, I mean, whose hair was black
    As the crow;
    Like the snow
  Her face and *brows shined* I ween;
    I saw a little one,
    A bonny pretty one,
  As bright, as buxom, and as sheen
    As was she
    On her knee
  That lulled the god," &c., &c.

I cannot help here digressing to observe that in *Midsummer Night's Dream*, Act v. Sc. 1, the true reading of

"These lily *lips*,
  This cherry nose,
These yellow cowslip cheeks," &c.

can be recovered from this passage; for *lips* undoubtedly read *brows*. I believe that this play in several places alludes to Greene and his writings; in fact, Oberon *The King of the Fairies* seems to be taken from Greene's *James IV*.

Doron's only other poetical production is his *Description of Samela*; a short sample will suffice :—

> "Like to Diana in her summer weed
> Girt with a crimson robe of brightest dye
> Goes fair Samela.
>
> Whiter than be the flocks that straggling feed,
> When washt by Arethusa faint they lie,
> Is fair Samela.
>
> As fair Aurora in her morning grey,
> Deckt with the ruddy glister of her love
> Is fair Samela.
>
> Like lovely Thetis in a calmed day,
> Whereas her brightness Neptune's fancy move
> Shines fair Samela," &c., &c.

Such was the poetry of Lodge according to Greene. S. Walker and Dyce, if one may judge by their emendations, have taken these rhymes as seriously meant for good writing. But that they are intended for burlesque will be evident if we compare them with Greene's other verses in the same work; for instance, with *Sephestia's* exquisite song, of which I subjoin one verse :—

> "Weep not, my wanton! smile upon my knee;
> When thou art old, there's grief enough for thee,
> Mother's wag, pretty boy,
> Father's sorrow, father's joy,
> When thy father first did see
> Such a boy by him and me,
> He was glad, I was woe;
> Fortune changed made him so;
> When he left his pretty boy,
> Last his sorrow, first his joy."

If we refer to Greene's *Never Too Late*, the burlesque is still more palpable; here is *Mullidor's Madrigal*:—

" Dildido, dildido, O love, O love,
I feel thy rage rumble below and above.
In summer time I saw a face,
    Trop belle pour moi, hélas, hélas!
Like to a stoned horse was her pace,
    Trop belle pour moi; voilà mon trépas.
Was ever[1] young man so dismay'd?
Her eyes like wax torches did make me afraid.
Thy beauty, my love, exceedeth supposes;
Thy hair is a nettle for the nicest roses.
    Mon Dieu, aide moi!
That I with the primrose of my fresh wit
May tumble her tyranny under my feet.
    Hé donc, je serai un jeune roi."

This is enough, I think, to show the *animus* of the writer. From the unpleasing contemplation of such a captious and perverse ill-feeling, let us turn to the more genial task of examining what Marlowe and Peele were doing during these years. Marlowe, we know, wrote the following works, and almost certainly in the order that has been universally assigned to them, which agrees exactly with that determined by metrical tests.

Probable Dates.			Certain Dates.
1585.	1.	Tamberlane, part i.	before 1587.
1586.	2.	Tamberlane, part ii.	before 1587.
1587.	3.	Faustus.	
1588.	4.	Jew of Malta.	
1589.	5.	Massacre of Paris	(1589*b*).
1592.	9.	Edward II.	(1592–3).
1593.	10.	Dido (left unfinished)	(1593).

In addition to these it is highly probable that he wrote

1589.	6.	Taming of a Shrew (with Shakespeare).	
1590.	7.	Andronicus	about 1590.
1591.	8.	Henry VI. (with Peele)	before 1592.

[1] *i.e.* yeoman.

If we suppose that **he wrote** one **play a** year the chronology of his works will exactly correspond with that we have assigned to Greene's; beginning with *Tamberlane* in **1585,** and ending with *Dido* in the order of the prefixed figures. The wretched condition of the text of *The Massacre of Paris* will also be now explicable.

For as I have stated **above,** the company for which Marlowe wrote his first plays was the Admiral's; for it he **wrote all the first five in** the above list (with the possible, not **probable,** exception of *The Jew of Malta*); but *The Massacre of* **Paris,** which was certainly the last play he wrote before joining the companies of Sussex and Pembroke, must have been produced **after the death of Henri III.** (August 1589), since **this incident** forms part of the plot, **and it is** most probable from **the nature** of the play that **it was** produced almost directly after **this event**; but the Admiral's company **was** under prohibition in 1589.[1] This play if interrupted by the prohibition would **remain** incomplete (it has but three acts), and after Marlowe had **broken** with that company he would **not care to complete it.** As, however, we have here not to discuss Marlowe's works, but only to show that **the chronology we assign to his plays is** consistent with that we have given to Greene's **we pass on to Peele.**

Peele in 1584 produced his *Arraignment of Paris* for the children of the Queen's chapel. In subsequent years he wrote various plays for some company not mentioned, **which I suspect to have been Lord** Strange's, as no other **poet is mentioned in** connexion with those players, and each of the other **companies then** playing in London had its own poet attached to it. **In 1586 he** perhaps aided C. **Tylney** in *Locrine,* but **more** likely in **1587 he** edited and finished that play which ridiculed **Greene's early works.** In 1588-9 or thereabouts he probably wrote *Alcazar* for the Admiral's company; in 1590, after **Greene's** retirement, as we have seen reason **to believe** above, he was **engaged by the** Queen's company, and **wrote for** them *The Old Wives' Tale,* and probably *The Troublesome* **Reign of** *King John* in the following year. After **this his share** in plays assigned to Shakespeare (*Richard III., Romeo and Juliet, Henry VI.*) has been discussed by me elsewhere. He may also have written part of *Edward III.;* certainly not *Sir Clyamon and Sir Clamydes,* nor the older *Leir,* both of which have been inconsiderately assigned

---

[1] Note that 1589 ends at Easter 1590.

to him. We have no difficulty then in adjusting the chronology of his works as well as Marlowe's to our general scheme. *The Old Wives' Tale* is the play that has for us in the present subject the greatest interest. In Greene's *James IV.*, the King of the Fairies, who acts as presenter along with Bohan, a Scot, has called up for his amusement two boys of Bohan's, who dance jigs for him, &c. In the play itself, which is supposed to be enacted for Oberon's delectation, these boys are actual *Dramatis Personæ*, and one of them has to be rescued from hanging by the intervention in the play of Oberon, for whom the play is being performed. This gross confusion is ridiculed by **Peele** in his fairy tale, where he shows Greene how a folkstory ought to be told, and **how such** a confusion can be legitimately introduced. His old woman begins to **tell the tale**, and while she is telling **it, the** personages of the narration **come** in and continue the **story**—exactly as we often experience in dreams—when we cannot distinguish between the book we are **reading and the vision we are seeing.** Peele's drama is a real Midsummer Night's Dream. His intention in this exquisite production to ridicule Greene is unmistakable.

All things then cohere and agree with our main theory as to Shakespeare's life during this period (1585-1594). I have diligently examined every source of **information within my** reach and have concealed nothing. **As**, however, in so large a mass of detail it **has** been impossible **for me to avoid** some confusion in exposition from having to mingle arguments **and** facts, I will here sum up in **a** concise narrative the theatrical history of these ten years; in this narrative it must be understood that hypothesis and proven fact are mingled; the grounds of the hypothetical part being given **above. In all other portions of** the **chapter** theoretical statements are carefully distinguished from authorized history, however **strong the** evidence may **be in their favour.** We come then to

THE STORY OF THE STAGE (1585-1594).

In the year 1585 William Shakespeare, pressed by the needs of fortune and an increasing family, attained his majority. Under the patronage of some great man, probably, **who was** passionately attached to the stage, as were at that time many noblemen, some of whom even acted as amateurs gratuitously in **theatrical pieces,** he came to London in 1585-6 and joined the **company of Ferdinando Lord Strange**. At this time John Lyly was well known as a writer of comedies, courtly in style, patronized by the Queen, but introducing in his dramas many political and personal allusions, which had at least once got him into trouble. George Peele was also well known by his Pastoral of *The Arraignment of Paris*, which was in like manner distinguished by palpable personalities. Both these writers had been employed by boys' companies; the latter by the Children of the Chapel, the former by the Children of Paul's as well. But in this year appeared a drama which was the first of a series which were to replace the old comedies in prose or doggrel, and the old pastorals in rhyme. Marlowe then produced his *Tamberlane*, the first English tragedy worthy of the name. In it he modulated blank-verse, not in the stiff formal manner of Surrey's *Virgil*, or Sackville and Norton's *Ferrex and Perrex*, but in a comparatively free and flowing rhythm such as the necessities of stage-dialogue require. In the Prologue to this play he says:—

> "From jigging veins of rhyming mother wits,
> And such conceits as clownage keeps in pay
> We'll lead you to the stately tent of war."

This new vein was successfully struck, miner after miner tried it, there was a rush to the gold diggings. The first arrival was Robert Greene, who wrote his *Alphonsus of Aragon* in direct rivalry with *Tamberlane*, for Lord Strange's (?) company; it was a dead failure. Not so the second part of *Tamberlane*, written in 1586, like the first by Marlowe for the Admiral's company. In this year W. Kempe, one of "the jigging vein," left England for Denmark, leaving the Queen's company under the management of Dutton and Lanham. They naturally sought for a play-writer who would supply them with tragedies of the new kind. Greene and Peele both offered for the office, and Greene was chosen, and wrote his *Orlando Furioso*. Peele, who was known for the older kind of drama, the Pastoral, and who had also written a Scriptural play, *David and Bathsheba*, perhaps even an historical one, *Edward I.*, was rejected, and joined Lord Strange's (?) company.

In 1587 Marlowe wrote his masterpiece, *Doctor Faustus*; Greene ridiculed the conjuror in his best play, *Friar Bacon*; Peele, on the other hand, in conjunction with Charles Tilney, had elaborated in 1586, his **mock-heroic** travesty of *Locrine* in ridicule of Greene's tragedies of the two preceding seasons. In this play Shakespeare, or some **other** actors of the same company with him, acted; and excited Greene's wrath by the way in which his mottos, or Latin posies, his "presenters," &c. were held up to public derision. Kyd meanwhile **was** emulating Marlowe in his *Jeronimo*, and Lyly was going on his **old** road unmoved as yet by the new theatrical **heresies.**

But in **1588**, while Marlowe was initiating a new kind of comedy in his *Jew of Malta*, the precursor of the *Merchant of Venice* of eight **years** after, Greene's indignation **burst out.** He saw that he could neither rival nor ridicule successfully Marlowe's tragic or comic power; he determined to employ prose **satire as** his vehicle. In his *Perimedes* he attacked **the** actors in and writers **of** *Locrine*, **and introduced the personal characters of** Peele and Marlowe into his **attack,** accusing one of **debauchery, the** other of blasphemy. At **the same time** finding **his failure as** Marlowe's competitor **to be** complete, he attempted **competition with** Peele in **a** historical piece, *James IV.* **Peele was** not **so easily to** be outdone; he firstly took his revenge on Greene's old **tragedies by another** mock heroic **(entirely his** own this time**)**, *The Battle* **of** *Alcazar*, **which** he wrote **anonymously for the Admiral's men; and in the** following year, 1589, ridiculed *James IV.*, **as we have seen already.** In 1589*b* Marlowe began his *Massacre of Paris* for **the** Admiral's company, but did not finish it; that company as well as Lord Strange's being **closed** by authority for the licenses they had used in taxing public characters. That they had taken great liberties is manifest from what we have seen as to the plays *Locrine* and *Alcazar*. The latter play had **ridiculed Kyd as** well as Greene. **In** consequence **of this** Shakespeare and Marlowe, thrown for a while out of employment, wrote in conjunction *Hamlet* and *The Taming of a Shrew* for **the** Earl of Pembroke's **company.** Greene, **who had called** Thomas Lodge **to his aid, wrote in** 1588-9 *The Looking-Glass for London*, **and still finding his** dramatic **success** unsatisfactory, determined to leave the stage altogether and **betake himself** to Prose Romance, in **which he was** supreme. Lyly **followed** suit, and along with Nash, who had **just** come **to** London, formed **a** band of satirical **pamphleteers, who were from** the sixteenth to the nineteenth century unsurpassed for abusive sarcasm and shameless impudence. Greene was further incited to this course by the preference given to Peele in this year by the Queen's Company, for whom he wrote *The Old Wives' Tale*, a delicate, carefully-chiselled satire on his *James IV*. Shakespeare up to his time had been unknown as a dramatic author; he was known as a poet probably among his friends, for he had written his *Venus and Adonis* in 1588. He published nothing till 1593. He was as far as the stage is concerned looked on merely as an actor. But now comes a great change. His career begins, and although he did not originate any one kind of dramatic composition, it soon became evident that he would be a formidable rival in all.

In 1590 Marlowe wrote *Titus Andronicus* for the Earl of Sussex's men; Shakespeare for Lord Strange's probably a play (now lost) on the same subject, and Peele *The Troublesome Reign of King John* for the Queen's. But Lord Strange's men, in spite of their late prohibition, are producing the two plays in which Greene's competitions with Peele for the favour of the Queen's company are delineated, namely, *Fair Emm* and *The London Prodigal*. Here personal satire on the stage reaches its climax. Greene is attacked, as he richly deserved, in his personal character as well as through his published writings; his aspersions on Marlowe and Peele are doubly redoubled on himself. His title to his recent prose work, "Never Too Late," is thrown back at him with a "Physician, heal thyself" kind of denunciation. Greene, in a passion, next year complains of *Fair Emm* in his *Farewell to Folly*, vilifies its author, and of all charges for Greene the profligate ex-parson to make, says it contains *abusing of Scripture*. He is as scurrilous against him though not as clever as his coadjutor Nash had shown himself in his preface to *Menaphon* (1599) in his abuse of Shakespeare. Greene also has attacked Lodge as a rustic, half-educated, strutting tragedian, under the characters of Mullidor in *Never Too Late* (1590), and Doron in *Menaphon* (1589). Nash has accused Shakespeare of being a runaway lawyer, a shifting companion, a would-be tragedian, a botcher of blank verse, a taffaty fool decked with poet's feathers, and all the terms of vituperation which could be found in an age, when that art had only been partially cultivated. Meanwhile Shakespeare was quietly doing his work, making money and gaining respect from every one by taking no part in all this controversy.

In 1591 set in a rage for historical plays; Marlowe and Peele united their forces to produce *The Contention of York and Lancaster* and *The True Tragedy of the Duke of York*, for the Earl of Pembroke's company; in 1593 Shakespeare and Lodge (?) wrote *Edward III.*; in the same year Marlowe's *Edward II.* was acted; in 1594 Peele began *Richard III.*, afterwards finished and elaborated by Shakespeare; some years before this 1 *Henry VI.* was written by Marlowe and Lodge, and during the same period (1590-1594) the old play of *Leir* and *The True Tragedy of Richard III.* were written by unknown writers for the Queen's players. But Greene did not allow this new turn of public favour to grow up unassailed. In his *Groatsworth of Wit* (1592) he endeavoured to detach the men he had so bitterly inveighed against from the *novus homo*, whom he hated still more. With the insincerity usually to be found in men of unbridled tongue and unrestrained passions, he put himself forward as their *quondam* acquaintance, and on the ground of old friendship endeavoured to injure their new and real friend in their estimation; and failed. The details are familiar and need no repetition. Notice, however, how in this work the motive of his jealousy shows up. It is the fact that the player's "properties" are worth 200*l.* that excites the wrath of this graceless spendthrift; it was the vain hope to do likewise that took him from his former sphere to play-writing. Hence the abuse of Shakespeare for leaving his previous profession. The old, old story. And this is the last we have to do with Robert Greene. He died the same year; he had sought to separate friends, and no friend stayed by him; no one by him but the poor outcast he had consorted with and her husband, who saved him from starving in the street. Next year died Marlowe in a brawl; his unfinished play *Dido* was completed by Nash for the Chapel Children in 1594. Three years after died Peele, diseased and unreformed. Shakespeare, the only one of these great rivals (for they were great), then only was beginning to show his strength. They had all preceded him in order of development; all to the outward view had excelled him; but the forest oak had withstood the frost, outbraved the lightning, and survived the canker that had killed the more symmetrical rapidly developed tropical palms; he and he only attained to the fulfilment of his natural powers.

Not that he was idle, however, during these years between 1590 and 1596;[1] he had written *Love's Labour's Won* (?), *Love's Labour's Lost* (afterwards enlarged in 1597), *Midsummer Night's Dream* (probably also enlarged afterwards), *The Comedy of Errors*, and *Richard II*. Besides this he had re-written *The Two Gentlemen of Verona* and *King John*, and finished, corrected, and partly re-written *Richard III*. and *Romeo and Juliet*. Of these early works of Shakespeare nothing is so noticeable here as this. During the time his friends were alive he wrote in his own way; he ignored Marlowe's system of rejecting rhyme, and Peele's mixture of comedy in historical plays. But when he can no longer be a rival to them, when they have left the scene of competition and he can no longer hurt them even in supposition by adopting their methods, he drops his rhymes, his doggrel, his purely tragical histories unmixed with prose, and writes his *Merchant of Venice* to rival *The Jew of Malta*; and his *Henry IV*. to rival *Edward I*. From this time to the end of his career he uses the plots of his predecessors, their prose stories, their characters, their metre, but he fuses all that he takes from them into such a homogeneous mass that the alloy is transmuted into the truest virgin gold. No such alchemist as Shakespeare is known in the annals of any literature.

Such is a sketch of the history of these missing portions of the annals of the stage as far as we can at present make out. No doubt some details are erroneously stated, some sequences wrongly inferred. But the advantage to a student of a working hypothesis is very great. It gives definiteness to the grouping of a mass of details otherwise indistinguishable; it forms a basis for future research; it relieves the monotony of what would otherwise be a sandy expanse of lifeless desert. And the hypothesis here presented has this advantage: that it is not based on or limited by the facts that we know concerning Shakespeare himself. Every detail known of his dramatic contemporaries has been ransacked; none have been knowingly neglected; and thus for the first time a consistent narrative (if not exactly true in every minutia) has been evolved.

[1] In 1594 Lord Strange's men were incorporated with the Chamberlain's, to which company Shakespeare henceforth belongs.

CHAPTER XIV.

ON "EDWARD THE THIRD."

THIS play consists of two parts—one, which forms the main bulk of the play, relates to the foreign wars of King Edward; the other, which consists of two scenes and part of a third, contains a narrative of an attempted seduction of the Countess of Salisbury by the same monarch. These parts are distinctly different in general style and poetic power; so much so, that none but the dullest of prosaic readers could fail to note the differences; they are also clearly separated by metrical characteristics of the most pronounced kind. They are equally distinguished by the use or disuse of special words; and the personages common to the two portions of the play—for example, the Black Prince—have different characters in those portions, and are unequally developed. In my opinion, the episode is by Shakespeare; the main part of the play not. I will first consider the episode. From the entrance of the king in Act i. Sc. 2 to the end of Act ii. Sc. 2, this play is not taken from the chronicles of Holinshed, but from Painter's *Palace of Pleasure*. This is the part from which Mr. Collier has happened to select *all* his quotations given in the *Athenæum* to prove that the drama is Shakespeare's from *end to end*; that it is *no doubtful play*; that the three last acts are all conducted with *true Shakespearian energy and vigour*. To give the reader a fair chance of judging on this point, I give passages from both parts of the play.

"*Edw.* When she would talk of peace, methinks her tongue
    Commanded war to prison; when of war,

It waken'd Cæsar from his Roman grave
To hear war beautified by her discourse.
Wisdom is foolishness but in her tongue;
Beauty a slander but in her fair face:
There is no summer but in her cheerful looks,
No frosty winter, but in her disdain."
                Act ii. Sc. 1. (*Quoted by* MR. COLLIER.)

"*John.* At sea we are as puissant as the force
Of Agamemnon in the haven of Troy:
By land with Xerxes we compare of strength,
Whose soldiers drank up rivers in their thirst:
Then, Bayard-like, blind overweening Ned,
To reach at our imperial diadem,
Is either to be swallow'd of the waves,
Or hackt apieces when thou com'st ashore."
                Act iii. Sc. 1. (*Not* SHAKESPEARE'S.)

"*Count.* For where the golden ore doth buried lye,
The ground undeckt with nature's tapestry,
Seems barren, sere, unfertile, fruitless, dry,
And where the upper turf of earth doth boast
His pied perfumes and party-coloured cost,
Delve there, and find this issue and their pride
To spring from ordure and corruption's side."
                Act i. Sc. 2. (SHAKESPEARE'S.)

"*Cit.* The sun, dread lords, that in the western fall,
Beholds us now low brought through misery,
Did in the orient purple of the morn
Salute our coming forth, when we were known;
Or may our portion be with damned fiends."
                Act v. Sc. 1. (*Not* SHAKESPEARE'S.)

I might fill pages with passages like these, but these, I think, are enough; the difference is felt at once. The second and fourth are totally unlike Shakespeare; the first and third are just what he might have written between *Richard II.* and *John.* In the episode we also find expressions such as *hugy, vasture, muster men, via, imperator*, *encouch*, which are either of frequent occurrence in Shakespeare, or have the true ring of his coinage in them. We find, moreover, two new characters introduced (Derby and Audley), who appear indeed in the after parts of the play, but developed after a totally different fashion from the masterly sketch of their first appearance; and above all, we find one character, Lodowick, the king's poet-secretary, introduced in the episode only, who in a play entirely from Shakespeare's hand would certainly not have dropped out of sight so early, but have been utilised to the very end. The delicious pedantry of the man, whose attempt at verse consists of the two lines,

" More fair and chaste than is the queen of shades,
More bold in constancy than Judith was;"

who talks in inversions:

"! Of what condition or estate she is,
'Twere requisite that I should know, my Lord;"

who tells the king, when inquiring for the above poem,

" I have not to a period brought her praise,"

is worthy, if not of the author of Polonius' advice to his son, at least of the author of the scene of Pandarus' love-song.

But it will be objected, Why do you give us these vague unscientific statements? Where be your rhyme-tests and double endings? Where your un-Shakespearian words that can be counted and tabulated? They are all at hand, good reader. Here they are.

In the episode, the proportion of rhyme-lines to verse-lines is one to seven; in the other parts of the play, one to twenty; in the episode, the proportion of lines with double endings to verse-lines is one to ten; in the rest of the play it is one to twenty-five. These differences are far too great to allow the play to have been all written by one author at one period; and if the play be Shakespeare's work throughout, it would be necessary to suppose that the worst part of the play was written in his later time, with *Lear* and *Othello*; or, if I may not be allowed to presume so far on the results of my applications of metrical tests (though to the development of Shakespeare's work they are, I am certain, our surest guide), then I appeal to a different kind of evidence altogether.

In the main part of this play there are many words used that never occur in undoubted Shakespearian plays, however often certain of them may be found in Marlowe and other early dramatists. For instance, *bonny*, which occurs in 1 *Henry VI.* and 3 *Henry VI.*, but is unknown in Shakespeare, occurs in Act i. Sc. 2 three times, and *bonnier* in Act iii. Sc. 1. So the strange verb *to patronage* occurs in Act iii. Sc. 3, and in 1 *Henry VI.*, never in Shakespeare; *hórizon* (Act v. Sc. 1), *Ave Caesar* (Act i. Sc. 1), *whinyard* (Act i. Sc. 2a), *Bayard* (Act iii. Sc. 1), *Nemesis* (Act iii. Sc. 1), *martialist* (Act iii. Sc. 3), *plate*, in the Spanish sense of silver (Act i. Sc. 2, Act iv. Sc. 4), *solitariness* (Act iii. Sc. 2), *quadrant* (Act v. Sc. 1), *ure* (Act i. Sc. 1), are all words unknown to Shakespeare's vocabulary. *Battle-'ray* occurs in Act iii. Sc. 3, and Act iv. Sc. 3; Shakespeare does not even admit the common form *'ray* for *array*, while *'rayed* is found in the part of *The Taming of the Shrew* not Shakespeare's. *Burgonet*, another word in this play, occurs only once in Shakespeare in a very late play, *Antony and Cleopatra*, while it is found in 2 *Henry VI.* three times. So the anomalous word *expulsed*, which we find in 2 *Henry VI.*, but not in Shakespeare, will be seen in Act iii. Sc. 2 of this play of *Edward III.*; and in Act v. Sc. 1 the unusual verb *to quittance*, as in 1 *Henry VI.*, but not in Shakespeare. *Cataline* in *The True Tragedy of the Duke of York* has been replaced by *Machiavel* in 3 *Henry VI.*, but remains undethroned in Act iii. Sc. 1 of our play.

But I must not enlarge on this; I must return to our play. I recommend anyone who has been deluded by Capell, or his German copiers, or his English reproducers at third hand, into the belief that this work is all Shakespeare's, to read from the entrance of the King in Act i. Sc. 2, to the end of Act ii. by itself, and judge if that part be Shakespeare's, as I say it is; then to stop awhile, and read all the rest of the play by itself, noting the monotonous thud of the antique stop-line and the un-Shakespearian words I have given above, and judge if any part of that be Shakespeare's. If he say yes, he is not one I should care to argue the point with, for to such a one even the scientific metrical test would be of no avail for his enlightenment. He might even agree with Mr. Collier in saying, "I might quote the whole quarto, for *it is all his.*"

CHAPTER XV.

EXTRACTS REPRINTED FROM THE "ATHENÆUM."

To the first of the subjoined letters on Aetion I have only to add that **Marcus** Antoninus uses αἴτιον in the sense in which the Elizabethans used ἰδέα, namely, that of "form without matter; exemplar." The other letter requires no comment.

Is Aetion Shakespeare?

The passage in Spenser's *Colin Clout's Come Home Again*,

"And there though last not least is Aetion ;
A gentler shepherd may nowhere be found :
Whose Muse like his high **thought's** invention
Doth like himself heroically sound,"

was supposed to allude to Shakespeare by Malone, on the grounds, 1, that Shakespeare was called *gentle;* **2,** that his Muse was full of high thought's invention ; **3,** that the name Shake-spear sounds heroically. Mr. Hales has added a fourth argument. "The name was adopted for its own intrinsic significance, as Spenser interpreted it. He has in his mind the Greek ἀετός ; and, seeing in the rising Shakespeare **a poet** whose imagination **was to** soar aloft, **he** styled him *The Eaglet*." **To** this another argument may be added : the **Falcon in** Shakespeare's arms might be alluded to as the Eaglet, for **eagles were ranked as** a species **of** the **genus** Falcon or Hawk in **Shakespeare's time.** Thus, in the translation of Pomey's *Universe in Epitome*, by **A.** Lovell, we find Eagle, Falcon, and Marlin grouped **together under the** head of Birds for Hawking ; and in Ryder's

Latin Dictionary, Eagle, Falcon, and Merlin expressly called Hawks; and under *Falco*, Hawk and Falcon are given as synonymous. On the other hand, Todd, and, after him, Mr. Minto, have asserted that Aetion is Drayton. In support of his claim it has been urged that Drayton's assumed poetical name, *Rowland*, sounds more heroically than Shakespeare, and that Lodge, in 1596, a year after *Colin Clout* was published, mentions Drayton but not Shakespeare, which would be strange if Spenser had already mentioned Shakespeare but not Drayton: to this I add, that in Drayton's *Sonnets*, published in 1594, he calls one *an allusion to the Eaglet:* it begins—

"When like an *eaglet* I first found my love."

As these pastoral names were often taken from the *writings* of the poet alluded to, Aetion may easily have originated from this sonnet. Again, there is no reason why, in 1595, Drayton should not have written and circulated in MS. one or more of *England's Heroicall Epistles*, published in 1598, which would account for his "heroically sounding Muse." But all this depends on the assumption that *Colin Clout* was written in 1594-5. If, as Prof. Morley thinks (and I agree with him), the main part of it was written in 1591, and this verse was part of that early portion, then we have a third claimant, *Marlow;* for his name was written *Marlen* or *Marlin* oftener than *Marlow;* he is called *Marlin* in Beard's *Theatre of God's Judgments* (1597); he was entered at college under this same name in 1580; he took his degree as *Marlyn* in 1583; and is mentioned as *Marlyn* as late as Latham's *Falconry* (1618). By the way, the mention of this book reminds me that Lady Juliana Berners expressly calls the Eagle a kind of Hawk. Now that *Marlyn* and *Eaglet* were considered as synonymous, there is proof in an allusion in Petow's *Hero and Leander* (a continuation of Marlow's). He says of Marlow:—

> "Oh had that king of poets breathed longer,
> Then had fair beauty's forts been much more stronger;
> His golden pen had closed her so about
> No *bastard eaglet's* quill the world throughout
> Had been of force to mar what he had made."

Here Marlyn the true eaglet is distinctly contrasted with the false one; so that whether Aetion is Marlow or not, Marlin is certainly an eaglet. That he was a "gentle shepherd" is shown in the quotation by Dyce from the *New Metamorphosis*, by J. M. (1660), where he is called "kind Kit Marlow." That Marlin recalling the great Arthurian enchanter "sounds heroically" is clear enough, and we know how his verse was estimated as far as his plays are concerned by the allusions to his "sounding lines." It may be said that Spenser must have cut out this notice on publishing in 1595, because Marlow was dead: but we do not always do all we ought; and Spenser may have remembered to alter his verses on Ferdinand Lord Derby, the poet's patron, and forgotten to do so for the humbler Marlow. I have, I think, fairly stated above the views that can be held on Mr. Hales's hypothesis, that Aetion means *eaglet*, and shown that it does not follow that Aetion must mean Shakespeare. I am bound now to give my own view. I believe that Aetion is not derived from ἀετός, but from αἴτιος, as Malone suggested in a note. For the line,—

"And then, though last, not least is Aetion,"

requires us to read Ætion in three syllables, and not Aëtion in four. I know some scansionists may deny this; but no poet will. And again, who has ever seen the word Aëtion anywhere else in English literature? Is the obscure Greek painter mentioned in English except in classical dictionaries? Or has any author used it for "eaglet"? Ætion, on the other hand, was so common a word in Elizabethan Latin, that it is given in the Latin dictionaries for schoolboys. In Ryder's Dictionary, I find "Ætion αἴτιον et ætia ætiorum, causa principium et origo—*an originall, beginning, or cause.*" It is much more likely, then, that Malone's derivation is right, than that the ingenious conjecture made by Mr. Hales is. But what can Ætion mean as a poet's name? Is any work of Shakespeare or Drayton called αἴτιον? I think there is. Drayton's pastoral name for his mistress is Idea, ἰδέα; *Idea est eorum quæ natura fiunt exemplar æternum.* So Drayton calls his mistress the example or pattern from whom all other women derive their excellence by participating in hers. As Cooper's *Thesaurus* has it, under Idea, "Pattern of all other sort or kind, as of one seal proceedeth many prints." But Drayton was not content with a mere allusion. Of the three works he had published before 1595, one was called *Idea*, and another *Idea's Mirrour*. What, then, more natural than to indicate Drayton by Ætion, the synonym for Idea? I conclude that the interpretation of Todd and the derivation of Malone are the correct ones, and that the only point they did not see was that Ætion meant "The original, the exemplar, the first, though here the last mentioned; the *formal cause.*" So Giles Fletcher uses *Idea* in *Christ's Victory and Triumph*, st. xxxix.—

> "In midst of this city celestial,
> Where the eternal temple should have rose,
>   Light'ned th' *Idea* beatifical,
> End and *beginning of each thing that grows.*"

Carew uses the word "cause" just in the same way :—

> " Ask me no more where Jove bestows,
> When June is past, the fading rose,
>   For in your beauty's orient deep
>   These flowers, *as in their causes*, sleep."

If anyone objects to my supposition that the *Heroicall Epistles* were in circulation as early as 1595, I would refer him to Drayton's *Address to the Reader*. "Seeing these Epistles are *now* to the world made public," &c., which distinctly implies that they had been written, and were known to have been written for some time; and again, in the *Catalogue of the Heroical Loves*, he says,—

> " Their several loves since I before have shown,
>   Now give me leave at last to sing my own."

This implies that the *Heroicall Epistles* were written before his love poems to Idea, for in no other poems does he "sing his own loves." But *Idea* and *Idea's Mirrour* were published in 1593 and 1594.

Shakespeare's Arms.

So far as I am aware, no attempt has hitherto been made to explain the charges in Shakespeare's arms. Yet from the presence of "spear" in them, it is evident at a glance that they belong to the class of *armes parlantes*, canting or punning arms. In the original instrument in the College of Heralds they are thus blazoned:—"In a field of gould upon a bend sables a speare, the poynt upward, headed argent, and for his crest or cognizance *a falcon with his wings displayed*, standing on a wrethe of his coullers supporting a speare armed hedded or stieled sylver fyxed uppon a helmet with mantell and tassels." Here is the *spear* plain enough; but where is the *shake?* In the words I have italicized, I think. For how could the name, or rather this part of the name, be expressed in the charge? There is no means of representing *shake* but by something shaking; and no inorganic thing can be so drawn; nor among living creatures can I find anything that can represent shaking excepting a bird *shaking its wings previously to flying*, which can heraldically be expressed. The connection between shaking and "with wings displayed" may be gathered from the following considerations. Lady Juliana Berners, in her work on Hawking, especially warns her readers never to say of a falcon that "she shakes," but always to say "she rouses." And in accordance with this, a bird shaking its wings in preparation to fly, that is to say, "with wings displayed," was often blazoned in the heraldic books as *rousant*. If we refer to the old dictionaries we find this confirmed; for instance, in Ryder's Latin Dictionary, to rouse is translated *corusco;* and in referring to *corusco*, we find "Corusco πάλλω κραδαίνω vibro, oculorum aciem perstringo. To shine, glisten, or lighten. To brandish. c. gladium vel hastam, Virg. to brandish or shake." So that the very word used by our ancestors in Latin to express the shaking of a spear was also used by them for the displaying the wings in heraldry. It is, therefore, to me certain that "Garter and Clarencieulx" in granting John Shakespeare his arms gave him a canting bearing, a kind which is rightly said in the *Penny Cyclopædia* to have been one of the most frequent as well as the most ancient descriptions of charges, and as worthy of respect as any other. The representation of *Shake* in Shakespeare (not Shakspere) by a rousing falcon is confirmed by the arms of Crispinus or Cri-spinas in the *Poetaster*, "a face *crying* in chief and beneath it a bloody toe between three thorns pungent." Marston, as well as Crispinus, is here indicated. *Mars* is red or bloody (compare *Mars ochre*) and *toen* is toes : together forming Marston. Both puns are equally bad. So again in *Every Man out of his Humour* Sogliardo's arms, "On a chief argent between two ann'lets sable, a boar's head proper," indicate Burbage (*Boar-badge*) ; badge (*bague*) being a ring, garland, or annulet.

The following list of managers, &c., will be useful for reference :—

Company.	Managers, &c.
Sir R. Lane's	Laurence Dutton (1573).
Sir R. Dudley's	James Burbage, John Perkyn, John Lanham, William Johnson, Robert Wilson (1574).
Earl Warwick's	Laurence Dutton, John Dutton (1576).
Earl Darby's	Robert Brown (1579).
Queen's	John Dutton, John Lanham (1590).
Chamberlain's	John Heminges, Thomas Pope (1597) ; Heminges alone (1600).
Admiral's	Robert Shaw, Thomas Downton, Philip Henslow, William Allen (1598).

Children.	Masters.
Paul's	Sebastian Westcott (to 1586) ; Thomas Giles (to 1600) ; Edward Piers.
Chapel	Richard Bowyer (to 1572) : John Honnys (to ?) ; William Hunnis.
Westminster	John Taylor (to 1579), William Elderton.
Windsor	Richard Ferret.
Merchant Taylors'	Richard Mountcaster.

THE END.

February, 1876.

A Catalogue of Educational Books, Published by MACMILLAN and Co., Bedford Street, Strand, London.

CLASSICAL.

Æschylus.—THE EUMENIDES. The Greek Text, with Introduction, English Notes, and Verse Translation. By BERNARD DRAKE, M.A., late Fellow of King's College, Cambridge. **8vo.** 3s. 6d.

Aristotle. — AN INTRODUCTION TO ARISTOTLE'S RHETORIC. With Analysis, Notes, and Appendices. By E. M. COPE, Fellow and Tutor of Trinity Coll. Cambridge. 8vo. **14s.**

ARISTOTLE ON FALLACIES; OR, THE SOPHISTICI ELENCHI. With Translation and Notes by E. POSTE, M.A., Fellow of Oriel College, Oxford. 8vo. 8s. 6d.

Aristophanes.—THE BIRDS. Translated into English Verse, with Introduction, Notes, and Appendices, by B. H. KENNEDY, D.D., **Regius** Professor of Greek in the University of Cambridge. Crown **8vo.** 6s.

Belcher.—SHORT EXERCISES IN LATIN PROSE COMPOSITION AND EXAMINATION PAPERS IN LATIN GRAMMAR, to which is prefixed a Chapter on Analysis of Sentences. By the **Rev. H.** BELCHER, M.A., Assistant Master in King's College School, London. 18mo. 1s. 6d. Key, 1s. 6d.

Blackie.—GREEK AND ENGLISH DIALOGUES FOR USE IN SCHOOLS AND COLLEGES. By JOHN STUART BLACKIE, Professor of Greek in the Univ. of Edinburgh. Second Edition. Fcap. 8vo. **2s. 6d.**

Cicero. — THE SECOND PHILIPPIC ORATION. With Introduction and Notes. From the German of KARL HALM. Edited, with Corrections and Additions, by JOHN E. B. MAYOR. M.A., Fellow and Classical Lecturer of St. John's College, Cambridge. Fourth Edition, revised. **Fcap.** 8vo. 5s.

THE ORATIONS OF CICERO AGAINST CATILINA. With Notes and an Introduction. From the German of KARL HALM, with additions by A. S. WILKINS, M.A., Owens College, Manchester. New Edition. **Fcap.** 8vo. 3s. 6d.

Cicero—*continued.*

THE ACADEMICA OF CICERO. The Text revised and explained by JAMES REID, M.A., Assistant Tutor and late Fellow of Christ's College, Cambridge. Fcap. 8vo. 4s. 6d.

Demosthenes.—ON THE CROWN, to which is prefixed ÆSCHINES AGAINST CTESIPHON. The Greek Text with English Notes. By B. DRAKE, M.A., late Fellow of King's College, Cambridge. Fifth Edition. Fcap. 8vo. 5s.

Ellis.—PRACTICAL HINTS ON THE QUANTITATIVE PRONUNCIATION OF LATIN, for the use of Classical Teachers and Linguists. By A. J. ELLIS, B.A., F.R.S. Extra fcap. 8vo. 4s. 6d.

Goodwin.—SYNTAX OF THE MOODS AND TENSES OF THE GREEK VERB. By W. W. GOODWIN, Ph.D. New Edition, revised. Crown 8vo. 6s. 6d.

Greenwood.—THE ELEMENTS OF GREEK GRAMMAR, including Accidence, Irregular Verbs, and Principles of Derivation and Composition; adapted to the System of Crude Forms. By J. G. GREENWOOD, Principal of Owens College, Manchester. Fifth Edition. Crown 8vo. 5s. 6d.

Hodgson.—MYTHOLOGY FOR LATIN VERSIFICATION. A brief Sketch of the Fables of the Ancients, prepared to be rendered into Latin Verse for Schools. By F. HODGSON, B.D., late Provost of Eton. New Edition, revised by F. C. HODGSON, M.A. 18mo. 3s.

Homer's Odyssey.—THE NARRATIVE OF ODYSSEUS. With a Commentary by JOHN E. B. MAYOR, M.A., Kennedy Professor of Latin at Cambridge. Part I. Book IX.—XII. Fcap. 8vo. 3s.

Horace.—THE WORKS OF HORACE, rendered into English Prose, with Introductions, Running Analysis, and Notes, by JAMES LONSDALE, M.A., and SAMUEL LEE, M.A. Globe 8vo. 3s. 6d.; gilt edges, 4s. 6d.

THE ODES OF HORACE IN A METRICAL PARAPHRASE. By R. M. HOVENDEN, B.A., formerly of Trinity College, Cambridge. Extra fcap. 8vo. 4s. 6d.

Jackson.—FIRST STEPS TO GREEK PROSE COMPOSITION. By BLOMFIELD JACKSON, M.A. Assistant-Master in King's College School, London. 18mo. 1s. 6d.

Juvenal.—THIRTEEN SATIRES OF JUVENAL. With a Commentary. By JOHN E. B. MAYOR, M.A., Kennedy Professor of Latin at Cambridge. Second Edition, enlarged. Vol. I. Crown 8vo. 7s. 6d. Or Parts I. and II. Crown 8vo. 3s. 6d. each.
"*A painstaking and critical edition.*"—SPECTATOR.

CLASSICAL.

Marshall.—A TABLE OF IRREGULAR GREEK VERBS, classified according to the arrangement of Curtius' Greek Grammar. By J. M. MARSHALL, M.A., Fellow and late Lecturer of Brasenose College, Oxford; one of the Masters in Clifton College. 8vo. cloth. New Edition. 1s.

Mayor (John E. B.)—FIRST GREEK READER. Edited after KARL HALM, with Corrections and large Additions by JOHN E. B. MAYOR, M.A., Fellow and Classical Lecturer of St. John's College, Cambridge. New Edition, revised. Fcap. 8vo. 4s. 6d.

Mayor (John E. B.)—BIBLIOGRAPHICAL CLUE TO LATIN LITERATURE. Edited after HÜBNER, with Large Additions by Professor JOHN E. B. MAYOR. Crown 8vo. 6s. 6d.

"*An extremely useful volume that should be in the hands of all scholars.*"—ATHENÆUM.

Mayor (Joseph B.)—GREEK FOR BEGINNERS. By the Rev. J. B. MAYOR, M.A., Professor of Classical Literature in King's College, London. Part I., with Vocabulary, 1s. 6d. Parts II. and III., with Vocabulary and Index, 3s. 6d., complete in one vol. New Edition. Fcap. 8vo. cloth, 4s. 6d.

Nixon.—PARALLEL EXTRACTS arranged for translation into English and Latin, with Notes on Idioms. By J. E. NIXON, M.A., Classical Lecturer, King's College, London. Part I.—Historical and Epistolary. Crown 8vo. 3s. 6d.

Peile (John, M.A.)—AN INTRODUCTION TO GREEK AND LATIN ETYMOLOGY. By JOHN PEILE, M.A., Fellow and Tutor of Christ's College, Cambridge, formerly Teacher of Sanskrit in the University of Cambridge. Third and Revised Edition. Crown 8vo. 10s. 6d.

"*A very valuable contribution to the science of language.*"—SATURDAY REVIEW.

Plato.—THE REPUBLIC OF PLATO. Translated into English, with an Analysis and Notes, by J. LL. DAVIES, M.A., and D. J. VAUGHAN, M.A. Third Edition, with Vignette Portraits of Plato and Socrates, engraved by JEENS from an Antique Gem. 18mo. 4s. 6d.

Plautus.—THE MOSTELLARIA OF PLAUTUS. With Notes Prolegomena, and Excursus. By WILLIAM RAMSAY, M.A., formerly Professor of Humanity in the University of Glasgow. Edited by Professor GEORGE G. RAMSAY, M.A., of the University of Glasgow. 8vo. 14s.

"*The fruits of that exhaustive research and that ripe and well-digested scholarship which its author brought to bear upon everything that he undertook are visible throughout.*"—PALL MALL GAZETTE.

Potts, Alex. W., M.A.—HINTS TOWARDS LATIN PROSE COMPOSITION. By ALEX. W. POTTS, M.A., late Fellow of St. John's College, Cambridge; Assistant Master in Rugby School; and Head Master of the Fettes College, Edinburgh. New Edition, enlarged. **Extra** fcap. 8vo. cloth. 3s.

Roby.—A GRAMMAR OF THE LATIN LANGUAGE, from Plautus to Suetonius. By H. J. ROBY, M.A., late Fellow of St. John's College, Cambridge. In Two Parts. Second Edition. Part I. containing :—Book I. Sounds. Book II. Inflexions. Book III. Word-formation. Appendices. Crown 8vo. 8s. 6d. Part II.—Syntax, Prepositions, &c. Crown 8vo. 10s. 6d.
"*Marked by the clear and practised insight of a master in his art. A book that would do honour to any country.*"—ATHENÆUM.

Rust.—FIRST STEPS TO LATIN PROSE COMPOSITION. By the Rev. G. RUST, M.A. of Pembroke College, Oxford, Master of the Lower School, King's College, London. New Edition. 18mo. 1s. 6d.

Sallust.—CAII SALLUSTII CRISPI CATILINA ET JUGURTHA. For Use in Schools. With copious Notes. By C. MERIVALE, B.D. New Edition, carefully revised and enlarged. Fcap. 8vo. 4s. 6d. Or separately, 2s. 6d. each.
"*A very good edition, to which the Editor has not only brought scholarship but independent judgment and historical criticism.*"—SPECTATOR.

Tacitus.—THE HISTORY OF TACITUS TRANSLATED INTO ENGLISH. By A. J. CHURCH, M.A., and W. J. BRODRIBB, M.A. With Notes and a Map. New and Cheaper Edition. Crown 8vo. 6s.
"*A scholarly and faithful translation.*"—SPECTATOR.

TACITUS, THE AGRICOLA AND GERMANIA OF. A Revised Text, English Notes, **and** Maps. By A. J. CHURCH, M.A., and W. J. BRODRIBB, M.A. New Edition. Fcap. 8vo. 3s. 6d. Or separately, 2s. each.
"*A model of careful editing,' being at once compact, complete, and correct, as well as neatly printed and elegant in style.*"—ATHENÆUM.

TACITUS.—THE ANNALS. Translated, with **Notes** and Maps, by A. J. CHURCH and W. J. BRODRIBB. Crown 8vo. 7s. 6d.

THE AGRICOLA AND GERMANIA. Translated into English by A. J. CHURCH, M.A., and W. J. BRODRIBB, M.A. With Maps and Notes. Extra fcap. 8vo. 2s. 6d.
"*At once readable and exact; may be perused with pleasure by all, and consulted with advantage by the classical student.*"—ATHENÆUM.

Theophrastus.— THE CHARACTERS OF THEOPHRASTUS. An English Translation from a Revised Text.

CLASSICAL.

With Introduction and **Notes.** By R. C. JEBB, M.A., Public Orator in the University of Cambridge, and Professor of Greek in the University of Glasgow. Extra fcap. 8vo. 6s. 6d.

"*A very handy and scholarly edition of a work which till now has been beset with hindrances and difficulties, but which Mr. Jebb's critical skill and judgment have at length placed within the grasp and comprehension of ordinary readers.*"—SATURDAY REVIEW.

Thring.—Works by the Rev. E. THRING, M.A., Head Master of Uppingham School.

A LATIN GRADUAL. A First Latin Construing Book for Beginners. New Edition, enlarged, with Coloured Sentence Maps. Fcap. 8vo. 2s. 6d.

A MANUAL OF MOOD CONSTRUCTIONS. Fcap. 8vo. 1s. 6d.

A CONSTRUING BOOK. Fcap. 8vo. 2s. 6d.

Thucydides.—THE SICILIAN EXPEDITION. Being Books VI. and VII. of Thucydides, with Notes. New Edition, revised and enlarged, with Map. By the Rev. PERCIVAL FROST, M.A., late Fellow of St. John's College, Cambridge. Fcap. 8vo. 5s.

"*The notes are excellent of their kind. Mr. Frost seldom passes over a difficulty, and what he says is always to the point.*"—EDUCATIONAL TIMES.

Virgil.—THE WORKS OF VIRGIL RENDERED INTO ENGLISH PROSE, with Notes, Introductions, Running Analysis, and an Index, by JAMES LONSDALE, M.A. and SAMUEL LEE, M.A. Second Edition. Globe 8vo. 3s. 6d.; gilt edges, 4s. 6d.

"*A more complete edition of Virgil in English it is scarcely possible to conceive than the scholarly work before us.*"—GLOBE.

Wright.—Works by J. WRIGHT, M.A., late Head Master of Sutton Coldfield School.

HELLENICA; OR, A HISTORY OF GREECE IN GREEK, as related by Diodorus and Thucydides; being a First Greek Reading Book, with explanatory Notes, Critical and Historical. Third Edition, with a Vocabulary. 12mo. 3s. 6d.

"*A good plan well executed.*"—GUARDIAN.

A HELP TO **LATIN** GRAMMAR; or, The Form and Use of Words in Latin, with Progressive Exercises. Crown 8vo. 4s. 6d.

THE SEVEN KINGS OF ROME. An Easy Narrative, abridged from the First Book of Livy by the omission of Difficult Passages; being a First Latin Reading Book, with Grammatical Notes Fifth Edition. Fcap. 8vo. 3s. With Vocabulary, 3s. 6d.

"*The Notes are abundant, explicit, and full of such grammatical and other information as boys require.*"—ATHENÆUM.

FIRST LATIN STEPS; OR, AN INTRODUCTION BY A SERIES OF EXAMPLES TO THE STUDY OF THE LATIN LANGUAGE. Crown 8vo. 5s.

ATTIC PRIMER. **Arranged for the** Use of Beginners. Extra fcap. 8vo. 4s. 6d.

MATHEMATICS.

Airy.—Works by SIR G. B. AIRY, K.C.B., Astronomer Royal :—
ELEMENTARY TREATISE ON PARTIAL DIFFERENTIAL EQUATIONS. Designed for the Use of Students in the Universities. With Diagrams. New Edition. Crown 8vo. cloth. 5s. 6d.

ON THE ALGEBRAICAL AND NUMERICAL THEORY OF ERRORS OF OBSERVATIONS AND THE COMBINATION OF OBSERVATIONS. New edition, revised. Crown 8vo. cloth. 6s. 6d.

UNDULATORY THEORY OF OPTICS. Designed for the Use of Students in the University. New Edition. Crown 8vo. cloth. 6s. 6d.

ON SOUND AND ATMOSPHERIC VIBRATIONS. With the Mathematical Elements of Music. Designed for the Use of Students of the University. Second Edition, Revised and Enlarged. Crown 8vo. 9s.

A TREATISE OF MAGNETISM. Designed for the use of Students in the University. Crown 8vo. 9s. 6d.

Airy (Osmund).—A TREATISE ON GEOMETRICAL OPTICS. Adapted for the use of the Higher Classes in Schools. By OSMUND AIRY, B.A., one of the Mathematical Masters in Wellington College. Extra fcap. 8vo. 3s. 6d.
"*Carefully and lucidly written, and rendered as simple as possible by the use in all cases of the most elementary form of investigation.*"—ATHENÆUM.

Bayma.—THE ELEMENTS OF MOLECULAR MECHANICS. By JOSEPH BAYMA, S.J., Professor of Philosophy, Stonyhurst College. Demy 8vo. cloth. 10s. 6d.

Beasley.—AN ELEMENTARY TREATISE ON PLANE TRIGONOMETRY. With Examples. By R. D. BEASLEY, M.A., Head Master of Grantham Grammar School. Fourth Edition, revised and enlarged. Crown 8vo. cloth. 3s. 6d.

Blackburn (Hugh).—ELEMENTS OF PLANE TRIGONOMETRY, for the use of the Junior Class of Mathematics in the University of Glasgow. By HUGH BLACKBURN, M.A., Professor of Mathematics in the University of Glasgow. Globe 8vo. 1s. 6d.

Boole.—Works by G. BOOLE, D.C.L., F.R.S., late Professor of Mathematics in the Queen's University, Ireland.

MATHEMATICS.

Boole—*continued.*

A TREATISE ON DIFFERENTIAL EQUATIONS. New and Revised Edition. Edited by I. TODHUNTER. Crown 8vo. cloth. 14s.

"*A treatise incomparably superior to any other elementary book on the same subject with which we are acquainted.*"—PHILOSOPHICAL MAGAZINE.

A TREATISE ON DIFFERENTIAL EQUATIONS. Supplementary Volume. Edited by I. TODHUNTER. Crown 8vo. cloth. 8s. 6d.

This volume contains all that Professor Boole wrote for the purpose of enlarging his treatise on Differential Equations.

THE CALCULUS OF FINITE DIFFERENCES. Crown 8vo. cloth. 10s. 6d. New Edition, revised by J. F. MOULTON.

"*As an original book by one of the first mathematicians of the age, it is out of all comparison with the mere second-hand compilations which have hitherto been alone accessible to the student.*"—PHILOSOPHICAL MAGAZINE.

Brook-Smith (J.)—ARITHMETIC IN THEORY AND PRACTICE. By J. BROOK-SMITH, M.A., LL.B., St. John's College, Cambridge; Barrister-at-Law; one of the Masters of Cheltenham College. New **Edition, revised.** Complete, Crown 8vo. **4s. 6d.** Part I. 3s. 6d.

"*A valuable Manual of Arithmetic of the Scientific kind. The best we have seen.*"—LITERARY CHURCHMAN. "*An essentially practical book, providing very definite help to candidates for almost every kind of competitive examination.*"—BRITISH QUARTERLY.

Cambridge Senate-House Problems and **Riders**, WITH SOLUTIONS :—
1848-1851.—RIDERS. By JAMESON. 8vo. cloth. 7s. 6d.
1857.—PROBLEMS AND RIDERS. By CAMPION and WALTON. 8vo. cloth. 8s. 6d.
1864.—PROBLEMS AND RIDERS. By WALTON and WILKINSON. 8vo. cloth. 10s. 6d.

CAMBRIDGE COURSE OF ELEMENTARY NATURAL PHILOSOPHY, for the Degree of B.A. Originally compiled by J. C. SNOWBALL, M.A., late Fellow of St. John's College. Fifth Edition, revised and enlarged, and adapted for the Middle-Class Examinations by THOMAS LUND, B.D., Late Fellow and Lecturer of St. John's College, Editor of Wood's Algebra, &c. Crown 8vo. cloth. 5s.

Candler.—HELP TO ARITHMETIC. Designed for the use of Schools. By H. CANDLER, M.A., Mathematical Master of Uppingham School. Extra fcap. 8vo. 2s. 6d.

EDUCATIONAL BOOKS.

Cheyne.—Works by C. H. **H. CHEYNE**, M.A., F.R.A.S.
AN ELEMENTARY TREATISE ON THE PLANETARY THEORY. With a Collection of Problems. Second Edition. Crown 8vo. cloth. **6s. 6d.**

THE EARTH'S MOTION OF ROTATION. Crown 8vo. 3s. 6d.

Childe.—THE SINGULAR PROPERTIES OF THE ELLIPSOID AND ASSOCIATED SURFACES OF THE NTH DEGREE. By the Rev. G. F. CHILDE, M.A., Author of "Ray Surfaces," "Related Caustics," &c. 8vo. **10s. 6d.**

Christie.—A COLLECTION OF ELEMENTARY TEST-QUESTIONS IN PURE AND MIXED MATHEMATICS; with Answers and Appendices on Synthetic Division, and on the Solution of Numerical Equations by Horner's Method. By JAMES R. CHRISTIE, F.R.S., late First Mathematical Master at the Royal Military Academy, Woolwich. Crown 8vo. cloth. **8s. 6d.**

Cuthbertson—EUCLIDIAN GEOMETRY. By FRANCIS CUTHBERTSON, M.A., LL.D., late Fellow of Corpus Christi College, Cambridge; and Head Mathematical Master of the City of London School. Extra fcap. 8vo. **4s. 6d.**

Dalton.—Works by the Rev. T. DALTON, M.A., Assistant Master of Eton College.

RULES AND EXAMPLES IN ARITHMETIC. New Edition. 18mo. cloth. **2s. 6d.** *Answers to the Examples are appended.*

RULES AND EXAMPLES IN ALGEBRA. Part I. 18mo. **2s.** *This work is prepared on the same plan as the Arithmetic.*

Day.—PROPERTIES OF CONIC SECTIONS PROVED GEOMETRICALLY. PART I., THE ELLIPSE, with Problems. By the Rev. H. G. DAY, M.A., Head Master of Sedburgh Grammar School. Crown 8vo. **3s. 6d.**

Dodgson.—AN ELEMENTARY TREATISE ON DETERMINANTS, with their Application to Simultaneous Linear Equations and Algebraical Geometry. By CHARLES L. DODGSON, M.A., Student and Mathematical Lecturer of Christ Church, Oxford. Small 4to. cloth. **10s. 6d.**

"*A valuable addition to the treatises we possess on Modern Algebra.*" —EDUCATIONAL TIMES.

Drew.—GEOMETRICAL TREATISE ON CONIC SECTIONS. By W. H. DREW, M.A., St. John's College, Cambridge. Fifth Edition, enlarged. Crown 8vo. cloth. **5s.**

SOLUTIONS TO THE PROBLEMS IN DREW'S CONIC SECTIONS. Crown 8vo. cloth. **4s. 6d.**

MATHEMATICS.

Edgar (J. H.) and Pritchard (G. S.)—NOTE-BOOK ON PRACTICAL SOLID OR DESCRIPTIVE GEOMETRY. Containing Problems with help for Solutions. By J. H. EDGAR, M.A., Lecturer on Mechanical Drawing at the Royal School of Mines, and G. S. PRITCHARD, late Master for Descriptive Geometry, Royal Military Academy, Woolwich. Third Edition, revised and enlarged. Globe 8vo. 3s.

Ferrers.—AN ELEMENTARY TREATISE ON TRILINEAR CO-ORDINATES, the Method of Reciprocal Polars, and the Theory of Projectors. By the Rev. N. M. FERRERS, M.A., Fellow and Tutor of Gonville and Caius College, Cambridge. Third Edition. Crown 8vo. 6s. 6d.

Frost.—Works by PERCIVAL FROST, M.A., formerly Fellow of St. John's College, Cambridge; Mathematical Lecturer of King's College.

AN ELEMENTARY TREATISE ON CURVE TRACING. By PERCIVAL FROST, M.A. 8vo. 12s.

THE FIRST THREE SECTIONS OF NEWTON'S PRINCIPIA. With Notes and Illustrations. Also a collection of Problems, principally intended as Examples of Newton's Methods. By PERCIVAL FROST, M.A. Second Edition. 8vo. cloth. 10s. 6d.

Frost.—SOLID GEOMETRY. By PERCIVAL FROST, M.A. A New Edition, revised and enlarged, of the Treatise by FROST and WOLSTENHOLME. In 2 Vols. Vol. I. 8vo. 16s.

Godfray.—Works by HUGH GODFRAY, M.A., Mathematical Lecturer at Pembroke College, Cambridge.

A TREATISE ON ASTRONOMY, for the Use of Colleges and Schools. New Edition. 8vo. cloth. 12s. 6d.

AN ELEMENTARY TREATISE ON THE LUNAR THEORY, with a Brief Sketch of the Problem up to the time of Newton. Second Edition, revised. Crown 8vo. cloth. 5s. 6d.

Hemming.—AN ELEMENTARY TREATISE ON THE DIFFERENTIAL AND INTEGRAL CALCULUS, for the Use of Colleges and Schools. By G. W. HEMMING, M.A., Fellow of St. John's College, Cambridge. Second Edition, with Corrections and Additions. 8vo. cloth. 9s.

Jackson.—GEOMETRICAL CONIC SECTIONS. An Elementary Treatise in which the Conic Sections are defined as the Plane Sections of a Cone, and treated by the Method of Projection. By J. STUART JACKSON, M.A., late Fellow of Gonville and Caius College, Cambridge. 4s. 6d.

Jellet (John H.)—A TREATISE ON THE THEORY OF FRICTION. By JOHN H. JELLET, B.D., Senior Fellow of Trinity College, Dublin; President of the Royal Irish Academy. 8vo. 8s. 6d.

Jones and Cheyne.—ALGEBRAICAL EXERCISES. Progressively arranged. By the Rev. C. A. JONES, M.A., and C. H. CHEYNE, M.A., F.R.A.S., Mathematical Masters of Westminster School. New Edition. 18mo. cloth. 2s. 6d.

Kelland and Tait.—INTRODUCTION TO QUATERNIONS, with numerous examples. By P. KELLAND, M.A., F.R.S., formerly Fellow of Queen's College, Cambridge; and P. G. TAIT, M.A., formerly Fellow of St. Peter's College, Cambridge; Professors in the department of Mathematics in the University of Edinburgh. Crown 8vo. 7s. 6d.

Kitchener.—A GEOMETRICAL NOTE-BOOK, containing Easy Problems in Geometrical Drawing preparatory to the Study of Geometry. For the Use of Schools. By F. E. KITCHENER, M.A., Mathematical Master at Rugby. New Edition. 4to. 2s.

Morgan.—A COLLECTION OF PROBLEMS AND EXAMPLES IN MATHEMATICS. With Answers. By H. A. MORGAN, M.A., Sadlerian and Mathematical Lecturer of Jesus College, Cambridge. Crown 8vo. cloth. **6s. 6d.**

Newton's PRINCIPIA. Edited by Professor Sir W. THOMSON and Professor BLACKBURN. 4to. cloth. 31s. 6d.
"*Undoubtedly the finest edition of the text of the 'Principia' which has hitherto appeared.*"—EDUCATIONAL **TIMES.**

Parkinson.—Works by S. PARKINSON, D.D., **F.R.S., Tutor** and Prælector of St. John's College, Cambridge.
AN ELEMENTARY TREATISE ON MECHANICS. For the Use of the Junior Classes at the University and the Higher Classes in Schools. With a Collection of Examples. Fifth edition, revised. Crown 8vo. cloth. 9s. 6d.
A TREATISE ON OPTICS. Third Edition, revised and enlarged. Crown 8vo. cloth. 10s. 6d.

Phear.—ELEMENTARY HYDROSTATICS. With Numerous Examples. By J. B. PHEAR, M.A., Fellow and late Assistant Tutor of Clare College, Cambridge. Fourth Edition. Crown 8vo. cloth. 5s. 6d.

Pirie.—LESSONS ON RIGID DYNAMICS. By the Rev. G. PIRIE, M.A., Fellow and Tutor of Queen's College, Cambridge. Crown 8vo. 6s.

Pratt.—A TREATISE ON ATTRACTIONS, LAPLACE'S FUNCTIONS, AND THE FIGURE OF THE EARTH. By JOHN H. PRATT, M.A., Archdeacon of Calcutta, Author of "The Mathematical Principles of Mechanical Philosophy." Fourth Edition. Crown 8vo. cloth. 6s. 6d.

Puckle.—AN ELEMENTARY TREATISE ON CONIC SECTIONS AND ALGEBRAIC GEOMETRY. With Numerous Examples and Hints for their Solution; especially designed for the Use of Beginners. By G. H. PUCKLE, M.A. New Edition, **revised** and enlarged. **Crown** 8vo. cloth. **7s. 6d.**

MATHEMATICS.

Rawlinson.—ELEMENTARY STATICS, by the Rev. GEORGE RAWLINSON, M.A. Edited by the Rev. EDWARD STURGES, M.A., of Emmanuel College, Cambridge, and late Professor of the Applied Sciences, Elphinstone College, Bombay. Crown 8vo. cloth. 4s. 6d.

Reynolds.—MODERN METHODS IN ELEMENTARY GEOMETRY. By E. M. REYNOLDS, M.A., Mathematical Master in Clifton College. **Crown** 8vo. 3s. 6d.

Routh.—AN ELEMENTARY TREATISE ON THE DYNAMICS OF THE SYSTEM OF RIGID BODIES. With Numerous Examples. By EDWARD JOHN ROUTH, M.A., late Fellow and Assistant Tutor of St. Peter's College, Cambridge; Examiner in the **University of** London. Second Edition, enlarged. Crown 8vo. cloth. 14s.

WORKS
By the REV. BARNARD SMITH, M.A.,
Rector of Glaston, Rutland, late Fellow and Senior Bursar of St. Peter's College, Cambridge.

ARITHMETIC AND ALGEBRA, in their Principles and Application; with numerous systematically arranged Examples taken from the Cambridge Examination Papers, with especial reference to the Ordinary Examination for the B.A. Degree. Thirteenth Edition, carefully revised. Crown 8vo. cloth. 10s. 6d.

"*To all those whose* **minds are** *sufficiently developed to comprehend the* **simplest** *mathematical reasoning,* **and** *who have* **not** *yet thoroughly mastered the principles of Arithmetic* **and** *Algebra, it is calculated to be of great advantage.*"—ATHENÆUM. "*Mr. Smith's work is a most useful publication. The rules* **are stated** *with great clearness. The examples are well selected, and worked out with just sufficient detail, without being encumbered by* **too** *minute explanations : and there prevails throughout it that just proportion of theory and practice which is the crowning excellence of an elementary work.*"—DEAN PEACOCK.

ARITHMETIC FOR SCHOOLS. New Edition. Crown 8vo. cloth. 4s. 6d. Adapted from the Author's work on "Arithmetic and Algebra."

"*Admirably adapted for instruction, combining just sufficient theory with a large and well-selected collection of exercises for practice.*"—JOURNAL OF EDUCATION.

A KEY TO THE ARITHMETIC FOR SCHOOLS. Tenth Edition. **Crown** 8vo. cloth. 8s. 6d.

EXERCISES IN ARITHMETIC. With Answers. Crown 8vo. limp cloth. 2s. 6d.
Or sold separately, Part I. 1s.; Part II. 1s.; Answers, 6d.

SCHOOL CLASS-BOOK OF ARITHMETIC. 18mo. cloth. 3s.
Or sold separately, Parts I. and II. 10d. each; Part III. 1s.

KEYS TO SCHOOL CLASS-BOOK OF ARITHMETIC. Complete in one volume, 18mo. cloth, **6s.** 6d.; or Parts I., II., and III., 2s. 6d. each.

Barnard Smith—*continued.*

SHILLING BOOK OF ARITHMETIC FOR NATIONAL AND ELEMENTARY SCHOOLS. 18mo. cloth. Or separately, Part I. 2*d*.; Part II. 3*d*.; Part III. 7*d*. Answers, 6*d*

THE SAME, with Answers complete. 18mo. cloth. 1*s*. 6*d*.

KEY TO SHILLING BOOK OF ARITHMETIC. 18mo. cloth. 4*s*. 6*d*.

EXAMINATION PAPERS IN ARITHMETIC. 18mo. cloth. 1*s*. 6*d*. The same, with Answers, 18mo. 1*s*. 9*d*.

KEY TO EXAMINATION PAPERS IN ARITHMETIC. 18mo. cloth. 4*s*. 6*d*.

THE METRIC SYSTEM OF ARITHMETIC, ITS PRINCIPLES AND APPLICATION, with numerous Examples, written expressly for **Standard V.** in National Schools. Fourth Edition. 18mo. cloth, sewed. 3*d*.

A CHART OF THE METRIC SYSTEM, on a Sheet, size 42 in. by 34 in. on Roller, mounted and varnished, price 3*s*. 6*d*. Fourth Edition.

"*We do not remember that ever we have seen teaching by a chart more happily carried out.*"—SCHOOL BOARD CHRONICLE.

Also a Small Chart on a Card, price 1*d*.

EASY LESSONS IN ARITHMETIC, combining Exercises in Reading, Writing, Spelling, and Dictation. Part I. for Standard I. in National Schools. Crown 8vo. 9*d*.

Diagrams for School-room walls in preparation.

"*We should strongly advise everyone to study carefully Mr. Barnard Smith's Lessons in Arithmetic, Writing, and Spelling. A more excellent little work for a first introduction to knowledge cannot well be written. Mr. Smith's larger Text-books on Arithmetic and Algebra are already most favourably known, and he has proved now that the difficulty of writing a text-book which begins ab ovo is really surmountable; but we shall be much mistaken if this little book has not cost its author more thought and mental labour than any of his more elaborate text-books. The plan to combine arithmetical lessons with those in reading and spelling is perfectly novel, and it is worked out in accordance with the aims of our National Schools; and we are convinced that its general introduction in all elementary schools throughout the country will produce great educational advantages.*"—WESTMINSTER REVIEW.

EXAMINATION CARDS IN ARITHMETIC. (Dedicated to Lord Sandon). With Answers and Hints.

Standards **I.** and **II.** in box, 1*s*. 6*d*. **Standards III. IV.** and **V.** in boxes, 1*s*. 6*d*. each. Standard VI. in Two Parts, in boxes, 1*s*. 6*d*. each.

A and B papers, of nearly the same difficulty, are given so as to prevent copying, and the Colours of the A and B papers differ in each Standard, and from those of every other Standard, so that a master or mistress can see at a glance whether the children have the proper papers.

MATHEMATICS.

Snowball.—THE ELEMENTS OF PLANE AND SPHERICAL TRIGONOMETRY; with the Construction and Use of Tables of Logarithms. By J. C. SNOWBALL, M.A. Tenth Edition. Crown 8vo. cloth. 7s. 6d.

SYLLABUS OF PLANE GEOMETRY (corresponding to Euclid, Books I.—VI.) Prepared by the Association for the Improvement of Geometrical Teaching. Crown 8vo. 1s.

Tait and Steele.—A TREATISE ON DYNAMICS OF A PARTICLE. With numerous Examples. By Professor TAIT and Mr. STEELE. New Edition, enlarged. Crown 8vo. cloth. 10s. 6d.

Tebay.—ELEMENTARY MENSURATION FOR SCHOOLS. With numerous Examples. By SEPTIMUS TEBAY, B.A., Head Master of Queen Elizabeth's Grammar School, Rivington. Extra fcap. 8vo. 3s. 6d.

WORKS
By I. TODHUNTER, M.A., F.R.S.,
Of St. John's College, Cambridge.

"*Mr. Todhunter is chiefly known to students of Mathematics as the author of a series of admirable mathematical text-books, which possess the rare qualities of being clear in style and absolutely free from mistakes, typographical or other.*"—SATURDAY REVIEW.

THE ELEMENTS OF EUCLID. For the Use of Colleges and Schools. New Edition. 18mo. cloth. 3s. 6d.

MENSURATION FOR BEGINNERS. With numerous Examples. New Edition. 18mo. cloth. 2s. 6d.

ALGEBRA FOR BEGINNERS. With numerous Examples. New Edition. 18mo. cloth. 2s. 6d.

KEY TO ALGEBRA FOR BEGINNERS. Crown 8vo. cloth. 6s. 6d.

TRIGONOMETRY FOR BEGINNERS. With numerous Examples. New Edition. 18mo. cloth. 2s. 6d.

KEY TO TRIGONOMETRY FOR BEGINNERS. Crown 8vo. 8s. 6d.

MECHANICS FOR BEGINNERS. With numerous Examples. New Edition. 18mo. cloth. 4s. 6d.

ALGEBRA. For the Use of Colleges and Schools. Seventh Edition, containing two New Chapters and Three Hundred miscellaneous Examples. Crown 8vo. cloth. 7s. 6d.

KEY TO ALGEBRA FOR THE USE OF COLLEGES AND SCHOOLS. Crown 8vo. 10s. 6d.

AN ELEMENTARY TREATISE ON THE THEORY OF EQUATIONS. Third Edition, revised. Crown 8vo. cloth. 7s. 6d.

Todhunter (I.)—*continued*.

PLANE TRIGONOMETRY. For Schools and Colleges. Fifth Edition. Crown 8vo. cloth. 5s.

KEY TO PLANE TRIGONOMETRY. Crown 8vo. 10s. 6d.

A TREATISE ON SPHERICAL TRIGONOMETRY. Third Edition, enlarged. Crown 8vo. cloth. 4s. 6d.

PLANE CO-ORDINATE GEOMETRY, as applied to the Straight Line and the Conic Sections. With numerous Examples. Fifth Edition, revised and enlarged. Crown 8vo. cloth. 7s. 6d.

A TREATISE ON THE DIFFERENTIAL CALCULUS. With numerous Examples. Seventh Edition. Crown 8vo. cloth. 10s. 6d.

A TREATISE ON THE INTEGRAL CALCULUS AND ITS APPLICATIONS. With numerous Examples. Fourth Edition, **revised and** enlarged. Crown 8vo. cloth. 10s. 6d.

EXAMPLES OF ANALYTICAL GEOMETRY OF THREE DIMENSIONS. Third Edition, revised. Crown 8vo. cloth. 4s.

A TREATISE ON ANALYTICAL STATICS. With numerous Examples. Fourth Edition, revised and enlarged. Crown **8vo.** cloth. 10s. 6d.

A HISTORY OF THE MATHEMATICAL THEORY OF PROBABILITY, from the time of Pascal to that of Laplace. 8vo. 18s.

RESEARCHES IN THE CALCULUS OF VARIATIONS, principally on the Theory of Discontinuous Solutions: an Essay to which the Adams Prize was awarded in the University of Cambridge in 1871. 8vo. 6s.

A HISTORY OF THE MATHEMATICAL THEORIES OF ATTRACTION, AND THE FIGURE OF THE EARTH, from the time of Newton to that of Laplace. 2 vols. 8vo. 24s.

"*Such histories are at present more valuable than original work. They at once enable the Mathematician to make himself master of all that has been done on the subject, and also give him a clue to the right method of dealing with the subject in future by showing him the paths by which advance has been made in the past . . . It is with unmingled satisfaction that we see this* **branch** *adopted as his special subject by* **one** *whose cast of mind and self culture have made him one of the most accurate, as he certainly is the most learned, of Cambridge Mathematicians.*"—SATURDAY REVIEW.

AN ELEMENTARY TREATISE ON LAPLACE'S, LAME'S, AND BESSEL'S FUNCTIONS. Crown 8vo. 10s. 6d.

Wilson (J. M.)—ELEMENTARY GEOMETRY. Books I. II. III. Containing the Subjects of Euclid's first Four Books. New Edition, following the Syllabus of the Geometrical Association. By J. M. WILSON, M A., late Fellow of St. John's Col-

Wilson (J. M.)—*continued.*

lege, Cambridge, and Mathematical Master of Rugby School. Extra fcap. 8vo. 3s. 6d.

SOLID GEOMETRY AND CONIC SECTIONS. With Appendices on Transversals and Harmonic Division. For the use of Schools. By J. M. WILSON, M.A. Second Edition. Extra fcap. 8vo. 3s. 6d.

Wilson (W. P.)—A TREATISE ON DYNAMICS. By W. P. WILSON, M.A., Fellow of St. John's College, Cambridge, and Professor of Mathematics in Queen's College, Belfast. 8vo. 9s. 6d.

"*This treatise supplies a great educational need.*"—EDUCATIONAL TIMES.

Wolstenholme.—A BOOK OF MATHEMATICAL PROBLEMS, on Subjects included in the Cambridge Course. By JOSEPH WOLSTENHOLME, Fellow of Christ's College, sometime Fellow of St. John's College, and lately Lecturer in Mathematics at Christ's College. Crown 8vo. cloth. 8s. 6d.

"*Judicious, symmetrical, and well arranged.*"—GUARDIAN.

SCIENCE.
ELEMENTARY CLASS-BOOKS.

IT is the intention of the Publishers to produce a complete series of Scientific Manuals, affording full and accurate elementary information, conveyed in clear and lucid English. The authors are well known as among the foremost men of their several departments; and their names form a ready guarantee for the high character of the books. Subjoined is a list of those Manuals that have already appeared, with a short account of each. Others are in active preparation; and the whole will constitute a standard series specially adapted to the requirements of beginners, whether for private study or for school instruction.

ASTRONOMY, by the Astronomer Royal.

POPULAR ASTRONOMY. With Illustrations. By SIR G. B. AIRY, K.C.B., Astronomer Royal. New Edition. 18mo. cloth. 4s. 6d.

Six lectures, intended "*to explain to intelligent persons the principles on which the instruments of an Observatory are constructed, and the*

Elementary Class-Books—*continued.*

principles on which the observations made with these instruments are treated for deduction of the distances and weights of the bodies of the Solar System."

ASTRONOMY.

ELEMENTARY LESSONS IN ASTRONOMY. With **Coloured** Diagram of the Spectra of the Sun, Stars, and Nebulæ, and numerous Illustrations. By J. NORMAN LOCKYER, F.R.S. New Edition. 18mo. 5s. 6d.

"*Full, clear, sound, and worthy of attention, not only as a popular exposition, but as a scientific 'Index.'*"—ATHENÆUM. "*The most fascinating of elementary books on the Sciences.*"—NONCONFORMIST.

QUESTIONS ON LOCKYER'S ELEMENTARY LESSONS IN ASTRONOMY. For the Use of Schools. By JOHN FORBES-ROBERTSON. 18mo. cloth limp. 1s. 6d.

PHYSIOLOGY.

LESSONS IN ELEMENTARY PHYSIOLOGY. With numerous Illustrations. By T. H. HUXLEY, F.R.S., Professor of Natural History in the Royal School of Mines. New Edition. 18mo. cloth. 4s. 6d.

"*Pure gold throughout.*"—GUARDIAN. "*Unquestionably the clearest and most complete elementary treatise on this subject that we possess in any language.*"—WESTMINSTER REVIEW.

QUESTIONS ON HUXLEY'S PHYSIOLOGY FOR SCHOOLS. By T. ALCOCK, M.D. 18mo. 1s. 6d.

BOTANY.

LESSONS IN ELEMENTARY BOTANY. By D. OLIVER, F.R.S., F.L.S., Professor of Botany in University College, London. With nearly Two Hundred Illustrations. New Edition. 18mo. cloth. 4s. 6d.

CHEMISTRY.

LESSONS IN ELEMENTARY CHEMISTRY, INORGANIC AND ORGANIC. By HENRY E. ROSCOE, F.R.S., Professor of Chemistry in Owens College, Manchester. With numerous Illustrations and Chromo-Litho of the Solar Spectrum, and of the Alkalies and Alkaline Earths. New Edition. 18mo. cloth. 4s. 6d.

"*As a standard general text-book it deserves to take a leading place.*"—SPECTATOR. "*We unhesitatingly pronounce it the best of all our elementary treatises on Chemistry.*"—MEDICAL TIMES.

A SERIES OF CHEMICAL PROBLEMS, prepared with Special Reference to the above, by T. E. THORPE, Ph.D., Professor of Chemistry in the Yorkshire College of Science, Leeds. Adapted for the preparation of Students for the Government, Science, and Society of Arts Examinations. With a Preface by Professor ROSCOE. 18mo. 1s. Key. 1s.

SCIENCE.

Elementary Class-Books—*continued.*

POLITICAL ECONOMY.
POLITICAL ECONOMY FOR BEGINNERS. By MILLICENT G. FAWCETT. New Edition. 18mo. 2s. 6d.

"*Clear, compact, and comprehensive.*"—DAILY NEWS. "*The relations of capital and labour have never been more simply or more clearly expounded.*"—CONTEMPORARY REVIEW.

LOGIC.
ELEMENTARY LESSONS IN LOGIC; Deductive and Inductive, with copious Questions and Examples, and a Vocabulary of Logical Terms. By W. STANLEY JEVONS, M.A., Professor of Logic in Owens College, Manchester. New Edition. 18mo. 3s. 6d.

"*Nothing can be better for a school-book.*"—GUARDIAN.
"*A manual alike simple, interesting, and scientific.*"—ATHENÆUM.

PHYSICS.
LESSONS IN ELEMENTARY PHYSICS. By BALFOUR STEWART, F.R.S., Professor of Natural Philosophy in Owens College, Manchester. With numerous Illustrations and Chromoliths of the Spectra of the Sun, Stars, and Nebulæ. New Edition. 18mo. 4s. 6d.

"*The beau-ideal of a scientific text-book, clear, accurate, and thorough.*" EDUCATIONAL TIMES.

PRACTICAL CHEMISTRY.
THE OWENS COLLEGE JUNIOR COURSE OF PRACTICAL CHEMISTRY. By FRANCIS JONES, Chemical Master in the Grammar School, Manchester. With Preface by Professor ROSCOE. With Illustrations. New Edition. 18mo. 2s. 6d.

ANATOMY.
LESSONS IN ELEMENTARY ANATOMY. By ST. GEORGE MIVART, F.R.S., Lecturer in Comparative Anatomy at St. Mary's Hospital. With upwards of 400 Illustrations. 18mo. 6s. 6d.

"*It may be questioned whether any other work on Anatomy contains in like compass so proportionately great a mass of information.*"—LANCET.
"*The work is excellent, and should be in the hands of every student of human anatomy.*"—MEDICAL TIMES.

STEAM.—AN ELEMENTARY TREATISE. By JOHN PERRY, Bachelor of Engineering, Whitworth Scholar, etc., late Lecturer in Physics at Clifton College. With numerous Woodcuts and Numerical Examples and Exercises. 18mo. 4s. 6d.

MANUALS FOR STUDENTS.

Flower (W. H.)—AN INTRODUCTION TO THE OSTEOLOGY OF THE MAMMALIA. Being the substance of the Course of Lectures delivered at the Royal College of Surgeons of England in 1870. By W. H. FLOWER, F.R.S., F.R.C.S., Hunterian Professor of Comparative Anatomy and Physiology. With numerous Illustrations. Globe 8vo. 7s. 6d.

Hooker (Dr.)—THE STUDENT'S FLORA OF THE BRITISH ISLANDS. By J. D. HOOKER, C.B., F.R.S., M.D., D.C.L., President of the Royal Society. Globe 8vo. 10s. 6d.

"*Cannot fail to perfectly fulfil the purpose for which it is intended.*"—LAND AND WATER.—"*Containing the fullest and most accurate manual of the kind that has yet appeared.*"—PALL MALL GAZETTE.

Oliver (Professor).—FIRST BOOK OF INDIAN BOTANY. By DANIEL OLIVER, F.R.S., F.L.S., Keeper of the Herbarium and Library of the Royal Gardens, Kew, and Professor of Botany in University College, London. With numerous Illustrations. Extra fcap. 8vo. 6s. 6d.

"*It contains a well-digested summary of all essential knowledge pertaining to Indian botany, wrought out in accordance with the best principles of scientific arrangement.*"—ALLEN'S INDIAN MAIL.

Other volumes of these Manuals will follow.

NATURE SERIES.

THE SPECTROSCOPE AND ITS APPLICATIONS. By J. NORMAN LOCKYER, F.R.S. With Coloured Plate and numerous illustrations. Second Edition. Crown 8vo. 3s. 6d.

THE ORIGIN AND METAMORPHOSES OF INSECTS. By SIR JOHN LUBBOCK, M.P., F.R.S. With numerous Illustrations. Second Edition. Crown 8vo. 3s. 6d.

"*We can most cordially recommend it to young naturalists.*"—ATHENÆUM.

THE BIRTH OF CHEMISTRY. By G. F. RODWELL, F.R.A.S., F.C.S., Science Master in Marlborough College. With numerous Illustrations. Crown 8vo. 3s. 6d.

"*We can cordially recommend it to all Students of Chemistry.*"—CHEMICAL NEWS.

THE TRANSIT OF VENUS. By G. FORBES, M.A., Professor of Natural Philosophy in the Andersonian University, Glasgow. Illustrated. Crown 8vo. 3s. 6d.

THE COMMON FROG. By ST. GEORGE MIVART, F.R.S., Lecturer in Comparative Anatomy at St. Mary's Hospital. With numerous Illustrations. Crown 8vo. 3s. 6d.

Nature Series—*continued.*

POLARISATION OF LIGHT. By W. SPOTTISWOODE, F.R.S. With many Illustrations. Crown 8vo. 3*s.* 6*d.*

ON BRITISH WILD FLOWERS CONSIDERED IN RELATION TO INSECTS. By SIR JOHN LUBBOCK, Bart., F.R.S. With numerous Illustrations. Second Edition. Crown 8vo. 4*s.* 6*d.*

Other volumes to follow.

Ball (R. S., A.M.)—EXPERIMENTAL MECHANICS. A Course of Lectures delivered at the Royal College of Science for Ireland. By R. S. BALL, A.M., Professor of Applied Mathematics and Mechanics in the Royal College of Science for Ireland. Royal 8vo. 16*s.*

Blanford.—THE RUDIMENTS OF PHYSICAL GEOGRAPHY FOR THE USE OF INDIAN SCHOOLS; with a Glossary of Technical Terms employed. By H. F. BLANFORD, F.R.S. Fifth edition, with Illustrations. Globe 8vo. **2*s.*** 6*d.*

Gordon.—AN ELEMENTARY BOOK ON HEAT. By J. E. H. GORDON, B.A., Gonville and Caius College, Cambridge. Crown 8vo. 2*s.*

Huxley & Martin.—A COURSE OF PRACTICAL INSTRUCTION IN ELEMENTARY BIOLOGY. By Professor HUXLEY, F.R.S., assisted by H. N. MARTIN, M.B., D.Sc. Crown 8vo. 6*s.*

SCIENCE PRIMERS FOR ELEMENTARY SCHOOLS.

In these Primers the authors have aimed, not so much to give information, as to endeavour to discipline the mind in a way which has not hitherto been customary, by bringing it into immediate contact with Nature herself. For this purpose a series of simple experiments (to be performed by **the teacher***) has been devised, leading up to the chief truths of each Science. Thus the power of observation in the pupils will be awakened and strengthened. Each Manual is copiously illustrated, and appended are lists of all the necessary apparatus, with prices, and directions as to how they may be obtained. Professor Huxley's introductory volume* **has been** *delayed through the illness of the author, but it is now expected to appear very shortly. " They are wonderfully clear and lucid in* **their** *instruction, simple in style, and admirable in plan."—*EDUCATIONAL TIMES.

PRIMER OF CHEMISTRY. By H. E. ROSCOE, Professor of Chemistry in Owens College, Manchester. With numerous Illustrations. 18mo. 1*s.* New Edition.

PRIMER OF PHYSICS. By BALFOUR STEWART, Professor of Natural Philosophy in Owens College, Manchester. With numerous Illustrations. 18mo. 1*s.* New Edition.

PRIMER OF PHYSICAL GEOGRAPHY. By ARCHIBALD GEIKIE, F.R.S., Murchison-Professor of Geology and Mineralogy at Edinburgh. With numerous Illustrations. New Edition. 18mo. 1s.

PRIMER OF GEOLOGY. By PROFESSOR GEIKIE, F.R.S. With numerous Illustrations. New Edition. 18mo. cloth. 1s.

PRIMER OF PHYSIOLOGY. By MICHAEL FOSTER, M.D., F.R.S. With numerous Illustrations. New Edition. 18mo. 1s.

PRIMER OF ASTRONOMY. By J. NORMAN LOCKYER, F.R.S. With numerous Illustrations. New Edition. 18mo. 1s.

PRIMER OF BOTANY. By J. D. HOOKER, C.B. F.R.S., President of the Royal Society. With numerous Illustrations. 18mo. 1s.

In preparation:—

INTRODUCTORY. By PROFESSOR HUXLEY. &c. &c.

MISCELLANEOUS.

Abbott.—A SHAKESPEARIAN GRAMMAR. An Attempt to illustrate some of the Differences between Elizabethan and Modern English. By the Rev. E. A. ABBOTT, M.A., Head Master of the City of London School. For the Use of Schools. New and Enlarged **Edition**. Extra fcap. 8vo. 6s.

"*A critical inquiry, conducted with great skill and knowledge, and with all the appliances of modern philology* . . . ."—PALL MALL GAZETTE. "*Valuable not only as an aid to the critical study of Shakespeare, but as tending to familiarize the reader with Elizabethan English in general.*"—ATHENÆUM.

Baldwin.—INTRODUCTION TO PRACTICAL FARMING FOR THE USE OF SCHOOLS. By T. BALDWIN, M.R.I.A. Superintendent of the Agricultural Department of National Education in Ireland. 18mo. 1s. 6d.

Barker.—FIRST LESSONS IN THE PRINCIPLES OF COOKING. By LADY BARKER. 18mo. 1s.

"*An unpretending but invaluable little work* . . . . *The plan is admirable in its completeness and simplicity; it is hardly possible that anyone who can read at all can fail to understand the practical lessons on bread and beef, fish and vegetables; while the explanation of the chemical composition of our food must be intelligible to all who possess sufficient education to follow the argument, in which the fewest possible technical terms are used.*"—SPECTATOR.

Berners.—FIRST LESSONS ON HEALTH. By J. BERNERS. 18mo. 1s. Fourth Edition.

Besant.—STUDIES IN EARLY FRENCH POETRY. By WALTER BESANT, M.A. Crown 8vo. 8s. 6d.

" *In one moderately sized volume he has contrived to introduce us to the very best, if not to all of the early French poets.*"—ATHENÆUM.

Breymann.—Works by HERMANN BREYMANN, Ph.D., late Lecturer on French Language and Literature at Owens College, Manchester, **and now** Professor of Philology in the University of Munich.

A FRENCH GRAMMAR BASED ON PHILOLOGICAL PRINCIPLES. Second Edition. Extra fcap. 8vo. 4s. 6d.

" *We dismiss the work with every expression of satisfaction. It cannot fail to be taken into use by all schools which endeavour to make the study of French a means towards the higher culture.*"—EDUCATIONAL TIMES. " *A good, sound, valuable philological grammar. The author presents the pupil by his method and by detail, with an enormous amount of information about French not usually to be found in grammars, and the information is all of it of real practical value to the student who really wants to know French well, and to understand its spirit.*"—SCHOOL BOARD CHRONICLE.

FIRST FRENCH EXERCISE BOOK. Extra fcap. 8vo. 4s. 6d.

SECOND **FRENCH** EXERCISE BOOK. Extra fcap. 8vo. 2s. 6d.

Calderwood.—HANDBOOK OF MORAL PHILOSOPHY. By the Rev. HENRY CALDERWOOD, LL.D., Professor of Moral Philosophy, University of Edinburgh. Fourth Edition. Crown 8vo. 6s.

" *A compact and useful* **work** .... *will be an assistance to many students outside the author's own University.*"—GUARDIAN.

Delamotte.—A BEGINNER'S DRAWING BOOK. By P. H. DELAMOTTE, F.S.A. Progressively arranged. New Edition, improved. Crown 8vo. 3s. 6d.

" *A concise, simple, and thoroughly practical work.*"—GUARDIAN.

Fawcett.—TALES IN POLITICAL ECONOMY. By MILLICENT GARRETT FAWCETT. Globe 8vo. 3s.

" *The idea is a good one, and it is quite wonderful what a mass of economic teaching the author manages to compress into a small space.*"—ATHENÆUM.

Goldsmith.—THE TRAVELLER, or a Prospect of Society; and THE DESERTED VILLAGE. By OLIVER GOLDSMITH. With Notes Philological and Explanatory, by J. W. HALES, M.A. Crown 8vo. 6d.

EDUCATIONAL BOOKS.

Hales.—LONGER ENGLISH POEMS, with Notes, Philological and Explanatory, and an Introduction on the Teaching of English. Chiefly for use in Schools. Edited by J. W. HALES, M.A., Lecturer in English Literature and Classical Composition at King's College School, London, &c. &c. Third Edition. Extra fcap. 8vo. 4s. 6d.

"*The notes are very full and good, and the book, edited by one of our most cultivated English scholars, is probably the best volume of selections ever made for the use of English schools.*"—PROFESSOR MORLEY'S *First Sketch of English Literature.*

Helfenstein (James).—A COMPARATIVE GRAMMAR OF THE TEUTONIC LANGUAGES. By JAMES HELFENSTEIN, Ph.D. 8vo. 18s.

Hole.—A GENEALOGICAL STEMMA OF THE KINGS OF ENGLAND AND FRANCE. By the Rev. C. HOLE. On Sheet. 1s.

Jephson.—SHAKESPEARE'S "TEMPEST." With Glossarial and Explanatory Notes. By the Rev. J. M. JEPHSON. Second Edition. 18mo. 1s.

Literature Primers.—Edited by JOHN RICHARD GREEN, Author of "A Short History of the English People."
ENGLISH GRAMMAR. By the Rev. R. MORRIS, LL.D., President of the Philological Society. 18mo. cloth. 1s.

"*A work quite precious in its way. . . . An excellent English Grammar for the lowest form.*"—EDUCATIONAL TIMES.
THE CHILDREN'S TREASURY OF ENGLISH SONG. Selected and arranged with Notes by FRANCIS TURNER PALGRAVE. In Two Parts. 18mo. 1s. each.
ENGLISH LITERATURE. By the Rev. STOPFORD BROOKE, M.A. 18mo. 1s.

In preparation :—
    LATIN LITERATURE. By the Rev. Dr. FARRAR, F.R.S.
    GREEK LITERATURE. By PROFESSOR JEBB, M.A.
    SHAKSPERE. By PROFESSOR DOWDEN.
    PHILOLOGY. By J. PEILE, M.A.
    BIBLE PRIMER. By G. GROVE, D.C.L.
    CHAUCER. By F. J. FURNIVALL, M.A.
    GREEK ANTIQUITIES. By the Rev. J. P. MAHAFFY, M.A.

Martin.—THE POET'S HOUR: Poetry Selected and Arranged for Children. By FRANCES MARTIN. Second Edition. 18mo. 2s. 6d.
SPRING-TIME WITH THE POETS. Poetry selected by FRANCES

"*By many degrees the most useful Dictionary that the student can obtain.*"—EDUCATIONAL TIMES.

"*A book which any student, whatever may be the degree of his advancement in the language, would do well to have on the table close at hand while he is reading.*"—SATURDAY REVIEW.

Morris.—Works by the Rev. R. MORRIS, LL.D., Lecturer on English Language and Literature in King's College School.

HISTORICAL OUTLINES OF ENGLISH ACCIDENCE, comprising Chapters on the History and Development of the Language, and on Word-formation. Third Edition. Extra fcap. 8vo. 6s.

"*It makes an era in the study of the English tongue.*"—SATURDAY REVIEW. "*A genuine and sound book.*"—ATHENÆUM.

ELEMENTARY LESSONS IN HISTORICAL ENGLISH GRAMMAR, Containing Accidence and Word-formation. Second Edition. 18mo. 2s. 6d.

PRIMER OF ENGLISH GRAMMAR. 18mo. 1s.

Oliphant.—THE SOURCES OF STANDARD ENGLISH. By J. KINGTON OLIPHANT. Extra fcap. 8vo. 6s.

"*Mr. Oliphant's book is, to our mind, one of the ablest and most scholarly contributions to our standard English we have seen for many years. . . . The arrangement of the work and its indices make it invaluable as a work of reference, and easy alike to study and to store, when studied, in the memory.*"—SCHOOL BOARD CHRONICLE. "*Comes nearer to a history of the English language than anything that we have seen since such a history could be written without confusion and contradictions.*"—SATURDAY REVIEW.

Oppen.—FRENCH READER. For the Use of Colleges and Schools. Containing a graduated Selection from modern Authors in Prose and Verse; and copious Notes, chiefly Etymological. By EDWARD A. OPPEN. Fcap. 8vo. cloth. 4s. 6d.

Otté.—SCANDINAVIAN HISTORY. By E. C. OTTÉ. With Maps. Globe 8vo. 6s.

"*A readable, well-arranged, complete, and accurate volume.*"—LITERARY REVIEW.

Palgrave.—THE CHILDREN'S TREASURY OF ENGLISH SONG. Selected and Arranged with Notes by FRANCIS TURNER PALGRAVE. In Two Parts. 18mo. 1s. each.

"*While indeed a treasure for intelligent children, it is also a work which many older folk will be glad to have.*"—SATURDAY REVIEW.

Pylodet.—NEW GUIDE TO GERMAN CONVERSATION: containing an Alphabetical List of nearly 800 Familiar Words followed by Exercises, Vocabulary of Words in frequent use, Familiar Phrases and Dialogues; a Sketch of German Literature, Idiomatic Expressions, &c. By L. PYLODET. 18mo. cloth limp. 2s. 6d.

Reading Books.—Adapted to the English and Scotch Codes for 1875. Bound in Cloth.

PRIMER. 18mo. (48 pp.) 2*d.*
BOOK I. for Standard I. 18mo. (96 pp.) 3*d.*
,, II. ,, II. 18mo. (144 pp.) 4*d.*
,, III. ,, III. 18mo. (160 pp.) 6*d.*
,, IV. ,, IV. 18mo. (176 pp.) 8*d.*
,, V. ,, V. 18mo. (380 pp.) 1*s.*
,, VI. ,, VI. Crown 8vo. (430 pp.) 2*s.*

Book VI. is fitted for higher Classes, and as an Introduction to English Literature.

Sonnenschein and Meiklejohn.—THE ENGLISH METHOD OF TEACHING TO READ. By A. SONNENSCHEIN and J. M. D. MEIKLEJOHN, M.A. Fcap. 8vo.

COMPRISING :

THE NURSERY BOOK, containing all the Two-Letter Words in the Language. 1*d.* (Also in Large Type on Sheets for School Walls. 5*s.*)

THE FIRST COURSE, consisting of Short Vowels with Single Consonants. 3*d.*

THE SECOND COURSE, with Combinations and Bridges, consisting of Short Vowels with Double Consonants. 4*d.*

THE THIRD AND FOURTH COURSES, consisting of Long Vowels, and all the Double Vowels in the Language. 6*d.*

"*These are admirable books, because they are constructed on a principle, and that the simplest principle on which it is possible to learn to read English.*"—SPECTATOR.

Taylor.—WORDS AND PLACES ; or, Etymological Illustrations of History, Ethnology, and Geography. By the Rev. ISAAC TAYLOR, M.A. Third and cheaper Edition, revised and compressed. With Maps. Globe 8vo. 6*s.*

Already been adopted by many teachers, and prescribed as a text-book in the Cambridge Higher Examinations for Women.

Thring.—Works by EDWARD THRING, M.A., Head Master of Uppingham.

THE ELEMENTS OF GRAMMAR TAUGHT IN ENGLISH, with Questions. Fourth Edition. 18mo. 2*s.*

THE CHILD'S GRAMMAR. Being the Substance of "The Elements of Grammar taught in English," adapted for the Use of Junior Classes. A New Edition. 18mo. 1*s.*

SCHOOL SONGS. A Collection of Songs for Schools. With the Music arranged for four Voices. Edited by the Rev. E. THRING and H. RICCIUS. Folio. 7*s.* 6*d.*

Trench (Archbishop).—Works by R. C. TRENCH, D.D., Archbishop of Dublin.

HOUSEHOLD BOOK OF ENGLISH POETRY. Selected and Arranged, with Notes. Extra fcap. 8vo. 5s. 6d. Second Edition.

"*The Archbishop has conferred in this delightful volume an important gift on the whole English-speaking population of the world.*"—PALL MALL GAZETTE.

ON THE STUDY OF WORDS. Lectures addressed (originally) to the Pupils at the Diocesan Training School, Winchester. Fifteenth Edition, revised. Fcap. 8vo. 4s. 6d.

ENGLISH, PAST AND PRESENT. Ninth Edition, revised and improved. **Fcap.** 8vo. 5s.

A SELECT GLOSSARY OF ENGLISH WORDS, used formerly in Senses Different from their Present. Fourth Edition, enlarged. Fcap. 8vo. **4s. 6d.**

Vaughan (C. M.)— A SHILLING BOOK OF WORDS FROM THE POETS. By C. M. VAUGHAN. 18mo. cloth.

Whitney.—Works by WILLIAM D. WHITNEY, Professor of Sanskrit and Instructor in Modern Languages in Yale College; first President of the American Philological Association, and hon. member of the Royal Asiatic Society of Great Britain and Ireland; and Correspondent of the Berlin Academy of Sciences.

A COMPENDIOUS GERMAN GRAMMAR. Crown 8vo. 6s.

A GERMAN READER IN PROSE AND VERSE, with Notes and Vocabulary. Crown 8vo. 7s. 6d.

Yonge (Charlotte M.)—THE ABRIDGED BOOK OF GOLDEN DEEDS. A Reading Book for Schools and General Readers. By the Author of "The Heir of Redclyffe." 18mo. cloth. 1s.

HISTORY.

Freeman (Edward A.)—OLD-ENGLISH HISTORY. By EDWARD A. FREEMAN, D.C.L., late Fellow of Trinity College, Oxford. With Five Coloured Maps. Fourth Edition. Extra fcap. 8vo. half-bound. 6s.

"*I have, I hope,*" *the author says,* "*shown that it is perfectly easy to teach children, from the very first, to distinguish true history alike from legend and from wilful invention, and also to understand the nature of historical authorities and to weigh one statement against another. I have throughout striven to connect the history of England with the general history of civilized Europe, and I have especially tried to make the book serve as an incentive to a more accurate study of historical geography.*" *In the present edition the whole has been carefully revised,*

and such improvements as suggested themselves have been introduced.
"The book indeed is full of instruction and interest to students of all ages, and he must be a well-informed man indeed who will not rise from its perusal with clearer and more accurate ideas of a too much neglected portion of English History."—SPECTATOR.

Green.—A SHORT HISTORY OF THE ENGLISH PEOPLE. By JOHN RICHARD GREEN. With Coloured Maps, Genealogical Tables, and Chronological Annals. Crown 8vo. 8s. 6d. Thirty-fourth Thousand.

"Stands alone as the one general history of the country, for the sake of which all others, if young and old are wise, will be speedily and surely set aside."—ACADEMY.

Historical Course for Schools.—Edited by EDWARD A. FREEMAN, D.C.L., late Fellow of Trinity College, Oxford.

The object of the present series is to put forth clear and correct views of history in simple language, and in the smallest space and cheapest form in which it could be done. It is meant in the first place for Schools; but it is often found that a book for schools proves useful for other readers as well, and it is hoped that this may be the case with the little books the first instalment of which is now given to the world.

I. GENERAL SKETCH OF EUROPEAN HISTORY. By EDWARD A. FREEMAN, D.C.L. Fourth Edition. 18mo. cloth. 3s. 6d.

"It supplies the great want of a good foundation for historical teaching. The scheme is an excellent one, and this instalment has been executed in a way that promises much for the volumes that are yet to appear."—EDUCATIONAL TIMES.

II. HISTORY OF ENGLAND. By EDITH THOMPSON. Fifth Edition. 18mo. 2s. 6d.

"Freedom from prejudice, simplicity of style, and accuracy of statement, are the characteristics of this little volume. It is a trustworthy text-book and likely to be generally serviceable in schools."—PALL MALL GAZETTE. "Upon the whole, this manual is the best sketch of English history for the use of young people we have yet met with."—ATHENÆUM.

III. HISTORY OF SCOTLAND. By MARGARET MACARTHUR. 18mo. 2s.

"An excellent summary, unimpeachable as to facts, and putting them in the clearest and most impartial light attainable."—GUARDIAN. "Miss Macarthur has performed her task with admirable care, clearness, and fulness, and we have now for the first time a really good School History of Scotland."—EDUCATIONAL TIMES.

IV. HISTORY OF ITALY. By the Rev. W. HUNT, M.A. 18mo. 3s.

"It possesses the same solid merit as its predecessors . . . . the same scrupulous care about fidelity in details. . . . It is distinguished, too, by

Historical Course for Schools—*continued.*
information on art, architecture, and social politics, in which the writer's grasp is seen by the firmness and clearness of his touch."—EDUCATIONAL TIMES.

V. HISTORY OF GERMANY. By J. SIME, M.A. 18mo. 3s.
" *A remarkably clear and impressive History of Germany. Its great events are wisely kept as central figures, and the smaller events are carefully kept, not only subordinate and subservient, but most skilfully woven into the texture of the historical tapestry presented to the eye."*—STANDARD.

VI. HISTORY OF AMERICA. By JOHN A. DOYLE. With Maps. 18mo. 4s. 6d.
" *Mr. Doyle has performed his task with admirable care, fulness, and clearness, and for the first time we have for schools an accurate and interesting history of America, from the earliest to the present time."*—STANDARD.

The following will shortly be issued:—
    FRANCE. By CHARLOTTE M. YONGE.
    GREECE. By J. ANNAN BRYCE, B.A.

History Primers.—Edited by JOHN RICHARD GREEN. Author of "A Short History of the English People."

ROME. By the Rev. M. Creighton, M.A., Fellow and Tutor of Merton College, Oxford. With Eleven Maps. 18mo. 1s.
" *The Author has been curiously successful in telling in an intelligent way the story of Rome from first to last."*—SCHOOL BOARD CHRONICLE.

GREECE. By C. A. Fyffe, M.A., Fellow and late Tutor of University College, Oxford. With Five Maps. 18mo. 1s.
" *We give our unqualified praise to this little manual."*—SCHOOLMASTER.

In preparation:—
    EUROPE. By E. A. FREEMAN, D.C.L., LL.D.
    ENGLAND. By J. R. GREEN, M.A.
    FRANCE. By CHARLOTTE M. YONGE.
    GEOGRAPHY. By GEORGE GROVE, D.C.L.

Michelet.—A SUMMARY OF MODERN HISTORY. Translated from the French of M. Michelet, and continued to the Present Time, by M. C. M. Simpson. Globe 8vo. 4s. 6d.
" *We are glad to see one of the ablest and most useful summaries of European history put into the hands of English readers. The translation is excellent."*—STANDARD.

Yonge (Charlotte M.)—A PARALLEL HISTORY OF FRANCE AND ENGLAND: consisting of Outlines and Dates. By CHARLOTTE M. YONGE, Author of "The Heir of Redclyffe," "Cameos of English History," &c. &c. Oblong 4to. 3s. 6d.
" *We can imagine few more really advantageous courses of historical study for a young mind than going carefully and steadily through Miss Yonge's excellent little book."*—EDUCATIONAL TIMES.

Yonge (Charlotte M.)—*continued.*
CAMEOS FROM ENGLISH HISTORY. From Rollo to Edward II. By the Author of "The Heir of Redclyffe." Extra fcap. 8vo. Third Edition, enlarged. 5*s.*
*A book for young people just beyond the elementary histories of England, and able to enter in some degree into the real spirit of events, and to be struck with characters and scenes presented in some relief. "Instead of dry details, we have living pictures, faithful, vivid, [and striking."—*Nonconformist.

A Second Series of CAMEOS FROM ENGLISH HISTORY. The Wars in France. Third Edition. Extra fcap. 8vo. 5*s.*
*" Though mainly intended for young readers, they will, if we mistake not, be found very acceptable to those of more mature years, and the life and reality imparted to the **dry** bones of history cannot fail to be attractive to readers of every **age**."—*John Bull.

EUROPEAN HISTORY. Narrated in a Series of Historical Selections from the Best Authorities. Edited and arranged by E. M. Sewell and C. M. Yonge. First Series, 1003—1154. Third Edition. Crown 8vo. 6*s.* Second Series, 1088—1228. Crown 8vo. 6*s.* Third Edition.
*" We know of scarcely anything which is so likely to raise to a higher level the average standard of English education."—*Guardian.

DIVINITY.

*** For other Works by these Authors, see Theological Catalogue.

Abbott (Rev. E. A.)—BIBLE LESSONS. By the Rev. E. A. Abbott, M.A., Head Master of the City of London School. Second Edition. Crown 8vo. 4*s.* 6*d.*
" Wise, suggestive, and really profound initiation into religious thought." —Guardian. *" I think nobody could read them without being both the better for them himself, and being also able to see how this difficult duty of imparting a sound religious education may be effected."—*Bishop of St. David's at Abergwilly.

Arnold.— A BIBLE-READING FOR SCHOOLS. The Great Prophecy of Israel's Restoration (Isaiah, Chapters 40—66). Arranged and Edited for Young Learners. By Matthew Arnold, D.C.L., formerly Professor of Poetry in the University of Oxford, and Fellow of Oriel. Fourth Edition. 18mo. cloth. 1*s.*
*" There can be no doubt that it will be found excellently calculated **to** further instruction in Biblical literature in any school into which it may be introduced; and we can safely say that whatever school uses the book, it will enable its pupils to understand Isaiah, a great advantage compared with other establishments which do not avail themselves of it."—*Times.

Arnold.—ISAIAH XL.—LXVI. With the Shorter Prophecies allied to it. Arranged and Edited with Notes by MATTHEW ARNOLD. Crown 8vo. 5*s*.

Golden Treasury Psalter.—Students' Edition. Being an Edition of "The Psalms Chronologically Arranged, by Four Friends," with briefer Notes. 18mo. 3*s*. 6*d*.

Hardwick.—A HISTORY OF THE CHRISTIAN CHURCH. Middle Age. From Gregory the Great to the Excommunication of Luther. Edited by WILLIAM STUBBS, M.A., Regius Professor of Modern History in the University of Oxford. With Four Maps constructed for this work by A. KEITH JOHNSTON. Fourth Edition. Crown 8vo. 10*s*. 6*d*.

For this edition Professor Stubbs has carefully revised both text and notes, making such corrections of facts, dates, and the like as the results of recent research warrant. The doctrinal, historical, and generally speculative views of the late author have been preserved intact. "As a manual for the student of ecclesiastical history in the Middle Ages, we know no English work which can be compared to Mr. Hardwick's book."—GUARDIAN.

A HISTORY OF THE CHRISTIAN CHURCH DURING THE REFORMATION. By ARCHDEACON HARDWICK. Fourth Edition. Edited by Professor STUBBS. Crown 8vo. 10*s*. 6*d*.

Maclear.—Works by the Rev. G. F. MACLEAR, D.D., Head Master of King's College School.

A CLASS-BOOK OF OLD TESTAMENT HISTORY. Eighth Edition, with Four Maps. 18mo. cloth. 4*s*. 6*d*.

"*A careful and elaborate though brief compendium of all that modern research has done for the illustration of the Old Testament. We know of no work which contains so much important information in so small a compass.*"—BRITISH QUARTERLY REVIEW.

A CLASS-BOOK OF NEW TESTAMENT HISTORY, including the Connexion of the Old and New Testament. With Four Maps. Fifth Edition. 18mo. cloth. 5*s*. 6*d*.

"*A singularly clear and orderly arrangement of the Sacred Story. His work is solidly and completely done.*"—ATHENÆUM.

A SHILLING BOOK OF OLD TESTAMENT HISTORY, for National and Elementary Schools. With Map. 18mo. cloth. New Edition.

A SHILLING BOOK OF NEW TESTAMENT HISTORY, for National and Elementary Schools. With Map. 18mo. cloth. New Edition.

These works have been carefully abridged from the author's larger manuals.

Maclear—*continued.*

CLASS-BOOK OF THE CATECHISM OF THE CHURCH OF ENGLAND. New and Cheaper Edition. 18mo. cloth. 1s. 6d.

"*It is indeed the work of a scholar and divine, and as such, though extremely simple, it is also extremely instructive. There are few clergymen who would not find it useful in preparing candidates for Confirmation; and there are not a few who would find it useful to themselves as well.*"—LITERARY CHURCHMAN.

A FIRST CLASS-BOOK OF THE CATECHISM OF THE CHURCH OF ENGLAND, with Scripture Proofs, for Junior Classes and Schools. 18mo. 6d. New Edition.

A MANUAL OF INSTRUCTION FOR CONFIRMATION AND FIRST COMMUNION. With Prayers and Devotions. Royal 32mo. cloth extra, red edges. 2s.

"*It is earnest, orthodox, and affectionate in tone. The form of self-examination is particularly good.*"—JOHN BULL.

THE ORDER OF CONFIRMATION, WITH PRAYERS AND DEVOTIONS. 32mo. 6d.

FIRST COMMUNION, WITH PRAYERS AND DEVOTIONS FOR THE NEWLY CONFIRMED. 32mo. 6d.

Maurice.—THE LORD'S PRAYER, THE CREED, AND THE COMMANDMENTS. A Manual for Parents and Schoolmasters. To which is added the Order of the Scriptures. By the Rev. F. DENISON MAURICE, M.A. 18mo. cloth limp. 1s.

Procter.—A HISTORY OF THE BOOK OF COMMON PRAYER, with a Rationale of its Offices. By FRANCIS PROCTER, M.A. Twelfth Edition, revised and enlarged. Crown 8vo. 10s. 6d.

Procter and Maclear.—AN ELEMENTARY INTRODUCTION TO THE BOOK OF COMMON PRAYER. Re-arranged and supplemented by an Explanation of the Morning and Evening Prayer and the Litany. By the Rev. F. PROCTER and the Rev. G. F. MACLEAR. New Edition. 18mo. 2s. 6d.

Psalms of David Chronologically Arranged. By Four Friends. An Amended Version, with Historical Introduction and Explanatory Notes. Second and Cheaper Edition, with Additions and Corrections. Crown 8vo. 8s. 6d.

"*One of the most instructive and valuable books that has been published for many years.*"—SPECTATOR.

Ramsay.—THE CATECHISER'S MANUAL; or, the Church Catechism Illustrated and Explained, for the use of Clergymen, Schoolmasters, and Teachers. By the Rev. ARTHUR RAMSAY, M.A. Second Edition. 18mo. 1s. 6d.

Simpson.—AN EPITOME OF THE HISTORY OF THE CHRISTIAN CHURCH. By WILLIAM SIMPSON, M.A. Fifth Edition. Fcap. 8vo. 3s. 6d.

Swainson.—A HANDBOOK to BUTLER'S ANALOGY. By C. A. SWAINSON, D.D., Canon of Chichester. Crown 8vo. 1s. 6d.

Trench.—SYNONYMS OF THE NEW TESTAMENT. By R. CHENEVIX TRENCH, D.D., Archbishop of Dublin. New Edition, enlarged. 8vo. cloth. 12s.

Westcott.—Works by BROOKE FOSS WESTCOTT, B.D., Canon of Peterborough.

A GENERAL SURVEY OF THE HISTORY OF THE CANON OF THE NEW TESTAMENT DURING THE FIRST FOUR CENTURIES. Fourth Edition. With Preface on "Supernatural Religion." Crown 8vo. 10s. 6d.

"*Theological students, and not they only, but the general public, owe a deep debt of gratitude to Mr. Westcott for bringing this subject fairly before them in this candid and comprehensive essay. . . . . As a theological work it is at once perfectly fair and impartial, and imbued with a thoroughly religious spirit; and as a manual it exhibits, in a lucid form and in a narrow compass, the results of extensive research and accurate thought. We cordially recommend it.*"—SATURDAY REVIEW.

INTRODUCTION TO THE STUDY OF THE FOUR GOSPELS. Fifth Edition. Crown 8vo. 10s. 6d.

"*To learning and accuracy which commands respect and confidence,* **he unites** *what are* **not** *always to be found in union with these qualities, the no less valuable faculties of lucid arrangement* **and** *graceful and facile expression.*"—LONDON QUARTERLY REVIEW.

THE BIBLE IN THE CHURCH. A Popular Account of the Collection and Reception **of the Holy** Scriptures in the Christian Churches. **New** Edition. 18mo. cloth. 4s. 6d.

"*We would recommend every* **one who** *loves and studies the* **Bible to read** *and ponder this exquisite little* **book.** *Mr. Westcott's account of the 'Canon'* **is true** *history in its highest sense.*"—LITERARY CHURCHMAN.

THE GOSPEL OF THE RESURRECTION. Thoughts on its Relation to Reason and History. New Edition. Crown 8vo. 6s.

Wilson.—THE BIBLE STUDENT'S GUIDE to the more Correct Understanding of the English translation of the Old Testament, by reference to the Original Hebrew. By WILLIAM WILSON, D.D., Canon of Winchester, late Fellow of Queen's College, Oxford. Second Edition, carefully Revised. 4to. cloth. 25s.

"*For all earnest students of the Old Testament Scriptures it is a most valuable Manual. Its arrangement is so simple that those who possess only their mother-tongue, if they will take a little pains, may employ it with great profit.*"—NONCONFORMIST.

Yonge (Charlotte M.)—SCRIPTURE READINGS FOR SCHOOLS AND FAMILIES. By CHARLOTTE M. YONGE, Author of "The Heir of Redclyffe." FIRST SERIES. Genesis to Deuteronomy. Globe 8vo. 1s. 6d. With Comments. Second Edition. 3s. 6d.

SECOND SERIES. From JOSHUA to SOLOMON. Extra fcap. 8vo. 1s. 6d. With Comments, 3s. 6d.

THIRD SERIES. The KINGS and the PROPHETS. Extra fcap. 8vo. 1s. 6d. With Comments, 3s. 6d.

Actual need has led the author to endeavour to prepare a reading book convenient for study with children, containing the very words of the Bible, with only a few expedient omissions, and arranged in Lessons of such length as by experience she has found to suit with children's ordinary power of accurate attentive interest. The verse form has been retained, because of its convenience for children reading in class, and as more resembling their Bibles; but the poetical portions have been given in their lines. When Psalms or portions from the Prophets illustrate or fall in with the narrative they are given in their chronological sequence. The Scripture portion, with a very few notes explanatory of mere words, is bound up apart, to be used by children, while the same is also supplied with a brief comment, the purpose of which is either to assist the teacher in explaining the lesson, or to be used by more advanced young people to whom it may not be possible to give access to the authorities whence it has been taken. Professor Huxley, at a meeting of the London School Board, particularly mentioned the selection made by Miss Yonge as an example of how selections might be made from the Bible for School Reading. See TIMES, *March* 30, 1871.

www.ingramcontent.com/pod-product-compliance
Lightning Source LLC
Chambersburg PA
CBHW031424230426
43668CB00007B/429